BIBLIA PAUPERUM

BIBLIA PAUPERUM

A FACSIMILE AND EDITION

BY

AVRIL HENRY

SCOLAR PRESS

First published in 1987 by
SCOLAR PRESS
Gower Publishing Company Limited
Gower House, Croft Road
Aldershot GU11 3HR

British Library Cataloguing in Publication Data

Biblia pauperum : a facsimile of the
forty-page block book.
1. Bible——Picture Bibles
I. Title
220'.022'2   Z241.B6

ISBN 0-85967-542-4

Publication of this book has been aided by a grant from the
Millard Meiss Publication Fund of the College Art
Association of America

Typeset by Gloucester Typesetting Services
and printed and bound in Great Britain at
the University Press, Cambridge

Contents

FOR MY FATHER
12.3.1907–18.1.1985

Acknowledgements

GENTLEMAN: Help! Help! O help!
EDGAR: What kind of help?

My primary obligations are to those who provided money and means for this edition. A British Academy grant laid the project's foundation; the University of Exeter supplied facilities for research.

The major materials for the facsimile were provided by the Sächsische Landesbibliothek, Dresden (where Professor Dr Burgemeister and Dr Alschner patiently answered questions), and by Musée Condé, Chantilly. Permission to publish material illustrating the Introduction was kindly given by the St Florian Stiftsbibliothek (Fig. 1); Herold of Vienna, publishers of Röhrig, *Der Verduner Alter* (Fig. 7); the Dean and Chapter of Canterbury Cathedral (Fig. 8); the Bodleian Library, Oxford, for the use of a frame from the filmstrip (Roll 155) of their *Bible Moralisée* (Fig. 9); the Provost and Fellows of Eton College, and the Bodleian Library, Oxford, for the use of a frame from their filmstrip of Eton College MS 177 (Fig. 10); Bibliothèque Royale Albert Iᵉʳ, Brussels, (Fig. 11); the British Museum (Fig. 13); the British Library (Figs 12, 14, 15, 16, 17, 19); the Nationalbibliothek, Vienna (Fig. 18); Mr J. D. C. Smith and the Dean and Chapter of Ripon Cathedral, for the use of Mr Smith's photograph of a Ripon misericord (Fig. 20A); the Rector of St Martin's Church, Stamford, and the National Monuments Record, for photographs of Stamford glass (Fig. 20C); and the Dean and Chapter of Exeter Cathedral (Fig. 21A).

Photographic material for research was provided by the Université de Liège, Bibliothèque Générale; Rijksuniversiteit Central Bibliotheek, Ghent; Stiftsbibliothek, St Gallen; Zentralbibliothek, Zurich; Walters Art Gallery, Baltimore; Pierpont Morgan Library, New York; Rijksmuseum Meermanno-Westreenianum and Koninklijke Bibliotheek, The Hague; Rijksmuseum, Amsterdam; The Louvre, Paris; Bayerische Statsbibliothek, Munich; Stadtbibliothek, Nuremberg; Museen der Stadt and Wallraf-Richartz-Museum, Cologne; Staatliche Museen, Berlin; and Muzeum Narodowe, Krakow.

Nearer home, I owe special thanks to staff at the University Libraries of Exeter, Oxford, Cambridge, and Glasgow, at the Ashmolean Museum Library and Blackfriars, Oxford, at the British Museum, Courtauld Institute, and Victoria and Albert Museum, London, and at the John Rylands Library, Manchester. All these showed their renowned generosity and courtesy in sharing their facilities and skills.

The late Professor E. J. Dobson, and Dr P. Gaskell, gave me valuable encouragement and advice at an early stage in the work. For later help I am most deeply indebted to Miss M. Knight, Mr W. J. Osborne, Mr R. Bowyer, and Mrs S. Bruni. The largest body of scholars to whom I owe thanks is formed by immediate colleagues, who generously answered questions and read drafts: Professor the Revd Canon J. R. Porter, the Revd A. H. B. Logan, the Revd D. L. Powell, Professor G. Yates, Professor P. Wiseman, Miss M. Dexter, Mr M. Jones, Dr G. H. A. Joynboll, Mr H. W. Stubbs, Mr M. Bennun, Mr A. Robertshaw, Miss S. Maitek, Mr J. R. P. McKenzie, and at Exeter College of Art, Mr M. Snow. I have drawn on friends' varied skills: from those of Mr M. Laczinski, who works in woodcut, to those of the Revd Patrick Rorke, S.J., who still has the Latin Mass and Breviary in his head. My students have cheerfully acted as guinea-pigs, and offered valuable criticism and insight.

Last in line but first in friendship's enthusiastic response to the idea of the *Biblia Pauperum* as a 'working book' are two friends and colleagues similarly interested in the wedding of word and image: Miss E. Cook, formerly of Homerton College, Cambridge, and Mrs M. Twycross of the University of Lancaster.

None of this varied advice could have been used without the most constant help of all—the unwavering interest and support of my father, who with his usual good humour tolerated my odd hours and antisocial preoccupation.

A.H.

Abbreviations

=	'represents' or 'is related to'
BL	British Library, London
BMQ	*British Museum Quarterly*
BP	*Biblia Pauperum*
Brev.	*Breviarium Romanum* (1876)
CC	Orchard, *A Catholic Commentary on Holy Scripture*
CE	Herberman, *The Catholic Encyclopedia*
DCC	*Dictionary of the Christian Church*
EETS	Early English Text Society
ES	Extra Series
JB	Jones, ed., *The Jerusalem Bible*
JEGP	*Journal of English and Germanic Philology*
JWAG	*Journal of the Walters Art Gallery*
JWCI	*Journal of the Warburg and Courtauld Institutes*
MLN	*Modern Language Notes*
MP	*Modern Philology*
NCE	*New Catholic Encyclopedia*
NT	New Testament
ODCC	*The Oxford Dictionary of the Christian Church*
OT	Old Testament
PG	Migne, *Patrologia Cursus Completus* (. . .) *Series Graeca*
PL	Migne, *Patrologia Cursus Completus* (. . .) *Series Latina*
ProcCAS	*Proceedings of the Cambridge Antiquarian Society*
RDK	Schmitt, *Reallexikon zur deutschen Kunstgeschichte*
RQ	*Renaissance Quarterly*
S.	Schreiber blockbook edition number (followed by roman numeral)
s.	*saeculo* (preceding a lower-case roman numeral indicating century—for example, s. xiv= fourteenth century—but appearing as S. at the beginning of sentences in notes to the commentaries)
SIAP	*Suffolk Institute of Archeology Proceedings*
sig.	signature (preceding a letter designating one of the pictures in the blockbook *Biblia Pauperum*)
SLI	*Studies in the Literary Imagination*
SS	Supplementary Series
ST	Thomas Aquinas, *Summa Theologica*
TLS	*The Times Literary Supplement*
TS	Typescript

INTRODUCTION

Introduction

Biblia Pauperum: name and nature

Biblia Pauperum is a dull title with which to encumber a good book. It means 'Bible of the Poor', but is inaccurate, as well as being uninviting in its Latin. The *Biblia Pauperum* is not a Bible (or a substitute for one[1]); clearly it was not for the simple poor, who did not buy books, let alone read Latin —especially heavily abbreviated Latin printed in black letter of peculiar illegibility.[2] *Biblia Pauperum* is not even likely to have been the original name. It does appear on two medieval copies of the work,[3] but so do other titles.[4] On the other hand, the name seems also to have been used for any kind of selected, vaguely biblical material, for it is occasionally given to medieval Bible indices, selections, and interpretations.[5]

The *Biblia Pauperum* is not an abstract of another work. It has a strong independent life of its own, offering, I believe, a carefully structured, meditative experience. The book's individuality and power have perhaps been obscured for us by its unattractive name, somehow suggesting a minimal Bible digest, its naivety of content equalled only by the mental and physical poverty of its intended readers. The heart of this edition, the facsimile with commentaries and notes, is designed to show how far this is from the truth: to reveal the density and sophistication of the work's verbal and visual design, and so perhaps offer even the specialist a new focus on a familiar work. This introduction, however, addresses the non-specialist, in the belief that anyone can, with a little help, enjoy this forbiddingly named book. However inappropriate, the name is unavoidable. *Biblia Pauperum* has been the accepted title since Heinecken first used it in print in 1769.[6] It is the title by which it is located in catalogues and described by scholars. The misnomer has been approved by mere usage. In any case, it is hard to invent a useful substitute, as the following brief description will show.

The *Biblia Pauperum* presented in this facsimile has forty pages, each composed of three principal pictures and short texts which are distributed round or between the three principal scenes. These pictures and texts are always arranged in the same general pattern. Each of the first twenty pages is identified by a letter just above the central scene, in a typical medieval twenty-letter alphabet: **a**–**v** (omitting *j*, *u*, *w*, *x*, *y*, and *z*). In the second half of the book, each page is identified by the same letters between dots: •**a**•–•**v**•.[7] Each page is dominated by three scenes, inside which additional texts occasionally occur, speech being shown within scrolls (Gabriel addressing Mary, for example, on the first page).

The central scene is usually from the New Testament. The two flanking scenes, usually from the Old Testament, show prefigurations or foreshadowings of the central scene, or 'Antitype'. For example, on sig. **e** the New Testament *Flight into Egypt* is flanked, with apparent predictability, by two Old Testament 'Types': *Jacob Flees Esau* and *David Flees Saul*. The tradition behind the use of Type and Antitype, and the *Biblia Pauperum*'s subtle use of it, are discussed on pp. 9–17: but for the moment it is only the sequence of Antitypes, the main central images, which is under consideration. The forty Antitypes tell a highly selective version of the story of God's relationship with man. The first thirty-six show events from the life of Christ from *Annunciation* to *Ascension*, ending with *Pentecost* and the *Coronation of the Virgin*. The last four treat our relationship with God after death (see the summary on p. 7). It is probably no accident that the Passion begins the second half of the book, at •**a**•. It would be hard to find a helpful title for even these summarised contents (unless it were *The Salvation of Man*, the title of one of *Biblia Pauperum*'s descendants).[8]

The book might be easier to name if we knew exactly what it was for. Its original purpose is not known (the possibilities are discussed on pp. 17–18). No medieval account of its use has been found, so any evidence which survives must be in the *Biblia Pauperum* itself, locked into its structure: in its design as a whole, in the relation between the two pages forming any opening, and in the linking of texts and images on each page. Perhaps, if used as originally intended, it may reveal its function, just as a sewing machine will stitch cloth but not grind grain. The central part of this edition, the facsimile pages and their facing commentaries, is meant to encourage *use* of the book, the best test of a hypothetical function.

Whatever that now mysterious purpose once was, it must have been important and popular, for the work has stood the test of time. The woodcut version of the *Biblia Pauperum* presented here is a blockbook, originally printed in its entirety, text and pictures, from wood-blocks.[9] It dates from about 1460 or a few years before,[10] making it among the earliest books printed.[11] But forms of it existed in manuscripts as early as the mid-thirteenth century, perhaps even as early as the late twelfth century:[12] the earliest to survive is a fragment *c.* 1300.[13] It became widely distributed throughout German- and French-speaking Europe. Some eighty-three exemplars are known, their texts in the original Latin or in German. The work's popularity did not cease in the mid-fifteenth century, however: our printed version was followed by a fifty-page edition of about 1480;[14] versions appeared in the sixteenth century; parts of it were used even in the nineteenth century.[15]

The manuscript ancestors and the format

Both the traditional and original elements in our fifteenth-century version of the *Biblia Pauperum* become clear if it is viewed as the descendant of its manuscript ancestors. Its overall plan is in some respects traditional. The original, lost manuscript (urexemplar) is thought to have contained only thirty-four main scenes, their subjects roughly coinciding with those in our version (the degree of coincidence is shown in the table in Fig. 5). Its descendant manuscripts divide into three 'families', from Austria, Weimar, and Bavaria. These are distinguished in three ways: by the *arrangement* of texts and images on the page; by the *number* of image-groups per page (some with two; some, like our version, with one); and by the *sequence* of images (as well as variations in details of iconography and text).[16] Several of these beautiful manuscripts are available in full-colour facsimiles splendid in their own right, and as background study to our version.[17] Perhaps the most immediate impact they make is in terms of the difference between the linear quality of a pen- or brush-drawn image and that of a woodcut, exemplified in our version. Fig. 1 shows an example of pages with two image-groups, from the earliest extant manuscript in the Austrian 'family'; the scenes illustrated correspond with those on the fifth, sixth, seventh and eighth pages of our facsimile.

It is obvious that whereas on a double-spread from our book two Antitypes and four Types are visually related, on a manuscript of the kind illustrated, four Antitypes and eight Types are seen at once. This makes the complexity of our book's visual effect look simple by comparison (and tells us something significant about the medieval capacity for absorbing multiple images). When Fig. 1 is compared with its equivalent pages in our version, it is also clear that even where subjects are common to both manuscript and book, their *compositions* differ.[18] The name *Biblia Pauperum* therefore refers to a kind of book, not a particular book.

That the *Biblia Pauperum* has vivid verbal elements will become clear later, but its images predominate. The main thought-structure of the book as a whole, and of each of its pages, is in terms of relationships among pictures. The sequence of Antitypes in our version has already been mentioned: thirty-six scenes from the life of Christ including *Pentecost* and the *Coronation of the Virgin*, followed by four scenes from the next world. Apart from this overall scheme, the only certain relationship between the pages is their pairing, as they appear in the open book.[19]

Fig. 4 shows a summary of the forty Antitypes (with the eighty Types, which will be discussed shortly). In the table, each central scene is identified in capitals. Under it are identified its two flanking pictures, first the one on the left and then the one on the right. The layout of the table shows the main pairs of Antitypes, which often share visual and thematic relationships (explained in the commentaries). For example, the *Annunciation* and its fulfilment in the *Nativity* (**a** and **b**) are to be read together, as they appear in Fig. 2 (Mary's position is similar in both); the *Magi* (**c**), showing the offering of gifts to the Child, is to be read, as in Fig. 3, with the *Presentation* (**d**), in which the Child is himself offered to God in the Temple (the position of Mother and Child is similar in both).

Thematic pairing is clear throughout the rest of the book. In **i** and **k** we see two conquests of sin: the first in the *Baptism*

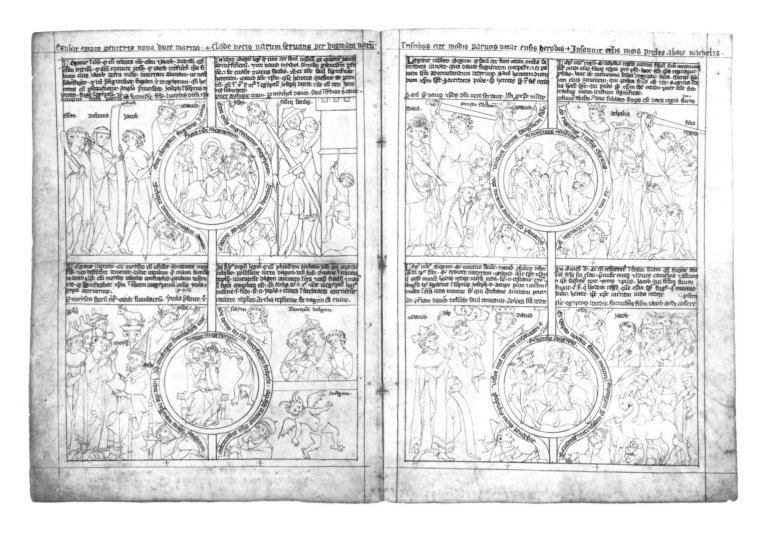

FIG. 1
St Florian, Stiftsbibliothek, MS.XI.80, ff. 2ᵛ–3ʳ.
f. 2ᵛ *Flight into Egypt* and *Egyptian Idols Fall*
f. 3ʳ *Massacre of the Innocents* and *Return from Egypt*

FIG. 2
Biblia Pauperum, sigs. **a** and **b**
Annunciation and *Nativity*

FIG. 3
Biblia Pauperum, sigs. **c** and **d**
Magi and *Presentation*

of Christ, the second in his resistance in the *Temptation*. Similarly, **l** and **m** show two contacts between this world and the next (the *Raising of Lazarus* and Christ's *Transfiguration*), while **n** and **o** show two different recognitions of Christ (Magdalene wiping his feet with her hair in penitence in *Mary Magdalene Repents*, and his acclamation as 'King' in the *Entry into Jerusalem*). In the Bible, there is a long interval between the expulsion of the traders from the Temple (Matt. xxi 12) and the conspiracy against Christ (Matt. xxvi 3–5); but here *Christ Purifies the Temple* is placed next to the Temple's High Priest plotting against Jesus, in the *Conspiracy* (**p** and **q**): Jesus's challenge to the Jewish 'establishment' is thus underlined. In **r** and **s** it seems no accident that *Judas is Paid* is next to his being identified at the *Last Supper* as the betrayer. In **t** and **v** those to whom Christ makes prophecies are shown first ignoring him, and then literally bowled over by his mere presence. In •**g**• Christ enters the confinement of the tomb, while in •**h**• he releases souls from the confinement of Hellmouth (the antithesis of *his* confinement is presented in •**i**•). The palpability of Christ's risen body is shown in •**n**•, *Doubting Thomas*, while its defiance of the laws of gravity follows in •**o**•, the *Ascension*. In •**p**• and •**q**• Mary heads the college of Apostles receiving the Holy Spirit in *Pentecost* and is then seen crowned in heaven in the *Coronation of the Virgin*. The *Crucifixion* appears twice, on each side of a double-spread (•**e**• and •**f**•): the echoed position not only of the Crucified but also of the onlookers is significant, as the commentary explains. Christ appears to Mary Magdalene and to his disciples, on each side of a double-spread (•**l**• and •**m**•), and so on.

This pairing is echoed even in the design of the formal controlling architectural frames which hold the elements on each page in such tight relation to each other. At a superficial glance these frames appear to be uniform throughout. In fact, those on the left-hand pages are quite distinct from those on the right-hand pages. On the left-hand pages the main pictures are set in arched architectural bays, the spandrels over the two central columns are filled by triangular motifs, the upper demi-figures in two cusped arches are framed by a rectangular round-cornered moulding, and the lower demi-figures are set in faintly ogee arches. On the right-hand pages the main pictures are set in flat-topped bays, the spandrels carry concentric circles, and the upper and lower demi-figures' cusped arches are each in a curved moulding.

In addition to the deliberate pairing, this printed book seems to show traces of division into thematic groups not of two but of four main subjects, following the pattern in many of the early manuscripts which showed two main subjects on a page (Fig. 1) and so four main subjects on an opening. These groups, dividing the woodcut version into ten 'chapters', are listed in Fig. 4, each to the right of the quartet they link. The four scenes are often linked in terms of optical as well as thematic design—for example, chapter 2 begins with the Holy Family moving left to right in flight, and ends with its return, right to left, as in the manuscript (Fig. 1); chapter 3 shows Christ conspicuously standing in all four central scenes. It is interesting to compare the chapters shown in the table in Fig. 4 with a list of the chapters in the original manuscript, which had only thirty-four main scenes. The tables in Fig. 5 show that a process which has been called 'optical editing' has taken place in the woodcut version:[20] subjects have been rearranged to give a different pattern of themes in the chapters making up the forty main scenes. For example, the first three chapters in the woodcut version are the same as those in the manuscript, except that the last scene of the twelve in the manuscript—*Mary Magdalene Repents* (and washes Christ's feet)—is replaced in the woodcut version by the *Raising of Lazarus*. This gives us the book's chapter 3:

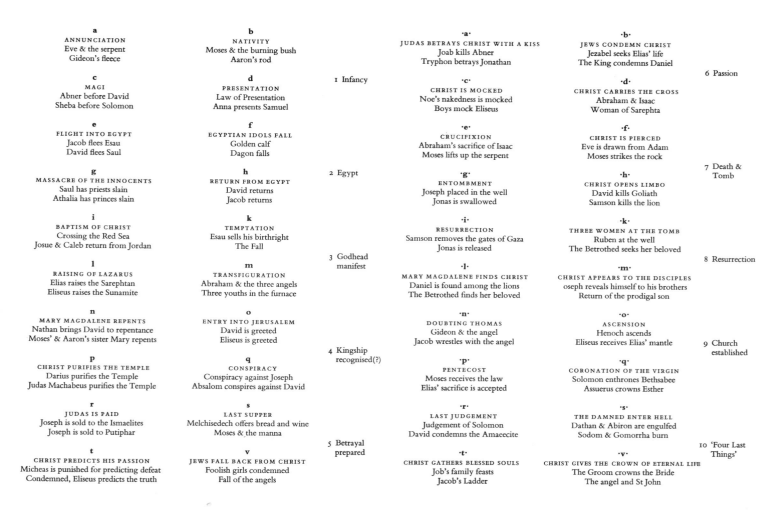

a ANNUNCIATION Eve & the serpent Gideon's fleece	b NATIVITY Moses & the burning bush Aaron's rod	1 Infancy
c MAGI Abner before David Sheba before Solomon	d PRESENTATION Law of Presentation Anna presents Samuel	
e FLIGHT INTO EGYPT Jacob flees Esau David flees Saul	f EGYPTIAN IDOLS FALL Golden calf Dagon falls	2 Egypt
g MASSACRE OF THE INNOCENTS Saul has priests slain Athalia has princes slain	h RETURN FROM EGYPT David returns Jacob returns	
i BAPTISM OF CHRIST Crossing the Red Sea Josue & Caleb return from Jordan	k TEMPTATION Esau sells his birthright The Fall	3 Godhead manifest
l RAISING OF LAZARUS Elias raises the Sarephtan Eliseus raises the Sunamite	m TRANSFIGURATION Abraham & the three angels Three youths in the furnace	
n MARY MAGDALENE REPENTS Nathan brings David to repentance Moses' & Aaron's sister Mary repents	o ENTRY INTO JERUSALEM David is greeted Eliseus is greeted	4 Kingship recognised(?)
p CHRIST PURIFIES THE TEMPLE Darius purifies the Temple Judas Machabeus purifies the Temple	q CONSPIRACY Conspiracy against Joseph Absalom conspires against David	
r JUDAS IS PAID Joseph is sold to the Ismaelites Joseph is sold to Putiphar	s LAST SUPPER Melchisedech offers bread and wine Moses & the manna	5 Betrayal prepared
t CHRIST PREDICTS HIS PASSION Micheas is punished for predicting defeat Condemned, Eliseus predicts the truth	v JEWS FALL BACK FROM CHRIST Foolish girls condemned Fall of the angels	

·a· JUDAS BETRAYS CHRIST WITH A KISS Joab kills Abner Tryphon betrays Jonathan	·b· JEWS CONDEMN CHRIST Jezabel seeks Elias' life The King condemns Daniel	6 Passion
·c· CHRIST IS MOCKED Noe's nakedness is mocked Boys mock Eliseus	·d· CHRIST CARRIES THE CROSS Abraham & Isaac Woman of Sarephta	
·e· CRUCIFIXION Abraham's sacrifice of Isaac Moses lifts up the serpent	·f· CHRIST IS PIERCED Eve is drawn from Adam Moses strikes the rock	7 Death & Tomb
·g· ENTOMBMENT Joseph placed in the well Jonas is swallowed	·h· CHRIST OPENS LIMBO David kills Goliath Samson kills the lion	
·i· RESURRECTION Samson removes the gates of Gaza Jonas is released	·k· THREE WOMEN AT THE TOMB Ruben at the well The Betrothed seeks her beloved	8 Resurrection
·l· MARY MAGDALENE FINDS CHRIST Daniel is found among the lions The Betrothed finds her beloved	·m· CHRIST APPEARS TO THE DISCIPLES oseph reveals himself to his brothers Return of the prodigal son	
·n· DOUBTING THOMAS Gideon & the angel Jacob wrestles with the angel	·o· ASCENSION Henoch ascends Eliseus receives Elias' mantle	9 Church established
·p· PENTECOST Moses receives the law Elias' sacrifice is accepted	·q· CORONATION OF THE VIRGIN Solomon enthrones Bethsabee Assuerus crowns Esther	
·r· LAST JUDGEMENT Judgement of Solomon David condemns the Amaeecite	·s· THE DAMNED ENTER HELL Dathan & Abiron are engulfed Sodom & Gomorrha burn	10 'Four Last Things'
·t· CHRIST GATHERS BLESSED SOULS Job's family feasts Jacob's Ladder	·v· CHRIST GIVES THE CROWN OF ETERNAL LIFE The Groom crowns the Bride The angel and St John	

FIG. 4
Table of Pairs and 'Chapters'

MS 'chapters'				*Blockbook 'chapters'* Scenes added in this version are capitalised, scenes moved are italicised
Annunciation. Nativity. Magi. Presentation.	**Infancy**	1	**Infancy**	Annunciation. Nativity. Magi. Presentation.
Flight. Egyptian idols fall. Massacre. Return.	**Egypt**	2	**Egypt**	Flight. Egyptian idols fall. Massacre. Return.
Baptism. Temptation. Transfiguration. Magdalene repents.	**Preparation**	3	**Godhead manifest**	Baptism. Temptation. *Lazarus*. Transfiguration.
Lazarus. Entry into Jerusalem. Temple purified. Last Supper.	**Ministry**	4	**Kingship recognised**	*Magdalene repents*. Entry into Jerusalem. Temple purified. *Conspiracy*.
Conspiracy. Judas paid. Judas kisses Christ. Pilate.	**Betrayal**	5	**Betrayal prepared**	Judas paid. *Last Supper*. CHRIST PREDICTS HIS PASSION. JEWS FALL BACK.
Christ mocked. Carrying the Cross. Crucifixion. Piercing.	**Passion**	6	**Passion**	*Judas kisses Christ*. JEWS CONDEMN CHRIST. Christ mocked. Carrying the Cross.
Burial. Limbo opened. Resurrection. Women at the Tomb.	**Tomb**	7	**Death & Tomb**	*Crucifixion. Piercing*. Burial. Limbo opened.
Magdalene meets Christ. Disciples. Thomas. Ascension.	**Appearances**	8	**Resurrection**	*Resurrection. Women at tomb*. Magdalene meets Christ. Disciples.
Pentecost. Coronation of Virgin.	**Virgin**	9	**Church established**	*Thomas. Ascension*. Pentecost. Coronation of Virgin.
		10	**Four Last Things**	LAST JUDGEMENT. HELL. BLESSED SOULS. CROWN OF ETERNAL LIFE.

FIG. 5
Table of Manuscript and Book 'Chapters'

Godhead Manifest. 'Optical editing' also alters emphases in the groups that follow: *Conspiracy* (the result of the High Priest of the Temple fearing a rival) becomes in the woodcut version part of a chapter concerned with recognition of Jesus's nature. Similarly, the woodcut version's chapter 9 brings *Doubting Thomas* as well as the *Ascension* into the group about the establishment of the Church (note that in each case the Types also stress these elements). Most important of all, the last group—which is in general terms about death and judgement, hell and heaven—is added in the blockbook.[21]

Hitherto we have looked at the structure formed by the forty Antitypes. We come now to the underlying structure within a page: the relationships created by the texts, and those created by the Antitype and its Types (not unnaturally called typological). In order to discuss these relationships we need a brief way of referring to each of the twelve interrelated elements on a page, as in the following diagram (which is found again on the bookmark).

The texts

Each page carries nine texts, of three different kinds and styles. Though the *Biblia Pauperum* may be enjoyed on the visual level alone, we would be wrong to regard it as purely visual. The texts play a part in the process which the page is designed to initiate. That process must be in part meditational, for of the nine texts, seven are always quite complex: they are not simply explanatory. First, under each of the three scenes is a caption known as a *titulus* (**8, 9, 12** on the diagram).[22] These are in verse: gnomic in compression, often punning, and usually meaning more than one thing at once.[23] All but six of the hundred and twenty in the book are thought to be the invention of the *Biblia Pauperum*'s authors (of manuscript and of wood cut versions). In themselves they are evidence of tradition-loving, but original and economical minds. (The pictures will reveal the same qualities, almost as if the *tituli* were created by the picture-designer.[24]) Consider •q•**12**, for example. The *titulus* to the *Coronation of the Virgin* is *Assumendo piam: veneraris christe mariam*. This is inadequately translated as 'By lifting her up you have honoured the loving Mary, O Christ', for Mary has not only, like her Types Bethsabee and Esther, been raised to the throne, she has also been literally assumed into heaven, uncorrupted by death, in a transition to the next world unique among mere mortals: *assumendo* bears much emphasis and two meanings. Similarly *piam*, for which 'dutiful' is too dry, 'good' too weak, and 'pious' too sentimental, carries all the classical connotations of fulfilment of obligation at all levels—to God and to man (Mary being acknowledged here as daughter, wife, mother, and queen extraordinary).

Second among the kinds of text on the page are the four Prophecies, two at the top and two at the bottom, in scrolls emanating from the four demi-figures representing Old Testament authors (**3, 4, 10, 11** on the diagram). These Prophecies are hardly less complex than the *tituli*. Usually from the Old Testament or the liturgy, they are related (mostly by

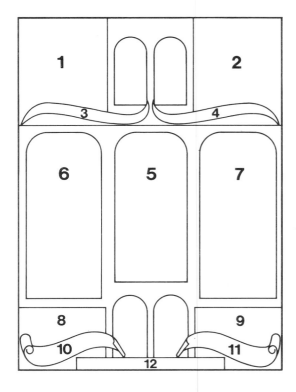

FIG. 6
Diagram of the twelve elements on a *Biblia Pauperum* blockbook page

tradition but sometimes with originality) to the main themes of the page. Their 'style' is that of the Vulgate, so that unlike other texts on the page they carry the authority of centuries of scriptural use and interpretation. Each of them speaks both on a literal and on a symbolic or typological level. This aspect of the words of prophets was explained to the disciples when after his Resurrection Jesus himself said: 'These are the words which I spoke to you while I was yet with you, that all things must needs be fulfilled which are written in the law of Moses and in the prophets, and in the psalms, concerning me'.[25]

The third kind of text is found in the little explanations known as *lectiones* (**1** and **2**). These two 'lessons' at the top left and right of each page describe only the simplest levels at which Types and Antitype relate. The top left-hand *lectio* explains how the left-hand Type relates to the Antitype, the right-hand one explains the other side: for example, the relationship between the *Coronation of the Virgin* (•q•**5**) and its second Type, *Assuerus Crowns Esther*, is described at its simplest level by •q•**2**: 'when Queen Esther had come to King Assuerus in his palace, King Assuerus himself placed her next to him to honour her. Esther the Queen signifies the Virgin Mary, whom Assuerus (that is, Christ) placed next to himself in celestial glory on the day of her assumption'. It is hard to believe that the *lectiones* are from the same mind as the *tituli*. Loosely connective in syntax, discursive for all their enforced brevity, only on rare occasions do they offer more than is obvious. In the example just quoted, no mention is made of the fact that Esther also prefigures Mary in her eloquent intercession for her people, in her humble confidence in her king, and in her recognition as his wife (Bethsabee, enthroned by her son Solomon in the other Type on the page, being acknowledged as mother). The first *lectio*, in sig. **a**, is a rare example containing material essential to the deeper sense of the page. Indeed, the first four *lectiones* happen to be unusually necessary to an understanding of the first two pages, which rely not on obvious parallels of event in Types and Antitypes, but on ancient theological interpretations of events either related directly to each other (God warning the serpent about Mary) or related only by quite subtle exegesis (*Moses and the Burning Bush* and *Gideon's Fleece* prefiguring the *Nativity*).

The shorthand represented in Fig. 6 is necessary to elucidate the relationships between picture and texts, because they are not so rigid and formalised as the page design might suggest. *Lectio* **1** does always explain the link between **5** and **6**, **2** does always explain the link between **5** and **7**; *titulus* **8** usually but not always describes **6** (though 'describe' is a narrow word for the additional insights which the *tituli* offer), **9** is similarly related to **7**, and **12** to **5**; but the Prophecies (**3**, **4**, **10**, **11**) may relate to any element on the page, and often to each other. Indeed, the Types may sometimes relate to each other: **r6** and **r7** are stages in the same story in which Joseph is twice sold.

Twelve elements on each page, therefore—three pictures and nine texts—interlock. A translation of the texts is supplied in the diagrams following each pair of facsimile pages. In these diagrams the position of each of the twelve elements is retained. The three capitalised titles in square brackets represent the three scenes; any text within scrolls in the pictures appears under the titles (**a**, **·k·**, **·l·**). The twelve elements' subtle interweaving is controlled by the underlying typology. The very position of the *lectiones* at the top of the page shows how fundamental to the book this typological mode is. Anyone unfamiliar with the images must identify them from the *lectiones*, and so understand the basic typological relationships they describe. The most important relationships in the book are those between Types and Antitypes.

Typology

Typology is the name given to a mode of thought which governs the relationship described at a simple level by the *lectiones*; strictly, it is distinct from the mode governing the kind of relationship represented by the four Prophecies on a *Biblia Pauperum* page. Types are commonly persons drawn from the 'history' books of the Bible (so Noah, Moses, and David are all familiar Types of Christ, according to subsequent interpretations of their activities); but a Type may also be an event or an object (in sig. **·e·5, 7** it is not Moses but the lifted serpent which is the Type of Christ on the Cross). Prophecy—certainly as found in the Prophecies in the *Biblia Pauperum*—is usually from the Bible's prophetic books or from the Psalms. It is easy to distinguish from typology when it is direct, a prophet referring specifically to the coming Messiah, as in

sig. **bII** when the prophet Micheas promises that the future king will come from Bethlehem, and his prophecy is quoted to Herod (Matt. ii 6). However, when a prophecy is indirect, being only an image later interpreted by the Fathers as a messianic reference—for example, Ezechiel's 'door which is to be kept closed', interpreted as the inviolate virginity of Mary (sig. **a10**)—it is hard to distinguish from a Type. Prophecy has produced even more pictorial schemes than typology (see n. 25). The Apostles and evangelists are ranged with the prophets in the apse windows at Bourges, for example, and the evangelists sit on the shoulders of the prophets in a window of the south transept of Chartres.

Typology differs also from allegory, in that details of a historical or quasi-historical event are examined for the light they throw on a later event,[26] whereas in allegory the first half of the equation is commonly invented. Bunyan creates Christian, his burden and his journey, to represent man's life: his hero has no qualities irrelevant to his meaning, none difficult to account for. In contrast, the cryptic story of Moses apparently making an idol of a snake on a stick must be *explored* as a Type of the Crucifixion (sig. **·e·**).

The typological habit of thought, which sees all time and history as part of God's patterned plan, is biblical. The Old Testament is understood not only as history, but also as a kind of elaborate code to the understanding of the New. In the Gospels, Christ himself created the Type just cited, saying of his coming Crucifixion: 'as Moses lifted up the serpent in the desert so must the Son of man be lifted up'.[27] Of his Resurrection he said: 'As Jonas was in the whale's belly for three days and three nights, so shall the Son of man be in the heart of the earth three days and three nights' (sig. **·i·**).[28] But Christ could only make use of such typological images because the concept of the past foreshadowing and fulfilled in the future is as old as Judaism.[29] His audience understood. These patterns of prefiguration are not the creation of a Church which 'could think of nothing better to do with the Old Testament'.[30] Indeed, to the Church, the parallels between the two Testaments were eternally *intended*, their pattern ultimately attributable to God, who created them, and to the Holy Spirit, under whose inspiration the Bible's writers worked.

The liturgy of the Church daily endorses this view even today. During the canon of the Mass (its central portion, which unlike the proper of the Mass remains essentially the same each day) the priest asks God to receive his sacrifice 'as once you accepted the gifts of your servant Abel, the sacrifice of Abraham, our father in faith, and the bread and wine offered by your priest Melchisedech' (sigs **·e·6** and **s6**).[31] The pages of the Breviary, the liturgical book containing the whole Divine Office recited by priests in daily portions until completed each year, are full of typology, often in passages drawn directly from Augustine and other Church Fathers: indeed the Breviary itself, rather than the Bible, appears to be the source of at least one of the Prophecies in our book (sig. **h4**).[32]

The tradition of scriptural typology is also unbroken in the writings of the Fathers. The notes to the commentaries in this edition show that many such images derive from the second-century Melito and third-century Tertullian, as well as from those founts of this kind of creative energy, Origen and the four 'Doctors': Augustine, Ambrose and Jerome in the fifth and Gregory in the sixth century. By the fifth century when Augustine made his much-quoted observation that 'the New Testament lies hidden in the Old, and the Old is fulfilled in the New' typology had long been implicit in art.[33] In early Christian frescoes on the walls of catacombs or on reliefs decorating sarcophagi, for example, resurrection would be implied by the presence of Jonas emerging from the fish (*Jonas Is Released*, sig. ·i·7).[34] The fifth-century carved doors of S. Sabina, Rome, equate the miracles of Moses and Christ, and the ascensions of Elias and Christ (sig. ·o·5, 7).[35] A famous sixth-century mosaic by the altar in S. Vitale, Ravenna, shows exactly the three events from the canon of the Mass mentioned in the previous paragraph.[36]

Typology soon became explicit. A well-known passage in Bede describes how the seventh-century Benedict Biscop brought from Rome to the English monastery and church of Jarrow typological paintings (representations of the 'Concordance of the Old and New Testaments')[37] which included as Types not only *Abraham's Sacrifice of Isaac* but also the previously mentioned *Moses Lifts Up the Serpent* (sig. ·e·6, 7). It is significant that this typological series was in a monastery, its audience therefore learned. Far from being a substitute language for the illiterate, iconography in general and typology in particular has always been rooted in the literary: the Latin (and Greek) Fathers *wrote*, so they were clearly not addressing the unlearned. That typological art was also found in public places does not necessarily mean that it was addressed primarily to the unlettered. One eleventh-century typological cycle planned for the Cathedral of Mainz in Germany, though never executed, is known to us only because it is recorded that the archbishop commissioned someone to compose Latin captions for it (this cycle, like that at Jarrow, also included the *Crucifixion* with *Moses Lifts Up the Serpent* as its Type)[38]. Most captions to surviving typological art are in Latin, as in Figs 7–11 below. (The question of audience is discussed further on pp. 17–18.)

The tradition maintained by the Fathers flowered in the twelfth century with the resurgence of scholarship in the great age of monasticism which immediately preceded the creation of the manuscript *Biblia Pauperum*.[39] The system was then sufficiently developed to surprise us by the 'ingenuity with which the most unpromising incidents in the Old Testament are pressed into the service': an ingenuity which 'often testifies to a really poetic imagination, exercised by generations of men determined to see Christ everywhere'.[40] Impetus to the typological system was given by writers such as the so-called Honorius of Autun (d. 1152), a prolific theologian whose lively sermons often showed an event of Christ's life in the light of all its possible Types.[41] Impetus was also given to the twelfth-century development of typology by the well-known work of Abbot Suger, who instigated the creation of several major typological schemes at St Denis. Among them was a great golden Cross which, though it does not survive, we know from descriptions to have borne sixty-eight typological scenes. Fragments of the superb scheme of typological stained glass at St Denis are, however, still accessible to us.[42] More familiar, perhaps, if only in the pioneering work of Mâle, are the twelfth- and thirteenth-century windows and west fronts of the great French cathedrals.

Typology proliferated in theology,[43] literature,[44] and art.[45] It is impossible as well as unnecessary to give here a complete account of typological representations in twelfth- and thirteenth-century Europe. Mention of some major examples, with illustration and discussion of a few of them, will simply offer a background against which the birth of the *Biblia Pauperum* may be seen, instead of viewing it in a void. They will incidentally illustrate the flexibility of typological equations and the influence of important schemes on designs in many media. Since the illustrated examples are also intended to act as a background against which to see our particular version of the *Biblia Pauperum*, they will be explained in some detail.

The most remarkable surviving example of a complete typological scheme predating the creation of the *Biblia Pauperum*, and the one most instructive to compare with it, is the so-called Altar of Nicholas of Verdun, in the monastery of Klosterneuburg, near Vienna.[46] Made in 1181, its exact original form is somewhat uncertain: it used to cover an ambo, a stand from which the Gospel and Epistle were read at Mass, so it was literally associated with the New Testament. It originally consisted of thirteen groups—each, as shown in Fig. 7, with a Type above and below it. Its present 'triptych' form as a great reredos of seventeen Antitypes, standing behind and above the high altar, dates from 1330, when after a fire it was extended by the two groups flanking the central *Crucifixion* (the *Betrayal* and the *Deposition*) and rearranged. Its purpose then is written into its Latin inscription: 'to make the results of redemption plain, and awaken in men consciousness of grace'. Fig. 7A shows one of the original groups, and Fig. 7B one of the later groups. Resplendent in blue enamel and black niello against gold, it communicates primarily by pictures, but the superb lettering of its brief Latin text (whose sources are usually liturgical) is a more important element in the beauty of the whole design than are the longer texts of the *Biblia Pauperum*. In total contrast to the book, the work's sheer size (it is about three and a half feet, or a hundred and eight centimetres, high) is most impressive, for it extends not only the length of the altar but also into two wings coming forward on either side to flank it. Yet in general concept it is very similar to the *Biblia Pauperum*, the purpose of which it may help us to understand. This great enamel was designed, if not simply for the glory of God, then surely for concentrated contemplation by man, as an aid to devotion. It is no portable *aide-mémoire* for sermon-givers, or a means of instructing the unlearned.

Unlike our book, the enamel consistently shows one Type from the period *ante legem* (before the law of Moses) and one

FIG. 7
Altar of Nicholas of Verdun, Klosterneuburg
A. *Abraham Gives Tithes to Melchisedech* and *Magi*
and *Solomon and Sheba*
B. *Cain Kills Abel* and *Judas Betrays Christ* and *Joab Kills Abner.*

sub lege (after the law of Moses)—the former above, the latter below the main scene, which is *sub gratia* (after the Redemption). It shares many subjects, but not all, with the *Biblia Pauperum* in its manuscript and woodcut forms: it therefore illustrates how typology, though schematised, is not rigid. In Fig. 7A, for example, the centre scene, the *Magi*, and the Type below it, *Solomon and Sheba*, are the equivalents of *Biblia Pauperum* sig. **d5, 7**, though different in composition from both manuscript and woodcut versions. The *titulus* to the main scene means 'Three wise men with gifts; the three kings give three symbolic gifts to the true God'. One of the Magi points to the guiding star; one doffs his crown; one kneels, crown on knee, to offer a gift. In a bold design device, this gift is only just within the architectural bay isolating the Virgin and Child. The Type below is 'The Queen of Sheba; by gifts, the queen symbolically indicates faith in Solomon'. Traditionally signifying the Church, the dark-skinned queen *stands*, almost dominating the design, the upper part of which is occupied by her head, Solomon's sceptre, and her courteous gesture. The Type above, however, is uncommon. It shows 'Abraham [and] Melchisedech; Abraham, conqueror of kings, gives tithes of everything [he has won]'. Here Melchisedech is acknowledged as king: it is the moment *after* his offering of bread and wine to Abraham—the common scene which both on this altarpiece and in the *Biblia Pauperum* prefigures the *Last Supper*, and in which Melchisedech is a Type of Christ not as king but as priest (sig. **s6**).

Fig. 7B shows one of the 1330 groups. Like Fig. 7A, it conveniently illustrates the variations often found in typology. Röhrig suggests (p. 43) that the source was one of the earliest extant manuscripts of the *Biblia Pauperum*: Vienna Nationalbibliothek Cod. 1198, probably made at Klosterneuburg, and itself derived from the St Florian manuscript, one opening of which is illustrated in Fig. 1. However, the style does not derive from the *Biblia Pauperum* manuscript: the 1330 goldsmith deliberately adopted an archaic manner, imitating that of the 1181 ambo. Also, he used the *Biblia Pauperum* selectively: the central *Judas Betrays Christ* is prefigured underneath by *Joab Kills Abner* (compare sig. **·a·5, 6**), but the Type above is *Cain Kills Abel*, not *Tryphon Betrays Jonathan*, as in the *Biblia Pauperum*. The altarpiece maintains the *ante legem* pattern in its upper scenes: *Tryphon Betrays Jonathan* (the *Biblia Pauperum* inscription from which is on the *back* of the panel) was no doubt rejected as *sub lege*. The *titulus* as it stands means 'Judas kisses the Lord. With a kiss, O Christ, this traitor betrays you' (a direct address to Christ perhaps suggesting devotional use). But the Latin *Osculo te Christi* . . . ('With a kiss O Christ . . .') is a restoration, and it is thought that the *titulus* originally echoed the manuscript *Biblia Pauperum* with *Per pacem Christe te* . . . ('By the Kiss of Peace, O Christ . . .'). All this gives an interesting insight into the early influence of the *Biblia Pauperum* on a work of art which may have originally influenced it.

Quite apart from the special relationship between the *Biblia Pauperum* and the 1330 enamels, the whole altarpiece scheme resembles the *Biblia Pauperum* in the care with which its designs have been made to interrelate. The pictures enrich each other in composition as well as in content. In the examples illustrated, Judas and Jesus are somehow alone in the crowded violence of *Judas Betrays Christ*. In clever contrast is the isolation in which the murders depicted in the Types occur. The *titulus* of the top one is 'The killing of Abel; like the serpent, Cain destroys Abel by what he says' (presumably a reference both to the Fall and to Cain's luring Abel into the fields to kill him). Almost in the centre, Abel's head is surrounded by vividly angular movements of rage and fear, the opposing lines of which are echoed in the tree. Effective contrast of another kind is made by the superficially passive group in the lower Type: 'The killing of Abner. Joab spoke to him pleasantly, and treacherously murdered him'. The thrust of Joab's blade into his unsuspecting victim's belly as he embraces him is the only discordant diagonal among the quietly standing figures.

The spandrels between the trefoil arches are occupied in the top register by angels, in the middle register by prophets, and in the bottom register by virtues. The altar shows the same esoteric use of prophecies as that shown by the *Biblia Pauperum*, though on the former only one (not four) is related to each Antitype. David, in the top left-hand spandrel, says 'in the house of my father'—a reference to Psalm liv 15, traditionally interpreted as alluding to Christ's anguish on being betrayed by one with whom he had shared friendship in his 'father's house'.[47] At the top right, Daniel's 'After this Christ shall be slain' refers to the *next* Antitype, towards which he looks—the *Crucifixion*.[48]

Austria and France were the great centres of early-twelfth-century typology, but in the late twelfth and thirteenth centuries 'a special interest in the collection of types . . . was a feature of English art in particular'.[49] Three great English cycles were larger than anything known to have existed in Austria or France at the time: two painted and one in glass, and all three related to each other in some way. An impressive series of typological paintings at Peterborough[50] can now only be imagined with the help of the Peterborough Psalter, which was influenced by them; its typological life of Christ is often echoed in the subjects (not the designs) of the *Biblia Pauperum*.[51] This cycle and its related Psalter (a page of which is reproduced in Fig. 11) are also related to the thirteenth-century stained glass at Canterbury, some of which appears in Fig. 8. Worcester Cathedral priory once had a series of ten typological subjects painted in the chapter house: the *tituli* and descriptions survive in a manuscript in the Cathedral library.[52] The Worcester cycle was related both to the Peterborough cycle and to the typological manuscript illustrated in Fig. 10. These two great cycles of paintings once at Peterborough and Worcester are known to us only from records in local manuscripts; however, some of the Canterbury stained glass, from the longest known cycle of the period, survives.

The beholder of the twelfth- and thirteenth-century typological glass at Canterbury may be unaware that its depth of colour is more than equalled by its depth of meaning.[53] The complete cycle once consisted of thirteen large windows. The glass shown in Fig. 8 is from the easternmost window (*c.* 1220) of the cathedral, the last in the cycle. The upper and lower half-roundels are from four Types surrounding what was once the *Crucifixion*. The latter was the lowest of the Antitypes in this 'Salvation' window, with the *Entombment*, *Resurrection*, *Ascension*, and *Pentecost* above, each with four Types. In these two half-roundels we see a tiny part of what is still a great, though incomplete, typological scheme.[54] At Canterbury these two little scenes are almost at eye level: for once, we know that the details visible to us were actually visible not only to God but also to the medieval observer, instead of being, as so often, beyond the range of eyes unaided by binoculars. Like some of the scenes on the Klosterneuburg Altar, these two scenes illustrate the variety found within typology, for here they form standard prefigurations of the *Crucifixion*; in contrast, the *Biblia Pauperum* rather eccentrically uses *Josue and Caleb Return from Jordan* (the lower scene) to prefigure the *Baptism of Christ* (sig. **i7**).

The *Josue and Caleb Return from Jordan* scene is a good example of the way in which such small panels, at first scarcely perceived as entities in the splendour of a whole window, show great care in their individual designs. First, the 'pendant' emphasis in the scene created by the burden of grapes is perfectly related to the 'pendant' semicircle, and then, within that, symmetrical colour and symmetrical composition fuse perfectly to convey the meaning of the scene. It is unfortunate that the colour, which is perhaps the major design element in any stained glass, cannot be shown in the illustration, for it is beautifully controlled (even in the small portions of restoration—the heads and parts of the drapery). However, some of this control is visible even in a black-and-white reproduction. For example, in the lower scene white plays a very important part in the pattern: against a rich blue sky, the grapes themselves are white, as are the pole bearing them, the bearers' heads and hands, the scarves flowing round them (and apparently being used as shoulder pads or tie-ropes), the staffs the bearers lean on, and the inscription explaining the relationship among all these white elements. For the pole is the Cross, and the fruit borne on it with such difficulty is Christ; the *titulus* means: 'The one [in front] refuses to look back at the cluster of grapes, the other thirsts to see it: Israel does not know Christ, the Gentile worships him'. The similarity of the pose adopted by the two figures creates a sense of the steady pace necessary in the support of such a weighty burden; so too does the symmetrical but not mechanical use of green for their legs, sleeves, and the ground on which they tread (their careful steps pointed by the way in which their feet obtrude into the red border and even into the white inscription itself). Only the tunics—the right-hand one red like the border inside the inscription, the left-hand one brown—vary the symmetry just enough to distinguish these symbols of Jew and gentile.

Above *Josue and Caleb Return from Jordan* (though divided from it by the *Crucifixion* in the original window) is *Abraham's*

FIG. 8
Canterbury Cathedral, Corona East Window No. 1
(the 'thirteenth' typological window)
Abraham's Sacrifice of Isaac
Josue and Caleb Return from Jordan

Sacrifice of Isaac. Like *Josue and Caleb Return from Jordan*, it is a traditional design—it may be compared with the same scene in Fig. 10, for example (as well as with *Biblia Pauperum* **·e·6**). It too is perfectly adapted to its semicircle, at the top of which the highest moment of the drama is caught as the angel of God seizes Abraham's sword. To the right and left, respectively, are Isaac lying on the cross-shaped faggots of his sacrificial altar, and the thicket-entangled ram which is to take his place. Instead of an explanatory inscription to this familiar scene there is a traditional border loosely based on Arabic lettering derived from the word for 'blessing' in Cufic script.[55] The overall economy is deceptively simple, art having been used to conceal art.

England produced not only the largest typological cycle of the period, but also the largest handbook of typological examples known, which possibly influenced the Canterbury glass. It may be contemporary with *Biblia Pauperum* in its earliest manuscript form. The long work by the Cistercian who called himself *Pictor in Carmine* ('Painter in Song' or perhaps 'Painter in Verse') is of about 1200.[56] This extraordinary work presents just the *tituli* for a hundred and thirty-eight Antitypes with over five hundred Types, in groups of varying sizes. In this respect, and in drawing for its Antitypes on the lives of Christ, John the Baptist, and the Apostles, it shows less formality than the *Biblia Pauperum* (the Types show an equal width of source material). Interestingly, the author's preface seems to suggest that it was intended to meet St Bernard's famous objection to fanciful and 'monstrous' artwork, which he regarded as inappropriate to monasteries.[57]

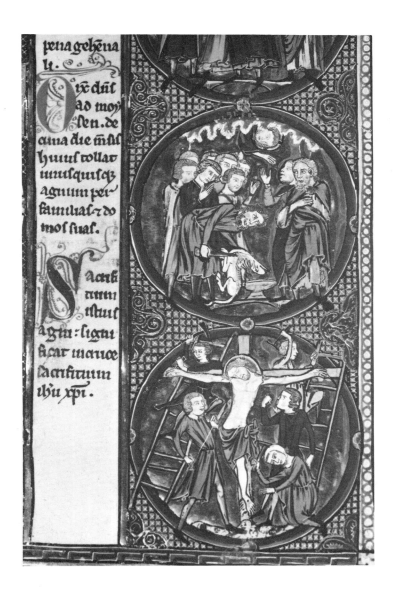

FIG. 9
Bible Moralisée
Oxford, Bodleian Library, MS. Bodley 270b, f. 45ᵛ
Top: *Paschal Lamb* Bottom: *Crucifixion*

FIG. 10
Figurae Bibliorum
Eton College, MS. 177, f. 5ʳ
Abraham's Sacrifice of Isaac and *Moses Lifts Up the Serpent*
Crucifixion
Jacob and Nahum Prophesy and *Elias Raises the Sarephtan*

For all its use of legend and other literature of the imagination (such as the Bestiary), it is conceived as a *rationalising* of decorative design. As one of the rare medieval texts directly related to art, it gives us another perspective on typological work.[58]

A moral aim different in kind from that stated in *Pictor in Carmine* is clear in the thirteenth-century French *Bible Moralisée*.[59] Vertical pairs of little roundels, eight to a large page, present in biblical order Old and New Testament scenes, each over an actual or invented scene illustrating its moral significance. For example, the creation of the birds on the sixth day of Creation signifies contemplatives who aspire to ascend to haven by prayer.[60] A brief text near the upper, main scene describes it, a similar one explains the moralising scene below. Not strictly a typological relationship, it sometimes becomes so, as when the sacrifice of the *Paschal Lamb* (as an Old Testament main scene) is explained in terms of the

Crucifixion (Fig. 9).[61] Here the top roundel's text is from Exod. xii 3, explaining that the Lord told Moses to distribute a sacrificial lamb among his people at the Passover. The lower roundel's text simply means 'The sacrifice of this lamb signifies the sacrifice of Jesus Christ on the Cross'. This beautiful book is an interesting contrast to the *Biblia Pauperum* in the comparative simplicity of its concepts. The upper roundels may be read as a picture-Bible, with the lower roundels as a kind of moral commentary. This is made easier by the fact that the related pictures are often deliberately similar in their directness of design: the central position of lamb and Cross is enough in this instance to relate them in the mind. Exactly the same kind of relationship between design elements has been observed in the Canterbury glass: 'the elements of such composition become visual equivalents of one another, and virtually interchangeable'.[62]

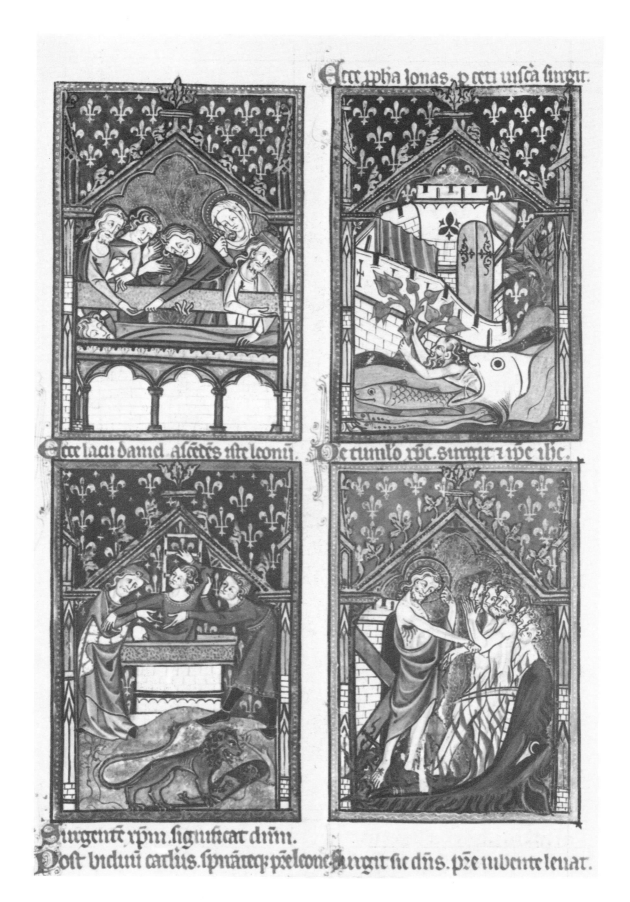

FIG. II
The Peterborough Psalter
Brussels, Bibliothèque Royale Albert Ier, MS. 9961–62, f. 64^v
Entombment and *Jonas is Released*
Daniel Leaves the Lions' Den and *Christ Opens Limbo*

The unique English manuscript known as *Figurae Bibliorum* (Fig. 10) bears a close relationship to the Worcester paintings, whose *tituli* we know.[63] It is also important because at *c.* 1250 it, like the *Bible Moralisée*, is near the date of the probable creation of the first *Biblia Pauperum* manuscript. It resembles the *Biblia Pauperum* in that its readers were clearly learned and deeply familiar with the typological and other iconographic ideas borne more by its pictures than by its minimal texts. At the top of the central roundel on the page shown in Fig. 10 Synagogue (the Old Law) is blindfold, while Ecclesia (the Church or the New Law) looks directly at Christ crucified. The *Crucifixion* is not as it appears in the *Biblia Pauperum*: to the right, the angel who banished Adam and Eve from paradise with his flaming sword here sheaths it in token of the new covenant between God and man made in the Atonement;[64] to the left, Ecclesia, probably representing both the Virgin at the Cross and the Church, collects Christ's blood in a chalice, for the Church distributes the sacraments which as St Augustine says, flowed from the side of Christ as he lay on the Cross.[65] Three of the associated roundels (at the top and at the bottom right) contain Types. The top Types, found also in our book, both prefigure the *Crucifixion*: *Abraham's Sacrifice of Isaac* and *Moses Lifts Up the Serpent* (sig. •e•). The roundel at the bottom left holds not a Type but a Prophecy of the Crucifixion: Jacob delivers part of his messianic prophecy (Gen. xlix 11), here applied to the crucified Christ: 'He shall wash his robe in wine [and his garment in the blood of the grape]', the prophet Nahum (i 14) saying 'I will make [it] thy grave, for thou art disgraced'—references to the effusion of Christ's blood, and to the ignominy of death on a cross. The roundel at the bottom right, however, is a Type of Entombment and Resurrection: *Elias Raises the Sarephtan*, which in our book prefigures the *Raising of Lazarus*, here recalls *both* Types in our book (sig. **l**), for the text mentions both Elias and Eliseus. Between the two lower roundels is Obedience, to remind us that man's disobedience at the Fall is atoned for in the Crucifixion.

The early-fourteenth-century Peterborough Psalter, bearing a close relationship to both the lost Peterborough cycle and to the Canterbury glass,[66] has many typological miniatures, though it does not present a complete scheme. It too is a splendid example of the variety within conformity which typology displays. At the top of Fig. 11 the *Entombment* is prefigured not as in the *Biblia Pauperum* (sig. •**g**•**5**, **7**) by *Jonas Is Swallowed*, but by *Jonas Is Released* (which in the *Biblia Pauperum* prefigures the *Resurrection*, sig. •**i**•). The Type here *anticipates* events. At the bottom, *Daniel Leaves the Lions' Den* prefigures *Christ Opens Limbo*, which in our book is prefigured (sig. •**h**•) by *David Kills Goliath* and *Samson Kills the Lion* (*Daniel Is Found Among the Lions* prefigures *Mary Magdalene Finds Christ*, sig. •**l**•). The four scenes may, however, be read in different relationships. The texts do not relate them horizontally, in the manner just described; they merely name each scene, or say something non-committal such as 'the Lord is signified by Daniel'. That all four scenes carry equal visual weight (unlike the three scenes on any page in our book)

allows them to be read not only horizontally but also vertically, so that Daniel's emergence from the den suggests Christ's rising from the tomb shown above, and Jonas's survival prefigures not only Christ's conquest of the tomb to harrow hell, but also the emergence of the souls from Hellmouth, in the scene below.

Typology is the product of a much-misunderstood perceptive and creative process which deserves a friendlier name, for it lies behind more medieval art than we expect. The *Biblia Pauperum* in its original manuscript form is the earliest, and in its printed form is the longest-surviving, illustrated book of the system. It is a treasure-house of the past, but it also had a profound influence on the future, itself affecting the tradition it preserved (see pp. 35–38). Herein lies both the delight and the danger in our approach to the book. Like an icon, it is ancient in ancestry, instant in appeal. Like an icon, it appeals to our self-consciously aesthetic twentieth-century taste as 'art' first and foremost: its images are powerful, with an exciting element of the esoteric. But with few exceptions, such as the *Nativity* or *Crucifixion*, the images themselves are unfamiliar, and the theological presuppositions underlying the choice of images are remote from us. Medieval art is often accessible to the eye or even the hand—we blink at it in stained glass, finger it in chiselled stone. But however easy its surfaces are to reach and enjoy, the underlying thoughts are elusive, the meaning is not apparent to the mind and heart as once it was. Yet precisely because our book is a compendium of images familiar for centuries, and traditionally associated, it is for us one of the quickest and most pleasurable ways of learning what its educated medieval reader already knew.

Typology in this book: the thought-pattern of the page

The unchanging relationships among the elements on the *Biblia Pauperum* page have been easily described, but the actual patterns of thought they create are more complex. It is time to consider the particular applications of typology in our book. To begin with, its Types relate to the Antitypes in varying ways.[67] First, the relationship may be an apparently simple parallel between externally similar events, as when the killing of Abner by Joab prefigures the betrayal of Christ by Judas (sig. •**a**•). Second, the Types may be drawn not from the Old Testament but from the New, as in parables of the Foolish Virgins of **v6**, or of the Prodigal Son of •**m**•**7**. Third, the relationship between Type and Antitype may be more elusive, deriving from ancient theological concepts, as is the case in **a7** and **b7**, where it is not at all obvious at first how *Gideon's Fleece* is a Type of the *Annunciation*, or *Moses and the Burning Bush* of the *Nativity*. Fourth, Types may relate causally to the Antitype. For example, **a6** actually depicts the warning that **a5** will occur—God warns the serpent of the Incarnation; **k6**, *The Fall*, is the reason why **k5**, the *Temptation of Christ*, is necessary. The *Law of Presentation* shown in **d6** is not typologically fulfilled in the *Presentation* in **d5**: it is *obeyed* in it. Some typological relationships refuse to be categorised—for example •v•7, where the angel and St John of the New Testament Apocalypse are more significant as the final image of the book than they are in terms of their relation to •v•5.

Even within truly prefigurative relationships, remarkable variations occur. The prefiguration may seem to be simply in terms of parallel events, as when Joseph is put into a well, as Christ is put into the tomb (•g•5, 6). Hitherto such parallels have been regarded as somewhat simple, even inappropriate: Joseph, for example, is put into the well by those who hate him, whereas Christ is buried by those who love him.[68] However, this kind of contrast within superficial resemblance is so common that it seems to be due not to carelessness or naivety, but to craftsmanship. There is little meditational profit in the thought that Joseph and Christ are exactly similar in their incarcerations, but it is moving to consider that unlike Joseph, Christ was dead and was buried by friends, as most men are. To take another case, it is surely significant that in sig. c the two Types show kings of this world acknowledged, while Christ the King is acknowledged by the Magi in another sense. It is unlikely to be accidental that in d7 Samuel remains in the service of the Temple, while the Child in d5 serves God in another way: he is bought back from God, according to the Law of Presentation, only to 'serve God' in his life and death outside among men. It seems to be intentional that David in h6 and Jacob in h7 return to their kingdoms, while in h5 Christ returns not to his birthplace but to Nazareth and persecution—his kingdom 'not of this world'. The whole point of i6 and i7 is that Moses and the Israelites come through water to a promised land on this earth, whilst the baptism shown in i5 admits us to a promised world hereafter. In k6 and k7 temptation wins, in k5 it is resisted. One of the most familiar of all Types—the sacrifice of Isaac by Abraham prefiguring the Crucifixion—is moving not because of the parallels between the two events, but because Christ died, while Isaac did not, and because Christ understood, while Isaac did not. We see the ultimate obedience which is asked of but not exacted from Abraham, actually demanded of God by God. The list of such contrasts-within-parallels is long.[69]

Occasionally a scene will bear two mutually illuminating but opposed meanings at the same time. A good example of this is •m•7, the Prodigal Son rather surprisingly prefiguring the appearance of the resurrected Christ to his disciples. The commentary explains that the point of this picture in its context is precisely that the welcomer and the home-comer are typologically interchangeable: the Prodigal Son and his father are each *both* Christ *and* the disciples. It is perhaps not surprising that one reader of the *Biblia Pauperum* observed grudgingly that the Type is incongruous: 'the Prodigal, I suppose, represents the disciples, who had fled from their master at his arrest, and the father stands for Jesus'.[70] That this is certainly not the only meaning of the picture is clear from the *lectio*, which affirms that the son stands for Jesus. A somewhat similar multiplicity of identity is found in •n•7, where *Jacob Wrestles with the Angel* is a Type of *Doubting*

Thomas: Christ is the angel in that he allows himself to be vanquished, but Christ is Jacob in that he receives the wound in the encounter between God and man.

Each page is like a series of chords—comprehensible only because based on recognised relationships, exciting in unexpected modulation by Prophecies and *tituli*. In •d•, for example, *Christ Carries the Cross* is flanked by ancient prefigurations: Isaac's shouldering of sticks for his own pyre, and the widow of Sarephta's two twigs (in art transformed by their prefiguring function into great branches), which she really gathered to flavour her starvation diet of broth. Traditional is the equation between Isaac's burden and Christ's. Traditional is the equation between the widow's two sticks and the Cross, which is our 'food', and also between her faith in the prophet and Christ's in his Father. Only the page context with its four Prophecies about sacrifice and silence, about trust in God's fearsome demands, and about feasting on the spoil of battle, brings all these themes together in echoing new relationships, so that somehow to shoulder a burden (•d•6) is to be fed (•d•7), and to give (•d•7) is to live (•d•6).

We have looked at the relation among the forty Antitypes in our book: their division into two parts at the start of the Passion, their division into ten thematic 'chapters', and their pairing on each double-spread. We have looked also at the wide variety of ways in which Type and Antitype illuminate each other. Finally we have looked at the varying ways in which the twelve elements on a page interrelate. Enough has been said to enable us to assess some theories about the original purpose of the *Biblia Pauperum*.

The purpose of the original book

It must be obvious by now that the *Biblia Pauperum* was not designed for use by children, as was once suggested, and that it was not intended as an aid 'by which . . . the preacher could assist the more stupid classes'.[71] It cannot, any more than can the great typological cycles or manuscripts, have been for the intelligent who could not read. Even recently the suggestion has been repeated that the *Biblia Pauperum* was to instruct the illiterate 'even as the façades of cathedrals instructed Villon's mother'[72] (a suggestion which implies comprehension of the pictures without their texts!). The surprisingly persistent notion that the medieval visual arts were designed to *instruct* the unlettered is based on a misconception. Little medieval art is merely instructive. Our modern response to medieval typology is sufficient evidence that pictures in this mode only 'instruct' if you already know what they mean. They then act as reminders of the known truth. It is not a bit of good staring at a picture of a man carrying two large doors on the outskirts of a city and expecting it to suggest the risen Christ. You are likely to take him for a builder's merchant or a removal man unless you already know that this is always Samson with the gates of Gaza (•i•6) and that like Christ he has, as it were, broken gaol. If you stare at a depiction of two self-consciously naked people picking fruit you are likely to mistake them for apple-gathering nature-worshippers if you do not already know (as most people do even today) that this is Adam and Eve, whose temptation and fall prefigures Christ's resistance to temptation (**k**).

Villon's mother was in any case not instructed by a façade: she was simply cheered and frightened by a picture of heaven and hell in her parish church.[73] It cannot have told her anything she did not already know (indeed, there is no way of depicting the joys of heaven which is even recognisable, let alone convincing, if the conventions are not familiar). Even a simple narrative series would have to show a known story to make sense: how far can we follow, say, Indian narrative art? To think it could teach directly is to confuse a medieval love of picture—a love inevitably informed and refined by daily contact with fine imagery, in contrast to the taste current in our unornamented environment—with a comic-strip mentality and method. On the other hand, illiteracy and ignorance were not synonymous in a world in which it was common to acquire knowledge aurally: through sermons alone a medieval observer would have been familiar with much typological thought that is strange to us.[74] Symptomatic of modern uncertainty about the book's use is the suggestion that far from being for the illiterate, it was for the use of preachers—a kind of pulpit *aide-mémoire* in the construction of arguments using illustrative examples.[75] This interpretation would be more convincing if sermons echoing whole *Biblia Pauperum* pages could be found. In any case, its elaborate pages do not seem to be conceived as 'notes' to aid the memory.

It is not possible to prove the purpose for which the *Biblia Pauperum* was made. One can, however, test hypothetical uses, as mentioned earlier. It has been suggested by Weckwerth that the *Biblia Pauperum* was propaganda against the Cathar heresy, which denied the authority of the Old Testament: its followers called themselves *pauperes Christi* or simply 'the Poor'. (The effect of this heresy on the French village of Montaillou in the thirteenth and fourteenth centuries has recently been brought to vivid life by Ladurie.) But the 'poor' may simply be the lesser clergy: Thomas purports to find internal evidence that the work was aimed by 'primitive' Franciscans against their more worldly brethren.[76] The real objection to these theories is that they regard as accurate a title which, as we saw at the outset, is unlikely to have been original. Schrade sensibly observed that the book appears to have been created by a 'learned theologian who assumed that readers would understand the theological concepts inherent in the images and inscriptions, for otherwise the book is almost incomprehensible'.[77] It seems at least possible that like its nearest earlier relative, the Altar of Nicholas of Verdun, the book was designed as an aid for personal meditation.[78] If the *Biblia Pauperum* performed a similar devotional function, it shows just the right balance of familiar and original imagery and text. Indeed, the balance between these two extremes is one of the most interesting aspects of the work, as if it were a consciously adopted device. Could our version with its forty pages have been intended for learned Lenten meditation—a page for each of the forty days? (Dodgson ingeniously suggested that since some surviving copies show adjoining pages printed so close together on their single sheet of paper that there was no space to accommodate binding between them, the sheets were meant to be pasted up on walls, not bound as a book at all.)[79]

The reader's growth of perception within the framework offered by a page or an opening is not a process that will be hurried. It seems unlikely, therefore, that the book was designed to be read cover to cover at a sitting. In that the *Biblia Pauperum* seems to demand time and silence, eliciting an essentially private kind of response, it rather suggests an illustrated Book of Hours. The strongest argument for the book's being intended for meditation is perhaps the way in which the twelve elements on each page (let alone the twenty-four on a double-spread, or the forty-eight in a 'chapter') interrelate. It is hard for us to practise the concentration, the receptive sensitivity to image and word, which is required to perceive their patterns: indeed, it is to assist such concentration that this edition is designed. But that difficulty should not blind us to the fact that the educated medieval mind was more likely than the modern mind to be trained in image interpretation, in recognition and understanding of half-quoted biblical texts, and above all in the process of meditation which is the prelude to prayer.

The purpose of this edition

There are several excellent facsimiles of manuscript versions of the *Biblia Pauperum*. They are inevitably very expensive.[80] They often give a transcript of the Latin or German text of the manuscript and often, if the original text is Latin, a translation into German. Berve, writing in German, is rare in giving not only a transcript of the German text in his manuscript, but also an explanation of the elements on the manuscript pages (some of which are reproduced in colour). Unfortunately, he presents only ten of its forty-one pages. There are two facsimiles of the woodcut version, but neither of them presents, as this edition does, Schreiber Edition I (S.I., see pp. 22–24 and n. 89) uncoloured. This is also the first edition of the blockbook to offer a transcription, English translation, commentary, and notes, and to consider the pictorial designs as part of the overall meaning.[81]

Two books are so misleading that they should be avoided. Berjeau's 'facsimile' of 1859 is (naturally, at that date) only a drawn copy of inevitable inaccuracy. It travesties the original woodcuts,[82] and so miscopies the Latin that it is frequently unintelligible.[83] Unfortunately, the only (partial) English 'translation' is based on Berjeau's errors: Didron not only compounds the errors, he occasionally translates not the text of the woodcut version or of Berjeau, but the Vulgate reading from which he hopes the former derives, in spite of the fact that the original text often consists of loose recollections rather than accurate quotations of the Bible.[84]

Much of the information brought together in the present edition is second-hand. There are iconographical dictionaries which give the history and development of traditional images;[85] there are discussions of these images as aesthetic objects, explaining the relation between their design and their meaning.[86] There are compilations which will reluctantly yield patristic precedents for the typology and theology;[87] there are books which examine the relationship between Types and Antitypes very skilfully (though even the best do not attempt to present the pictures they explain).[88] Hitherto no book has attempted, in however limited a fashion, to bring these pieces of information together in offering a guide to the whole *Biblia Pauperum*.

A few readers may wish to use the book in devotional meditation. Some of these rare readers may need to use only the facsimile: black letter and heavily abbreviated bad Latin will be no obstacle; inadequate accounts of Bible stories such as Joab's murder of Abner or Jezebel's threatening of Elias will serve to call the whole narrative to mind; fragmentary quotations from the Bible will be mentally completed. I am privileged to know one such reader: even where quotations are not from the Bible but from the Breviary, he hears the unwritten words, the Latin Office still echoing in his mind behind the now-universal vernacular. Soon there will be few indeed who remember the Latin liturgy. Where the material is not biblical, ancient legends such as the Fall of the Idols will be recalled to the minds of some readers by the pictures presenting them. Years of loving familiarity with the visual arts, on buildings and in books, will enable them instantly to distinguish traditional from original elements on any page. Most readers, however, now need a good deal of help in approaching the *Biblia Pauperum*.

It is primarily a picture-book, but not in a modern sense. It was for initiates, not infants. There is no modern analogue for a series of static images designed mainly to recall familiar facts and occasionally to impart new ones. Still less in our world of fast-moving film is there any parallel for a picture-series meant to be lovingly dwelt upon—pondered until new ideas crystallise even around the old. I should like to have been able to bridge this gap between ancient and modern more thoroughly, explaining fully in each commentary the art history and meaning of the images, the theology and literature associated with them and with the texts. There is inevitably a great gap between the ideal and what it has been possible to do in a reasonable space. Let me explain here what omissions are common in the commentaries.

I have sometimes, but not always, explained how some of the oldest images embody meaning in their time-tried design. In such images, which are indeed 'icons', meaning is carried by the very arrangement of elements and by the ancient language of gesture (ballet is the nearest modern analogue for this mode of communication). A few examples of typical devices will enable the reader to find many more. It is surprising how often the significance of a composition depends on the use of a dividing central vertical, actual or implied. In the *Annunciation* (**a**), Mary and Gabriel inhabit two worlds at the moment of those worlds' reunion. A similar division of 'worlds' is found in the *Baptism of Christ* (**i**), where the Baptist's action symbolically gives Christ access to the other world, represented by the angel standing, holding the towel or garment, on the other side of the central axis. This is what baptism, at least for ordinary readers, is about: a passage from the Old Law to the New. The separation by a vertical of Adam and Eve at *The Fall* (**k**) is, on the other hand, not unifying but divisive. Their personal unity, and that of the world they stand surrogate for, is broken by the serpent and the tree. Notable examples of the significance of gesture are sigs **t** and **·c·**, whose central scenes show several conflated events identifiable, as the commentaries explain, mostly by gestures. These are essentially traditional designs embodying traditional concepts. The hypothetical ideal edition would also point out the many occasions when the designs are not, apparently, traditional, but rely on the designer's creation of compositions which, though independent of tradition, succeed in conveying meaning. An example of this is sig. **n6**, where the penitential David lies at the bottom of a flight of twelve significant steps (see commentary). If there is precedent for this particular design, it is certainly not common.

It is also remarkable how frequently the three pictures on a page are designed as a unit. Often these clear relationships to each other are not merely formal or decorative, but full of meaning. I have already mentioned (pp. 5–6) examples of just the central scenes in paired pages echoing each other in design and theme. The first double-spread (sigs **a** and **b**) is, however, one example of page unity achieved by the repeating of a motif in all the pictures on the two pages: the upper elements in all six scenes are connected (see commentaries). Pages often show a pyramidal pattern, too: in sig. **o** strong diagonals in the two side scenes lead the eye to the top of the central scene, and to a man in a tree; in sig. **·i·6, 7** Samson on the left and Jonas on the right lead the eye up to the risen Christ; in sig. **·o·** the same structure is apparent, leading the eye to Christ ascending. Indeed, there is a sense in which this pyramidal structure controls every page: the central scene, though actually somewhat smaller than the Types, gives the impression of being higher, since it is, as it were, on an architectural 'plinth' in relation to the flanking scenes. The effect is of a triptych—an association which may be intended.

So far we have considered only the ideal treatment of the larger elements in the designs. The details also deserve equal and consistent attention, which cannot often be given. For example, is the bellying of the sail rudderwards on the ship from which Jonas is thrown (sig. **·g·**) simply impossible, a concession to compositional requirements (as the commentary suggests), or is it intended to imply that the ship has been 'taken aback'—blown rudderwards in a storm? Jonas is, after all, being thrown overboard to stop a storm, and the little pennant does suggest that the wind is blowing the ship backwards. Why, to take another example, is Gideon's shield so prominent in sig. **a7** (this designer does not as a rule treat foregrounds lightly)? Is it important that in sig. **b** Moses is in the presence not only of his flock and his sheepdog, but also of a cow? Why is the sceptre being handed to Absalom in sig. **q** passed through the centre of the crown? There is not space in the commentaries even to ask these questions.

Neither is there space systematically to comment on the content of the *lectiones*, which in spite of their apparent simplicity sometimes carry curious information (the first in sig. **r**, for example, explains the effect of inflation on the currency used to pay Judas). Still less is there space to give the full exegetic background of the Prophecies, whose ancient meanings are certainly as important as those they acquire here by context; often there is not room even to complete the sentences of which they represent a small part. The *tituli* are largely ignored; but there is some justification for this neglect, since with six exceptions they do not carry the weight of tradition borne by the pictures and Prophecies. Their meaning is accessible in the context of the page alone.

The notes to the commentaries are in no sense comprehensive. They do not, for example, attempt to identify the earliest, let alone all, patristic precedents for given interpretations. The Fathers are cited simply to show that these interpretations are not merely mine—though sometimes several references are given to indicate the popularity of a given idea. Each page of the *Biblia Pauperum* could, of course, be the basis for an entire book on its texts' and images' history and meaning.

The commentaries and their notes, then, do no more than selectively suggest approaches to each page. Sometimes one, sometimes another element among the twelve will receive the most attention. The brevity of the commentaries has been maintained in order to keep the matter of each within one page, and in order to allow mental room for the reader's responses. This brevity often demands quite hard work from the reader. Indeed, a certain amount of preparatory work is taken for granted. It is assumed that the reader knows or will discover the biblical or legendary stories on which the scenes are based: details of them, though unrecorded in the pictures or texts, are usually important to the overall meaning. Anyone who has read the background stories, looked at the pictures, and read the translation is in possession of at least some of the information which would have been commonplace to the original reader: he can ponder the relation among stories, pictures and texts. The most effective approach is as to a devotion, not a dictionary.

The facsimile

One object of this book is to offer the only facsimile of an unspoiled copy of the forty-page blockbook *Biblia Pauperum* known as S.I. What is meant by that designation (more importantly, what is *not* meant by it) will be clarified on pp. 22–24. At the moment it is only necessary to explain that the only other facsimile of 'Schreiber I', edited by Soltész (and now out of print), though splendid in other ways, is deficient in two. It destroys the original pairing of images (sig. **a** being absent, **b** and **c** are paired instead of **c** and **d**, and so on).[89] Second, it is unfortunately based on one of the hand-coloured copies.[90] Woodcut is an essentially linear medium, and the line in our cuts is of great refinement: even delicate colour-

ing upsets the flow of the imprinted line across the page and obscures relationships between the major and minor elements in the design. In most copies with contemporary colouring the whole tonal balance of the pictures is destroyed: in the Hungarian copy, for example, the open graves in sig. **•r•** are so dark that they distract attention from Christ in glory. Detail is often obscured too. Such detail is more than charmingly delicate; it is often a decisive element in the total meaning. Whole areas of lovely line are often obscured by a pale opaque green, rendering the overall composition unintelligible. In the examples below, the *Biblia Pauperum* plate number is followed by the Soltész facsimile page number, since the copy on which her facsimile is based shows heavy overwriting of the original little letters, just above each central scene, which identify the page. It is worth listing examples at some length to indicate the importance of close attention to the pictures. (The full significance of these details is explained in the commentaries.)

In sig. **k6** (Soltész 10), a bowl is touched, as a rough stone is touched in **k5**—we are meant to feel the different tactile sensations; but in the Hungarian copy, bowl and stone are almost invisible. In **p5** (15) the sheep borne shoulder-high out of the Temple is as significant as the silver and produce spilled in the foreground, but more important than either should be the three-thonged whip wielded by the Lord, which can hardly be seen. In **q6** (16) we cannot see the eloquent crumpling of cloth over Jacob's hands, covered to signify his silence and grief. In the little background scenes at the top of **t6** and **t7** (19), dogs lick under a cart and a man lies trampled by a crowd: both (if we know the biblical stories) indicate bloodshed—a central theme in the page—but both are obscured. Equally significant and equally invisible under the colour are the lions who fawn on Daniel in their den in **•l•6** (31), and the embracing lovers in the foreground of **•g•7** (36), whose erotic gestures are reduced, by the indiscriminate application of pigment, to a smudge.

Our facsimile, then, shows the state in the printing development of the forty-page woodcut version of the *Biblia Pauperum* known as S.I, in its uncoloured condition. This version was chosen for its beauty—for its extreme delicacy of craftsmanship which is, as we shall see, not necessarily the same thing as its artistry—and because there seems no good reason to doubt Schreiber's original intuition that this is an early state in the development of the book. The facsimile is as near as we can reasonably come to the early form of this state of the blockbook—though there may have been an earlier one still, no impression of which survives (see p. 22). We see it complete, uncoloured, undefaced, and little damaged by wear, worm, or rodent. To achieve this, the impression at Dresden, excellent in spite of water-stains acquired during the blitz of Dresden in World War II, has been used as base copy. It lacks only the last page (**•v•**). In the facsimile, this page and six imperfect other ones have been replaced by pages from the Chantilly impression. This will not please the purist, for whom a 'facsimile' accurately reflects the condition of one particular copy. But this book is not designed as a monument:

it is for use. Accuracy to any single impression has therefore been sacrificed to clarity. The text is complete, and the pictures clear. In these respects the book is more whole than any extant.

The Dresden impression has been used as the basis of this facsimile not only because it is clear, but also because it is the earliest of those suitable for use (i.e., uncoloured and relatively undamaged). Eleven impressions of S.I are known, and some fragments: they are listed in Appendix A. Only the first three complete or nearly complete impressions in the list were suitable candidates for facsimile. The Appendix offers only such descriptions as are necessary to explain the choice. That the Dresden copy is the earliest of those fit to use in facsimile is evident from comparison of the four usable impressions. The cumulative evidence resulting from this process of comparison is overwhelming.

It is helpful to understand how the order of impressions is established. In order to do this, we must consider the nature of woodcut, which also explains some of the editorial problems described later. Understanding of the craft of woodcut will also enable us more fully to enjoy the skill and artistry of the woodcutter whose work we study here. It will help to explain what is meant (and not meant) by saying that our copy belongs to S.I. Finally, it will account for some apparent 'faults' in the facsimile itself, which may otherwise appear to be the result of bad modern printing.

Woodcuts

A blockbook consists of pictures, text, or both, printed entirely from woodcuts. As a rule, each page (in the case of the *Biblia Pauperum*, each double-spread of pages) is cut from one block of wood and is printed in one process.[91] This lends a particular unity to the complete page design. The very quality of cut wood (usually the soft, fine-grained pear, apple, cherry, sycamore, or beech) produces a harmony not present when woodcut pictures are accompanied by text set in type or written in afterwards by hand.[92] The simultaneous inking of picture and text also ensures uniformity of ink colour and density.[93] Woodcuts (and wood-engravings) are relief as opposed to intaglio prints. In the latter, ink is held in channels cut by a pushed graving tool. In woodcut, a knife is pulled towards the user, in the plank surface, the surface parallel with the grain (in wood-engraving, the endgrain is used, allowing very fine detail). Ink is carried on the surface which is *not* cut away.[94] The method has several important effects. An understanding of it certainly produces an amazed respect for craftsmen who could create such fine and subtle detail using this apparently intractable plank-surface technique. (The quality of line produced has in fact been a major element in recent critical arguments about the nature of S.I [p. 23].)

Text and pictures are of course cut as mirror images of the desired print. This affects the very form of the letters. The natural writing movement of the hand is inhibited in creating, say, the swung descenders of *y* or *g*. The resulting letter forms are sometimes as difficult for the copyists as for the modern editor. For example, the third word in the caption at the bottom of sig. **d12** ends impossibly in *a*: no doubt it was *s* in the original, but as can be seen in *symeonis* two words later, the forms of *a* and *s* are similar, especially if, as was probably true of their cutter, you are reading them backwards and know no Latin to guide your interpretation.[95] The woodcut letter has a totally different appearance from one made by a pen, for another reason. The cutter must work in mirror image, often across the grain, and he must also work in negative, forming the letter by making several strokes round it instead of constructing it positively by a stroke or two of the pen. Penned letters reveal on close examination the very direction and order in which the ink strokes were made—even the order in which they were overlaid: their 'duct'. The reader of a printed letter lacks the guidance of a 'duct'. This guide is absent in any printed letter, of course, but in the case of woodcut the reader has also to contend with the effects of a technique which often obliges the cutter to make strokes in the 'wrong' order.

That the wood is cut plankwise also means that any thin ridges of wood left running vertically, across the grain, are particularly fragile. This explains why ascenders and descenders are so often missing, as in sig. **d1**'s *pauperes*, which appears to be *pauues* with a stroke under the second *u*. It is in fact all that remains (or was perceived) of *paupes*, containing *p*, the abbreviation for *per*. Confusion is therefore likely between such forms as *p* and *u*, *b* and *o*, *i* and *l*. Such confusions differ from those common in penmanship.

The fact that a woodcut-maker works on the plank surface of the wood can help us to determine the arrangement of pages as they were cut on the block. Some editions of the *Biblia Pauperum* show splits (giving white horizontal stripes running along the grain) which cut right across the two pages in a pair, suggesting that sigs **a** and **b**, **c** and **d** were cut in two pairs in one block.[96] Our copy is too early an impression to show such split damage, but the same phenomenon on a smaller scale often causes confusing stripes across words (in **h8**, for example, the caption to the left-hand picture). This pairing on the block explains the frequency with which the pages in our impression have been cropped, part of the text on the inner edges having been cut away. The two pages had to be close together on the block, already large. The resulting layout of printed pairs of pages has already been described (pp. 5–6). When the books were cut up and mounted (as in the case of many impressions, including that at Dresden) the narrow inner margins, perhaps binding damaged, were trimmed off.[97]

The overall format of our *Biblia Pauperum* (and most blockbooks of the period) may also be partly explained by the methods of manufacture. It was made not by inserting the blocks into a press (which might have explained their splitting), but by laying the inked blocks face upwards, placing damp paper on them, and pressing, rolling, or rubbing the paper down.[98] The result was an inked line sufficiently indented to make accurate printing on the back of the paper impractical.

This brief account of the woodcut method is necessary to an understanding of the sections below on editorial procedure. It is also relevant to the section immediately following them, on other blockbooks.

Schreiber's editions and some editorial difficulties

Mention has already been made (p. 20) of the reasons for choosing the Dresden and Chantilly impressions as the basis for this facsimile. To determine the order in which the impressions within an 'edition' were printed is relatively easy, since blocks deteriorate progressively: later impressions naturally show some blurring in definition, a greater number of splits (usually along the grain), and a much greater number of places where the fragile ridges of wood normally carrying the ink have broken. The grain direction accounts for the frequency with which the vertical borders of the pages break, providing one of the easiest ways of determining the order of impressions.

To determine the order in which *editions* were cut is much more difficult, yet it is necessary if one is to adopt the normal editorial procedure, deciding which version is more authoritative, and so which variant readings in the text are correct. This method has not been adopted here, for the following reasons.

Blockbook 'editions' are more accurately called 'states'. A new state is created if the whole set of blocks is recut (as may be the case with S.III).[99] A new state is also created if some whole pages are recut but not others. But blocks can be modified without being completely recut, new plugs of wood being inserted to replace, say, a worn portion of text.[100] Add to all this the possibility that some editions were printed from blocks belonging to various states, or were even made up of odd leaves from various states, and the room for editorial error is alarming.

An editor normally proceeds by the detection and removal of textual errors accumulated during repeated copyings (by scribes or, in the case of normal printed books, by type compositors).[101] This process is not much use in blockbooks: even where all forty blocks are recut, the process of copying is unlikely to produce detectable error. The reason for this lies in the method of transference. Transference of the old design to a fresh block involves processes different from those required to transfer an original design (be it drawing, illumination, or other source) to the block for the first time. At the moment it is merely necessary to realise that while the simplest method of making a new block copy is to print from the first block straight on to the second block, and then cut away everything but the print-mark, the result subsequently printed on paper is then in reverse. To avoid this, it is perfectly possible to transfer the print itself, 'first covering it in gum solution then laying it face downwards [i.e., in reverse] on the [fresh] block; then damping the back and fretting the body of the paper away, leaving the print on the block. This method was no doubt continually practised in old book-illustration to replace worn blocks'. The copier would then simply cut round the inked design on the new block. The final impression would be a very exact copy, though 'seldom so exact as not to disclose differences in detail'.[102] This is why even text rarely serves to determine the order of states: it remains essentially the same in transmission (I have elsewhere been able to demonstrate some corruption in S.VIII as compared with S.I, but it is not apparent in the less obviously separated editions, such as S.I, S.III, S.VI)[103].

We are now in a position to understand the problems Schreiber faced, and the conclusions to which he came in his cataloguing of editions.[104] It is important to do so because his findings have been challenged, with vital consequences for our view of the edition (S.I) chosen for this facsimile. Schreiber named ten editions by identifying groups of copies which shared certain variable features forming parts of the framework of the pictures: the column capitals and bases framing the three main scenes, their shading, the design of spandrels or circles above columns. The sheer mass of his evidence, in the days before microfilm and xerox, is remarkable.

The first point to observe is that Schreiber did not think that any of his ten editions (S.I–X) was the original from which all the others derive.[105] Perhaps he understandably thought the level of textual error in all his editions, even S.I, so high that the source was unlikely to be among them, but he does not say so. He inclined on somewhat slender evidence to believe that S.I, S.IV, and S.VI all derive from a lost first edition. We cannot be certain that there was an edition predating those we have, though the high level of their textual corruption may imply it. Conceivably it is implied by the slight but discernible superiority of woodcut line in such contemporary blockbooks as the *Grotesque Alphabet* and *Ars Moriendi* (Figs 13 and 14) in comparison with the *Biblia Pauperum*, even in S.I. It might also be implied by the presence of any pictorial peculiarities or misunderstandings that could be the result of forms or damage typical of woodcut. There is a faint possibility of such an oddity in sig. **v6**: a curious object in the top right-hand corner, against the border, remains unidentifiable. If it was once meant to be smoke from hell, perhaps there has been a loss of vertical (and so vulnerable) lines which in a lost edition linked it to the bottom of the picture.

The second point to observe is that Schreiber did not claim to know the order in which his editions had been created.[106] The variations upon which Schreiber chose to base his identification of editions are unfortunately no guide to chronological priority. There is no reason why a column-base with shading should precede, or follow, one without shading: the copier might have omitted something present in his exemplar, or corrected an omission in it. It would have been different had Schreiber found examples of corruption of truly pictorial details, misunderstood in transmission between extant editions. But he located only examples of omission, already shown to be an unreliable criterion: no irrefutable examples of real misunderstanding have yet been found. Subsequent scholars add little to Schreiber's observations: Hind speculated further about which extant edition might

FIG. 12
Biblia Pauperum (S.VIII and S.I)
Moses and the Burning Bush (sig. **b6**)
British Library, G. 12090 (S.VIII)

be the earliest; Musper attacked Schreiber's methods without making specific objections.

Since it is so difficult to establish the relationship among editions from the inevitably inadequate architectural details collected by Schreiber, or from comparison of texts, one tends to fall back on assessment of the quality of the drawings as a guide. This is perilous. 'Quality' is almost indefinable. It may refer to artistic concept in the basic designs (which does not materially alter through any of the editions), or to an elusive element in their execution. It is natural to assume with Schreiber that a first edition (or earliest extant edition) will be 'better'.[107] Schreiber (and Soltész) thought S.I 'better'—more delicate, more detailed—than any other. Hind agreed, though somewhat inclined to give priority to S.III. But there is no absolute reason why a copier should not cut more skilfully than the cutter of his exemplar. This does not seem likely (if only because a subsequent edition may not merit the employment of a craftsman as skilled as the one used for the first edition), but it cannot be ruled out. Indeed, Musper (1937 and 1961) thought the greater delicacy and detail in S.I a

symptom of its decadence, and attempted to show that S.VIII not only predates S.I but is the earliest edition extant. Soltész accepted his view, while deciding nevertheless to use S.I for her facsimile. I have used S.I, and reject his view, which is now discredited.[108] Not only the pictures but also more conclusively the texts of S.VIII show corruption in comparison with S.I, as I have already said (it is an unusually crude cutting, making such changes apparent). Nevertheless, it is helpful to juxtapose, as Soltész did, examples of a page from S.I and from S.VIII, to illustrate the difference of 'quality' under discussion (Fig. 12). It would be hard to tell from S.VIII[109] that Moses was pulling off one of his boots; it would even be hard to recognise as a dog the little animal to the right of his removed boot, or to see woolly sheep in the bristly beasts round him.

Faced with all these difficulties in establishing a correct text from extant blockbooks, one might reasonably expect to determine it by reference to the *Biblia Pauperum* manuscripts. This proves not to be possible either. It is clear from Schmidt's table of *tituli* that there is no consistent relationship between

the early manuscript families (or urexemplar) and the block-book.[110] In any case, the earliest extant complete manuscript, *c.* 1330, is already very corrupt after nearly a hundred years of transmission—and the urexemplar's text has yet to be established in a critical edition of a manuscript *Biblia Pauperum*.

The blockbook has been said most nearly to resemble the unique parchment-scroll *Rotulus Seragliensis 52*, but as already mentioned (note 18), I do not think its relationship to our book is understood yet, and in any case it lacks all text but for brief *tituli* to Old Testament scenes. One manuscript later than those compared by Schmidt that does resemble the blockbook very closely, in text as well as images, has already been mentioned too: evidence is inconclusive, but Hague MS. 10.A.15 is probably copied from the prints.[111]

Transcript

The Latin transcript printed here (pp. 152–8) is therefore, with few exceptions, simply that: it is not a critical edition.[112] In the transcript each of the twelve elements on the page is identified by a number in bold type, in accordance with the diagram on p. 8 (and on the bookmark). English captions for the scenes in **5, 6, 7** are inserted to recall the pictures and give context, particularly important where speech is present in a scroll, as in **a7**: 'GIDEON'S FLEECE *dominus tecum virorum fortissime*'. There has been no attempt to reconstruct an original text.[113] Only obvious nonsense is conjecturally emended, in accordance with biblical or liturgical precedent where appropriate. However, what are perhaps 'loose recollections' of the Bible or liturgy are retained, in which case the Vulgate reading, if appropriate, is recorded in the critical apparatus, where it is followed by 'V'. As a general rule this apparatus otherwise records only emendations and the readings in the blockbook. They are recorded in spite of easy access to the facsimile, as the level and incidence of such error is important. Readings derived from the liturgy rather than the Vulgate are discussed not in the apparatus but in the notes (**·p·3**, for example).

Distinctions between *u* and *v*, *i* and *j* are retained, as are punctuation and capitalisation. Word-separation is normalised. Expansion is silent except in words not proper nouns where *no* abbreviation mark is present, in which case square brackets indicate the irregularity. However, one abbreviation mark is frequently allowed to do the work of two, as when **·v·1** *spōsa* becomes *sponsam*. Proper nouns are the exception, sharing a confusing variety of abbreviations, often without an abbreviation mark: they are silently expanded to the expected form (e.g., *Duid* to *Dauid*). Late medieval forms such as *e* for *ae* or *oe* are retained, as is *c* where one would expect *ch* (*Crist*, *Mycol*, *Ezeciel*), but *x* is expanded to *Ch*, and I have, perhaps inconsistently, expanded to the normal form contractions which are marked (e.g., *hᶜ* becomes *haec* not *hec*).

Some groups of abbreviations present particular difficulties. First, to describe the relation between Type and Antitype, the author used in the *lectiones* forms of both *figurare* and *significare* (or even *signare*, though this is not found anywhere in full). Sometimes he is unambiguous, as in **a2**, **c1**, **e1**, **l2**, **m1**, **·d·2**. When abbreviated, however, forms of the two verbs are easily confused, *u* and *v* and *f* and *s* being even harder to distinguish in cut letters than in printed or written ones: see *fig^{u}bat* (**s2**, **·a·1**, **·b·1**, **·o·2**), *sig^{n}nture* (**·s·1**), *sig^{n}t* (**v2**). Second, the scribe is inconsistent in his use of cases after *in libro*, making expansion hazardous: sometimes he uses the ablative (*in libro exodo*), sometimes the genitive (*in libro iudicum*), and often the odd *in genesi* (which may be for *in genesim*). Lastly, prophets' names before chapter numbers may be nominative (*Sacharias ij*) or genitive (*Ysaiae ij*). I have assumed that those ending in -*e* (except for nominative *Osee*) are intended genitives. Biblical references are completed in the translation.

Translation

The object of the translation is to combine accuracy with brevity for the format, and to avoid archaism. Where appropriate, the Vulgate must be translated 'warts and all', since frequently readings now regarded as incorrect became part of medieval iconography and exegesis. This ruled out the Jerusalem Bible, and sometimes even Knox, both corrected from earlier biblical sources. However inaccurate in the light of the Hebrew and Greek, it is the Vulgate's form of Jeremias xi 19 (meaning 'Let us put wood in his bread') which for centuries has been seen as a reference to the Jews planning to kill Jesus by crucifixion (**d4**, **5**), so it would be useless to adopt the Jerusalem Bible's 'Let us destroy the tree in its strength'. The beautiful Knox version is used where convenient, except where it corrects Vulgate errors: for example, Psalm 71.6 (**a4**) refers in the Vulgate to *vellus* ('fleece') in the verse which links the Annunciation with the story of Gideon's fleece; Knox corrects to the Hebrew, 'fleece' becoming 'grass'. The old Douay-Rheims Bible, though translating the Vulgate complete with its errors (unlike the Authorised Version), is neither modern nor familiar. Even the 1955 revision of it—the 'Douay Bible', which represents the nearest thing we have to a modern rendering of the uncorrected Vulgate—offers archaisms: in sig. **a1** the Lord would say to the serpent: 'Upon thy breast shalt thou go' (even Knox's 'Thou shalt crawl on thy belly' has in our translation been purged of its 'thou'). The reader will doubtless find much to quarrel with. Perhaps the awkward Douay rendering here more accurately suggests the gracelessness of a Satan struggling to move with his chest on the ground, however happily the liquid sounds in the Knox evoke the picture of snake-like progress. Translation usually reduces the resonance of its original. In sig. **a11**, for example, *femina circumdabit virum* as a prophecy of the conception of Christ suggests not only that 'woman is to be the protectress of man' (Knox) but also that a woman for the first time 'shall compasse a man' (Douay)—with all the connotations of her being uniquely fitted to contain this boy-child, and her simultaneously embracing the whole of mankind. But modern idiom will not allow the use of 'compass', and no synonym seems available, so Knox's translation is adopted. Proper names are given in the Vulgate–Knox–Douay form, following the *Biblia Pauperum*: where this may lead to confusion in comparison with more familiar Authorised Version forms, the latter are added in square brackets, for example, 'Eliseus [Elisha]'. Biblical references in round brackets are not in the original text, but are relevant sources. For example, **c11** is composed not only of Numbers xxiv 17, cited in the blockbook, but of Isaias xi 1.

Translation of the prophecies is inevitably a compromise when their full sense is apparent only in the light of the rest of the unquoted passage. For example, **·d·10**: 'Come, make haste, run to the sacrifice' reflects the emended Latin printed, but this sense is not quite to be found in the whole sentence, which in the Vulgate means 'Gather round quickly, come together from all sides (to my victim which I slay for you—a great victim upon the mountains of Israel) to eat flesh and drink blood'. A compromise has also been adopted in translating the biblical references themselves. I have rendered such forms as *Prouerbiorum xxi* (**q10**) by 'Proverbs xxi' rather than the literal 'the 21st (Book of) Proverbs', but have occasionally felt the need for a greater circumlocution, as in **p11** *Zacharie vltimo*: 'From the last book of Zacharias (xiv 21)'. References

FIG. 14
Ars Moriendi (S.I)
British Library, IB.18, ff. 17–18
220 × 340 mm approx.

which in the blockbook (and transcript) are wrong, incomplete or absent have been silently corrected, completed or supplied here.

The blockbook context

Before considering in detail the actual designs in our book, it will be helpful to look very briefly at some other, contemporary Netherlandish blockbooks, in order to put the *Biblia Pauperum* in its immediate context, and give another background (different from that offered in the section on typology) against which to see its content, layout, compositions, linear quality, and function.[113] The rarest and perhaps most enigmatic 'blockbook' (which may never have been in book form —we know it only as a series of woodcuts) lacks any text at all, its whole meaning being conveyed by pictures. The *Grotesque Alphabet* consists of twenty-three letters of the alphabet (omitting *J*, *U*, and *W*) and a final page of decorative foliage. It is precisely dated 1464, very near the '*c.* 1460' of our blockbook, to which it has been compared.[114] Fig. 13 shows the letters *K*, *L*, and *M*, typical of its vivid composition and delicate drawing.

Its function is unknown. One's initial assumption that like a modern ABC it was for children or for the illiterate, is made uneasily, the same assumption having so often been made, with manifest inaccuracy, about the *Biblia Pauperum*. Modern pedagogic considerations may be quite irrelevant, but the subject-matter does not seem to be appropriate to children. The content of the letter *K*, for example, seems to be adult and sophisticated. Two lovers form the upright: the kneeling youth holds a scroll saying *Mon aues*, with a little heart drawn between the words, giving 'You have my heart'; the lady holds a chaplet of flowers suggesting the May rituals of courtly love. Could the book have been a pattern for designers? Could it have been an adult amusement, the pictures bearing some symbolic or topical meaning, or being used as the basis for a game of association? The letter *L* is famous for the words written by a contemporary hand on the sword of the attacker and the garment of his victim, the former reading *London* ('L is for London'?), the latter remaining stubbornly obscure.[115] Whatever the purpose of this delightful book, we can take pleasure in the imaginative vitality and humour of the letters. The letter *M* is typical of the way in which the grotesque and delicate are held in tension throughout: three figures wielding weapons ride mythical beasts in a balletic battle.

All the other major examples of blockbooks are religious.[116] The one commonly regarded as the most beautiful, the *Ars Moriendi* ('The Art of Dying'), is not, like the others, biblical. It shows affinity with both the *Grotesque Alphabet* (which Hind thinks is by the same cutter) and the *Biblia Pauperum*: they seem to share certain characteristics of composition, notably a love of using the main axes of a rectangle. Similar in date to the *Grotesque Alphabet*, the earliest extant edition of *Ars Moriendi* is *c.* 1465.[117] It consists of twenty-four leaves, arranged, like the *Biblia Pauperum*, to form printed openings alternating with blank ones. The first opening holds a prose preface, followed by eleven openings, each consisting of a picture with a facing text. As in our blockbook, there is a considered relationship between text and image. The first opening, the preface, tells us what the book is for: he who carefully ponders the book will be taught how to make a good death. This aim is not one easily understood in our society, which, though preoccupied with the causing of death, is reluctant to dwell on the experience of it. Hospices to help us die thoughtfully, with dignity, have only recently emerged as an alternative to the impersonal, asceptic rule. In the *Ars Moriendi* the dying person (which in a real sense means all of us) is invited to recognise five final temptations (to abandon faith, to give way to despair, impatience, pride, and avarice), and after each its divine 'antidote'. This occupies ten openings, followed by the twelfth and last, on the death agony.

Much of the book's appeal lies in its repeated mingling of familiar images of this world with visions of the next, as the dying man is surrounded by objects and persons from his imagination or his inner eye. As he is tempted to avarice, for example, we see his deathbed surrounded by glimpses of his fine horse and his full cellar, his heirs and his good angels; as he almost succumbs to impatience we see his ill-temper affecting his nurses and delighting his resident demons.

Fig. 14 shows the eighth opening, the antidote to the fourth temptation, pride. An angel admonishes the dying man: 'Be humble', while another points to Hellmouth yawning nearby to consume the proud. The text asks how man can be proud of his faith, his hope, and his powers of endurance, when all these are from God. The Fathers are cited: Augustine reminds us that God will visit the humble but abandon the arrogant; St Bernard assures us that once pride is overcome, all other sins will be more easily conquered, for it is the basis of all sin. Pride caused the angels' fall with Lucifer, who, once the loveliest of angels, became as a result the ugliest. In contrast, the Virgin's humility earned her a place even above the angels. From the top of the picture, the Virgin and Trinity look down in compassion. The text recalls how St Anthony (seen at the foot of the bed with his crutch and his bell for warding off demons) resisted the Devil's temptations to pride. We may be meant to recall that he is said to have had a vision of the world suspended in the Devil's net, and that crying out to know how to be saved from it, he was told 'Be humble'. Overcome by this appeal to God, to the Virgin and St

FIG. 15
Apocalypse (S.III)
British Library, C.9.d.1, f. 11(7)
265 × 195 mm approx.

Anthony, as well as to the Fathers' authority, a demon in the foreground cries 'I am beaten', and another takes refuge under the bed. The design effectively contrasts chaotic patterns made by the forces of evil, with orderly groups made by the celestial vision and by attentive angels at the beside.

The next two examples of contemporary blockbooks are directly biblical: the *Apocalypse* and the *Cantica Canticorum*. Like the *Biblia Pauperum* they carry brief legends as part of the pictures, and they too demand considerable background knowledge. The Netherlandish *Apocalypse* of *c.* 1430 contains fifty leaves, again arranged so that printed openings alternate with blank ones. The first two printed openings show scenes from the legendary life of St John the Divine, author of the Apocalypse (Book of Revelation) which the rest illustrate. The page shown in Fig. 15 is bounding with bold composition and free-flowing line—both perhaps reflecting its comparatively early date. Even the clutter of angular legends somehow contributes to a sense of urgency. The beauty of the woodcuts is startling, and it is easy to see why this book is regarded as artistically 'first among the block-books . . . holding a most honourable place in the great achievements of art'.[118]

Understanding the meaning of the pictures is less easy. Fig. 14 shows the left half of a double-spread of four scenes. The scenes are linked by their 'narrative' content (the 'narrative' of the last book of the Bible) rather than by typology. Yet full understanding depends, as in the *Biblia Pauperum*, on knowledge not only of the New Testament but also of the Old, and indeed of the Fathers, who interpreted both. As we shall see, the meaning of this page is almost impenetrable without prior knowledge of the commentaries which influenced it. Perhaps part of the pleasure in using this book (as in reading its biblical source) lay in the very mysteriousness of its messages. From its creation, the last book of the Bible received elaborate commentary by the Fathers: it is, after all, a vision requiring explanation, and its popularity as a text for exegesis and illustration lay in its mind-bending images of a world outside normal time and space, a world full of literally universal conflict resolved in final harmony. There are dozens of differing interpretations. By the thirteenth century, when the Apocalypse was illustrated in many magnificent manuscripts, commentaries by the ninth-century Berengaudus and the thirteenth-century Alexander of Bremen were in fashion. The blockbook derives from manuscripts which show the influence not only of Berengaudus but also of the twelfth-century compilation of the Fathers' comments on the Bible known as the *Glossa Ordinaria*, and of an unknown elaborator of Berengaudus: we have the biblical text trebly modified.[119]

The far from apparent theme of this page showing the Third and Fourth Horsemen of the Apocalypse is the relationship between the Old and New Testaments, and the importance of their exposition by the Fathers (important elements in the *Biblia Pauperum*, incidentally). At the top of the page, Luke's symbol, a marvellously active ox (the 'third living creature' of Apoc. vi 5), hands St John a text meaning 'Come, see and spiritually understand what you read in the prophets'; only the first two words here are biblical: the rest is based on Berengaudus.[120] The legend at the top right identifies the rider of the Third Horse:[121] 'the Lord', who carries scales which (says Berengaudus's legend under the horse) represent the equity of the judgement which demands a life for a life, an eye for an eye, a tooth for a tooth (Exod. xxi 23, 24). Berengaudus, in a passage *not used in the picture*, says the Black Horse represents either the Doctors of the Church (whose writings are 'dark' because of the difficulty of the law they taught) or those saved by the law. It is hard to reconcile this sense with the legend behind the horse: 'The devil rules men through their sins, as [he rules] the Church through the sins of its prelates'—and indeed this legend is, as Bing has shown, from Berengaudus' unknown elaborator, whose overall interpretation remains lost to us.

The lower scene shows the Fourth Horse, ridden by Death, in front of Hellmouth (*Infernus*): the Apocalypse tells us that 'hell followed him; and power was given to him over the four parts of the earth'. This time it is the eagle, symbol of John the Evangelist (with whom tradition identified John the Divine), which holds the text calling the onlooker to 'come,

see and spiritually understand'. The theme is again from Berengaudus, who is quoted in the legend held by John: the breaking of the Fourth Seal signifies the understanding of the prophets given to the Fathers. The lower text explains that the fire in the rider's hand (not in the biblical Apocalypse) represents the anger of the Lord against those who ignore the prophecies: hell consumes them. For this reason the Lord as Fourth Horseman is called Death: 'I will kill . . .' says the Lord in the legend at the top left, this again being a modification of Berengaudus, where the Lord says rather 'I am the life'.[122] All this shows us that the demands made by the *Biblia Pauperum* are not unique: these books function by requiring thoughtful recall of complex material rather than by simply imparting new information.

Fig. 16 shows the left half of the first opening of the Netherlandish *Cantica Canticorum*[123] (second edition, c. 1465), which in eight openings, each composed of two such double scenes, presents the allegorised version of the Song of Songs in which the bride represents not the Church, but the Virgin.[124] (It is on both these traditions that *Biblia Pauperum* sigs ·q· and ·v· draw, in the *Coronation of the Virgin* and *Christ gives the crown of Eternal Life*.) The Song of Songs achieved popularity as the Bible's most elaborate love-song, full of intimate and lyrical imagery of courtship and consummation, and in the allegorised version, of crucifixion and coronation too. Dom Leclercq has said that the Canticle is the poem of the pursuit which is the basis for monastic life, the search for God: 'The Canticle is the dialogue between the bridegroom and the bride who are seeking each other, calling to each other, growing nearer to each other and who find they are separated just when they believe they are finally about to be united.' He goes on: 'It is not pastoral in nature; it does not teach morality, prescribe good works to perform or precepts to observe . . . But with its ardent language and its dialogue of praise, it was more attuned than any other book in Sacred Scripture to loving disinterested contemplation'.

Here, the top scene shows the groom (Christ) leading the bride towards the allegorical garden, saying, 'I am come into my garden, O my sister, my spouse. I have gathered my myrrh, with my aromatical spices',[125] while she says, 'Let him kiss me with the kiss of his mouth: for thy breasts are better than wine'.[126] The 'garden' is a field: the crop is being reaped, tied, carried, threshed, ground, and stored: perhaps a reference to Cant. iii 3: 'The King hath brought me into his storerooms'. In the lower scene, three handmaidens say, 'Thy head is like Carmel. Thy neck is as a tower of ivory'.[127] It is already obvious that the biblical text is here used very freely, not in narrative order, as in the *Apocalypse*. The Virgin is presented here not in her earthly but in her heavenly guise, as if already in the pose of the Assumption by which she made her way to the other world at the end of her life. She says, 'I am black but beautiful, O ye daughters of Jerusalem, as the tents of Cedar, as the curtains of Solomon'.[128] There is a strong contrast between this abstracted, vision-like presentation of the Virgin, who claims spiritual beauty beneath her mere 'black' humanity, and the human, rural scene above it.

FIG. 16
Cantica Canticorum (S.II)
British Library, IB.46, f. 1ᵛ
255 × 180 mm approx.

FIG. 17
Speculum Humanae Salvationis
(S.II, the second Latin edition)
British Library, IB.47000 (G.11784)
Left: *Flagellation* and *Achior Bound*
Right: *Lamech Mocked* and *Job Beaten by his Wife and a Demon*
Woodblock on each page 100 × 195 mm approx.

lamech gfligit a mat hus vrozbus   Job flagellabat a dimone et ab vroze

Achioz fuit ligatus p holoferni satestites
Xps ligat? fuit ad colupnu p pilati milites
Achioz ipe veritate qd diceat fuit ligat?
Ihs ipe veritate qd pdicaneat fuid flagellat?
Achioz ligabat qz noluit hostm loq plac¯da
Xps ligat? e qz reph¯edis iudeos displicebat
Achioz e ligat? qa gloriadei magnificauit
Xps flagellat? e qz nom sui pris manifestabat
¶Notadu at qd due gétes xpm flagellauerut
et ille p duas vxoes lamech pfiguade fuerut
Due vxozes lamech appellabar cella z ada
Due gétes fuerut gétilitas z synagoga
cella z ada mariti sui vbi vbeibz afflixerut
gétilitas z synagoga saluatore suu flagellauert
Gétilitas vbeauit eu flagellis z virgis
Synagoga vbeauit eu lignis z verbis
¶Hec flagellacio i xpo duobz mdis ppetrata
Olim fuit in bto iobflagellacoe pfiguata
Brus iob fuit flagellat? duobus modis
Quia satha flagellauit eu vbeibz z vxor vti
De flagello sathane sustinuit doloze i carne
De flagello ligue habuit coturbacoem i corde
Nó suffecit dyabolo qz flagellauit carnē extia
Vita etia instigaret vxore qz irritaret cor itit?
Sic nó cotefedi mdeit qz xps cedebat flagellis
     Genelis iij capto

¶ili etia affligeret eu acutissis vermis
a planta pes vsz ad vtice i iab saitas no cat
Sic i carne xpi m gausu nichil remaebat
Et quato caro xpi eat nocilioz z tenerioz
Tanto fuit doloz ipius amarioz z asperioz
O hó cogito qtita sustinuit xps p te passione
Et ne tradas aiam tua iteru i pdicione
Attéde si vmqp tale pena audiuisti z vidisti
Qualis fuit passio dñi nri ihu xpm
Aduce quata habuit xps ad te dilcione
Qui tanta p tue salute sustinuit passione
Cosidera sili qtitu tu bta vice ipe xpm sustinuisti
Qñti gtitudis z qtiti seruicij tibi reddidisti
Dñe bonus qd fadis oietis dieb? vite tue
nó coruideti mime sanguis sue gutte
voli ergo nsiñae si cotigerit te modicu sustine
Sed sanguine ihu xpi odis metalibz ituere
Amaritudine tua cu sanguine xpi comiscere
Et videtur tibi qñlqp sustineris et dulce
Sustine i hac vita modica flagellacone
Et i futuro effugias ppetua dapnacione
Postula a dño ut i hoc selo ita corripiaris
Vt post morte regnu dei sm pea igregi mearis
O bóe ihu i hac vita gaute nos z flagella
Et post morte nram gustem? celica mella
     Job ij° capto

Tension throughout the book is, as in the Song itself, between eroticism and elegance of spiritual expression.

The *Speculum Humanae Salvationis*[129] in its manuscript form is later (*c.* 1317) than the original manuscript *Biblia Pauperum*, and indeed influenced the fifty-page woodcut version of the latter, which followed our forty-page form.[130] The *Speculum* was extraordinarily popular, surviving in over three hundred and ninety manuscripts, quite apart from the so-called block-book versions (which are with one exception printed in movable type with woodcuts above), and many other early editions. It consists of a prologue, prohemium, and forty-two Antitypes each with *three* Types, and three chapters based on the Hours (of the Passion and of the Virgin's Sorrows and Joys). It is rather an illustrated text than a series of explained pictures: the long texts can be understood without their illustrations. Superficially similar in that it presents Antitypes and Types with text, it is in fact quite different from our book, containing much more varied, obviously devotional material and using sources other than the Testaments for its Types. The scenes in Fig. 17 do not illustrate these particular differences of content, but their subjects have no parallel in the *Biblia Pauperum*, and they do show the different relationship between text and picture. In four severe and symmetrical designs (which are not typical in these respects), the *Flagellation* on the left is followed by its three Types.

The four blocks of verse are not precisely related each to the scene above: the text is one unit. It describes events (not always biblical) immediately preceding the Flagellation. Christ was taken before Pilate, and then was passed on to Herod who, disappointed by the silence of a man whom he hoped to see perform marvels, dressed him in the white robe of an idiot (not realising that whiteness also signified innocence) and sent him back to Pilate. There the Jews accused Christ of claiming to be able to destroy the Temple and rebuild it in three days, of saying that Caesar should not be given tribute, and of claiming to be king of the Jews. As Caesar's representative, Pilate was worried by his last claim, but learning that Jesus's kingdom was not earthly, he ordered him simply scourged. Bribed by the Jews, his tormentors scourged him beyond the legal requirement. The textual emphasis here is on narrative background to the picture, rather than its significance in itself.

In the second picture Achior (Jud. vi) prefigures Christ in four ways, we are told: both were bound by servants of their enemy; both were tortured for telling the truth; both had criticised their enemies; and both were punished for glorifying God. The accounts of Lamech and Job which follow draw on legendary as well as biblical material. In the third picture Lamech (Gen. iii) is berated by his two wives; this prefigures the double scourging of Christ, who suffered attacks from both paganism (the gentiles) and Synagogue (the Jews). In the last picture Job similarly suffers two-fold attack: a beating from the demon and a tongue-lashing from his wife. The text ends with a meditation on the torn flesh of Christ and the love it reveals. The reader is advised to accept a little 'flagellation' in life. Indeed, we are to ask Christ to strike us so sharply that without suffering the pains of purgatory, which are the debt of sin, we may 'taste the heavenly honey'. The four scenes are accompanied by a meditation on the universally experienced 'slings and arrows' (often, apparently, of a domestic kind), made not only bearable but desirable by Christ's example. The text, in contrast to the texts in the *Biblia Pauperum*, does most of the work for the reader, and is markedly moral in tone.

The designer and his designs

This brief selection from contemporary blockbooks has given a background against which to view the design and content of the *Biblia Pauperum* blockbook. It is first essential to be clear who is meant when discussing the designer. Whoever he is, behind him stand the shadowy figures of all those who contributed to the traditional iconography of many of the pictures, in which the relationships and meaning of major elements had for centuries been part of an international language. This tradition is the theme on which variations by individual designers are played.

At least four individuals may have contributed to the pictorial pattern we see on the page. First, there is the person who invented the compositions (he might, for example, have provided rough drawings for the printing atelier, or he might have been simply the originator of a set of pictures used without his knowledge as source material). Second, there is the person who modified these originals for the woodblock, adjusting their proportions, removing any detail impractical in the medium. Third, there is the person who transferred the original designs to the block. Fourth, there is the cutter. These four might in theory be one and the same.

Before attempting to discuss these elusive people further (and their identities cannot be clearly distinguished in the present state of scholarship), it clarifies the problem to look briefly at some of the attributions made in the past. On stylistic grounds our blockbook has been thought to be the product of the design-school which flourished in the areas controlled by Philip the Good (1419–67) and under the general influence of Jan Van Eyck.[131] As long ago as 1859 it was suggested that the designer was Roger van der Weyden or a member of his atelier; this suggestion was repeated in 1921,[132] and given support even in 1967.[133] Musper thought that the designs more closely resembled the work of two Dutch painters, Dirk Bouts (*c.* 1410–75) or Albert van Ouwater, of Haarlem-Leuven and Haarlem.[134] None of these painters' styles seems to me to be unequivocally echoed in our blockbook. That it is hard to find a convincing source for our prints among the Dutch and Flemish painters is hardly surprising, since even if our cutter is the same as our designer, his work as we see it has been transmuted into another medium. It is a lot to expect that the transference from painting or drawing to woodcut should preserve the subtleties which identify a painter's hand.[135]

In any case, the real parallels to our prints are to be found not in the great painters' work but in that of illuminators and

of other woodcutters.[136] Even the fashions depicted (which
are, of course, not directly related to the question of the
artist's style) are located in the work of the Flemish and Dutch
painters only in a scattered way,[137] whereas in the mid-
fifteenth-century manuscripts and other blockbooks from
the Haarlem and Utrecht areas these fashions are on every
page.[138] Several observers have noted examples of blockbook
designs derived from contemporary illuminations.[139] Recently, direct relationships between the woodcuts in S.I and
the work of several Utrecht illuminators have been identified.[140] Most interesting, because one of his manuscripts is
dated *c.* 1460, and so must represent a very early use of the
blockbook or a common source, are the links with the
Master of the Vederwolken (Master of the Cirrus Clouds, so
named because of his distinctive treatment of clouds, also
known as Master of the London Passional, because his work
appears in that manuscript. A scene from this Passional appears
in Fig. 18).[141]

What is relevant here is the insight such analogues give us
into the care with which we should consider what we mean
by the 'designer' of the blockbook. Comparison of two of
the Master of the Vederwolken's designs with their blockbook equivalents will make the point. It will also facilitate
discussion of the compositional habits of the designer or
cutter of the blockbook—habits thrown into sharp relief by
contrast with the work of the illuminator. The comparison
is exciting because in each case the subject and the general
composition of elements are the same, yet between illumination and woodcut there is a vital difference. The basic elements
in Fig. 18A and 18B are the same in both treatments of the
subject. All four figures are in both—and in both the two
outer figures are half out of frame. The bag on the floor
behind Christ, the roll of cloth under the stool being carried
off left, the bench and cloth on the right in the illumination
are absent in the book. The book shows a remarkable structure
to represent the Temple, the foremost pillars of which separate Christ from the other figures. The most obvious difference, common to all the analogues in the work of the Master
of the Vederwolken (though to a lesser degree in the illuminator's treatment of historiated initials), is the comparative
tightness and economy of the blockbook design. The effect
is of claustrophobia and violence. The illumination seems
relatively dispersed, diffuse, as if the scattering of the trades-
men in the Temple were of more significance than a sense of
struggle or crowding. One must beware at this stage of
assuming that any of these qualities necessarily indicates
priority. We are concerned only with the characteristic
attitudes of the blockbook designer. Already comparison of
two versions of a subject has shown how apparently small
shifts in the disposition of elements can totally alter the effect
of a composition. This is no news to those used to designing
—it is rather like the small but vital differences between a
beautiful face and a plain one—but it may surprise those unfamiliar with the way in which medieval artists constantly
modify and modulate extant compositions. They do the
same in literature: for example, Chaucer will take a *fabliau*—a

FIG. 18
Christ Purifies the Temple
A. Vienna, Nationalbibliothek, MS. 2772, f. 46ʳ
B. *Biblia Pauperum*, sig. **p**

FIG. 19
Presentation
A. British Library, MS. Add. 18162, f. 51ᵛ
B. *Biblia Pauperum*, sig. **d**

story already honed and polished by tradition—and add to it other details, or give to it another burnishing.

A similar economy is apparent in the blockbook if the two versions of the *Presentation* are compared (Fig. 19). Mary, Simeon, the Child and the altar are essentially the same in print and illumination, except that in the former, Mary's head is uncovered and the Child turns his head to Simeon. It is significant that in the context of the whole *Biblia* page, this turn of the head is particularly important: children similarly presented in the Types (the *Law of Presentation* and *Anna Presents Samuel*) do *not* make this gesture of recognition. This would seem, on the face of it, to be an argument for the priority of the illumination: there would have been no need to remove this detail were it there already, but there is every reason for the blockbook designer to insert it.[142] But again, what matters here is the cast of the print-designer's thought. It is typical of these comparisons that we find two figures (Joseph and another man) present in the manuscript but not in the book; less common is the presence of additional material in the book: another woman in the background and a tall candle. Both are, in the event, essential to the meaning of the whole, as explained in the commentary on this scene. Attention is focussed on the little boy, in a composition most effectively combining formal symmetry with the humanity of the Child's turning gesture.

The relationship between this illumination and the woodcut has illustrated the characteristic symmetry, the near austerity, of the blockbook designs. The love of symmetry and simplicity, with a strong inclination to make dramatic points by understatement, is typical of all the designs in the book. This economy is apparent first of all in a love of conflation: the fusing of traditional designs in one image to suggest two or more historically separate events at once. This is not uncommon in medieval art: for example, **·q·** shows a popular conflation: both the Crowning with Thorns (indicated by the stave used to avoid damage to the torturers from the thorny crown) and the Buffeting of Christ (indicated by the raised fist of an attacker). It is common also to find the Presentation conflated with the Meeting with Simeon (**d**). But as already observed our designer adds a candle to the design, thereby referring also to Candlemas, so that we have three events implied. A minor conflation occurs on the first page of our book, where Mary is seated in front of an object that suggests a bed, a throne, a Temple altar, or a baldachin (see notes to the commentary). The most remarkable example is in **t**, for which I know no precedent: Christ's Farewell to his Disciples is conflated with his Warning of the Pharisees—indeed the main theme of the page is warning, although the central scene is dominated by the gesture from Christ which signifies the farewell.

The designer's love of compactness and economy is perhaps apparent also in his arrangement of elements within each scene. Symmetry and a love of relating main movements in the designs to central verticals or to diagonals may seem a simple approach to composition. In this man's work it is elevated to something resembling a stylistic theme, unifying the whole book. A glance at the first page of pictures will show how important the central vertical is: in **a6** Eve holds the repeated apple in this position; in **a5** the Child is on the same imaginary central line; in **a7** the hands of the angel and Gideon lie on it. In **g7** this line divides good and evil queens, and the child being killed stands on it. In **i5, i7, k6**, in scene after scene, we are aware of this imaginary vertical either because important elements are sited on it or because it is made conspicuous as a space dividing elements in opposition: Christ and the mourners in **l5**; Abraham and the Trinity in **m6**; the youths in the furnace and the rest of the court in **m7**; the givers and receivers of instructions in **p6, 7**; the givers and receivers of messages or homage in **q6, 7**; Joab and his knife on either side of the victim Abner in **·a·6**; the king and his satraps in conflict over Daniel in **·b·7**; and so on. Many of these show traditional disposition of the figures, but that is only evidence that this designer exploited convention constructively.

He uses a horizontal division almost as often, notably in **b7** (so that the censer lies in fact on the junction of a suggested central vertical and a depicted horizontal, formed by the front of the altar). The grape-bearing bough in **i7** is similarly placed, so that at the junction of vertical and horizontal we become aware of the association between blood (the grapes which traditionally foreshadow the Crucifixion) and the water of the Jordan—the association of blood and water in the imagery of the Baptism being a major theme in the page. In **n** the table firmly separates Mary and Christ, emphasising her contact with him—the scene is about the breaking of barriers (and even conventions).

Often the designer unashamedly places important elements in the actual centre of his scene: a symbolic jug in **b5**, a censer in **b7**, an offering in **c5**, a touched stone in **k5**, a small celebratory bell in **o6**, a donkey head in **o5**, and so on. Diagonals are important too: the whole of **h** seems to be based on a pyramidal structure, as are **o, ·i·, ·o·**. Individual scenes often seem to utilize a diagonal movement in conveying their very meaning: David crowned and David abased in **n6**, for example, or the triple top-right–bottom-left diagonal in **·c·5, 6, 7**. It may be that this tightness and conciseness of pattern is one result of designing within a rigid architectural framework on the page, or the result of a second mind working on a given composition.

These purely linear, two-dimensional considerations should not blind us to the designer's skill in suggesting solidity. This is all the more apparent in contrast with the work of the Master of the Vederwolken, who in spite of using greater volumes of space—large rooms and more distance between people—creates a certain flatness of effect. It is extraordinary that even where the very lines of drapery on the manuscript and blockbook versions of a figure are identical, the woodcut version imparts to the figure a sculptural sense of form and weight. To succeed in this without disturbing the flow of the line on the page is no mean feat.

The *Biblia Pauperum* offers us a visual and verbal experience foreign to our fast-moving lives, and perhaps the more valu-able for that reason. Its apparent formality—its niched figures and sequential scenes—is metaphorically as well as literally a grid for the control of free-ranging ideas. As we have seen, the oldest of these ideas have their origins in Christian typology, indeed the words of Christ himself. Many more are rooted in the writings of the Fathers. More still derive from the language of images which became fully coherent in the twelfth century. Most originate in the lost ancestor of all the manuscript *Bibliae Pauperum*, which gave birth to the essential relationships among the pictures in the narrative series, and among Types Antitypes, and texts. But the final level of ideas was contributed by the designer of our book, who reformulated the ancient statements in line (and sometimes in Latin), so forming a work which in its own right influenced much art to follow.

The influence of the forty-page blockbook Biblia Pauperum on art and literature

The *Biblia Pauperum*'s influence can be traced in two ways: direct and indirect. It may be used as an actual model, from which designs are copied, or its scheme may be adopted, with new compositions. It is not possible to given an exhaustive list of the works of art in the former category, but some of the most notable examples are worth mentioning.

Three unillustrated manuscripts of the *Biblia Pauperum* itself are thought to derive directly from our blockbook version.[143] A fourth is illustrated: its similarity to the woodcuts has long been known, but the exact relationship between the two has only recently become clear.[144] (I have already mentioned [n. 18] the problem of the manuscript scroll *Rotulus Seragliensis 52*, whose relationship with the blockbook seems to me to be uncertain, and which may prove to derive from it.) These are all versions of the *Biblia Pauperum*. A surprising number of illuminations and border designs in manuscripts which are not versions of the *Biblia Pauperum* but derive directly from it is now known. They are in illustrated selections from the Bible, or occasionally Books of Hours, from Utrecht (which they suggest was the origin of our book). Two such illuminations whose relationship to the blockbook cannot be determined by internal evidence alone have already been discussed in another context (Figs 18 and 19); others demonstrably derive straight from the blockbook, sometimes by direct transfer (probably by pricking the woodcut design through on to the manuscript page).[145]

The blockbook's influence on manuscripts is perhaps to be expected. More surprising is its influence on other art forms. One of the earliest three-dimensional works to show direct influence of the blockbook must surely be a relief on a Louvain tomb of *c.* 1460 identified by Diane Scillia.[146] Another is a late-fifteenth-century casket in the Cluny Museum, the precise date of which is not known: it shows thirty-three scenes unmistakably from the blockbook, though modified by the demands of the medium (polychromed ivory).[147] By far the largest sculptural scheme derived directly from the blockbook *Biblia Pauperum* (and the blockbook *Speculum*

FIG. 20
Samson Removes the Gates of Gaza
A. Ripon Cathedral, Misericord
B. *Biblia Pauperum*, sig. •i•6
C. St Martin's, Stamford, Lincolnshire: south aisle window.

Humanae Salvationis) fills the voussoirs of the central portal in the west front of the Church of St-Maurice, Vienne.[148] According to Cornell, there is a stained-glass cycle of thirty-nine groups of pictures in the cloister of Hirsau, for which our book was the source.[149]

In spite of the fact that we have no written evidence of distribution of the *Biblia Pauperum* in England, some English examples of late-fifteenth-century glass and woodwork deriving directly from it are known. In view of their importance as evidence for the use of the book in England they are illustrated here, although like the Vienne sculptures they have been fully published elsewhere. Four Ripon misericords of the late fifteenth-century derive from our book: the one in Fig. 20A is typical of their accuracy to the woodcuts. Samson's posture, boots, headband, and burden clearly echo their source.[150] In Fig. 20C is an example from a series of stained-glass panels *c.* 1480, once in the church at Tattershall, Lincolnshire, and known to be English work. Six panels from it are now in windows of the south aisle of St Martin's, Stamford, four are in the great hall of Burghley House, Nottinghamshire, and fragments of *tituli* from it are in Warwick Castle Chapel.[151] All the panels have been mutilated to some extent, but the direct influence of the book is still apparent.

Also in England, though reputedly Flemish, are glass panels now in the south window of the Lady Chapel at Exeter Cathedral, from what may once have been full-scale typological series, though unfortunately the Continental origins of these windows, collected as part of the Costessey private collection, have not been traced.[152] Several of the Exeter panels show subjects found in the *Biblia Pauperum* or *Speculum Humanae Salvationis*, and even show a general resemblance of composition. One (Fig. 21) is a clear copy of one of our woodcuts, in spite of 'restorations' such as the background city which now provides an incongruous setting for a bed.

Indirect influence is of course much more common than this direct derivation. The *Biblia Pauperum* as a kind of book (as opposed to our particular blockbook version of it) may explain, for example, some of the windows at Fairford, Gloucestershire. The west window is the *Last Judgement*, the west windows of the aisles flanking it with the *Judgement of Solomon* on the north, and *David Condemns the Amalecite* on the south. The typology echoes sig. •r•, especially if the Types were originally reversed.[153] Of roughly the same date are the Flemish tapestries of 1518 in the Abbey of Chaise Dieu,[154] and those of 1530 in Rheims Cathedral, presenting the *Life of the Virgin*. The fifty-page blockbook *Biblia Pauperum* derived from our version was loosely used as the source for the typological scenes at the top of seven of the sixteen tapestries in the latter series.[155] The *Biblia Pauperum* underlies the scheme (though not the compositions) of the still later Flemish-designed stained glass of King's College Chapel, Cambridge.[156] More surprisingly, the book's typology has recently been shown to underlie the overall scheme of Michelangelo's Sistine Chapel ceiling.[157]

It is not possible to prove the *direct* influence of the *Biblia Pauperum* on literature, though the influence of the habits of

FIG. 21
Eliseus Raises the Sunamite
A. Exeter Cathedral, Lady Chapel (from the Costessey Collection)
B. *Biblia Pauperum*, sig. **l7**

thought it typifies is apparent everywhere. Without an understanding of the pervasiveness of this habit of thought we may make the mistake, as modern producers often do, of regarding the popular medieval play of *Abraham and Isaac* as at best a study in obedience and courage,[158] at worst an account of an old man torturing a boy because he is himself tormented by a cruel God (sigs •**e**• and •**f**•).[159] We shall think Chaucer contrived if not clumsy when he says that Moses saw the bush burning with red flames yet without a twig singed, as a sign of Mary's inviolate virginity (sig. **b6**):

> Moises, that saugh the bush with flawmes rede
> Brenninge, of which ther never a stikke brende,
> Was signe of thin unwemmed maidenhede.
> Thou art the bush on which ther gan descende
> The Holi Gost, the which that Moyses wende
> Had ben a-fyr; and this was in figure.[160]

We shall lose the full sense of the lovely line in the carol which sings of Jesus born 'as dew in Aprile' (sig. **a7**),[161] and shall probably underestimate the familiar but unbiblical ox and ass at Bethlehem, which we vaguely regard as some kind of scriptural authority for the love of animals (sig. **b**). Verses such as this from an early-fourteenth-century lyric addressed to the Virgin will be largely incomprehensible (sig. •**q**•):

> Thou art Hester, that swete thinge,
> And Asseuer, the riche kinge,
> Thee hath ichose to his weddinge,
> And quene he hath avonge:
> For Mardocheus, thy derlinge,
> Sire Aman was ihonge.[162]

These images appear in literature as if deeply familiar to their readers. They were to be recognised, not introduced as if to a stranger. It is no wonder that to us they often remain meaningless. The influence of the ideas embodied in the *Biblia Pauperum* is wider than we realise, and the ideas themselves are larger (and tougher) than our visually simplified and sometimes sentimental Western Christianity will easily admit. Though few may now use the *Biblia Pauperum* as an aid to meditation, anyone can use it as a guide to the medieval art which so often served that very purpose. It would be pleasant to think that, even if at two removes, it might perform the function for which it was originally designed.

Notes to Introduction

References are given in full only in the Bibliography. Unless otherwise stated, 'Schmidt' refers to Gerhard Schmidt (1959), 'Cornell' to Cornell (1925) and 'Röhrig' to Röhrig (1955).

1. As suggested, for example, by Hirsch, p. 128.

2. See p. 18 for another possible interpretation of 'the Poor'.

3. Wolfenbüttel, Herzog-August-Bibliothek, Cod.5.2.Aug.4; Munich, Bayerische Staatsbibliothek, Cod.lat.12717 (Schmidt, pp. 41–49, 119).

4. *Concordantia hystoriarum, Concordancie veteris et novi testamenti, Capitula bibliae excerpta* (Schmidt, pp. 118–19).

5. Schmidt, pp. 119–20; Berve, p. 8.

6. Heinecken, p. 117. For further discussion of the title see Engelhardt, p. 13; Schmidt, pp. 1, 117; Soltész, pp. VI–VII; Behrends, p. 73.

7. It is misleading to describe these letters as identifying 'pages', because of the format of the original books on which this facsimile is based: half the true 'pages' are blank and unlettered. The letters cannot be said to define 'folios' or 'leaves' for two reasons: fear of confusion with the varying folio numbers on which they appear in different copies (where the *Biblia Pauperum* may be bound up with another text, for example), and fear of confusion where apparent 'folios' are formed by sticking the blank backs of the original leaves together, so forming what appears to be one folio, from two—a common practice. I therefore refer to these identifying letters as 'signatures' and show the signature itself in bold type (e.g., sig. **a**). The word is not used in its technical sense to identify gatherings; but confusion is unlikely here, since gatherings proper do not exist in copies of *Biblia Pauperum*, which is composed of folded single sheets. The dots are unaccountably absent in •**n**•, •**o**•, •**r**•, •**s**• of the second alphabet in the edition on which this facsimile is based: they are silently included in references to these signatures.

8. *Speculum Humanae Salvationis*, literally 'The Mirror of Man's Salvation', is described on p. 32. The sequence of Antitypes has a long history in art. Narrative series based on the life of Christ had been current from at least the fifth century (for example, in the mosaics of S. Maria Maggiore, Rome, or in the sixth-century S. Apollinare Nuovo, Ravenna). Some later examples easily consulted in reproduction are the tenth-century Golden Gospels of Echternach (Metz), paintings in twelfth-century Bury St Edmunds (Parker), the fourteenth-century Duccio *Maestà* altarpiece (Wald), and the early-fifteenth-century Ghiberti bronze doors of the Florence Baptistry (Krautheimer).

9. Woodcuts and blockbooks are discussed on pp. 21, 22, 26–32.

10. Stevenson (*BMQ*, 1967) dated the edition known as Schreiber I (which he accepted as the earliest extant) '1465 or a little earlier' on the basis of the unicorn watermark on one of three pages from

a Schreiber I copy (·s·, ·t·, ·v·) bound up as part of a Schreiber VI in the British Library (IB.43): he had found one of these watermarks on paper in archives at Metz, fresh from its mould and firmly dated.

Schreiber editions (see pp. 22–23) are hereafter indicated by the prefix 'S.' (S.I, S.II, and so on).

S.I is likely to be 'earlier', for the impressions to which Stevenson refers are later than some others in the same edition which show different watermarks (see Appendix A). For example, the Alnwick Castle copy of the *Biblia Pauperum* S.I (not known to Stevenson) contains some perfect pairs of these same unicorns, and the Alnwick impression is certainly late: the blocks are badly worn. The author is engaged on a study of the paper of the forty-page *Biblia Pauperum*, based on the watermarks of all known copies; the aim of the study is to examine the relationships between impressions and editions, not to establish a new date, but it is likely to show that the Dresden copy (which Stevenson thought was lost) carries watermarks earlier than 1465.

Koch (1977) claims that the *Biblia Pauperum* is of about 1460, since illuminations by the Master of the London Passional (Master of the Vederwolken) in the (roughly) dated *Hours of Mary van Vronensteyn* derive from it—a relationship noted in 1975 by Smeyers. (Hoogewerff, I, pp. 531–47, suggests that the woodcuts of a book dated 1460 echo illuminations by the Master of the Vederwolken.) None of this defines for us the earliest date at which the (hypothetical) original forty-page blockbook *Biblia Pauperum* was printed, but if such an impression existed, costumes in the *Biblia Pauperum* preclude its being much earlier than 1460 (as Hind, I, p. 242, suggests, on the basis of its comparison with later Dutch illustrations).

11. The first printed Bible is of 1460. The earliest prints from woodblocks were c. 1400. The form and craft of early printed books are discussed by Haebler; Hind; Mongan and Wolf. See Field for medieval woodcuts; Hodnett for English ones; Hindman (1977) for the relation between manuscript and print.

12. The manuscripts are discussed in detail in the monumental works of Cornell, who also refers to the blockbook versions, and of Schmidt. Schmidt, pp. 77–87 and tables on pp. 141–47, 'reconstructs' a lost ancestor of all three manuscript families, dating it c. 1250. Cornell, pp. 152–53, suggests c. 1190–1250; Künstle, pp. 19–20, postulates the existence of an unillustrated *Biblia Pauperum* as early as 1050!

13. Munich, Staatsbibliothek, clm. 23425 (Cornell, p. 69, pl. 2).

14. Heitz and Schreiber introduce and explain a facsimile.

15. *Les Figures du vieil testament & du nouuel* was printed in Paris in 1504; Vavassore produced a sixteenth-century blockbook version in Italian. For the nineteenth-century use see Formby.

16. The three 'families' are described by Schmidt, pp. 31, 43, 54; diagrams of their varying arrangements on the page are on his p. 140. The disposition of images and texts on the blockbook page is similar to that in the Budapest sub-family among Austrian manuscripts (Schmidt, pls 7–14). Some manuscripts of the *Biblia Pauperum* consist of only text (perhaps because the pictures were sufficiently familiar to be present in the mind's eye), but pictures when present took precedence: they were drawn first, the texts added afterwards (Schmidt, p. 78; Behrends, p. 78).

17. Facsimiles of manuscripts in the Austrian family are presented by Unterkircher and Schmidt and by Forstner, and in the Weimar family by Gabelentz and by Behrends. The xylochyrographic

(woodcut pictures with manuscript text) version c. 1400 is presented by Kristeller (1906). For a 'facsimile' of the German-text 'Albertina' MS see Einsle and Schönbrunner.

18. Schmidt's plates illustrate the representative manuscripts. The 'four-group' per double-spread type is accessible in the Unterkircher and Schmidt facsimile, and in the Camesina and Heider 'facsimile'. It has been suggested by its editors (Deissman and Wegener, p. 46) that the parchment scroll *Rotulus Seragliensis 52* in the Topkapi Saray in Istanbul is dated 1450 or a decade earlier or later, that it shares a lost common source with the blockbook *Biblia Pauperum* (and that since it is in scroll form with small pictures bearing only brief *tituli* for Old Testament scenes, it was intended as a pattern-book for painters—a view rejected by Schmidt, p. 107). Soltész, pp. IX–X, discusses at length some of its similarities to our book, but does not question the editors' theory of its relationship to the book, although their dating largely relies on the perilous evidence of costume drawn in the scroll. I do not think the scroll's relationship to the blockbook is yet understood. The *Rotulus* is No. 51 in Deissmann's catalogue (1933).

19. The Pierpont Morgan Library copy of S.III of our blockbook is perfect: the sheets uncut and currently unbound. It shows **a** and **b**, and so on, printed on one sheet next to each other. I am indebted to Dr Paul Needham, Curator of Printed Books and Bindings, for confirming this. Most of our early editions have been cut up and mounted or, like the S.I at Chantilly, so tightly bound that their cut or uncut condition cannot be ascertained. That the two groups of pictures **a**, **b** are on one side of a sheet does not, however, mean that they were simultaneously printed: the copy of S.VII offered for sale at Sotheby's on 12 June 1978 (*Cat.* p. 9)—in June 1979 still the property of The Carl and Lily Pforzheimer Foundation—shows that only one of the two pages cut on a block was printed at a time, a frotton covering the one to be printed second: the paper frame for keeping the margins free of ink slipped sometimes, so that the outer frame of the adjoining page was accidentally printed in the wide margins of this copy. (I am indebted to Mr Poole-Wilson of Quaritch for the book's location.) The books were not always printed thus. Hind, I, p. 214, explains that later editions of the *Biblia Pauperum* show first and last pages printed on one leaf, the second and penultimate on another, and so on, the resulting folios being placed one inside the other in a single gathering—the basic procedure used in a modern multigathering book.

20. For 'optical editing' see Schmidt, pp. 79–81. Behrends, p. 77, discusses the process in the manuscript he edits. Most of the manuscripts show thirty-four main scenes (though Schmidt, p. 83, suggests that the 'urexemplar' may have been meant to contain more than its thirty-four subjects). Some, particularly those later than our blockbook, may approach the number in the fifty-page blockbook *Biblia Pauperum* (ed. Heitz and Schreiber). Three of the forty-page book's additional scenes are found in the early-fifteenth-century British Library MS. Kings V (very similar to the blockbook in text, though differing in designs [Cornell, pp. 111, 168, 229, pl. 70]). The blockbook adds these and **t**, **v**, ·v·. Cornell, pp. 174–78, lists all the scenes in the 'Western' family to which the blockbook is related (probably by derivation from a common source or by use of the blockbook as source).

21. The 'Four Last Things'—death, judgement, heaven and hell—are present in the four last main scenes: death and judgement in ·r·, hell in ·s·, heaven in ·t·, ·v·; they also comprise the last scenes on the Altar of Nicholas of Verdun at Klosterneuburg (see pp.

10–12). The meditational practice of considering the Last Things is embodied, for example, in the fifteenth-century lyric whose refrain is *Memor esto novissima* (R. T. Davies, p. 226). Schmidt, p. 81, observes that Judgement is absent from the 'urexemplar' because it did not fit the overall plan—it would have necessitated the development of its own 'four-group' (found in the blockbook).

22. Schmidt, pp. 84–85, 137; Cornell, pp. 11, 17–53. The blockbook *tituli* are preceded by the word *Versus*, emphasising their function as captions, which had for centuries tended to be in verse. Schlosser (1914) summarises his study of precedents in early art and poetry, showing that *tituli* pass into tradition with surprising infrequency. The hexameter caption (leonine in having an internal rhyme) is found as early as the tenth century (Cornell, p. 60) and on the Klosterneuburg Altar. By the late thirteenth century, Bible commentary itself was to be found in verse.

23. Cornell, p. 87, regards the *tituli* as clumsy, lacking elegance and spiritual content. In contrast, Buschhausen, pp. 26–28, finds the similar Verdun *tituli* (which are not, however, sources for most in the *Biblia*) effective compressions of complex theological ideas into the 'halting flow of the hexameter'.

24. Of the hundred and twenty *tituli*, five have known sources or analogues (see notes to commentaries): **a8**, **b8** are from the twelfth-century Peter de Riga; **s9**, **s12** are on the Hildesheim Chalice; **·a·8** is on the Klosterneuburg Altar (Cornell, pp. 12–13). It is not possible to determine whether text and pictures came from the same mind or not. Schmidt, p. 84, suggests that the unusually subtle *tituli* borrowed from Peter de Riga provided impetus for the rest, most of which the author (of the manuscript) invented.

25. Luke xxiv 44. All biblical translations except those following the facsimile pages in this edition (on which see pp. 25–26) are from the 1956 version of the Douay Bible (see Holy Bible). The Gospel as the fulfilment of Old Testament prophecy is a major iconographical theme: see Mâle (1913), pp. 158–65. It underlies, for example, the illustrative scheme of the mid-twelfth-century Hildesheim Missal and the cycle of paintings at Hildesheim with which the Missal is associated (see Beissel): the Missal's illuminations consist of two on the Creation, followed by a series of New Testament and apocryphal scenes, from the *Annunciation* to the *Assumption*. A number of its prophecies appear also in the *Biblia Pauperum*.

26. It is not helpful in this context to distinguish, as Meyers, pp. 145–46, does, between strictly historical characters and those, like the bride and bridegroom in the Song of Songs, who are not 'real': the distinction did not exercise the medieval mind.

The best brief account of typology up to the twelfth century is by Heitz and Schreiber; a more generally accessible account of it in the Fathers and in art is in Mâle (1913), pp. 131–51. For further treatments in theology, literature, and art see nn. 43–45.

27. John iii 14 (Num. xxi 8–9).

28. Matt. xii 40 (Jonas ii 1). See also Luke xvii 20 (Sodom and Gomorrah = the Last Judgement, sig. **·s·7**); I Cor. x 2 (the Crossing of the Red Sea = Baptism, sig. **i6**); Heb. vi 20, vii 1–3 (Melchisedech = Christ, sig. **s6** and the passages in the Pauline epistles which Auerbach [1959], p. 49, regards as still more important: I Cor. x 6, 11; Gal. iv 21–31; Col. ii 16ff.; Rom. v 12ff.; I Cor. xv 21; II Cor. iii 14; Heb. ix 11ff.). See Bowers for a demonstration of the flexibility with which the Jonas story was interpreted: a valuable paradigm for our approach to the *Biblia Pauperum*.

29. Mâle (1913), p. 134, traces the method to the Jews of first-century Alexandria. See Auerbach (1959), pp. 28–49, for the use of typology from Tertullian to Augustine.

30. Ph. Schmidt, p. 34: *Denn der Kattolizismus wusste mit dem Alten Testament eben nichts anderes anzufangen.*

31. Noted but not quoted in Meyers, p. 153.

32. See *Breviarium Romanum*. For accounts of the Breviary see Baudot; Batiffol: developing by the fourth century, its form was largely established by the sixth century.

33. *In Vetere Novum lateat, et in Novo Vetus pateat* (PL XXXIV 625) and *in Testamento vetere obumbratur novum . . . Quid est enim quod dicitur Testamentum vetus, nisi occultatio novi? et quid est aliud quod dicitur novum, nisi veteris revelatior?* (PL XLI 505). Migne, errors and all, has been used throughout for patristic references, as is still common practice in the iconographical dictionaries: when Glorieux has corrected a Migne attribution or date, the *PL* reference is asterisked. *Corpus Scriptorum Ecclesiasticorum Latinorum*, in progress, provides modern editions of many of the texts in *PL*.

34. Künstle, pp. 18–20.

35. S. Sabina's doors are illustrated in Gugliemi, pp. 89–91, where the whole is shown in black and white, with some panels in colour. See also Darsy.

36. The relevant mosaics of S. Vitale, Ravenna, are illustrated in Ricci, pls 90, 95, 96.

37. *Imagines de concordantia veteris et novi testamenti* (PL XCIV 720). For a recent suggestion that these were in fact panel-paintings, not simply manuscripts to be used as models, see Meyvaert.

38. Ekkehart IV was commissioned by Archbishop Aribos (d. 1031) to compose the *tituli* (see Steinmann, and 'Ekkehard IV. Tituli für den Dom zu Mainz' in Schlosser [1896], pp. 158–81). Late-eighth-century Carolingian frescoes at St Johann, Münster, Switzerland, correlate a David cycle with a Christ cycle: *Encyclopedia of World Art*, III, pl. 57, shows a scene from this cycle.

39. For an account of this resurgence see Knowles, pp. 69–149. It has been suggested (Weckwerth, pp. 232, 240–47) that this revival of typological interest was in part an answer to the twelfth-century revival of Manichaeism—the very heresy which had prompted Augustine to make his observations about the New Testament being concealed in the Old. In general terms this may be true, but I remain unconvinced by Weckwerth's theory that the *Biblia Pauperum* was conceived as a German Benedictine weapon against the heresy.

40. James (1951), p. 151, of the *Pictor in Carmine* (see pp. 13–14).

41. He called himself *Honorius Augustodunensis*: the place to which *Augustodunensis* refers is not now thought to be Autun. His works are in *PL* CLXXII (but see *DCC* for corrections).

42. Suger's part in the development of Gothic aesthetics is described in Frankl, pp. 3–24. Suger's own account of his work is translated in Panofsky (1946). Surviving fragments of the glass are reproduced in colour in Grodecki (1948), pls 1 (*The Ark of the Covenant*) and 2 (*Moses and the Burning Bush*). See Grodecki (1961) for a full account of the surviving glass.

43. See Barr; Daniélou (1950 and 1963); Lampe and Woollcombe; Lundberg; *NCE*, XIV, pp. 351–52. Strohem, though concluding that the Malmesbury roundels which contain many subjects often employed typologically are not based on typological correspondence, offers a useful background of English twelfth-century typology. The roundels are illustrated in Galbraith, pls XVII–XXVI.

4 4. See Hoëfer; Auerbach (1959, a translation of a 1944 article; 1949 and 1953). Keenan offers a bibliography of typology, in its widest sense, in English medieval literature: many entries concern typology in the strict sense. Miner edits essays on typology as transmuted in the post-medieval period, to the present day.

45. Cornell, pp. 120–53; Schmidt, pp. 88–97; *RDK*, III, col. 90; Réau (1955), I, ch. 4; Tietze; Goldkühle. A good, brief account is given by Bloch. Some major thirteenth-century French typological works of art are discussed by Mâle (1913), pp. 140–75.

46. See Röhrig for reproductions, transcript, commentary, and so on; Buschhausen for its sources in the liturgy; see also Cornell, pp. 134, 142; Schmidt, p. 89. In the altarpiece's present form, the *Crucifixion* is centrally over the altar (on which the eucharistic sacrifice is re-enacted). Other typological art objects of about the same date are often similarly liturgical or devotional: Pickering, pp. 257–65, discusses (and on his cover illustrates in colour) the Meuse Valley Cross also from the Verdun school; Bloch, col. 397, mentions the chalice bowl from the same school, in the Diocesan Museum, Cologne, and also portable altars such as that of Stablo, *c.* 1165, bearing Types of the Crucifixion, Eucharist, and Resurrection, or that in Munich with the sacrifices of Abel, Abraham, and Melchisedech as well as Moses Raising the Brazen Serpent as well as the base of the Cross of St Omer, *c.* 1160, bearing eight Types of the Crucifixion, four of the same subjects also being found on the Reliquary Cross in London, Victoria and Albert Museum. Relevant also is the Regensburg manuscript (clm. 14159), which searches all history for Types of the Cross. The Klosterneuburg Altar, however, has no known prototype.

47. The Psalm actually has *in domo Dei* ('in the house of God'), but is probably the source for the Prophecy, as this passage was traditionally associated with the Betrayal (*PL* XXI 863; Jerome, *PL* XXVI 1042, who specifically mentions Judas's visiting the Temple with Jesus; Cassiodorus, *PL* LXX 389).

48. Dan. ix 26 actually has *Et post hebdomades sexaginta duas occidetur Christus* ('And after sixty-two weeks Christ shall be slain'): the designer wisely replaced the cumbersome Latin for 'sixty-two weeks' with *hec* ('this'). The prophet's reference to Christ (which really means 'the anointed one') was taken as a direct reference to Jesus, who in Matt. xxiv 15 referred to this and the next verse. The relation between the verses and the Crucifixion and Resurrection is explicit in Theodoret, *PG* LXXXI 1483.

49. James (1901), pp. 145–46.

50. James (1897); Caviness, p. 121, has recently challenged Sandler's (1970) view that these were thirteenth-century paintings on choirstalls of 1233–1245, suggesting that twelfth-century panel-paintings were incorporated into the later stalls.

51. Facsimiles of the Psalter are presented by Gheyn and by Sandler (1974), who on pp. 112–15 tables the typological miniatures and *tituli* of the Psalter, and on pp. 110–11 discusses the different arrangements of the cycle and Psalter, concluding that the latter was motivated by, not directly derived from, the paintings.

52. James (1898–1903); Tristram, p. 155, lists both sets of *tituli*. Borenius refers to thirteenth-century cycles at Winchester and Windsor.

53. James (1901) lists some once visible *tituli*; the windows are described and illustrated in Rackham. Caviness (1977) conjecturally reconstructs the entire cycle of Canterbury glass: see especially pp. 115–68. Fragments of a major fourteenth-century typological scheme in stained glass survive at Malvern (Rushforth [1936], who

on pp. 33–44 discusses its relationship to the *Biblia Pauperum*). An excellent, brief account of typology in English medieval art, especially in glass, is in Marks (1975), pp. 191–93.

54. Caviness (1977), Appendix fig. 20, p. 174, shows a diagram of the whole reconstructed window's scheme; Rackham, pp. 72–80, describes the whole window, which is illustrated in colour in Connick, pl. XL, the lower portion to which the half-roundels in our plate belong being shown on p. 322. The inscription of the lower half-roundel is *BOTRVM RESPICERE NEGAT HIC. SITIT ISTE VIDERE: ISRAEL IGNORAT CHRISTVM; GENTILIS ADORAT.* For commentary on the image, see sig. **i** in this facsimile.

55. Rackham, p. 28n.

56. James (1951) prints the table of Antitypes and Types from the beginning of this lengthy work, and lists the Canterbury *tituli*, showing how often subjects are common to both; Strohem, p. 184, n. 9, is, however, unconvinced by James's contention that the *Pictor* and the cycles at Peterborough and Canterbury are closely related. The *Pictor* has been interpreted both as a guide to painters and as a literary work (Pickering, pp. 151–52, n. 1). Related to it are three important typological works, all showing some connection with the *Biblia Pauperum*: the *Concordantia Veteris et Novi Testamenti* (Schmidt, p. 92, explains that some of the *Biblia tituli* are found in one exemplar of it); the *Rota in Medio Rotae* presented by Röhrig (1965) and discussed by Schmidt, p. 92; and the mid-fourteenth-century *Concordantia Caritatis* by Ulrich of Lilienfeld (near Vienna), which has two hundred and thirty-eight Antitype groups and is related to the Weimar family of *Biblia Pauperum* manuscripts (Tietz; Schmidt, pp. 93–94). This important work (of which there is a full account in *RDK*) is basically a life of Christ, composed of pictures with texts, each Antitype being related not only to two Types and four Prophecies (as in the *Biblia Pauperum*) but also to two natural images drawn from the *Physiologus* or *Bestiary*. At the end is a section on the Commandments, Vices and Virtues, Creed, Sins, and various allegorical images. I have been unable to trace a facsimile and commentary apparently in progress in 1972 (Neumüller, p. 9: 'Eine Faksimile-Ausgabe des Lilienfelder Originals [mit Kommentar] ist in Vorbereitung und wird bei der Akademischen Druk- u. Verlagsanstalt Graz erscheinen.')

57. Holt, p. 21.

58. On ancient and medieval treatises on art see *Encyclopedia of World Art*, 14, cols 277–86. See Scheller for a survey of mainly architectural modelbooks.

59. Laborde edits the black-and-white facsimile of the manuscript from which Fig. 9 is taken. It was originally in four parts: Part I is in Oxford, Bodleian Library; Part II is in Paris, Bibliothèque Nationale, MS. Lat. 11560; Parts III and IV are in the British Library, MSS Harley 1526 and 1527. There is a microfiche edition of Part I, edited by W. O. Hassall, and a colour filmstrip of the same, sold by the Bodleian. This version of the *Bible Moralisée* (and the scenes shown here) belong to the longer 'B Redaction' identified by Haussherr (1972, p. 367), who also presents (1973) a full colour facsimile of one of the earlier, shorter versions, which has a slightly different layout. For a study of the artists who produced the four thirteenth-century manuscripts, see Branner (1977), pp. 52–57.

60. *Per aues significantur contemplatiui id est religiosi qui amant spiritualia* (f. 4ʳ).

61. These are roundels D1, D2, according to Laborde's method. The upper text is *Dixit dominus ad moysen decima die mensis huis tollat unusquisque agnum per familias et domos suas*; the lower is *Sacrificium istius agni significat in cruce sacrificium ihesu christi.*

62. Caviness, p. 120. The four-fold exegesis of Scripture, one level of which is moral, is described by Augustine (translated by Auerbach [1959], p. 42); by Honorius of Autun, *PL* CLXXII 359; and by Aquinas, *ST* 1ae, q.1.a.10. See Haussherr (1972) for an attempt to interpret the *Bible Moralisée* at other levels.

63. James (1898–1903) describes the paintings; the *tituli* are also listed in Tristram, p. 155. Cox relates the Worcester misericords to the Psalter (so relating the lost Peterborough cycle to the lost Worcester cycle from which the misericords probably derive); she has also noted (p. 168) the relationship between the Worcester cycle's recorded *tituli* and twenty-five of the texts in the *Figurae Bibliorum*, including some of those shown in Fig. 10 (also reproduced in Cox, pl. LI).

The texts in Fig. 10 read, left to right: 1. *Abraham. Quem peperit sara pater offert in crucis ara. Veruer mactatur. puer incolumnis reuocatur.* 2. *Moyses. Serpens christus necat ignipotentes. Serpentes.* 3. *Nos deus exemit fuso qui cruore redemit. Morte minus digna moriens a morte maligna.* 4. *Jacob. lauabit uino stolam suam. Naam. [Pon]am sepulchrum tuum quia inhonorat[us es].* 5. *Elyas. Sareptena. In cruce vita deus nos suscitat nunc elyseus. sic monstratura puero fuit ante figura.* Emendations in square brackets are made in the light of the Vulgate sources, Gen. xlix 11 and Nahum i 14. The meaning seems to be (the fifth roundel is difficult): 1. 'Abraham. The father offers on the altar of the cross him whom Sara bore; the ram is sacrificed, the boy is recalled unharmed'. 2. 'Moses. The Serpent Christ kills the fiery [serpents]. Serpents'. 3. 'God released us, who with his shed blood redeemed us from an evil death by dying a death without dignity'. 4. 'Jacob: "he shall wash his garment with wine". Nahum: "I shall make [it] your grave because you are disgraced"'. 5. 'In the Cross is life: God lifts us up; now Elyseus: the Type [of this] was formerly about to be shown in the boy'. At the bottom of the page, as on the other typological pages of the *Figurae Bibliorum*, is one of the commandments: *Non occides* ('Thou shalt not kill'); the effect is of deliberate paradox.

The patristic analogues of all but the fourth roundel are dealt with in the notes to the equivalent scenes in our book. The scene in the bottom left-hand roundel, not in the *Biblia Pauperum*, combines one well-known and one rare prophecy of Christ: Jacob's words are associated with the Crucifixion in the fifth century (*PL* L 1040), but I have not yet found a precedent for the prophetic treatment of Nahum's statement. (The author is engaged on a study of the *Figurae Bibliorum*—which is bound up with a thirteenth-century *Apocalypse* in the manuscript—with a view to producing an explanatory edition.)

64. The image appears also in the thirteenth-century window of Sens Cathedral north choir aisle. The Cistercian monk Guillaume de Deguileville's poem of 1330, *Le Pèlerinage de la Vie Humaine*, which is often typological, uses the image (Guillaume, lines 93–94); for a critical edition of the Middle English prose translation, *The Pilgrimage of the Lyfe of the Manhode*, see Henry (1985, 1988).

65. See sig. **·f·7** and commentary.

66. Sandler (1974) illustrates the parallels. Caviness, pp. 120–21, believes (unlike Sandler) that the scenes in the Canterbury glass, as well as their inscriptions, are directly related to the Psalter, probably through a common model.

67. Engelhardt, pp. 23–50, and Schmidt, pp. 109–14, analyse some of these ways (discussing the manuscripts, not the blockbook). Both indicate the flexibility of the typological methods employed.

68. Engelhardt notes this contrast but regards it as a flaw. He consistently interprets any contrasts within the Types negatively.

69. Bloch distinguishes between true prefigurations and relationships of this kind (such as Eve's being the Type of Mary), calling the latter 'antitheses'. I have not followed this practice, since contrasts so often appear within prefigurations which are primarily parallels.

70. Kendon, p. 82. The same interpretation appears in Schmidt, p. 110.

71. That it was for children is suggested by Engelhardt, pp. 14–15, who also summarises other suggestions, including the possibility that it was for the homiletic and catechistic education of the clergy, or a compendium for private study, or a basis for sermons. The suggestion that it was for the 'stupid classes' is by Conway, p. 3.

72. Bowers, p. 22, n. 5.

73. *Femme je suis povrette et anciënne, | Qui riens ne scay; oncques lettre ne lus. | Au moustier voy dont suis paroissienne | Paradis paint, ou sont harpes et lus, | Et ung enfer ou dampnez sont boullus: | L'ung me fair paour, l'autre joye et liesse* 'Le Grand Testament', lines 893–98 (written 1461–1462, very nearly the time at which our blockbook was printed): Villon, pp. 40–41. Villon puts his mother into a poem written for her; it is significant that he presents her as a 'simple soul'.

74. See Owst. No doubt it is this familiarity that explains the common assertion by medieval authorities that pictures are the books of the unlearned; see for example the seventh-century Gregory the Great (*PL* LXXVII 1128): *Nam quod legentibus scriptura, hoc idiotis praestat pictura cernentibus, quia in ipsa etiam ignorantes vident quid sequi debeant, in ipsa legunt qui literas nesciunt*, and ten other examples up to and including Villon, cited by Gougaud, most of which imply recognition of a known story. It is possible that the fourteenth-century movement known as *Devotio Moderna* (see Post, and *NCE* IV 31–32) contributed to the popularity of the *BP*, but there is no direct evidence for it (see Strand's article in his edition), and the *Devotio* developed too late, of course, to have been responsible for the earlier manuscript tradition.

75. Suggested by Schreiber, IV, p. 1, and cited even in recent years, for example in the catalogue describing the Paris copy of S.I (*Les Incunables . . .*; p. 34).

76. Hind, I, p. 230, also thought the 'Poor' were the lesser clergy. Koch (1979), p. 550, refers to it as 'a homiletic work for the benefit of poor preachers'.

77. Schrade, col. 499.

78. Behrends, p. 79, speaks of the need for a 'meditative digesting of the picture' (but in the context of a manuscript Apocalypse). M. Thomas is rare in having suggested (in a remark incidental to his thesis that it was the product of a Franciscan milieu) that the *Biblia Pauperum* was meant as an aid to meditation.

The possibility that it is meditational in function should be considered in the light of two major examples of literary meditation on the life of Christ: the *Meditationes Vitae Christi*, once attributed to St Bonaventura, by an anonymous thirteenth-century Franciscan (*S. Bonaventura Opera Omnia*. XII [Venice,

1756]; see *Meditations* for a translation); and a work based on but differing from it, the fourteenth-century German Ludolphus Saxoniensis' *Vita Christi*. The latter was translated into Dutch in 1400, and printed in 1487. This work is based not on typology but on speculation regarding what is *not* said in the biblical life of Christ, resulting in the invention of apocryphal material. For details of manuscripts, translations, and editions see Bodenstedt, pp. 11–23.

79. *Catalogue of XVth Century Books in the British Museum*, I.

80. See n. 17.

81. Isolated examples of such analysis occur: Soltész, p. XX, remarks (following Musper) on the pathos of **·k·6** and **·k·7**, for example. But these are analyses of the dramatic content of posture and gesture rather than of the design as a whole.

82. According to Hind, I, p. 236, by 'one of the copies in the British Museum', used as the basis for his book, Berjeau apparently meant the copy of S.I (see Appendix A).

83. Willshire, p. 174 (citing earlier work by Weigel), noted that Berjeau was unreliable. Berjeau transposes sigs **n** and **·n·** and **o** and **·o·**; examples of mistranscription are **f2** *virgo quae cum cristo* for *hoc quod cum christus*; **g3** *sacerdotum* for *sanctorum*; **h1** *surge et tolle* for *apparuit Attolle*; **h2** *furorem* for *timorem* with *quo* omitted; **·s·2** *extelancia* for *excecancia*. Pilinski's 'facsimile' is no better.

84. Didron, II, pp. 403–30.

85. Notably Schiller; Kirschbaum; Réau; *RDK*. Cornell (1924) is a good example of the kind of detailed individual study of particular images which may be found.

86. Panofsky is the authority on the relevant iconography; M. Davies lists other sources of interpretation.

87. See n. 33: in spite of their frequent errors, the Indices in *PL* CCXVIII–CCXX remain an unsurpassed tool in this process.

88. See n. 67.

89. Soltész: the pairing fault was noted by Heimann (1969). The only other true facsimile of the forty-page *Biblia Pauperum* (S.VIII) is Musper (1961).

90. Oxford, Bodleian Auct.M.III.B, a copy of S.X, is coloured with more than usual sensitivity, but I cannot agree with Soltész, pp. XXI–XXII, in her analysis of the effects of colour in the Hungarian copy. Response to such matters must be partly subjective, but I have wondered whether in some cases the colouring is by children or apprentices. Hind, I, p. 123, observes that printers must 'frequently have supplied uncoloured impressions for their customers to colour': on pp. 167–70 he gives general descriptive notes on colour in early woodcuts. There is room for research here.

91. What follows is derived from Hind, I. The craft of bookmaking itself is explained in Haebler and in Gaskell.

92. Compare the very different effects in the 'xylochyrographic' version of the *Biblia Pauperum* at Heidelberg (ed. Kristeller). Its pictures are printed individually from separate blocks, within a pre-printed framework, and the text is in manuscript.

93. But note the curious copy of S.I in the Pierpont Morgan Library, New York, in which the text is darker than the pictures, almost as if differently inked if not separately printed, though of course from the same block as the pictures. I am most grateful to Mrs Meg Twycross of the University of Lancaster for her inspection of this copy on my behalf.

94. Woodcut can usually be distinguished from intaglio by inden-

tation of the inked line. This is not a foolproof test: Hind, I, p. 78, explains that the action of damp pigment on vellum can cause shrinkage giving similar indentation.

95. We know little about the woodcutters (Conway; Hind, I, p. 107). If monastic, they would probably have known Latin, but the level of error in the original editions is unlikely to have been much less than in those extant—a level which suggests that the blockbook was not cut by a Latin speaker. Bühler describes the interaction of craftsmen in the making of the fifteenth-century book.

96. Hind, I, p. 234, of the British Library copy of S.IX (G.12090), **c** and **d**. This phenomenon is, however, open to misinterpretation. For example, in S.VIII (see Musper's facsimile) splits on **·a·**, **·b·**, **·c·**, **·d·** coincide in a way which might 'prove' various contradictory relationships among them on the blocks, depending on whether we interpret the splits as 'shakes' in the block-centre or splits at its outer edges caused by its having had something heavy placed centrally on it, which must have been the case here if the normal pairing was adopted. The prints appear thus:

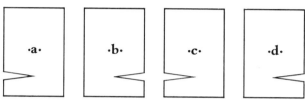

If the block had opened centrally one might think pairs were formed by **·a·** and **·d·**, **·b·** and **·c·**.

97. The Chantilly impression may be uncut, but unfortunately tight binding conceals the truth. The narrow margin between the two pages on the Pierpont Morgan Library's copy of S.III (see n. 19) is significant; a leaf from the British Museum fragment of the same edition is reproduced in Hind, I, p. 235.

98. Hind, I, pp. 4–5: this process naturally permits more control over variety in the pressure applied than is possible in the use of a press. Could it explain the differences in density of text and pictures in the Pierpont Morgan Library copy of S.I (n. 93)?

99. Hind, I, p. 236.

100. Bliss, p. 4, gives examples from 1490, 1494, 1575. It is possible that shrinkage has made one detectable in **c9** of S.VIII as it appears in Musper's facsimile (1961).

101. The principles are described by Maas.

102. Hind, I, pp. 17–18.

103. *Oud Holland*, 95, No. 3 (1981), 127–50.

104. The list of copies in Schreiber, IV, pp. 1–9, is supplemented by Hind, I, pp. 236–40, and Soltész, p. XXVI, n. 88. None of these compilers was aware of the copy in the possession of the Duke of Northumberland, or of the incomplete copy in Vienna, for notice of which I am grateful to Dr Eva Irblich (see Appendix A).

105. Schreiber, IV, p. 2. Musper (1972) suggests the 1440s as the date of the lost original, but gives no evidence for this; he was perhaps following Schretlen, p. 18, who thought that it must have been pre-1450.

106. Schreiber, IV, p. VIII: 'Il est pour la plupart impossible d'en fixer l'order chronologique' (ibid, p. 2).

107. Schreiber, IV, p. VIII: 'Il est vrai qu'une edition princeps faut être d'un prix plus elévé que ses copies'.

108. What Musper (1937 and 1961) regards as S.I's corruption of

S.VIII's treatment of the Baptist's halo and raised arm in the *Baptism of Christ* (**i5**) is in fact evidence of corruption in S.VIII (Koch [1977], n. 10, and see n. 103 above).

109. The British Library's copy of S.IX, identical with S.VIII except in **r, s, t, v**, has been used instead of a complete S.VIII, of which there is no copy in the U.K.

110. Schmidt, pp. 146–47: the table presents a selection of *tituli* and their variant readings as they appear not only in the 'urexemplar' but also in the prototypes of the Austrian and Bavarian manuscript families. The blockbook readings (not tabled by Schmidt) do not show a consistent pattern, sometimes reflecting the 'urexemplar', sometimes the separate families. Cornell, pp. 16–53, included the blockbooks in his examination of *tituli*, but found no consistent and unambiguous correlation either.

111. The Hague, MS 10.A.15: see Henry (1984) for a demonstration of the manuscript's derivation.

112. Full textual analysis of the forty-page *Biblia Pauperum* would be very expensive, requiring comparison not only of single impressions from each of the ten Schreiber editions, but of *all* impressions, in order to eliminate misreadings resulting from wear or replacement. For this edition I have simply ascertained that there is no Schreiber edition from which the textual errors apparent in S.I are absent.

113. Hind, I, pp. 216–64, gives an illustrated survey of the major blockbooks.

114. See the facsimile of *Grotesque Alphabet*, p. 16, the woodcuts of which are described by Willshire, I, p. 200. Two copies are known: this one in the British Museum, and the more perfect Dyson Perrins copy described in Dodgson (1910). In addition, there is a different version (probably a copy) in Basle. Hind, I, pp. 151–52, suggests that the cutter of the first version is the same as of the *Ars Moriendi* S.I, while the Basle copy of the *Alphabet* is by the cutter (or one of the cutters) of the *Biblia Pauperum* S.I. A splendid modern example of the genre 'grotesque alphabet' is in Beeke.

115. *Bethemsted, Bethinsted* (Dodgson [1899]), and *Westminster* (Dodgson [1910] and Hind, I, p. 151]) have been suggested.

116. For example, they include, in addition to those discussed, *Exercitum Super Pater Noster*, on the Lord's Prayer; *Symbolum Apostolicum*, on the Creed; *Das Zehn Geboten* on the Commandments (in an explanatory facsimile by Werner); the *Life of Saint Servatius*.

117. According to Hind, I, p. 227, the book was probably created *c.* 1450. He lists the fifteenth-century French and sixteenth-century English printed versions (II, pp. 660–63).

118. Hind, I, p. 224. The blockbook version is in a facsimile presented by Musper. For a study of the Apocalypse in thirteenth-century France see Deslisle and Meyer. For facsimiles of manuscript versions see *The Douce Apocalypse* and *The Trinity College Apocalypse*; the great Angers tapestry is reproduced in Planchenault.

119. For Alexander's commentary, which interprets the scene mainly in terms of the persecution of Christians by the Roman emperors, see Alexander Minorita (his other title). The *Glossa* is composed of marginal and interlinear glosses; the former are printed in *PL* CXIII–CXIV. For the relation between the manuscript and blockbook versions see Bing, who on pp. 154–55 discusses the scenes illustrated here. She shows that the Wellcome

manuscript shared a common thirteenth-century source with the blockbook, and that the source belonged to a 'family' which included BN MS Fr.403 and Bodleian MS Auct.D.4.17.

120. *PL* XVII 913: *Veni et vide; id est, intellige spiritaliter Scripturam legis*. Apoc. vi 1, 3, 5, 7 have only *Veni et vide*: 'Come and see'.

121. Both the rider and his position as Third Horseman show this to be the Black Horse (Apoc. vi 5–6), as in Berengaudus, *PL* XVII 913: *Sessor autem equi dominus est. Statera vero aequitatem judicii legalis demonstrat, ut est istud 'Animam pro anima, oculum pro oculo, dentem pro dente'*; at 914 he gives the second interpretation of the Black Horse: *per equum ii qui per legem salvi facti sunt designantur*. The blockbook legend, however, mentions *equus pallidus*, the Fourth Horse (which appears in the scene below), calling it *ypocrisis*, an interpretation perhaps derived from the *Glossa* (*PL* CXIV 722): *falsos fratres: qui sub habitu religionis obtinent* (Bing, p. 155).

122. *PL* XVII 920: he explains that those who ignore prophecies are swallowed by hell, and that the Lord is called Death because although he said *Ego sum vita*, he is also the death of the wicked. For some alternative explanations see *PL* V 329: the Black Horse is Hunger controlled by Antichrist; XXXV 2425: the Pale Horse is the Devil; XCIII 117: the Black Horse represents those who bear the appearance of honesty but deceive by it, and the Pale Horse represents heretics who pose as catholics; C 1124–25 and CXVII 1025: the Black Horse is the craving for evil which buys men with temporal rewards, and the Pale Horse is spiritual death, or the Devil; CLXV 635: the Black Horse represents persecutors of the Church, the rider bearing scales as a pretence of equity, the Pale Horse signifies the enemies of the Church, its rider the Devil; and so on.

123. For facsimiles of both coloured and uncoloured copies see *Cantica Canticorum*. The Berjeau 'facsimile' (1860) is, like his *Biblia Pauperum*, to be avoided.

124. Both interpretations are to be found, for example, in the work of the twelfth-century Honorius 'of Autun'. His *Speculum Ecclesiae* and *Expositio in Cantica Canticorum* equate the bride with the Church (though the *Expositio* is to be read, says its author, on the Feast of the Virgin, who is a Type of the Church); his *Sigillum Sanctae Mariae* (*PL* CLXXII 495–518) equates her throughout with the Virgin for 'everything said about the Church can also be said about the Virgin' (*PL* CLXXII 494). See Leclercq (1978), pp. 106–9, on the great monastic popularity of the Canticle (which, though called *Canticum Canticorum* ['The Song of Songs'] in the Vulgate, is commonly called *Cantica Canticorum* ['The Songs of Songs'] by the Fathers, because thought of as a collection of lyrics).

Hind, I, pp. 243–45, observes that the *Cantica Canticorum* S.I's cutter 'may well have been identical with one of the cutters of *Biblia Pauperum* S.I–IV'.

125. Cant. v 1. In his *Expositio in Cantica Canticorum* Honorius (*PL* CLXXII 492) explains that there are four gardens in the Canticle: the enclosed garden, the garden of fruits, the perfumed garden and the garden of nuts; the first, *hortus conclusus*, is the Virgin.

126. Cant. i 1.

127. Cant. vii 5 and vii 4 respectively.

128. Cant. i 4. Honorius explains (*PL* CLXXII 500) that the Virgin calls herself 'black' because born of poor parents. Compare the English morality play *Wisdom*, where the Soul, her white

spiritual garment covered by the black mantle of her humanity, sings *Nigra sum* . . . .

129. Facsimiles of manuscripts are presented by Lutz and Perdrizet; James (1926); Neumüller. There is a study by Perdrizet. The blockbook version (the Latin, not the later Dutch-text version which uses the same blocks for the illustrations) is presented in facsimile by Kloss. Silber's valuable thesis is unfortunately not published. Wilson and Wilson ostensibly offer a survey of the *Speculum* in all its forms, but see reviews by Silber and by Henry. The Middle English version of the Latin text is in Henry, *The Miroure of Mans Saluacioune*.

130. A facsimile of the fifty-page *Biblia Pauperum* blockbook is presented by Heitz and Schreiber.

131. Conway, p. 7, quoting M. Renouvier, *Histoire de l'origine et des progrès de la gravure dans les Pays-Bas. Mémoires couronnés par l'Academie royale de Belgiques*, X (Brussels, 1860), p. 62, which I have been unable to consult. Koch (1977, pp. 288–89) believed the 'fraternal betrayer' in **q** to represent Philip the Good. See also n. 138 below.

132. Kristeller, cited by Soltész, p. XIII, n. 54.

133. Graesse, III, p. 305; Stevenson (*BMQ* 1967), pp. 86–87.

134. Musper (1961), in the unpaginated English insert to the facsimile. He is cited by Soltész, p. XIII, who sensibly observes that the influence would be easier to test if authenticated works of those two painters from the early part of the fifteenth century had reached us, and that the influences on our designer would be better sought in the 'late manuscripts which must have been the wood-cutter's chief source of inspiration'.

135. An awful, and very appropriate, warning of the fate which style may suffer in a change of medium is to be found in the *Justice of Trajan* tapestry (1460–1470), a 'free copy after Roger van der Weyden' in which 'the style of Roger's composition is obscured by the flattening and schematising effect of a severely limited and *retardataire* medium' (Panofsky [1953], I, p. 264; II, pl. 283).

136. Schretlen, p. 5, most usefully observed that the nearest stylistic similarities are in the illuminators of the Haarlem school.

137. See Appendix B on the Prophets' Hats.

138. One of the best sources of information on costume and daily life of the mid-fifteenth century in the relevant area is the French translation of the Miracles of the Virgin made by Jean Miélot, secretary to the Burgundian Duke Philip the Good (1419–1467), as illustrated in Bodleian MS 374 (or in its facsimile, see Miélot [1885]). The whole question of the costume in the blockbook (partly considered in Soltész, pp. XI–XII, who is essentially showing its contemporary accuracy) deserves more attention than I have been able to give it. Certainly its use in any argument about dating requires the attention of an expert, since the available books on costume are inadequate to the task.

139. For example Ph. Schmidt, on the derivation of the Koberger-bibel woodcuts from the Berlin National Library Cod. Germ. 516.

140. See Smeyers (1975), Koch (1977), Henry (1983[2]); some additional examples are mentioned in the notes to the commentaries on pp. 131–51.

141. British Library MS Add. 18162. I have accepted the objections made by Vermeeren to the use of the name Master of the London Passional for the illuminator who contributed very little to that manuscript.

142. The illumination and the blockbook design in Fig. 18 are discussed by Koch (1977), p. 287, who believes that the illuminator 'expands from the corresponding scene in the block-book to accommodate a rectangular field'.

143. Two are in Latin, one in German: St Gallen Stiftsbibliothek, Cod. 605 (St Gallen 1–5); they clearly derive from the prints, not vice versa, as they have additional material drawn from the *Speculum Humanae Salvationis*, not found in our blockbook (Cornell, pp. 115, 174).

144. The Hague, Museum Meermanno-Westreenianum, MS 10.A.15. Cornell, p. 115, pl. 69, suggests that it is from the blockbook; Soltész, p. IV, recognises the alternative possibility; Koch (1977), pp. 287–88 (where he uses its old identification, Gr. fol. 13), regards it, on evidence offered privately by Delaissé, as derived from the blockbook. If it is a copy from the blockbook, as can, I think, be proved (Henry, 1984), the wheel has come full circle, manuscripts producing blockbooks which in turn produce manuscripts.

145. See n. 1: examples of direct transfer can be seen in Henry (1983).

146. Diane Scillia generously informed me of her discovery that the design in the *Biblia Pauperum* scene *Mary Magdalene Repents* (**n5**), which she calls *Christ at the House of Simon*, appears in a relief of *c*. 1460 at Lièges, probably made in Louvain, for the Epitaph of Canon Guillaume de Wavre, who died in 1457.

147. Koechlin, II, pp. 352–54, describes the casket, and in III, pl. CLXVIII, illustrates eight relevant scenes: *Judgement of Solomon* (sig. ·**r**·6), *Abraham and Isaac* (·**d**·6), *Entombment* (·**g**·5), *Jonas Is Released* (·**i**·7), *Resurrection* (·**i**·5), *Samson Removes the Gates of Gaza* (·**i**·6), *Christ Opens Limbo* (·**h**·5), *Daniel Is Found Among the Lions* (·**l**·6). Some panels have been misplaced in restoration, but it is clear that the basic plan presents each Antitype with one of its Types. The lowest register of panels shows the life of Job.

148. A list of art works influenced by the *Biblia Pauperum* is in Mâle (*de la fin*, 1925), pp. 237–46: the sculptures in the archivolts of the west central portal of Saint-Maurice at Vienne are mentioned on pp. 241–42. Bégule's subsequent work on the sequence (Bégule, pp. 144–68, with excellent plates) is developed by Koch (1950), who proves that both the forty-page blockbook *Biblia Pauperum* and the French translation of the *Speculum Humanae Salvationis* printed in Paris, 1478, were sources for the scheme. He illustrates among others the sculptures echoing the *Biblia Pauperum*'s *Christ Opens Limbo* (·**h**·5) and *Eliseus Receives Elias' Mantle* (·**o**·7). Koch also lists other art works influenced by both books: late-fifteenth-century stained glass in the Cathedral of Berne, frescoes in the Cathedral of Brixen in the Tirol, frescoes in Sweden, the *Life of Christ* tapestry at La Chaise-Dieu (see n. 154 below), the Rheims tapestries discussed below, sixteenth-century stained glass at Vic-le-Comte. The whole porch at Vienne, also *Aaron's Rod* (**b7**), *Pentecost* (·**p**·5), *Ascension* (·**o**·5), and *Elias' Sacrifice Is Accepted* (·**p**·7) are illustrated in Koch (1959), Figs 4, 5, 7. See also Cornell, pp. 189–210, for the influence of the *Biblia Pauperum*.

149. Cornell, p. 198. Excluded here is evidence from a number of articles demonstrating the derivation of wall-paintings from *BP*: see Clausen (1974) on wall-paintings dated 1496, in Bellinge Church (near Odense, Denmark); the overall design of this

sequence is further discussed by Banning (1980) and Haastrup (where unfortunately use of the fifty-page edition of the blockbook has falsified some comparisons—on pp. 153–54, for example, discussion of the *Last Supper* scenes depends on omission from the blockbook of the identification of Judas, which is clearly present in the forty-page version). Fučič (1979), illustrates fourteen late-fifteenth-century frescoes in the Istia peninsula, Yugoslavia (Trieste is just over the border). Banning (1979) describes and illustrates fragmentary inscriptions echoing *BP tituli*, on late-fifteenth- and early sixteenth-century wall paintings in Skåne (the peninsula at the extreme south of Sweden): here the painting in Hällestad Church is highly important because allegedly dated 1460—though the pictures themselves do not show derivation from *BP*. Saxtorph, pp. 116ff, discusses paintings in Hjembaek Church, Zealand.

150. Purvis speaks of the misericords' relationship to the *Biblia Pauperum* having 'been known for some time'. *Josue and Caleb Return from Jordan* (**i7**), *Jonas Is Swallowed* (**·g·7**), *Jonas Is Released* (**·i·7**), and *Samson Removes the Gates of Gaza* (**·i·6**). The last two are better illustrated in Smith, pp. 24, 25.

151. The Stamford panels are reproduced in colour in *The Town of Stamford*, pl. 35: from the south aisle, the windows represent *Moses Strikes the Rock* (**·f·7**), *Samson Removes the Gates of Gaza* (**·i·6**), *David Kills Goliath* (**·h·6**), *Crucifixion* (**·e·5**, **·f·5**), *Three Women at the Tomb* (**·k·5**), *Resurrection* (**·i·5**). The windows are imperfect, but the resemblances in all but the *Crucifixion* are striking. The whole series is discussed in depth by Marks (1975), pp. 194–98, 282–325, whose published illustrations (1979, pl. LIIIa) include the Burghley House panels: *Joseph Placed in the Well* (**·g·6**); *Christ Opens Limbo* (**·h·5**); *Eliseus Is Greeted* (**o7**)—which I suspect is a composite panel, perhaps containing figures from the two scenes showing Joseph sold (**r6, 7**)— and *Boys Mock Eliseus* (**·c·7**).

152. Drake discusses the Costessey collection. For the Exeter panels see an article in two parts by the author, in the *Friends of Exeter Cathedral Fifty-Third Annual Report* and that for the year after: note that the first two illustrations (not their captions) were transposed in printing.

153. Arnold, pp. 263, who does not mention the *Biblia Pauperum* as a reason for suspecting this reversal.

154. Some idea of this great sequence can be gained from the early engravings in Jubinal: see I, pp. 43–44, Pls 1–18; II, pp. 1–5, Pls 19–32.

155. Sartor, pp. 68–101: the seven are the *Marriage of the Virgin, Annunciation, Nativity, Magi, Presentation, Flight into Egypt, Coronation of the Virgin*. That the source is the fifty-page *Biblia Pauperum* is clear from the presence of the first and last of these, not in the forty-page version. The relationship between the tapestry designs and the woodcuts is very loose—merely an echo of typological subjects, not, as a rule, of composition, let alone detail. The series is more clearly illustrated in Loriquet, pp. 85–161.

156. See Wayment for a complete record of the glass and a discussion (p. 124) of its relationship in part to the *Biblia Pauperum*.

157. Leach argues that it is a late manifestation and modification of the stock typological patterns.

158. See the English mystery cycles (Beadle; Lumiansky and Mills; Block; England and Pollard). A number of medieval dramatic pieces are explicitly typological. Brooks (1936) describes a 1507 pageant of a series of Old Testament Types—Gideon and his fleece, Aaron and his rod, the Queen of Sheba, Jacob and Esau, and so on. To call their New Testament Antitypes chronologically to mind, they appear in the order of Pfister's (1463) version of the *Biblia Pauperum* (slightly different from our blockbook). Milchsack edits the Heidelburg Passionplay presenting both Types and Antitypes. Kolve, pp. 62–88, shows the importance (and the limitations) of typology as a 'principle of selection' underlying the English mystery cycles' structure; Meyers illustrates the surprising extent to which typology would have been familiar to the drama's audience through sermon and catechism.

159. See Woolf (1957 and 1972, ch. 4) for the typology of this play.

160. 'An ABC', lines 89–94: Chaucer's translation of Guillaume de Deguileville's poem of 1330. Meyers, p. 149, cites some other examples of the burning bush image in Middle English literature: *Towneley Plays*, ll. 359–67 (England and Pollard, p. 111); *Chester Plays*, ll. 81–88 (Lumiansky and Mills, p. 355); and Ross, Sermon 29, p. 221.

161. R. T. Davies, p. 155. This line in the lyric is clearly related to the image of Gideon's fleece, but I do not wish to suggest that typology in literature always follows the *Biblia Pauperum* interpretations; for example, *Ludus Coventriae*, ll. 129–36 (Block, p. 340):

> The dede styk was signifure
> How cryst pat shamfully was deed and slayn
> As pat dede styk bare frute ful pure
> So cryst xuld ryse to lyve a-geyn;

in the *Biblia Pauperum* Aaron's rod signifies not the Resurrection but the Virgin Birth (sig. **b**).

I have made no attempt to cite literary examples of typology in other European literature, but mention should be made of the *c.* 1120 redaction of the Early Middle High German *Ezzolied*, which makes it a major device in celebrating Christian history from Creation to the Resurrection; the poem in both redactions is discussed and edited in Maurer, pp. 269–303.

162. R. T. Davies, p. 34. This poem is full of images also in the *Biblia Pauperum*: Mary is the burning bush (**b**), the stone which killed Goliath (**·h·**), the rod of Aaron (**b**), Ezechiel's closed gate (**a**).

BIBLIA PAUPERUM

According to Genesis iii 14, the Lord said to the serpent: 'You shall crawl on your belly' and later, in the same place, of the serpent and the woman: 'She shall crush your head, and you will lie in wait for her heel'. Now this is fulfilled in the annunciation to the glorious Blessed Virgin Mary.

a

According to Judges vi 36–8, Gideon prayed for a sign of victory in the fleece being filled with a fall of dew which prefigured the glorious Virgin Mary made pregnant without violation, by the pouring out of the Holy Spirit.

Isaias vii 14
See, a virgin shall conceive and bear a son

David, Psalm 71.6
The Lord shall descend like rain on a fleece

[EVE & THE SERPENT]

[ANNUNCIATION]
Luke i 28, 36
'Hail, you who are full of grace; the Lord is with you' 'Here is the servant of the Lord; let it be done to me'

[GIDEON'S FLEECE]

'The Lord is with you, bravest of men'

The serpent loses power, a virgin bearing without labour

Earth remained dry: the fleece is wet with dew

Ezechiel xliv 2
This gate shall be shut, and not be opened

Jeremias xxxi 22
The Lord has created a new order of things on earth: woman is to be the protectress of man

The virgin is acknowledged: inviolate, she conceives

All three scenes show divine announcements, God or his messenger being at the top left. The Types prefigure the Annunciation of Christ's conception in different ways: the first by contrast, the second by parallel. The contrast is between **6** and **5**, causally related to each other, the Annunciation being one result of the Fall: Eve subjects man to evil by her disobedient trust in the serpent, Mary reverses that by her obedient belief in Gabriel's message.[1] In **6** Eve stands by her apparent equal, but the *versus*, **8**,[2] refers to God's warning to the serpent (**1**):[3] as the Virgin grows big with child, the snake will shrink, the Devil's power diminish. Perhaps the sinuous lines of the specious serpent ('erect like a man'[4] because as yet uncursed by God, who watches from the tree) are deliberately balanced in the central scene by scrolls bearing acknowledgement of Mary, and her humble reply.[5] Gabriel's words 'the Lord is with you' are used by the angel addressing Gideon (**7**),[6] pointing the fact that both bring messages of victory: of salvation by Christ and of conquest signified by the filled fleece.[7] Mention of Gideon's bravery also implies Mary's courage in accepting the unexplained will of God: Gideon, after all, asked for a miracle, Mary simply received one.

The contrast was between **5** and **6**; the parallel is between **5**

and **7**, between the Virgin's conceiving, and the filling of the fleece: the 'rain'[8] of **4** and 'dew' of **2** and **9** are images of the silent appearance of a life-giving gift from God (a parallel familiar in a carol: 'He cam also stylle ther as his moder was / As dew in Aprylle . . .'.[9]. The earth which 'remained dry' (**9**) suggests not only the barrenness of the Christless, serpent-dominated world before the Incarnation,[10] but also the miraculously preserved virginity of Mary, the central theme of the next page.[11]

As in each of the Infancy scenes (**a–h**), the suffering of the adult Christ is implicit: the Baby following the Spirit down the shaft of light leading to Mary already shoulders his Cross.[12] The other paradoxes of the page are underlined by the four Prophecies: the miraculous conception in **4**, this and the virginity in **3**,[13] the perpetual virginity in **10**,[14] and the mystery of God incarnate in **11**, which in context suggests not only the natural miracle in any woman's bearing a son, but the special place of this woman as all men's spiritual mother.[15] Following **12**, we are to acknowledge her unique position—as did God, through Gabriel. As a common medieval pun has it: 'Eva' has become 'Ave'.[16]

According to Exodus iii 1–14, Moses saw the burning bush, and it did not burn, and he heard the Lord speaking to him from the bush. The burning bush which is not consumed prefigures the blessed Virgin bearing a child without defilement of her body. A virgin, she gave birth and remained pure.

b

According to Numbers xvii 1–11, the rod of Aaron burst into leaf and blossom one night. This rod prefigured the Virgin Mary who, unfertilised by male seed, was to bring forth the everblessed Jesus Christ.

Daniel ii 34–35
From the mountain-side was struck a corner-stone no hands had quarried

Isaias ix 6
To us a child is born, a son is given

[MOSES & THE BURNING BUSH]

[NATIVITY]
Matthew i 25 Luke ii 1–7

[AARON'S ROD]

It glows and kindles
but the bush is not consumed by fire

This is against nature: a rod bears a blossom

Habacuc iii 2
Lord, I have heard what you said, and am afraid

Micheas v 2 (Matthew ii 6)
Bethlehem of the land of Juda, you are not least among the princes of Juda

O Virgin Mary, you bear a child without the pain caused by man

---

Here is the mystery of Mary's perpetual virginity[1]—in conceiving, in childbirth, and thereafter (**1, 2, 12**[2]). The page also presents Incarnation in which death is implicit. Virginity is central to both ancient Types. The burning bush is multiple in meaning. Like Aaron's rod heralding a new era in the Old Law, it came to represent the Incarnation. The flame was the Spirit by whose divine power Mary remained unhurt at the conception of Jesus (**a**),[3] then the burning of desire by which she was untouched;[4] finally, the bush became Mary inviolate at impregnation and parturition.[5] Bush and rod (which burst not into flame but into flower as a sign of Aaron's priesthood) relate not only to the Virgin Birth but also to Christ as 'first priest'.[6] The rod's leaves and blossom (mentioned in **2**) are his protection and sweetness;[7] the God speaking from the bush is (unbiblically, but in accordance with the nativity symbolism) the cross-nimbed second Person of the Trinity.[8]

The central scene is apparently mundane: in contrast to **6** (where Moses removes his shoes on holy ground, shading his eyes against literal and metaphorical illumination[9]) Joseph comfortably holds shod feet to a small fire.[10] But the Child's divinity is indicated even here. Ox and ass, not in the Bible story, represent recognition of God: they derive from 'the ox knows its owner and the ass its master's crib, but Israel has not known me, and my people have not understood'.[11] Their very position derives from the linking

of this verse with Habacuc's: 'You will make yourself known between two living creatures'.[12]

The topmost elements in all the scenes also imply sacrifice. In **7** the rod suggests a Christian altar crucifix: indeed, the symbolism of leaves and flowers already quoted, derives from the rod's comparison to the Cross bearing Christ as fruit.[13] Christ in **6** is even like a burnt offering: the bush's flame is the Passion.[14] In **5** he lies on a 'manger-altar', a common device to suggest the sacrifice of his birth (God emptying himself to become man), as well as death. There may even be an echo of the tradition in which ox and ass eat hay or lick the Child as if in symbolic 'communion' at the sacrifice of the Mass.[15]

Prophecy **3** recalls the Virgin Birth: the mountain the Mother, the stone Christ.[16] The others prophesy Christ: **4** directly,[17] **11** celebrating his birthplace.[18] **10** is most resonant: the prophet is afraid 'because the Word by which all things were made was laid in a manger';[19] alternatively, the Son himself 'fears' the Incarnation he will undertake.[20] Anguish and awe are thus implicit in **5**'s tranquil domesticity. Indeed, central to each scene is a sign of its awesomeness: Moses's double gesture of dazzlement and humility (**6**), the divinity-honouring censer swung by Aaron (**7**), and in **5** a little water-jug, symbol of Christ as life-source.[21]

Legit̃ in lib̃ leuitici · xṽ ·
ca̅ g̃ oĩs mulier pariẽs · pri
mo geiti ipm̃ r̃dimie cũ
ouẽ debet : pauper at̃ g̃
oue no̅ here pterat : tur
tures aduos pullos colũ
bari p puero offerre d̃bat
et hoc p sua purificatoe cũ
virgo glosa implerut qui
us purgaco̅ no̅ idiguit

Legit̃ in pmo lib̃ regu · i
ca̅ g̃ cũ ãna mater samuel̃
ipm̃ samuele ablactãs obtulit
eũ hely sacdoti in tabernaculo
dei ⁊ oblatio iisig̃bat oblatoes
dei in teplo ⁊mulo fcm̃

Dauid   **Malac · iij ·**

Dñs in templo s̃co suo   d veẽt ad teplũ s̃cm̃ suũ d̃iator q̃ vos q̃rit

Hic psentatur · ṽs
prioz ṽt redimatur

ṽs Oblatum x̃m samuel
te d̃uotat istũ

Sach̃   Ecc̃ c̃ ṽenoz habita
· iij ·   ta in medio tuĩ

Sopho
· iij ·

Rex url̃ d̃ñuinus
in medio tuĩ

ṽs Virgo hbana x̃m symeonis recipit istum

According to 2 Kings iii 6–21, Abner, captain of Saul's army, came to David in Jerusalem to restore to him all the people of Israel who followed the house of Saul. This prefigured the coming to Christ of the magi, who showed him reverence with ceremonial gifts.

C

According to 3 Kings x 1–12, the Queen of Sheba (who was a Gentile), having heard reports of Solomon, came into Jerusalem to show him reverence with great gifts. This clearly prefigured the Gentiles who came a great distance to show the Lord reverence with gifts.

David, Psalm 71.10
Kings of Tharsis and the islands shall offer gifts

Isaias lx 14
And they shall worship your footsteps

[ABNER BEFORE DAVID]

[MAGI]
Matthew ii 1–12

[SHEBA BEFORE SOLOMON]

These people denote the nations
wishing to be united to Christ

This figuratively denotes the gentiles
coming to Christ

Isaias ii 2–3
All nations shall flock to him, and many people go there

Balaam, Numbers xxiv 17 (Isaias xi 1)
A star shall rise out of Jacob, and a stem spring from the root

Christ is adored; gold, frankincense and myrrh are set out

Much of the central scene's meaning lies in its contrast with Types remarkably similar to each other in design:[1] both **6** and **7** show crowned, enthroned kings with conspicuous sceptres, someone kneeling with an offering, and two figures in the background. In **5**, canopied thrones are replaced by Mary's lap and a thatched roof: Christ's kingdom is not earthly. The sceptres' position is occupied by the Child; he *is* the 'sceptre' prophesied by Balaam in a verse partly used in **11**: 'A star shall rise out of Jacob, and a sceptre spring up from Israel'.[2] The 'star' in the corner of **5** is pointed out by a Wise Man, but in **6** and **7** the equivalent corner, to which both sceptres point, is empty. The star signifies Christ's kingship (as does the sceptre) and his divinity, manifested only in the New Testament.[3] Mary's 'throne' forms a frame out of which Jesus reaches as if from one world to another.[4] Central to the page is a ciborium-like vessel whose upper portion, touched in acceptance by Jesus, resembles an orb, symbol of royal authority.[5]

The Three Wise Men (Magi)[6] were 'the first heathen to whom God revealed himself';[7] later they represent Europe, Asia, and Africa:[8] the world offering homage to Christ the King. Un-biblically, they appear as kings: three 'Kings of Tharsis . . . of the Arabians and of Saba' were identified with the Magi by the third century.[9] Earthly kings recognise a higher power (the removed crown of one of them is in the foreground); as Wise Men they acknowledge a greater wisdom. Homage offered by Jews is represented by Abner (**6**) bringing a rival faction to acknowledge David (the Child's ancestor and the first king of all Israel).[10] The covenant David accepts is the equivalent of the gift accepted by the Child in **5**. The queen of Sheba (**7**) is a common Type of the gentiles acknowledging Christ, and of the Church composed of all races.[11] Jesus himself contrasted her willingness to make a long journey to learn from Solomon with the Jews' reluctance to hear him at all.[12] Her rank, and her desire to learn by asking Solomon questions, echo the humility of the Wise 'Kings'.

All three scenes are analogues of spiritual journey. Pilgrimage to wisdom is implied in Prophecies more obviously concerned with homage—**3**, **4**, and **10**: the latter goes on 'and he will teach us his ways and we will walk in his paths . . .'[13] Prophecy **4** has been related to converted persecutors of Christians (an echo of **6**, where Abner makes peace), and to the Apostles who travel preaching.[14]

The Magi's familiar gifts are not identifiable here, but the Feast of Epiphany says that gold is for kingship, incense for priesthood, myrrh for burial: Christ is honoured as King, God, and man.[15] The gifts represent the very 'gifts' he offers to man: his kingdom 'not of this world',[16] his godhead constrained in babyhood, his humanity to be sacrificed. The first moment of his glory already suggests his grave.

According to Leviticus xii, every woman bearing a firstborn must buy him back with a sheep; the poor, however, who would have no sheep, were obliged to offer two turtle-doves or two young pigeons for the boy; and this was for purification. The glorious Virgin carried this out although she did not need to be purified.

d

According to 1 Kings i 21–25, Anna the mother of Samuel, weaning this Samuel, offered him to Heli the priest in the temple of God. This offering prefigured the presentation of God to Simeon in the temple.

David, Psalm 10.5
The Lord is in his holy temple

Malachias iii 1
The ruler whom you seek shall come to his holy temple

[LAW OF PRESENTATION]

[PRESENTATION]
Luke ii 22–39

[ANNA PRESENTS SAMUEL]

This firstborn child is presented in order to be bought back

This Samuel denotes Christ himself offered

Zacharias ii 10
See, I am coming and shall live among you

Sophonias iii 15
The king of Israel, the Lord, is among you

The Virgin, making an offering to Simeon, receives back Christ himself

---

In **c**, offering was made to God; in **d**, God himself is offered to the priest in accordance with the law that every first-born child be given to God and redeemed by payment.[1] As **12** implies, only by surrendering our own does it become truly ours. Sacrifice is central to the New Law in a new way: the Redeemer is himself redeemed. Four separate events are suggested in the central scene: Simeon's prophecy; the Child's Presentation by its father after thirty days; the Purification, after forty days, of the mother, ritually unclean after childbirth under Mosaic Law; and the Feast of Candlemas. Luke's conflation of the second and third events is found in **1**: birds would be offered not 'for the boy'[2] (at the Presentation) but at the Purification. Conflation is natural: in both, the law is humbly fulfilled.[3]

The centrality of the Presentation (mentioned in **2**) is clear from **6**, illustrating Leviticus's law (mother replacing father, to relate the scene to **5** and **7**). This very abstraction, unrelated to a story, shows the importance of this sacrificial act.[4] Indeed, all three designs show a child on an 'altar', suggesting the Christian immolation of God at death and in the Eucharist:[5] **d** (like **a**, **b**, and **c**) prefigures the Passion. The second Type (**7**) shows not Samuel's presentation by his father,[6] but as **2** says, his mother giving him to the Temple (unlike Jesus, given to God very differently).[7]

Before the Presentation, Christ's death is prophesied not by the priest but by Simeon (named in **2** and **12**).[8] He foresees Jesus's importance, and Mary's heart pierced by a 'sword'.[9] This recognition is indicated by the boy's turn (a contrast with **6** and **7**)—the focal point to a lovely group of heads and eloquent hands.[10] The second woman is Anna the prophetess, who recognised Christ too. Recognition of God again links **d** with **a**, **b** and **c** (Gabriel, ox and ass, and Magi). That the Purification is also represented is clear from **1**, and from the large candle signifying Candlemas, celebrated on the Feast of the Purification and associated with Simeon, who saw the 'light to lighten the Gentiles'.[11]

The Prophecies mainly recall the Presentation, the Child being received back into the world he is to redeem. The keeping of the Old Law introduces the New. The last Old Testament prophet is the very Malachias quoted in **4** by Jesus, saying of the Baptist: 'For this is he of whom it is written: "Behold, I sent my angel before thy face, who shall prepare the way before thee" '.[12] Both **10** and **11** express joy in the Messiah.[13] The Prophecies also suggest his purity,[14] echoed in his mother's Purification: the 'temple' of **3** and **4** is not only the Church,[15] but also the human body.[16] Christ inhabits his body as a priest his temple: in it he makes his sacrifice,[17] and is offered in the Eucharist. In various ways the page celebrates grace made newly accessible in Christ.

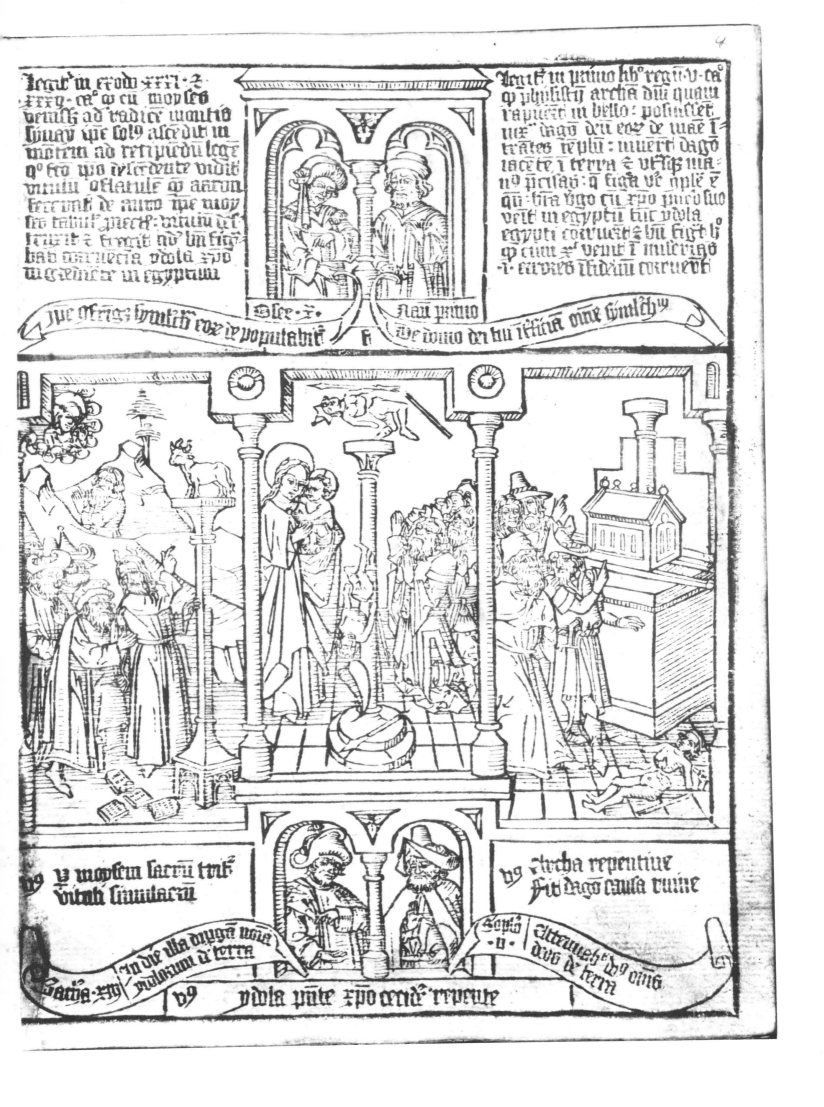

Legitur in exodo xxxi. z
xxxiiij. capitulo qd cum moyses
venisset ad radices montis
synai ipe solus ascedit in
montem ad recipiendu legem
qd deo ipo descendente vidit
vmulu oftacule qd aaron
fecerat de auro ipe moy
ses tabulas fregit: vmulu ds
fregit z fregit hoc vn figu
bat corruptia ydola xpo
nascente in egyptum

Legitur in primo libro regum v. ca
qd phylistii archa dm quam
rapuerat in bello: posuerut
vxta dago deu eoz de mane in
tratis templu: inuenerut dago
iacete in terra z vtrasq ma
nu prcisas: q figla vc nplet z
qn bria ydo cu xpo puero suo
venit in egyptu tunc ydola
egypti corruerut vn figla h
qd cum xpo venit in miserigo
i corues ydui corruerut

Osee · x. Reu primo

Que offerz vmlich eoz ip populabit
vir de domo dei vn iessim ome vmlchiii

ij moysem sacru vol
vilali simulacru

vq archa repentiue
fit dago causa ruine

in die illa dirigam vole
ydoloru de terra

Sopho
nie · ij

Attriueh dos dos ome
dos de terra

Sacia xiij
vq ydola pure xpo cedis rupente

According to Genesis xxvii 41–45, when Rebecca the Mother of Esau and Jacob heard that Jacob might shortly be murdered, she sent Jacob her son from his own country into a foreign land, to avoid death. This aptly pre- figured Christ's flight into Egypt, when the moment he was born, Herod sought him to destroy him.

e

According to 1 Kings xix 9–12, King Saul sent guards to find and murder David. However, David's wife Michol let him down from a window by a rope, and so he evaded those looking for him. Now King Saul signifies Herod, who sought Christ to kill him, when Joseph led him into Egypt with Mary and so he escaped the hands of those seeking him.

Isaias xix 1
See, the Lord will enter Egypt and the idols shall be dislodged

David, Psalm 54.8
See, I have gone a long way in flight and lived in solitude

[JACOB FLEES ESAU]

[FLIGHT INTO EGYPT]
Matthew ii 13–15

[DAVID FLEES SAUL]

In fear of his brother Jacob left his father's house

Through Michol, David escaped Saul's plots against him

Jeremias xii 7
I have abandoned my house and left my home

Osee v 6
They shall look for the Lord and not find him

The boy Christ flees from the terrible anger of Herod

Like **a–d**, **e–h** form a group, being bounded by the *Flight into Egypt* and the *Return from Egypt*.[1] Events within the group are linked: **e3** refers directly to **f5**, the *Egyptian Idols Fall*, itself a kind of parallel with the human massacre in **g**. The Flight, the second of Christ's sufferings (the first, the Circumcision, is implied in the Presentation) will in **f**, **g**, and **h** lead to the manifesting of God to heathen and finally to Jews. The Flight, however, is about escape. We sense the aggressors traditionally absent from the central scene because they are dominant in the Types: Isaac and Esau (identified by his bow, as he is in **k6**) fill the foreground of **6**, while Jacob is a relatively small figure in the background saying farewell to his mother before taking flight. In **7** David (identified by the clothing he wears in **4** as Psalmist) escapes the crowding troops of Saul. The design of **5**, in which mother protects son while husband leads and protects both, is as old as the sixth cen- tury.[2] The Types also show a mother's concern for her son (Rebecca and Jacob) and a wife's concern for her husband (Michol and David); this points not only to the strong sense of family typical of the Flight, but perhaps also to the paradox by which Mary, a unique mother and wife, is concerned for the boy she bore, who is also the God by whom she conceived.

The traditional Flight design conveys a sense not only of family, but also of urgency—the ass stepping smartly from left to right,

Joseph moving out of the picture, a lovely curving diagonal, top left to bottom right, accentuating this direction.[3] In all three scenes, evil is to be avoided, even at the expense of material security—perhaps only by the abandonment of it. In both Types, threats to the persecuted originate in jealousy roused by a threat to the persecutor's authority, as in the case of Herod. Yet there is little precedent for either Type's relation to the Flight.[4] However, in other contexts Jacob is a common Type of Christ: his leaving home is compared in general terms with Christ's going among gentiles,[5] and Esau's hatred is compared with that of Jews for Christians,[6] so it is only a small imaginative leap to see Jacob's journey as a Type of the first journey made by Jesus.[7] Similarly, the association of the Flight with David's escape is predictable, the reign of Saul being equated with evil and that of David with good.[8]

With one exception, association of the Prophecies with the Flight is also new. The exception is **3**: in the eighth and ninth centuries these idols are equated with those that fall in the pre- sence of the Child.[9] **4** has a double meaning: in the fourth century it was seen as a reference to the 'holy flight' from worldliness,[10] and later to David's flight from Saul (**7**).[11] Prophecies **10** and **11** are also concerned with escape and asceticism.[12]

According to Exodus xxii and xxxii, when Moses had come to the foot of Mount Sinai he went along on to the mountain to receive the law. Having done this and come down he saw the cast image of a calf, which Aaron had made in gold. Moses, having thrown down the tables of the law, tore down the calf and broke it up, which aptly prefigures the falling of the idols when Christ went into Egypt.

f

According to 1 Kings v 1–5, the Philistines had placed the ark of the Lord, which they had seized in battle, next to Dagon their god. Entering the temple in the morning, they found Dagon lying on the ground, and both hands broken off. This prefiguration was truly fulfilled when the blessed Virgin came into Egypt with Christ her son; then the idols of Egypt fell, and aptly signify that when Christ came, images (that is, errors of the unbelieving) fell.

Osee x 2
He shall break down their idols, he shall destroy

Nahum i 14
I will destroy every image in the house of your god

[GOLDEN CALF]　　　　　[EGYPTIAN IDOLS FALL]　　　　　[DAGON FALLS]

The image of the calf is crushed by
Moses the holy

The ark of the covenant causes
Dagon's unexpected downfall

Zacharias xiii 2
At that time I shall eradicate the names of the idols from the earth

Sophonias ii 11
The Lord will bring low all the gods of the earth

In the presence of Christ, the idols suddenly fell

The Fall of the Egyptian Idols, mentioned in **e**, is from eighth- and ninth-century legends of the type which, though condemned as early as the fifth century,[1] retained great popularity in literature and art.[2] Affrodosius, governor of Sotinen, kneels, converted by a miracle designed to reveal God to the heathen: 'he went up to the blessed Mary, who was carrying the Lord in her bosom, and worshipped him, and said to his whole army and to all his friends "If he were not the God of our gods, our gods would not have fallen on their faces before him" '.[3]

Commentators, commonly restricting their attention to biblical material,[4] give no precedent for the Types' relation to the Fall of the Idols.[5] However, Dagon's fall (**7**) is often allegorised: the holy Ark, shown on the altar crowned by the empty pillar from which the Philistine god fell, is the Gospel taken to gentiles.[6] Dagon's fall itself is idolatry giving way to faith, his broken hands are the curtailed deeds of idolaters, his detached head (not shown) is the broken pride of the Devil or of idolatry's rule,[7] his torso flight.[8]

The *Golden Calf*'s relation to **5** is less simple. Moses, having broken the Tables of Law received from God on Mount Horeb (**6**, top left), orders the calf's destruction.[9] Interestingly, we do not see what **8** describes: the idol broken (as in **5** and **7**) to signify vanquishing of devil-worship.[10] The only broken objects shown are the Tables, that is, the Old Law superseded by the New.[11] If these are the real equivalent of the broken idols in **5** and **7** the design may relate to **5** and **7** in another way: the calf representing evil is, in another tradition, the sacrificial victim, Christ himself.[12] It may, then, simultaneously suggest false gods and the true God replacing them. In this case it is significant that in **7** the pedestal is empty, in **5** the idols fall from it, but in **6** the calf is still in place, because it is both the conquered and the conqueror.

The source of the Fall of the Idols mentions it as a fulfilment not of any of the *Biblia Pauperum* Prophecies, but of Isaias xix 1: 'Behold the Lord . . . shall come into Egypt and the idols of Egypt shall be moved'.[13] The *Biblia Pauperum* Prophecies are not connected by tradition even with the Types.[14] In view of the calf's ambivalence, **10** is interesting in that it follows a Messianic prophecy of the crucifixion: 'They will look on the one they have pierced'. The page thus suggests the miracle-working power of God, the superseding of the Old Law by the New, the suppression of literal and doctrinal idolatry, and perhaps the coming sacrifice sealing all these.

According to 1 Kings xxii 11–18, King Saul had all the priests of the Lord in Nobe killed because they had harboured the fugitive David and had given him holy bread to eat. Saul signifies Herod, for David signifies Christ, and indeed the priests signify the innocent boys whom Herod had had killed on account of Christ.

g

According to 4 Kings xi, Queen Athalia, seeing her son dead, had all the sons of the king killed lest they rule in their father's place. However, the sister of the king then secretly took away the younger son, who was afterwards made king. The cruel queen signifies Herod, who because of Christ had the boys killed; the boy secretly saved from death signifies Christ secretly saved from death at the hands of King Herod.

David, Psalm 78.10
Avenge, O Lord, the blood of your holy men which has been shed

Proverbs xxviii 15
A wicked ruler of poor people is like a roaring lion and a hungry bear

[SAUL HAS PRIESTS SLAIN]

[MASSACRE OF THE INNOCENTS]
Matthew ii 16

[ATHALIA HAS PRINCES SLAIN]

On account of David, Saul slaughtered the Lord's anointed

The royal stock was established by stealth because one had been saved

Jeremias xxxi 15
(Matthew ii 18)
A voice was heard in Rama: lamentation and mourning

Osee viii 4

They have reigned, and not with my authority

These were taken from this world in place of Christ

The apparently crowded design of the *Massacre of the Innocents* (5) is really in three traditional parts: Herod's command, children's deaths, mothers' lament.[1] The sequence of events is contracted, suggesting a timeless view of these 'protomartyrs', who did not suffer for Christ but 'on his account' (1).[2] Each element of the design is cleverly pointed by a strong diagonal movement from top left to bottom right: Herod's authoritative sceptre gestures to a lamenting mother, isolated in her grief. Its direction is echoed in the sword-thrust of the soldier[3] and in the body of a child being killed, hanging sprawled, surrounded by gestures of violence, fear, and entreaty.

For Matthew, the Massacre fulfilled the Prophecy of Jeremias (10),[4] which so stresses formal lamentation, while 3, 4, and 11 emphasise its two other elements: the violent deaths and Herod's tyranny.[5] Herod's fear of the house of David is echoed in the first Type (6): Saul has the priests of Nobe killed for harbouring David himself (we recall that the Innocents by their numbers unwittingly protected Jesus). There appears to be no precedent for this scene as a Type of the Massacre—surprisingly, since it is a good parallel: when Doeg has slain the eighty-five priests, Saul goes on to have the town of Nobe 'put to the sword, men and women, children and infants, cattle and donkeys, and sheep'.[6]

The destructive insecurity of the tyrant is shown also in Athalia

(7).[7] Here we are aware not only of the victims but also of the survivor, Jehoash, the Type of Jesus. The very pose of Jehosheba, carrying the rescued boy, recalls the Virgin and Child: it does not naturalistically show a woman concealing a boy to save him.[8] Contrasted with the crowded order of the central scene is a formalism in which two dead children lie symmetrically in the foreground, the next victim behind them, while the two women stand opposed across a significant central space.

The two Type designs balance each other beautifully: 6 has a strong diagonal movement from top right to bottom left, along which the sweep of the executing sword would pass; 7 shows an opposite movement stressed by Athalia's condemning gesture. Both find their echo in the pyramidal structure of 5, the apex of which is formed by the destroying soldier's fist.

We may wonder why so many children had to die so that the infant Jesus should escape. The uncompromising traditional answer is perhaps implied in 12: they did not simply die, they were 'taken from this world in place of Christ'—almost as a privilege, since they would be better off in the next world than they could possibly be in this.[9] The ultimate effect is to remind us that the Christ-child escaped only to die more horribly as a man: once again the Passion is implicit in the Infancy.

According to 2 Kings ii 1–4, King Saul being dead, David consulted the Lord, who answered that he should return to the land of Juda. David signifies Christ, who returned to the land of Juda after the death of Herod. So indeed the evangelist testifies, saying: 'The angel of the Lord appeared: "Take the boy and his mother and go, etc; truly, those who sought the boy's life are dead"'.

h

According to Genesis xxxi and xxxii, Jacob, returning to his country, from which he had fled in fear of his brother Esau, sent sheep and cattle, camels and asses ahead, and himself followed with his wives and sons. Jacob, who fled from his brother, signifies Christ, who fled from King Herod (whom Esau represents). When Herod was dead, Christ returned to the land of Juda.

David, Psalm 105.4
Come to us Lord, on your deliverance

Osee
Egypt, do not weep: the Lord has had pity on you

[DAVID RETURNS]

[RETURN FROM EGYPT]
Matthew ii 19–21

[JACOB RETURNS]

Saul being dead, David returned to his country

Jacob fears his brother but longs to see his father

Osee xi 1
I have called my son out of Egypt

Zacharias i 16
I shall return to Jerusalem bringing mercy

Jesus leaves Egypt and returns to the holy places

The *Return from Egypt*, mentioned briefly in the Bible, is important here: it ends not only the group bounded by the *Flight into Egypt* and the *Return from Egypt* (e–h), but also the Infancy of Christ (a–h, a fifth of the whole). Matthew says the Flight took place so that the Return might fulfil Osee's Prophecy (10). The Return is distinguished from the Flight by the Child's being old enough to walk. Both Types, though rare,[1] are wholly appropriate in context: The flights of Jacob and David (e6 and e7) prefigured the Flight; here their returns prefigure the Return: all three designs in **e** move left to right, here all three move right to left.

The Types suggest that the central scene shows the beginning of Jesus's authority. In **6** David (identified as the Psalmist of **3** by his hat, and by the harp on his shield) returns to be crowned. We recall that Christ's kingship is 'not of this world'. Jacob (**7**) received divine orders to leave exile,[2] as David, and Jesus (through Joseph), had done. He, too, returns with new authority, represented here by his wealth: 'sheep and cattle, camels and asses, wives and sons'. The group of small animals at the bottom, the lines of larger animals' heads and of people behind (one looking back as if to those following) suggest a great company. The whole is firmly controlled by a strong central vertical. The *titulus* (**9**) adds

more meaning: Jacob returns 'longing for his father's house',[3] but fearing his brother.[4] Jesus is now to go about his father's business too, in the face of opposition. Joseph, afraid of Herod's son, did not take his family back to Bethlehem:[5] Jesus became 'of Nazareth' as a refugee, but his new authority is suggested in **5** by Joseph's being barely in frame, leaving the Child dominant.[6]

The Prophecies also imply the end of an exile or the beginning of an era, a duality pointed in **12**. Osee's Prophecy (**10**) originally referred to the Israelites' exodus from Egypt (itself a Type of the Redemption): a deliverance and new departure. The Psalm (**3**) also suggests escape and renewal.[7] Initially confusing in its mention of compassion for Egypt, which in **5** is the place of exile, **4** may echo the Advent Office: 'Egypt, do not weep, your sovereign will come to you . . .',[8] where Egypt signifies those awaiting Christ's advent into their lives.[9] Return from exile, and renewal, are thus related to redemption: indeed Zacharias's Prophecy (**11**) was related to Crucifixion and (since it goes on 'and my temple shall be rebuilt there') Resurrection.[10] Like those preceding it, the last Infancy scene looks to the Passion, which is to crown the ministry—the next section.

According to Exodus xiv, when Pharoah was following the Israelites with chariots and horsemen, he went after the Israelites into the Red Sea, and the Lord brought back the waters of the sea over them. In this way he freed his people from the hand of the pursuing enemy. In the same way he has even now freed the Christian people from the bonds of Original Sin, by the waters of baptism made holy by Christ.

i

According to Numbers xiii 1–28 (and xiv 6–7), when the scouts sent to spy out the promised land came back, they cut a cluster of grapes, carried it over a pole, and crossing the Jordan, brought the cluster back as evidence of the richness of that land. This signifies that if we wish to enter the kingdom of heaven we must first pass through the waters of baptism.

Isaias xii 3
With joy you shall draw water from the saviour's springs

David, Psalm 67.27
You from the springs of Israel, bless the Lord in the churches

[CROSSING THE RED SEA]

[BAPTISM OF CHRIST]
Matthew iii 13–17

[JOSUE & CALEB RETURN FROM JORDAN]

The enemies are on the road: they are overwhelmed by the sea

The river is crossed and the land of honey is approached

Ezechiel xxxvi 25
I shall pour out pure water upon you

Zacharias xiii 1
At that time there shall be an open spring for the house of David

Baptism is made holy when Christ is baptised

Jesus is baptised by immersion in water; John pours baptismal oil.[1] The gentle ceremony has violent connotations: the anointing is as if for a journey or contest. The Messianic mission is about to begin,[2] and then the Passion in which it will culminate: the Baptism even suggests burial.[3] Not only Christ's death but also the end of all things is called to mind: the 'baptism of fire' which John said would be given by Christ.[4] The formal action of the first sacrament[5] is completed by the laying on of hands. An angel standing by with a cloth acts as deacon,[6] while heaven opens,[7] shedding light. The scene resembles **a5**, the *Annunciation*. In both the Trinity is manifested (here in Christ, in the Spirit as dove, and in the Father saying 'This is my Son, the beloved');[8] in both a task is accepted, an angel is present, and some kind of birth is announced. Jesus (who called his Passion a baptism)[9] also called his Baptism a rebirth,[10] and early theologians, relating the Father's words above to Psalm 2.7 ('Thou art my Son, this day I have begotten thee') saw Christ's own baptism as a 'birth'.[11]

Traditionally the Prophecies have been related not to the Baptism of Christ but to him as source of spiritual life: **3** through Christ's 'Let him who thirsts come to me and drink',[12] **4** through 'He who drinks the water I shall give shall never thirst'.[13] In **10** and **11** have been seen baptism purging the soul, the 'waters of doctrine', rebirth in Christ, and the baptism of blood offered on the cross.[14]

Bloodshed as well as cleansing water is a major meaning of **6**, the Red Sea having long been equated with the red blood of Christ.[15] Pharoah (the Devil[16]) is destroyed by the sea: foundering, he fails to save his men. In contrast Moses, like Christ, leads his people out of bondage (in a balancing contrary movement). The sea is a literal and metaphorical boundary, as is the river Jordan in **7** and **5**. Just as the Israelites now begin a forty-year journey in the wilderness, Christ now begins a forty-day fast in the wilderness and is then tempted (**k**).

The other Type (**7**) normally foreshadows the Crucifixion, grapes hanging on the wood like Christ on the Cross.[17] It is not at first clear how it prefigures baptism, apart from the baptism of blood. The two scouts did bear back their burden over the Jordan (in the background of **7**), but it is a different crossing of this river which is usually seen as a Type of baptism: that in Joshua iii, where the river, like the Red Sea, miraculously parts to let the Israelites into their new land.[18] *Biblia Pauperum* brilliantly conflates two events to stress the bloodshed implicit in the Baptism. The main scene and its Types are primarily concerned not with the Trinity, as are early examples of the subject,[19] but with new life, purification, the end of one era and the start of another, and the death that makes them all possible.

According to Genesis xxv 29–34, Esau, in exchange for a soup his brother Jacob had made, sold his birthright (that is, the privilege due to the firstborn), and lost the paternal blessing. In the same way, the devil tricked the First Parents by means of gluttony and pride, saying: 'The moment you eat you shall become like gods, knowing good and evil'.

k

According to Genesis iii 1–6, Adam and Eve were tricked by the serpent, who tempted them with gluttony because the devil tricks us, misleading us as it were by a device. This aptly prefigured the temptation which the devil presented to Christ, when he tempted Christ, saying: 'If you are the son of God, command these stones to become bread'. This temptation excited appetite.

David 34, Psalm 34.16
They tempted me, they mocked at me with scorn

Isaias xxix 16
The thought is unnatural, as if clay were to oppose the potter

[ESAU SELLS HIS BIRTHRIGHT]

[TEMPTATION]
Matthew iv 1–3

[THE FALL]

Out of a liking for lentil soup, he utterly lost his personal privilege

The serpent overcame Adam so that he sucked the forbidden food himself

2 Kings (2 Samuel) vii 9
I have slain all your enemies

Job xvi 10
My enemy has looked at me with terrible eyes

Satan tempted Christ so that he might overcome him

In Bible and *Biblia Pauperum* Christ's Baptism is followed by forty days of fasting and solitude[1] culminating in triple temptation: gluttony, pride, and power (to turn stones into bread, to throw himself from the Temple-top so that angels would save him, and by worshipping the Devil to acquire the world visible from a mountain). The main scene shows not only the first, but all three, since Temple and mountain form the background.[2]

All the pictures focus on food. In **5** Jesus touches a proffered rock, not turned to bread. In **7** the twice depicted fruit, in line with heads and hands, appeals to sight, smell, and touch. In **6** Esau, back from hunting, takes the soup: sides of meat on the wall and a cauldron on the fire suggest a cosy kitchen, all part of the temptation (like Christ's) to reward the body after deprivation. The apparently unnecessary column between Jacob and Esau in **6** has a clever double function, stressing the difference between the men (one losing, the other gaining status, as soup is exchanged for seniority) and echoing the design of *The Fall*, where the central tree points an ominous *similarity* between Adam and Eve: both lose their 'birthright'—a privileged relationship with God.[3] Their sin is not preceded by deprivation: it causes it.

Although the fruit is not yet bitten, they cover their nakedness, as if the serpent (said to have adopted a woman's face to obtain Eve's confidence, even to appear as her very self[4]) confronted them with sexuality as well as making subtler insinuations., Gluttony traditionally results in lust; it is also associated, in **6** and **7** as

well as **5**, with pride and love of power. Jacob wants power, Eve hopes that knowledge of good and evil will make Adam and herself 'like gods'. But we are meant to obey God, not be gods. Christ replies to the first temptation: 'Man is not fed by bread alone, but by every word that comes from the mouth of God'. Obedience nourishes us.[6]

The Fall is more than a Type of the Temptation. Precisely because the first man was overcome by gluttony, lust for power, and pride, Christ the 'second Adam' conquers by abstinence, poverty, and humility:[7] a victory uniquely made the theme of **10** and **11**.[8] The other Prophecies are equally original in application.[9] The image in **4** (derived from Genesis ii 7, where God makes man from clay) relates to Fall and Temptation. Its Bible context is the impossibility of secrecy from God (recalling Adam and Eve's futile attempts to hide): ' "Who can see us? Who can recognise us?" The thought is unnatural, as if the clay were to oppose the potter'. But St Paul quotes it in a new context: 'What right have you, a human-being, to cross-examine God? The pot has no right to say to the potter "Why did you make me this way?" '[10] We have no right to complain of temptation, neither can we hope to hide or totally avoid sin, being free and fallible.

The page suggests temptation's subtlety, the interrelationship of sins, their horrible consequences, the duty to fight them by following Christ's example, and the privilege so gained—our natural dignity and the final vision of God.[11]

According to 3 Kings xvii 17–23, Elias [Elijah] the prophet carried the dead boy on to the hill and prayed, saying: 'I beg that the soul of the boy may return'; and it was so, and he gave the boy back to his mother alive. This aptly prefigured the raising of Lazarus, whom the Lord raised from the dead and restored to his sisters, that is, to Mary Magdalene and Martha.

1

According to 4 Kings iv 8–37, Eliseus [Elisha] the prophet saw that the son of the widow with whom he used to lodge was dead, and he prostrated himself on the boy, and the body of the boy grew warm and came to life. Eliseus prefigures Christ: and indeed the boy whom he raised from the dead represents Lazarus, restored to life before the Jews' eyes.

Deuteronomy xxxii 39
I will kill and make live, I will strike and I shall heal

David, Psalm 29.4 (?)
Lord, you have freed my soul from the dead

[ELIAS RAISES THE SAREPHTAN]   [RAISING OF LAZARUS]   [ELISEUS RAISES THE SUNAMITE]
John xi 1–45

The widow's son is brought to life
by Elias

By means of your gifts, O God,
Eliseus gave him life

Job xiv 14
Do you think that a dead man can live again?

1 Kings (1 Samuel) ii 6
The Lord kills and makes live

By you, O Christ, this Lazarus is brought to life again

The *Raising of Lazarus* shows God's power to overcome the death of both body and soul.[1] Lazarus, raised incorrupt, foreshadows the soul's recall from sin,[2] the general resurrection,[3] the return of Christ's soul from the other world at the Harrowing of Hell (after his death and before his Resurrection),[4] and Christ's own rising. The latter (·i·) is full of vitality, but here an onlooker covers his nose against the stench of decay,[5] and a woman[6] raises her hand to her face in the gesture of mourning (Jesus himself wept in sympathetic sorrow).[7] This gloom is banished by the command 'Lazarus, come out', indicated by Jesus's raised hand (carefully placed in a central space and seeming to lift Lazarus by its relation to his clasped hands).

The Prophecies echo these themes. God's control over the life and death of soul and body is affirmed in **3**[8] and **11**. The Harrowing of Hell is the main association of **11** and **4**,[9] the former also referring to Christ's Resurrection.[10] The general resurrection is related to **10**, **11**, and **4**.[11]

The Types stress all these except the Harrowing. It is not surprising that they are similarly interpreted: the raising of the Sarephtan by Elias (Elijah) and of the Sunamite by Eliseus (Elisha) are as confusingly similar as the several names.[12] In both a poor widow is miraculously fed, and a prophet repays her hospitality by resuscitating her son, prostrating himself on the child lying dead on the prophet's bed. Are these the rewards of admitting God to house and heart, as Lazarus's family did? Designs for the two are often similar: the difference between them here may mean that in creating **6**, the artist worked from the text **2**, which oddly has the boy carried 'on to the hill' (instead of the bed).[13]

The Sarephtan resurrection was related to Lazarus early: both glorify God.[14] In legend the boy is Jonas, to be 'resurrected' a second time from the whale (a prefiguration of Christ's Resurrection, as in ·i·**7**).[15] The Sunamite is related to Christ's Resurrection too,[16] sometimes as humanity resurrected in Christ.[17] But he is usually humanity saved not by the Resurrection but by the Incarnation: Christ identifies himself with us, just as Eliseus lay and breathed on the body.[18] The widow is the Church; the upper room the height of her faith. Even the bed, table, and stool[19] are explained: as spiritual search, unity of faith, and the power of teaching.[20] Perhaps, since in **3** Moses (author of the *Song of Moses* in Deuteronomy xxxii) holds his rod, we are to recall the rod which Eliseus had placed on the dead boy first, without success: the Old Law can correct but not revivify.[21] The whole page powerfully presents the superiority of the New Law. The prophets' miracles required considerable effort: Lazarus, dead longer than the boys, is raised by one command.[22]

According to Genesis xviii 1–3, Abraham saw three youths (that is, angels) who had accepted his hospitality: 'he saw three and worshipped one'. The three angels signified the trinity of Persons, but in that he worshipped one, he indicated the singleness of its Nature. In the same way, Christ in his transfiguration showed himself to be one true God in Nature, and of three Persons.

m

According to Daniel iii 91–92, Nabuchodonosor the King of Babylon sent three youths into a fiery furnace, and when he approached the furnace to watch them in the fire, he saw with them a fourth like a Son of God. The three youths represented the trinity of Persons, the fourth the singleness of their Nature. In his transfiguration Christ showed himself truly single in Nature, three in Persons.

David, Psalm 44.3
More beautiful than the sons of men

Isaias lx 1
Jerusalem, your light has come, and the glory of the Lord has risen over you

[ABRAHAM & THE THREE ANGELS]

[TRANSFIGURATION]
Matthew xvii 1–9

[THREE YOUTHS IN THE FURNACE]

Abraham saw three, worshipped one

Look! The Glory of Christ is revealed to that gentile

From the last book of Malachias, iv 2
For you who fear my name the sun of justice shall rise

Habacuc iii 4
His brightness shall be like light and horns shall be on his hands

Three represent the glorified son of God

This page, as *lectiones* and Types show, is about the mystery of three Persons in one divine Nature: the Trinity.[1] In **6** Abraham, somehow understanding three apparent angels to be one, and divine, addresses them in the singular: 'Lord . . .'.[2] In **7**, three youths unharmed by the furnace signify the Trinity,[3] and **2** says that a fourth visible among them (not shown in the picture) represents God's single nature.[4] For once, the relation between Types and Antitype is very odd.[5] Visual parallels and **12** suggest that in the Transfiguration (**5**), Moses, Christ, and Elias represent the unity of the Trinity. If intended, this is idiosyncratic: not surprisingly, commentators do *not* equate Moses and Elias with the first and third divine Persons. It is true that the Transfiguration (like the Baptism) reveals the Trinity. God the Father speaks, indicating something like human love within the Trinity itself: 'This is my beloved Son, who has my approval'; the power of the Son is shown in the brightness of Jesus and the presence of long-dead prophets; the Spirit is in the 'bright cloud'.[6] But this triplicity is clearly not illustrated in **5** (though it often is in Transfigurations, and certainly is in the Baptism, **i**).

There is, however, a confused association in some commentators between the three standing figures and the Trinity: almost as if the familiar image (fully evolved by the sixth century)[7] suggested that the three figures were analogous to, though not to be equated with, the three Persons. Two ninth-century writers, for example,

accuse the disciple Peter of stupidity in suggesting a tent each for Christ, Elias, and Moses: 'the three tents should have been one, as the Trinity is one'. Jesus himself, the triple God incarnate, had required only one 'tent'—the human body.[8] Perhaps the Transfiguration reveals a world in which distinction between persons is less simple than in ours: Christ speaks immediately after it as if Elias and the Baptist are in some sense the same.[9]

All three scenes present a visionary perception of the supranatural. All three emphasise light and beauty (two of the disciples show traditional dazzlement). The *Transfiguration* tells us something about the 'glorified' body (a contrast with the rather macabre *Raising of Lazarus* preceding it).[10] Light and beauty are the four Prophecies' themes, and **11** has been related to the Transfiguration.[11] One (**10**) is concerned not only with light but also with doomsday and judgement, strongly suggesting the fiery furnace of **7**, and the resurrection of the glorified body: Malachias's chapter begins: 'For behold, the day shall come kindled like a furnace, and all the proud and all who do evil shall be burned like stubble . . . but for you that fear my name the Sun of justice shall rise . . .'.[12] All three scenes transcend time: Abraham sees the then unrevealed Trinity; in **7** Nabuchodonosor sees a portent of it; at the Transfiguration, Old and New Testaments come together, suggesting fulfilment in eternity.

According to 2 Kings xii 1–13, Nathan the prophet was sent to David to reprove him: and indeed King David, moved by repentance, obtained mercy from God. Now the penitent David denotes the penitent Mary Magdalene, who obtained forgiveness for all her sins.

n

According to Numbers xii, Mary the sister of Moses and Aaron was made leprous for her sins, and was cured of her uncleanness by Moses. Now Moses signified Christ, who cleansed Mary Magdalene of all the impurity of her sins, as he himself testifies in Luke, saying: 'Your sins are forgiven you' etc.

Ezechiel xviii 22
Whenever a man shall repent they shall not record all his offences

David, Psalm 50.19
O God, you will not ignore a contrite and humble heart

[NATHAN BRINGS DAVID TO REPENTANCE]

[MARY MAGDALENE REPENTS]
Luke vii 37–50

[MOSES' & AARON'S SISTER MARY REPENTS]

Impressed by Nathan's argument
King David mends his evil ways

This woman was made clean,
leprosy having been her punishment

From the first book of Zacharias, i 3
Turn towards me and I shall turn towards you

David, 2 Kings (2 Samuel) vii 22
There is none like you among the gods O Lord

The source of goodness absolved this woman from sins

Guilt, repentance, penance, mercy, and the Passion, which alters their nature, meet in the main scene because it conflates two occasions when Jesus was anointed by a woman while at table.[1] The first, relating to the Passion, is suggested by this page's position between the *Raising of Lazarus* (1), and the start of the Passion sequence at the *Entry into Jerusalem*, which (in *Biblia Pauperum* as in John) follows immediately.[2] At Bethany with Simon the leper, Lazarus and Martha see their sister Mary anoint Jesus, wiping his feet with her hair.[3] When the disciples protest at the waste of valuable oil, Jesus justifies its use 'as if for his burial'. The main motif, forgiveness (stressed in 3), derives, however, from the different occasion, at the house of Simon the Pharisee.[4] A sinner—associated with the prostitute Mary Magdalene (as in 2) only by tradition[5]—anoints Jesus's feet, weeps on them, and dries them with her hair. The figure on the right is the Pharisee.[6] Secretly scandalised that Christ should allow such a person to touch him, he is told, as Christ's raised hand suggests, that her gesture of humility and love is related to her sins.[7] She is not punished; Christ pays her debt.

In contrast, David (6) and Moses's sister, Mary (7), do severe penance.[8] At the top of 6, Nathan accuses David of having murdered his wife's first husband to obtain her. At the bottom, under a startling blank wall round an enclosure emphasising isolation and self-abasement, the king, crownless in penance, fasts and stays awake for seven days to persuade God to save the sick child of his sinful union. The child dies, and David accepts God's will. The stairs dominating the design suggest the Twelve Steps of Humility leading a repentant soul to heaven, or perhaps the Twelve Steps of Pride[9] descended. Mary (7) is struck by leprosy for criticising Moses's marriage, and banished for seven days until she recovers. Guilty of accusing God's prophet of sexual irregularity, she (unlike David) receives intercession from Aaron and eventually from Moses himself.[10] Hands raised to Moses form a vertical with the tree above, separating supplicants from auditors, as David is isolated by the extraordinary wall and steps,[11] and as the woman in 5 is separated from Christ by the table (a barrier she breaks by touching him).[12]

The Prophecies stress the power of penitence: 4 has been put into the mouth of David during his self-abasement after Nathan's rebuke (shown in 6),[13] while 11 is part of his thanksgiving for Nathan's later very different message, promising him a line of descendants fulfilled in Christ.[14] According to Aquinas, 10 shows the subtle relation (highly relevant to the page) between grace and free will: man turns to God freely, yet not unless God turns to him.[15] Similarly in 12, Magdalene, the archetypal source of penitential tears, is absolved by the 'source' of goodness.

According to 1 Kings (1 Samuel) xvii (and xviii 6), when David had ſtruck down Goliath he cut off his head and carried it in his hand. As he was coming from the combat, women ran to him with tambourines, singing and dancing. Full of joy, they took him back to Jerusalem in great glory. Now David signifies Chriſt, whom the young men of the Hebrews took into Jerusalem shouting in a loud voice and saying: 'Blessed is he who comes in the name of the Lord'.

O

According to 4 Kings ii 13–15, when Eliseus [Elisha] was returning to the city the boys ran to meet him, bringing him in and praising him with great glory and honour. Eliseus signifies Chriſt, whom the young men of the Hebrews took in with great honour and glory as he came to Jerusalem.

David, Psalm 149.2
Let the daughters of Sion rejoice in their king

Canticles iii 11
Go out daughters of Sion, and see King Solomon

[DAVID IS GREETED]

[ENTRY INTO JERUSALEM]
Matthew xxi

[ELISEUS IS GREETED]

David, who threw down the enemy, is praised in song

O son of God, this glory of Eliseus is appropriate to you

Zacharias ix 9 (Matthew xxi 5)
Tell the daughter of Sion, see, your king comes meekly to you

Zacharias ix 9
Himself like a poor man riding on a humble donkey

The song of the good Hebrews praises you, O Chriſt

Victory and authority are celebrated. David (6) is so praised by the women of Jerusalem for killing Goliath that King Saul says he all but won the crown.[1] Like David met by music (one of the bells is central to 6, a triangle is nearby), Christ enters Jerusalem as saviour-king, to shouts of acclamation.[2] Eliseus (7), who has just inherited Elias's authority including his awesome power to save or destroy, is greeted outside Jericho by prophets.[3] Praying hands are central to 7, a contrast with the mood created by the fashionable women greeting David. Like Eliseus, then, Christ is acknowledged as a prophet. But the Types' very simplicity reveals paradoxes inherent in Christ's reception. King and conqueror,[4] he rides a common donkey (fulfilling Prophecy 11),[5] a symbol of humility whose head is central to the page.[6] The people think Jesus a temporal king, whereas his kingdom 'not of this world' is won by victory through defeat on the Cross.

The Types mirror each other in design, formally flanking the page with David and Eliseus. The crowds (women and prophets) and the hills behind them form a triangle at the apex of which is a man in a tree, conspicuous also because his gesture of homage completes a circle (round that symbolic donkey head) of figures, thrown-down clothes, and leaves. He also tops a vertical axis: donkey foreleg, Christ's body and blessing hand, the tree.

This figure, if not cutting palms, may be Zacheus, who climbed to see Jesus enter not Jerusalem but Jericho.[7] Conflation of the two

occasions is common,[8] and this design does give remarkable prominence to the figure: he, not the gate of Jerusalem, is the real equivalent of Jerusalem and Jericho, which in 6 and 7 heroes are to enter. In the conflated action, Christ enters not only Jerusalem (a Type of the City of Heaven) but also the house of Zacheus, the despised tax-collector. Defying public opinion, he draws attention to his chosen host: 'Zacheus, make haste and come down: I must stay in your house today'. He enters not merely a city or house but a heart, for Zacheus promptly returns his unjust profits. This conversion of Zacheus—a true triumph, unlike the Entry into Jerusalem—leads Jesus to declare his true purpose: to save the lost, not rule a realm. Zacheus rightly dominates the page.

The Prophecies, like the page, are symmetrical. The lower two actually form one verse quoted in the Gospel account of the Entry. Unlike them, the upper two are not traditionally related to these scenes, but both refer to 'daughters of Sion',[9] with an effect of unanimous acclaim. Like the Entry and its Types, these two point paradoxes: 3 is related both to the priest and sacrificer[10] who is to become the triumphant King of Heaven,[11] and to the Church rejoicing with the 'music' of Christ's pains on the Cross;[12] 4 exhorts us to contemplate Christ,[13] leaving worldly things for him (like Zacheus).[14] It is also a reference to his receiving from his mother the paradoxical crown of human life and suffering.[15]

Fieiam oius de domo mea • Ze·N· Dauid • Solo domus tue g̃medit me

vℊ Templu̅ mūdari iubeti h̃ et festa uocari

vℊ Et tua sc̃a deℊ mūdare studet machabeℊ

Amos ·v· Odio habuer̅t ĩ porta corripientem

Sacheℑ vltio Non erat ult̃ m̃coi ĩ domo dn̅i

vℊ Cristus uendentes te̅plo repellit ementes

Legitur in genesi xxxvii capitulo quod fratres Joseph miserunt ad patrem suum Jacob inunciando quod dicerent quod fera pessima devoravit filium suum Joseph hoc et facer dolose aspirantes in morte fratris sui. Joseph dolose venditus a fratribus suis christi figura qui a iudeis dolose venditus fuit in morte sine culpa.

Legitur in 2 libro regum capitulo decimo quod Absolon filius david stetit ad istum portae civitatis israel, et ipso ingrediente loquebatur donec constituit iudicium: et inclinauit corda virorum qui serua spiritates eius contra patrem suum david cum in rege constituerent contra patrem suum p scripto ipsa occideret et interficeret: Ista absolon malicia perditione surgit cum in morte christi cum iudeis conspirauit

In oculum eorum non veniet aia mea · · · geiu Jacob xlii · Dauid · Quid dii guemiret gilibati li accipe aias

virta maligitur fratrum puer notatur · · · Mititur iu causa pris ples scelerata

Non est sapia regs ... pdrucis xli · · · Ihennie xi · Super me cogitauerint orilia

vg Ju mortem cristi ospirant fratres ihu

According to 1 Esdras the Scribe vi 16–22 King Darius told Esdras the Scribe to go to Jerusalem, and how to purify the Temple. Now King Darius signified Christ, who drove the buyers and sellers out of the Temple. In this way he cleansed the Temple of the Lord of forbidden things, giving us to understand by this that the Temple of the Lord is a house of prayer and not of buying and selling.

p

According to 1 Machabees iv 36–58, Judas Machabeus told the Jews they should cleanse the Temple of forbidden things and make it holy, since it had been defiled in defiance of the law. Machabeus signifies Christ who, making a whip of cords, threw out of the Temple those who were buying and selling in it, and drove them away, saying: 'Do not make my father's house a place of business'.

Osee ix 16
I will throw them out of my house

David, Psalm 68.10
Enthusiasm for your house fires me

[DARIUS PURIFIES THE TEMPLE]

[CHRIST PURIFIES THE TEMPLE]
John ii 13–17

[JUDAS MACHABEUS PURIFIES THE TEMPLE]

He commands that the temple be cleansed and celebrations held

Machabeus is eager to purify your holy places, O God

Amos v 10
They hated the one who rebuked them at the entrance

From the last book of Zacharias (xiv 21)
No longer shall the trader be in the house of the Lord

Christ drives the buyers and sellers from the Temple

The Passion sequence begun with the *Entry into Jerusalem* appears, as in Mark,[1] to be interrupted at once by the Purification of the Temple: Christ's one recorded act of physical violence.[2] In fact it is directly related to his coming Death and Resurrection. Explaining his right to act in this way in God's house, Christ tells the Jews: 'Destroy this temple and in three days I will raise it up'.[3] A marked contrast with the next twelve scenes of subsequent humiliation before Jesus's next triumphal appearances, *Christ Opens Limbo*—the Harrowing of Hell (·h·)—and the *Resurrection* itself (·i·), its violence is underlined by the Types' formality.[4] Both show the mere issue of orders for earlier purifications of the Temple, whereas the central scene shows Christ's own action. It is crowded in design. Instead of being outside the Temple as in **6** and **7**,[5] we are inside: only here do we see what defiles the holy building. Two pillars in the foreground simultaneously increase our sense of enclosure, and separate Christ from the money-makers he expels with their stalls, produce, and animals—his whip raised, their money prominent in the foreground at his feet.[6]

The Types throw light on the central scene in less obvious ways. Since **1** refers both to Darius and to the purification of the Temple by Esdras, **6** must conflate events.[7] Darius orders the rebuilding of the Temple after the Jewish exile;[8] Christ's rebuilding of the 'Temple' is his Resurrection after the Redemption. But it is the later Artaxerxes[9] who commissions Esdras 'the great and growing hero of Judaic tradition'[10] to go to Jerusalem and reform Jewish law,[11] a process Esdras himself calls a 'glorifying of the house of the Lord'. He achieves this, as Christ does, by moving the people to repentance.[12]

Like Esdras, Judas Machabeus (**7**) is a hero of his people.[13] The picture looks quiet: Judas Machabeus's commanding gesture is central, like the sceptre of Darius and Esdras's gesture of acceptance in **6**. But unlike Esdras, who merely preaches, Judas Machabeus, like Christ, uses force to restore the sacrificial function of the Temple, ordering soldiers to fight off the enemy while the Temple is purified, and building an undefiled altar to replace one polluted. Christ acts like Darius, Esdras, and Judas Machabeus, but he is himself to be the sacrifice crowning his preaching and his purging of the Temple.

In the Prophecies, **4** is actually spoken by Christ at the Purification of the Temple,[14] **3** and **11** are directly related to the central subject even by the fifth century.[15] In view of Christ's condemnation of commercial abuse of that which should be venerated, **10** is a relevant attack on corrupt administration of the law: lawyers sitting in judgement at city gates (or officials in the Temple) hate anyone questioning their authority, especially if pleading the cause of the innocent.[16] Purification of the Old Law by the New, of the world by God, or of body and soul by the individual (all implicit in the Purification of the Temple) is inevitably painful.[17]

According to Genesis xxxvii 3–20, Joseph's brothers sent a certain messenger to his father Jacob saying that a terrible beast had devoured his son Joseph. They did this, to tell the truth, deceitfully plotting the death of their brother. Joseph cunningly sold by his brothers signifies Christ who, guiltless, was cunningly sold by Judas to his death.

q

According to 2 Kings (2 Samuel) xv (–xvii 3) Absalom the son of David stood at the entrance to the gate of the city of Jerusalem and spoke to the people going in: 'Who will make me a judge?'; and he influenced the minds of the men who were conspiring with him against his father David—they set him up as king, and then pursued the father, intending to kill him.

Jacob, in Genesis xlix 6
My heart shall not join in their plot

David, Psalm 30.14
While they assembled for evil purposes they plotted to take life

[CONSPIRACY AGAINST JOSEPH]

[CONSPIRACY]
Matthew xxvi 3–4, 14–16

[ABSALOM CONSPIRES AGAINST DAVID]

The group of brothers wickedly arranged that the boy is picked upon

The vicious child works against his father's achievements

Proverbs xxi 30
There is no wisdom, there is no good sense

Jeremias xi 19
They devised plots against me

Those people plotted the death of Christ together

This page is remarkable in two ways. First, it seems unnecessary, being followed by Judas's payment: to include his planning of this betrayal places curious stress on treachery.[1] Yet it has been included deliberately, not by mere tradition. The main scene in **r** is rare, but this one (with its Types) is rarer:[2] but for **1** and **2** we might not even recognise it.[3] After the violent *Christ Purifies the Temple*, it is understated: the only movement is the echoing gesture of Caiphas and Judas, suggesting shared intentions. As on the previous page, only the main scene is indoors: the effect here is of secrecy. Ominously, the Temple High Priest's enthronement suggests *God in Majesty* or the *Last Judgement*.[4] Caiaphas feels threatened by Jesus; his posture parodies the very power he fears (as often in the Mystery Plays).

The Types also show status-conscious conspirators: brothers plot against an envied brother (**6**); a son attempts his father's throne (**7**). In **5**, Judas betrays 'brother' and 'father'—his friend and his God. The rare Joseph scene, as well as foreshadowing **5**,[5] contrasts with it: the brothers invent the tale of the wild beast to *avoid* killing Joseph and incurring blood-guilt. He not only lives, he is later reconciled to them (·**m·6**). Judas desires Jesus's death. For him there is no reconciliation: his fatal sin is this failure to reapproach God. The over-elegant man addressing the silent Jacob (**6**), not named in *Biblia Pauperum* or the Bible, may be the brother who advised selling Joseph: Judas, linked with Judas Iscariot.[6] Like **5**, this scene is understated: not even Joseph's coat, which the brothers spattered with animal blood, is shown.[7]

Absalom (**7**) and Judas Iscariot are also compared, in treachery and in death (both, significantly, hanged from a tree).[8] Absalom attempts David's throne, having himself illegally declared judge,[9] then 'king'. The Jews' 'judgement' of Christ the true Judge is equally improper. Usurped authority is recalled by the crown and sceptre in **7**, as it is by the enthroned priest in **5**.

Brilliantly, the thoughts of the victims in the understated main scenes are in the Prophecies: Jacob's (**6**) and David's (**7**) in **3** and **4**, Christ's in **10** and **11**. Jacob's address to his treacherous sons in **3**[10] is attributed to Christ, aware of but ignoring the conspiracy.[11] With similar neatness, **7** is related to **4**, interpreted as David's complaint against Absalom.[12] The cryptic **10** and **11** are clear only if we mentally complete them. 'No human plan can prevail against the will of God', says **10**,[13] with the deeper sense that God utilises even evil for our redemption.[14] Prophecy **11** also refers to the Redemption. 'I was carried to the slaughter like an unresisting lamb, unaware that they devised plots against me', is traditionally said by Christ.[15] It is heavily ironic: directly or by implication, **3**, **4**, and **10** reveal God's will fulfilled through the plots he permits.

According to Genesis xxxvii 25–28, Joseph's brothers sold him to the Ismaelites for thirty pieces of silver. The good Joseph sold by his own brothers though innocent, denotes the innocent Christ treacherously sold by Judas—the Judas who sold Christ himself to the Jews for thirty pieces of silver (and these were thirty denarii for which Joseph was sold—one of which was worth ten of the common denarii).

r

According to Genesis xxxix 1–2, when the Ismaelites who had bought Joseph arrived in their land leading Joseph with them, they sold him in Egypt to the leader of the king of the Egyptians' army, called Putiphar. The boy Joseph signifies Christ, sold by the wicked Judas.

David, Psalm 108.8
May his days be numbered and his official position etc

Solomon, Proverbs xvi 30
He who with fixed eyes plans evil things

[JOSEPH IS SOLD TO THE ISMAELITES]

[JUDAS IS PAID]
Matthew xxvi 14–15

[JOSEPH IS SOLD TO PUTIPHAR]

That young son who was sold signifies you, O Christ

Whatever was done to that boy applies to Christ

Aggeus i 6
He who collected wages put them in a bag full of holes

Zacharias xi 12
And they weighed out the payment in thirty pieces of silver

O Judas, you who sell Christ are on your way to hell

The preceding page reveals envy and ambition as motives for betrayal. Here the motive is merely money. Central to the page is Judas's outstretched hand taking a coin; his other clutches a pouch. The three conspirators contemplate the thirty pieces of silver which the Gospel describes by quoting Zacharias (**11**): God's complaint against being offered poor payment.[1] Central to **6** is the coin-offering hand of Joseph's Ismaelite purchaser. His other hand is in his money-bag, in evidence again when he appears cap-in-hand before Putiphar in **7**. Even *lectio* **1** stresses money: Christ's betrayal for the price of a slave is doubly ignominious, as Joseph, a mere boy, was sold for thirty *denarii*,[2] worth ten times the value they had in Jesus's time.[3]

The Types are uniquely from one story,[4] giving a horrifying sense of a child twice sold, at the beginning and at the end of a long journey (camels in the background of **6** recall that he is carried with the goods, 'spices and balm, and myrrh', they bear).[5] Christ is 'sold' more than once by each of us. The double use of the one tale facilitates contrast: **5** and **6** centre on money, but at the heart of **7** are touching hands. The child turns to his purchaser with something like a gesture of affection; indeed, his seller makes a similar gesture.[6] This recalls that the outcome of this sale was happy, Joseph contributing to the prosperity of Egypt and eventu-

ally being reconciled with his brothers. The outcome of Christ's 'journey' on earth is the same:[7] **9** says 'whatever was done to that boy applies to Christ'.[8] The whole Joseph story is in fact a lesson in how providence thwarts men's plots, utilising their malice.[9] Throughout the Infancy we are reminded of the coming Passion; throughout the Passion we are promised joy.

It is through the Prophecies that the horrible effect of his crime on Judas himself is expressed: above all in **3**, which like **11** is quoted in the Gospel account of Judas (not at his payment, but at his suicide and replacement among the Apostles by Matthias).[10] His days are indeed numbered, and his official position taken by someone else. Failure to grasp the implications of sin is a theme in **4**: a picture of a man contemplating evil with staring eyes, chewing his lips (as the rest of the verse tells us), and as guilty as if he had done the deed.[11] In spite of this anguish, he remains ignorant of the outcome. Uncertainty is suggested even in the apparently simple warning of **10**: money is a short-lived reward, useless if one's spiritual life is in ruins,[12] unreliable in effect.[13]

The whole page thus recalls not only the horror of the betrayal-payment and the effects of such sin on the soul—but also the true payment Christ makes for us.[14]

According to Genesis xiv 14–20, when Abraham returned from the land of his enemies, to bring with him the great plunder which he had wrested from his enemies, Melchisedech the high priest of God offered him bread and wine. Melchisedech signifies Christ, who at supper offered bread and wine (that is, his body and blood) to his disciples to eat and drink.

S

According to Exodus xvi 3–18, the Lord instructed Moses to tell the people that everyone should pick up enough of the manna which came from heaven, to last him for that day. Now the heaven-sent manna which the Lord gave to the Israelites signified the holy bread (that is, of his most holy body) which he himself gave to his disciples at supper, when he said: 'Take this, all of you etc'.

David, Psalm 77.25
Man has eaten the bread of angels

Proverbs ix 5
Come, eat my bread

[MELCHISEDECH OFFERS
BREAD & WINE]

[LAST SUPPER]
John xiii 1–2, 20–30

[MOSES & THE MANNA]

The holy things which Melchisedech
gave him denote Christ

He holds himself in his hand:
himself the food he feeds himself

Isaias lv 2
Listen to me carefully and eat that which is good

Wisdom xvi 20
You gave them bread from heaven

The king sits at supper together with all the twelve

As in the Bible, the *Last Supper* follows Judas's payment.[1] The central scene surprisingly shows not the Institution of the Eucharist (which the Types clearly prefigure) or the Communion of the Apostles, but Christ identifying his betrayer.[2] This, the third consecutive page treating betrayal, underlines one of Christ's severest sufferings (St Peter, on Christ's right, reminds us of the betrayal by him, soon to follow).[3] 'The disciple whom Jesus loved', his head on his Lord's breast, asks who was to betray his master; Christ replies: 'the one to whom I shall give the wine-sop'.[4] Judas, distinguished by the absence of a nimbus and by the money-pouch in his left hand, is in the foreground, head tipped back to receive the sop of wine.[5] John, over whom Jesus reaches towards Judas, points the contrast between the love Jesus deserves and the treatment he receives from his betrayer. Judas's cringing suggests not only his hypocrisy but the terrible fate of the unworthy recipient of such bread.[6]

Indeed, aligned on the vertical axis of the scene are Christ, St John's head, Judas, and yet another element unusually important in the *Biblia Pauperum* context: the dish holding the remains of the paschal lamb, literally and metaphorically central to the page as a whole.[7] The sacrificial atonement of the Passover meal is actually celebrated, as well as the sacrifice of Christ on the Cross and in the Mass.[8]

Vertical movement is strong and significant in **6** and **7** too.

Melchisedech (**6**) and manna (**7**) are eucharistic Types in the New Testament.[9] Central to **6** (and the visual equivalent of the lamb in **5**) is the bread offered by Melchisedech, to whom the author of Hebrews compares Christ.[10] Melchisedech is king and priest of Salem, meaning 'peace' (the city prominent in the background), and his name means 'righteousness'.[11] Melchisedech, shown as a bishop holding Host and chalice, means that we see Christ as priest at the Last Supper.[12]

Jesus himself said: 'I am the bread of life. Your fathers ate manna in the desert and are dead, but this bread comes down from heaven so that a man may eat it and not die . . . the bread I shall give is my flesh for the life of the world'.[13] *Biblia Pauperum* makes the eucharistic parallel obvious by making the manna host-like.[14] This gift (celebrated in **3**[15] and **11**[16]) was given on a journey to the promised land; similarly, communion feeds the soul on its life-journey.

Because the Types are so authoritative, the Prophecies are readily related to them and to the Eucharist: **4** is attributed both to Melchisedech and to Christ.[17] Only **10**, offering salvation under the figure of food and drink, is not traditionally related to the scenes,[18] but the verse before it invites 'those who have no silver' to dine, perhaps a deliberate reminder of those who, like Judas, love money more than God; it is then still clearer the central scene juxtaposes images of sacrifice and selfishness.

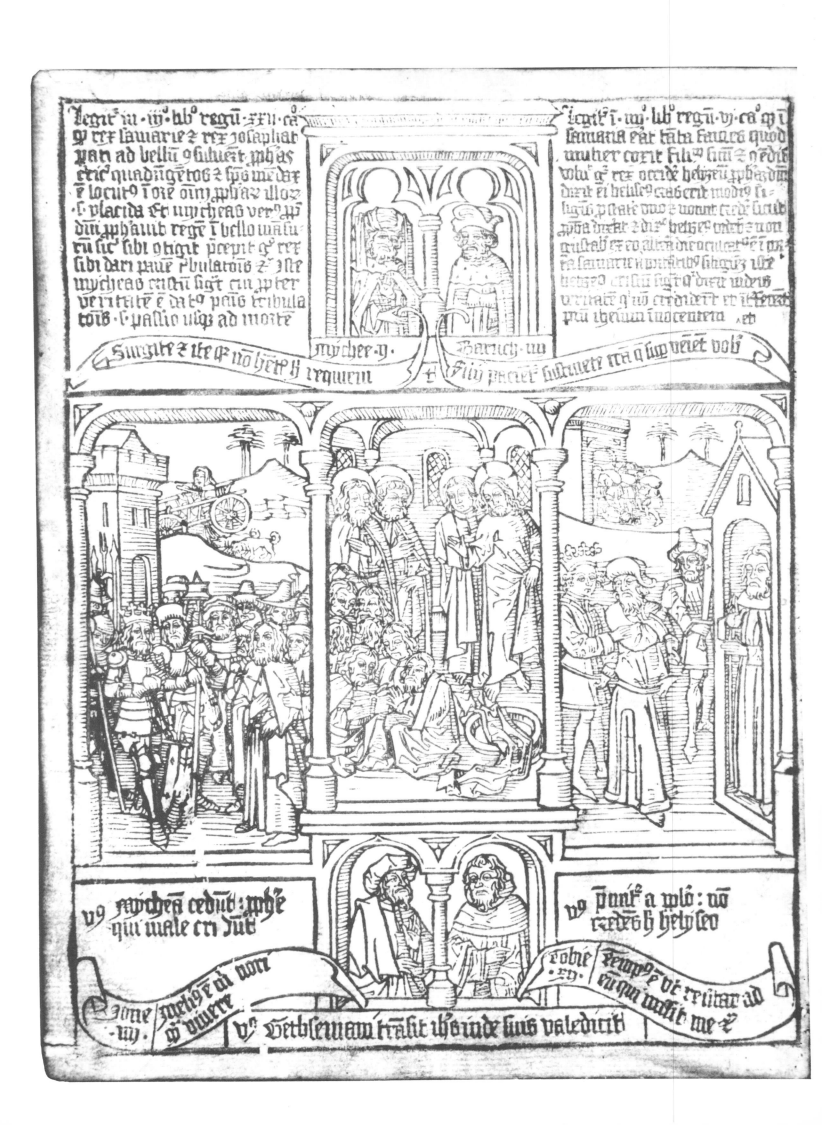

According to 3 Kings xxii 1–35, the King of Samaria and King Josaphat being prepared for war consulted about four hundred prophets, and an evil spirit spoke in the mouth of all those prophets, thus: 'Don't worry'. And Micheas, a real prophet of the Lord, prophesied that the king's fortune in war would be what did in fact happen to him. The king ordered him to be given a starvation diet, etc. Micheas signifies Christ to whom, on account of the truth, the bread of suffering (that is, agony bringing death itself) was given,

According to 4 Kings vi 24 (–vii 20), there was such a famine in Samaria that a woman boiled her son and ate him. The King therefore wanted to kill Eliseus [Elisha] the prophet of the Lord. Eliseus said to him: 'Tomorrow a measure of fine wheat flour shall cost one small silver coin'; and [a man] did not want to believe what the prophet had said, and Eliseus said: 'You shall see but not taste any of it'. And the next day the man was trampled on at the gate of Samaria by those carrying the flour. Eliseus signifies Christ who told the truth to the Jews, who did not believe, and killed the good, innocent Jesus.

t

Micheas ii 10
Get up and go away for you shall have no peace here

Baruch iv 25
My children, endure patiently the anger which has fallen on you

[MICHEAS IS PUNISHED FOR PREDICTING DEFEAT]

[CHRIST PREDICTS HIS PASSION]
Matthew xxvi 36–37
John viii 12–24, xiii 4–16

[CONDEMNED, ELISEUS PREDICTS THE TRUTH]

Those who disbelieve the prophet Micheas abandon him

This man, not believing Eliseus, is trampled by the people

Jonas iv 3
It is a better thing for me to die than to live

Tobias xii 20
It is time for me to return to him who sent me, etc

On going away to Gethsemane Jesus said his farewell

The page is complex. The central scene cleverly conflates several events, notably Jesus's Farewell to the Disciples (mentioned in 12), and one of his warnings about belief in him, which as 1 and 2 explain is echoed in Types showing true prophets' suffering and disbelievers' death. The main design shows the Farewell.[1] Jesus goes to Gethsemane with Peter, James, and John, telling the rest: 'Sit here while I go to pray'.[2] But the huddled men reading are unnimbed, inattentive, and indoors, whereas the disciples (never at this time reading) would be nimbed, attentive, and on Mount Olivet. The inattentive men are actually referred to in the Farewell (echoed in 11): 'I shall not be with you much longer, and *as I told the Jews*, you cannot come where I am going'.[3] This refers to his warning Pharisees teaching in the Temple: 'I am going away . . . you cannot come where I am going . . . if you do not believe that I am He, you will die in your sins'.[4] On one level the huddle is of Pharisees.

It is this doom of unbelievers that the Types echo (as does 3, rejecting an unwelcome prophet). In 6 and 7 kings punish prophets, and the outcome is a death, shown in the background. Micheas (6) is to be imprisoned on bread and water for warning the king of defeat: 'I have seen all Israel scattered on the mountains like sheep without a shepherd'.[5] But in the background is the king's corpse (mortally wounded in battle, he had been strapped upright and died like that): 'blood from the wound ran into the

bottom of the chariot . . . dogs licked up the blood'.[6]

Christ's farewell echoes Micheas: 'You will lose all faith in me this night, for it is written "I shall strike the shepherd and the sheep of the flock shall be scattered" '.[7] Christ, too, suffers for truth, and the deaths he foresees (of unbelievers and of himself) do occur. Unlike the dead king in 6 who seems alive, Christ will indeed live, his blood not licked by dogs in defeat, but venerated in victory.

In 7 a warning and promise are disbelieved (as in Christ's prophecies). The king sends a swordsman to kill Eliseus, who is blamed for famine. Eliseus promises an end to it next day. 'One of the lords on whose arm the king leaned' accuses the prophet of lying, but in the background this lord lies next day at the city gate, crushed by a stampede for cheap flour.[8] Christ promises us true 'bread' (s).

The conspicuous tubs and cloth in 5 (from the Washing of the Feet at the Last Supper),[9] balance the little death scenes in 6 and 7, not with blood but with water. The Washing can signify purification.[10] Augustine speaks of the cloth wiping away sin and foreshadowing Christ's empty graveclothes.[12] Thus in front of Christ's Farewell and prophecy of death is a symbol of his return and our redemption (promised in 4 and 10).i/ The Washing also recalls the new commandment of love which followed it, promising the Spirit and peace.[13] This is indeed the end of conflict (6) and famine (7).

According to Matthew xxv 1–13, the door (that is, the door to eternal salvation) was closed to the foolish girls without oil in their lamps. The girls signify the Jews who in a similar way fell back when asked by the Lord on the Mount of Olives: 'Who are you looking for?'. That is to say, in despair and deadness of heart they fell back, and as a result, not believing, they are in hell.

V

According to Apocalypse xiii 9 and Isaias xiv 12–15, Lucifer fell from heaven with all his followers, because of pride. The proud devils signify the Jews who were afraid of losing their position and land, and so crucified and killed the good and humble Jesus; and they themselves fell into the pit they had themselves made, that is to say, they are alive in hell, as is written in Psalm 14.

Lamentations ii 16
This is the day we were waiting for: we have found it

Isaias liii 2, 3
We longed for him, despised and most abject of men

[FOOLISH GIRLS CONDEMNED]   [JEWS FALL BACK FROM CHRIST]   [FALL OF THE ANGELS]

John xviii 4–6
Matthew xxvi 36

Hope, given to those who are aware, is snatched away from the foolish girls

Thrust away from his position the old serpent falls back

Jeremias xiv 3
They carried back their vessels empty

Baruch vi 26
If they fall to the ground they do not get up again by themselves

Those ready to capture Christ are laid low in this way

Gethsemane is over. His Passion imminent, Jesus asked: 'Father, if it is possible, let this cup pass me by; nevertheless, let your will, not mine, be done'.[1] Rock, fence, and trees suggest Gethsemane and draw the eye up to the hand of God accepting sacrifice in the Agony, Passion, and Eucharist[2] (recalled in the Host over the 'cup of sorrow'). This hand tops a triangle formed by steps in **6** and the downward slide of the damned in **7**: the theme is acceptance of and by God.[3] Unlike the foolish girls (**6**) and the damned (**7**), Jesus humbly accepts the painful will of God. However, **5** shows not Christ's abasement but a flash of his divinity.[4] Guards seeking him drop back and fall down at his: 'I am He'.[5]

Christ's hand is raised in judgement, the Types' theme: 'What will the man do when he is our Judge, if he can do this when himself about to be tried?'[6] The 'despair and deadness of heart' in *lectio* **1** echoes Paul: 'Your hardness and impenitence of heart adds to the anger God will show ... when his just judgements are known he will repay each one as his deeds deserve'. The 'lamb about to be sacrificed roars like a lion' at those who do not fear him, echoing the awesome words with which God once identified himself: 'I am who am'.[7]

In **6**, idle bridesmaids in the Judgement parable are banished from the house of the bridegroom, Christ. Richly dressed, dead lamps reversed, they fill a stair of superhuman scale, Hellmouth gaping under it.[8] Surprisingly, **7** shows not the Last Judgement but the First Fall, of the angels.[9] Use of this scene gives, in addition to Judgement at the end of history implied in **6**, a judgement at its beginning (the angels' Fall lying behind the Fall of man). Half-way through *Biblia Pauperum* the justice of God is seen to span time.[10]

The *Fall of the Angels* is also appropriate because Christ once referred to his divinity by telling the disciples: 'I watched Satan fall like lightning from Heaven. Yes, I have given you power to tread underfoot serpents and scorpions and the whole strength of the enemy'.[11] This is the divinity revealed at his arrest. The bright Lucifer (**7**) is thrust down by Michael, wings and fingers growing webbed as he falls, his enormity of arrogance echoed in deformity of body until he becomes Satan, monstrous as a mere demon.[12]

Darkness pervades; in **5** guards carry 'lanterns and torches and weapons', in **6** virgins leave the light (suggested by a shuttered window), in **7** angels drop into gloom lit only by fire. Prophecies suggest horrible fulfilment of expectation: **3** is a cry of vengeance interpreted as God's reaction to sinners,[13] **4** is the Jews' dismay at the humble appearance of the Messiah,[14] **10** refers to the foolish girls who could not buy more oil (grace). Only **11** offers hope:[15] those who 'fall' on earth cannot rise unaided but, unlike lost souls, may repent with God's help. Christ's right hand leads the eye to the Father, his left to the cup of sorrow: judgement and mercy are in fact balanced.

87

According to 2 Kings iii 26–27, Joab the leader of David's army went to Abner to speak deceitfully to him, and pierced him with a sword while speaking softly and with cunning. Joab, who spoke cunningly to Abner, signifies Judas, who deceitfully kissed Christ and gave him to the wicked Jews to be crucified.

•a•

According to I Machabees xix 39–49, Tryphon came to the men of Juda and Israel to speak to them deceitfully and capture them. Tryphon signifies that traitor Judas who, coming deceitfully to Christ, kissed him hypocritically and so handed him over to the wicked Jews to be killed.

David, Psalm 40.10
The man who gives me peace, in whom I trusted

Solomon, Proverbs xvii 20
He who lies falls into evil

[JOAB BETRAYS ABNER]

[JUDAS BETRAYS CHRIST
WITH A KISS]
Matthew xxvi 49

[TRYPHON BETRAYS
JONATHAN]

Joab spoke softly, and wickedly
killed him

Uttering soft words, Tryphon
prepares horrible weapons

Isaias iii 11
Curses on the wicked man: he shall be given what his actions deserve

Jeremias ix 8
With his mouth he speaks peace to his friend

The betrayer leads you to them with a greeting, O Christ

The central scene follows tradition in conflating three events. Judas kisses Jesus to identify him to the Temple guards, one of whom is making the arrest, holding the arm which Jesus extends to Malchus to heal the ear St Peter cut off in a misplaced attempt to defend his master. Malchus's lantern tells us it is night, his club, futile in the foreground, suggests the supremacy of love over violence.[1] The main theme is hypocritical greeting to disguise malice. All three scenes cleverly focus attention on the 'greetings'. In the background of **5** a distant spire marks the apex of the inverted 'V' formed by the slopes of Mount Olivet, which leads the eye to Christ. In **7** a similar shape is formed by the walls of Ptolemais, a bastion marking the meeting of Tryphon and Jonathan. In **6** the strong vertical of one tower draws the eye to the betrayed Abner and the symbolically fashionable Joab (his mantle dagged and tunic slit), but the gatehouse pulls attention to the dagger in Abner's back.[2] Jesus reaches through a false embrace and an armoured grasp to the kneeling Malchus, whose severed ear he holds. The compassion Christ shows at the very moment of his betrayal is highlighted by the absence of any parallel to it in the Types.

There are, however, elements in both which illuminate the main story. Abner, like Christ, was on his way 'to rally all Israel to my Lord the King', and King David's lament over him stresses his having died unbound but unresisting, just as Christ refuses to use violence. In **7** Jonathan (on the right, his men without weapons) is being persuaded to send home most of his army before entering the city, apparently surrendered to him, but where he will in fact be imprisoned so that his friends think him dead. In contrast Christ's disciples simply flee at his betrayal, and he does in fact die. The horrible obscurity (or mere meanness) of Judas's motive is highlighted by Tryphon's clear desire for the crown, and by Joab's simple revenge, disguised as support of the authorities.[3]

The main theme of hypocritical greeting sounds in Prophecy **11**, whose peacemaker is 'in his heart plotting a trap for him'. The others are related also to the fate of Judas: **4** and **10** obviously,[4] and **3** ('the man who gives me peace in whom I trusted, the one who ate my bread with me, has rebelled') by Jesus himself at the Washing of Feet: 'Happiness will be yours if you behave properly. I am not referring to all of you: I know those I have chosen; but what scripture says must be fulfilled: "He who eats my bread will rebel against me" '.[5] This Prophecy recalls Judas's feigning of friendship at the Last Supper, already illustrated in **s**.[6]

According to 3 Kings xix 1–2, when she had killed the prophets of the Lord, Queen Jezabel eventually wanted to kill the prophet Elias [Elijah]. This evil queen signified the evil Jews, who cruelly and enviously intended to kill the true Elias (that is, Christ) because he revealed their own malice to them by preaching.

·b·

According to Daniel xiv 1–29, the wicked Babylonian people came to king Nabuchadonosor and they said: 'Hand over Daniel the innocent to us'. This people signifies the Jews who shouted to Pilate violently with insistent voices: 'Crucify, crucify him!' and then 'If you let him go you are not a friend of Caesar'. Moreover, the king signifies Pilate who, fearing the Jews, handed over the innocent Christ to them.

Isaias v 20
Cursed be those who call evil good, and good evil

Proverbs xviii 5
It is no use accepting an evil-doer as judge

[JEZABEL SEEKS ELIAS' LIFE]

[JEWS CONDEMN CHRIST]
Matthew xxvii 11–26

[THE KING CONDEMNS DANIEL]

Thus the harsh, impious woman condemns that anointed one

This cruel people engineers Daniel's death

Job xxxvi 17
Your cause has been judged as if that of a wicked man

Amos v 7
You who turn judgement and justice into wormwood

The savage crowd dared to condemn Jesus without cause

The page shows men condemned by perverted justice; it shows judges (**5** and **7**) with divided minds, aware of their victims' innocence but powerless before public protest; it shows silence and prayer in application, and implies survival of the death-sentence we all receive. Three of the Prophecies are about perversion of justice: **10** clearly refers to Christ's innocence;[1] **4** is related by context (and **3** by commentators[2]) to the release of Barabbas, requested immediately before the moment shown in **5** and granted immediately after it. But between the Betrayal and Pilate's washing to dissociate himself from the crucifixion,[3] Jesus is led to Annas, to Caiaphas representing the Jewish court, to Pilate the Roman procurator, to King Herod,[4] and back to Pilate.[5] During this bureaucratic buck-passing Jesus is silent until he answers Pilate's: 'Are you the king of the Jews?' with the affirmative: 'It is you who say it'. Prophecy **11** suggests this silence: the prophet warns perverters of justice to think of God, observing that in corrupt times 'the prudent man will stay silent'.[6] Jesus's answer and the warning message from Pilate's wife (the jug and bowl may be held by her messenger)[7] increase Pilate's culpability in not protecting an innocent man.[8] Jesus stands in resumed passivity, bound and held. Pilate twists awkwardly to wash while watching him:[9] Christ's inactivity is an enigma.

In his protracted trial Christ confronts religious, secular, Jewish, and Roman power. The Types' threats to authority are comparatively simple. Jezebel (**6**) threatens Elias for support of a God challenging her authority.[10] Remaining silent (as his hidden hands indicate) he flees, then immediately wishes to die: his very weakness, ashamed though he is of it, saves his life for God.[11] Christ, condemned, does not flee: death he fears, wills, and suffers. Daniel's relevance (**7**) is more complex. Like Pilate,[12] his king is an unwilling judge.[13] Officials jealous of Daniel persuade the king to forbid prayer to anyone but himself, or be thrown to the lions. Daniel (wearing the hat he has in **b3**) is at home praying. Like Elias and Christ he is in stillness, not suffering. The officials, finding him thus, have come twice to the king who must unwillingly obey his own irrevocable 'laws of the Medes and Persians'. However, Daniel survives in the den of lions, an angel sealing their jaws. (The underworld will be similarly powerless to swallow Christ.[14]) This story is Daniel vi. But **2** cites Daniel xiv, recalling Daniel's other sojourn with lions (for having exposed idolatry by bursting what one is tempted to imagine as a feline dragon-god, by feeding it flavoured fur-balls'.[15] All these exploits silently affirm that Christ is God.

legitur in genesi· ix· cum qp noe
cum dormiret in tabuaculo suo ia
cuit in terra nudatus qp cum vidisset
filius eius cham derisit eum sed alij filij
eius vultus noluerit et eorum oculos
obtexerit: Noe xpm significat qp videi
deridentes ipsi coronauerut et
deuudauert et sic fideles filij
xpm tamq stultum sublauauert

Dominus videntes me deriserut me

David · c ·

prouerbior· xix·
pater sit deriforibus iudicia et mallei percutient

legitur in· iiij· libro regum· ij· cã
qp cum helyseus prophetā ascendisset
in montem bethel occurrerit ei
pueri in ciuitate et sublansandi
eu deriserit et dixit ascede calue
lue ascede caluue: helyseus significat
xpm qp sui pueri· i· videi in
conatioue et passioue deriserit

vox Nuda verecundiat: pius
dum cham male ridet

vox Percutit ira dei:
derisores helysei

Ysaie
primo
Blaſphemauit
ſecū dicit

Error
iij·

ecclesia ideriberū o
nulo meo

vox Pro nobis criste: probrum pateris pie triste

According to Genesis ix 22–23, Noe lay on the ground naked when he went to sleep in his tent. When his son Cham saw this he mocked him, but the other sons did not wish to see, and covered their eyes. Noe signifies Christ, whom the mocking Jews crowned and stripped—and similarly the untrustworthy sons jeered at him as if at a fool.

According to 4 Kings ii 23–24, when Eliseus [Elisha] the prophet went up the hill to Bethel, boys ran towards him and mocked him with shouting and jeering, and they said: 'Get on, baldy! Get on, baldy!' Eliseus signifies Christ, whose own boys (that is, the Jews) mocked him in his crowning and suffering.

•C•

David, Psalm 21.8
All those seeing me jeered at me

Proverbs xix 29
Sentences and beatings were prepared for mockers

[NOE'S NAKEDNESS IS MOCKED]

[CHRIST IS MOCKED]
Matthew xxvii 27–31, xxvi 67

[BOYS MOCK ELISEUS]

When Cham saw his father's naked genitals he sniggered

The anger of God struck the mockers of Eliseus

Lamentations iii 14
I am made a mockery to all my people

Isaias i 4
They have blasphemed the holy one of Israel

For our sake you suffer shameful abuse, O good Christ

The central scene refers both to the Buffeting and the Crowning with Thorns, between which Jesus is stripped, whipped, and again stripped. The humiliating nakedness and mockery is shadowed in **6**, the Crowning in **7**. The Buffeting occurs after he appears before Caiaphas, whose attendants mock his prophetic powers, asking him to guess who strikes him. It is identified by the binding, the blindfold, and the attackers' raised hands.[1] The Crowning with Thorns occurs after Pilate's sentence (•**b**•). This scene's position in *Biblia Pauperum*, and the stick traditionally used to thrust down the thorns on Jesus's head,[2] mean that the Crowning is the major event in the scene, even though the crown is not shown. (If depicted alone, the Crowning usually shows Roman soldiers jibing at 'kingship' with mock crown, sceptre, royal robes, and homage, and Christ unbound, holding a reed, with someone kneeling at his feet.[3])

Three Prophecies have long been related to the Mocking of Christ: **10** in general terms,[4] **3** to the abuse on the Cross,[5] **11** to the Jews at Pilate's judgement rejecting the very kingship mocked in the Crowning, and to the other insults.[6] The application of **4** appears to be original.

Both Types are ancient. Though Eliseus has just performed a miracle for the city, purifying its water, boys mock his baldness: like Christ, he bears a symbol of humiliation on his head.[7] The saving power of Christ is also insulted. To the Fathers, however, Eliseus foreshadows the mockery of Christ crucified: the boys' taunt '*Ascende calve*' punningly foreshadows the Jews' 'Crucify him' at Pilate's judgement, as if they had said '*Ascende crucem in loco Calvariae*' ('Get on to your cross on Calvary').[8]

Punishment of mockers is important in **7**, **4**, and **6**.[9] Having cursed the boys, Eliseus summons bears to savage them.[10] Cham (**6**) enters his father's tent and sniggers at his drunken self-exposure.[11] Gleefully he fetches Shem and Japhet, but with averted eyes they back towards their father and cover him. As **8** and **9** make clear, Noe (like Eliseus) curses his mocker. The picture does not follow the Bible. We see one brother mock (he points at Noe); one dutiful brother lifts his hands in horror (a gesture echoed by Eliseus in **7**), while the other respectfully covers his father, with the compassion so absent from **5** and **7**.[12]

The biblical setting is modified too: Noe's tent is omitted; we see his vine.[13] To the Fathers the vine is Israel which brought about its master's downfall,[14] the wine is the 'cup of sorrow' drunk in the Passion,[15] Noe's nakedness is Christ's stripping, the sleep his death.[16] But the vine is also the visual equivalent of the city (or mountain source) whose water Eliseus purifies, and of the blows Christ receives. The parallel suggests himself as vine, his cleansing blood as wine,[17] mixed with water at Mass to signify his mingling with humanity.[18]

According to Genseis xxii 1–6, when Abraham and Isaac went on together Abraham carried a sword and the fire: it was Isaac who carried the pieces of wood by which he was himself to be sacrificed. This Isaac who carried the wood signifies Christ who on his own body carried the wood of the cross on which he wanted to be sacrificed for us.

·d·

According to 3 Kings xvii 8–12, Elias [Elijah] called to a woman who was going to the field to collect sticks to make a meal for herself, who said in reply: 'Well, I am collecting two sticks so that with them I can make a meal for myself and my son'. The two sticks which this woman collected signified the wooden pieces of the cross, which Christ picked up to carry on his own body.

Isaias liii 7 (Acts viii 32)
He was led like a sheep to the slaughter

Jeremias xi 19
Come, let us put wood in his bread

[ABRAHAM & ISAAC]　　　[CHRIST CARRIES THE CROSS]　　　[WOMAN OF SAREPHTA]
John xix 16–17

The boy carrying the pieces of wood prefigures you O Christ

The two pieces of wood belonging to this woman are mystical symbols of the cross

Ezechiel xxxix 17
Come, make haste, run to the sacrifice

Jeremias xi 9
But I was like a most docile lamb carried as a sacrifice

Here Christ, thinking it appropriate for him, carries the wood of the cross

---

Jesus, crowned with the thorns implicit in the last picture, divested of the mock-royal mantle,[1] is both led and driven, like an animal.[2] Yet he is obedient: the goad-carrying figure above him is idle.[3] As 3[4] and 11[5] say: 'The Lord burdened him with the sins of all of us; he was offered by his own will, and he did not open his mouth; he was led like a sheep to the slaughter' and he 'was like a most docile lamb carried to be a sacrifice'.[6] The next part of this same verse forms 4: the victim is unaware that they 'plotted against me, saying "Come, let us put wood in his bread"'. This points Christ's total *awareness* that the poisonous 'wood' in his 'food'—the Cross—will kill.

These virtues—awareness, self-sacrifice, and faith—show in Isaac's similarly bearing the means of his own immolation (6).[7] But unlike Christ, neither Abraham nor his son fully understands the terrible command they obey. The design's purposeful processional quality contrasts with the oppressed effort in 5 (further highlighted by the static quality of 7): indeed, Abraham's firebrand to light the fuel resembles the candle carried to Mass by a deacon.[8] Torch and sword lift the eye up to the altar on the mountain, while in the background the ram is conspicuous:[9] the sacrificial victim in Prophecies and central scene, it also represents Christ because, caught in thorns as he was crowned in them,[10] it took Isaac's place in death as Christ took ours.[11]

Eucharistic imagery is strong in the story of the woman of Sarephta (7). Her two sticks resembling the Cross seem at first feebly contrived. In the Gospel, the event shows merely that a prophet is ignored in his own country: Elias is sent far from home to assist the starving.[12] The Fathers first saw him as a Type of Christ simply in his generosity: since the woman fed him, Elias made her remnants of food miraculously sufficient.[13] But later, the sticks in which she put her faith (in the story, mere twigs gathered to flavour a starvation diet) are the Cross:[14] spiritual food to us, as it had been 'poison' to Christ (4). With twigs in her broth the woman can face death; trusting her incomprehensible orders, she escapes it[15].

Faith, food, and conquest are superbly fused in 10, suggesting Christ's victory through defeat in death. Literally, God promises his people triumph in battle; they are to summon birds and beasts for a feast on enemy carrion: 'Come, make haste, run to the sacrifice which I am killing for you; a great sacrifice on the mountains of Israel. You will eat flesh and drink blood, and will eat the flesh of heroes and drink the blood of princes of the earth'. In the *Biblia Pauperum* context, the sacrifice is Christ moving to Calvary, the implication eucharistic.[16] At another level 10 announces his victory at the end of the world: the apocalyptic angel quotes it, shouting to the blessed to celebrate the end of evil.[17] Those in heaven 'feast' on God.[18]

Legitur in geñsi·ij·cõ cū
adam obdormiuiss dñs costā
de latere ei9 tulit et formauit de
ea mlierē: adam dormiens
cruciem iā in cruce mortuum
sigñt de cui9 latere p nobis flu-
ere sacramēta cū multis lacri-
mis latus cristi aperiut

Legitr in exod·xvij·cõ q
cū moyses ipsin p dñt seruum
israel duxissz desint e te illā aq
p aq penuria moyses cum virga quā in manu tenebat liber
penuciebat z exiuert aq lar-
gissie velut de abisco vmlta
silex siue lapis xpo sigñt qui
nobis aq̄s salutares·t·sacra-
mēta de suo latere effudit cū
illo·sacra multis in cruce
aperiri punisit

Dauid   **Sacha·xij**

Sup dolorē vlneru meorū addidert ·E· Nut sñ plage iste ī medio manuū tuarū

Feminā primā vñ: de costē cepit oriri   Est sacramēti: cristi dñs petsz fluē tem

O vos oms qui trāsitis p vñā attendite t videte   In die illa occidet sol z radios suos abscondet

Amos·vñ·

vs De cristo multa: cū sāguine pstluit vnda

According to Genesis xxii 7–18, when Abraham had raised his sword to sacrifice his son, an angel of the Lord prevented him from heaven, saying: 'Do not lift your hand against the boy'. Abraham signifies the heavenly Father, who sacrificed his son (that is, Christ) on the cross for us all, so that in this way he might give an indication of the Father's love.

·e·

According to Numbers xxi 4–8, when the Lord wanted to free from serpents the people whom the serpents had bitten he instructed Moses to make a brass serpent and hang it upon a stake so that whoever looked at it would be rid of serpents. The serpent hung up and stared at by the people signifies Christ on the cross, whom every believing person who wishes to be rid of the serpent (that is, the devil) should gaze upon.

David, Psalm 21.17
They have pierced my hands and my feet

Isaias liii 7, 11
He was sacrificed because he himself wished it, and he bore our sins

[ABRAHAM'S SACRIFICE OF ISAAC]

[CRUCIFIXION]
Matthew xxvii 23–54, Mark xv 39

[MOSES LIFTS UP THE SERPENT]

The father sacrifices this boy who signifies Christ

The hurt are healed when they look at the serpent

Job xl 20
Can you capture Leviathan with a hook?

Habacuc iii 4
There are horns on his hands: there his strength is hidden

The suffering of Christ snatches us from the gloomy abyss

The book gives extraordinary emphasis and impact to an image which familiarity tends to blur.[1] It does this by presenting not one but two *Crucifixions* (·e· and ·f·); it does it by giving them strikingly similar structures with totally different meanings, by stressing observers of each scene (two pointing to the Crucified), and by giving not a chronological sequence of events from ·e· to ·f·, but an almost symbolic suspension of time in which the contents of two pages must be read as one.[2] For simplicity, the two central scenes will be discussed with ·e·, and the four Types and eight Prophecies with ·f·.

In both *Crucifixions* Christ is already dead, his side showing the wound opened to prove his death. But the moments immediately before he died are suggested not in ·e· but in ·f·: crying out in thirst, he was given vinegar in a sponge thrust on a spear, by a man about whom nothing else is said. In ·f·, the action is over: Stephaton[3] on the right holds spear and sponge in his right hand, the bucket of the 'sour drink of the roman soldier' held nearby.[4] The act was probably meant as a kindness, but the Gospels interpret it as ironic malice.[5] Stephaton's gesture is probably one of mockery; it differs from that by the equivalent figure in ·e·, being made with the left hand, across the body, instead of in the 'display' or 'gesture of witness' manner. The designer conflates Stephaton's traditional role with the earliest of the events suggested: Christ's mockery by passersby, priests and elders, the crucified robbers, and nearby soldiers.[6] The mockery is associated with Jesus' indirect claim, at Pilate's judgement, to be King of the Jews (the title 'INRI' at the top of the Cross).[7] The next historical event is suggested in ·e·. As Jesus dies, eclipse, earthquake, and the Temple curtain torn in two move a centurion to say: 'Surely this was the Son of God'. He makes the 'gesture of witness' towards the title on the Cross; the very similarity of his pose to Stephaton's (as he, too, speaks to someone behind him) emphasises his contrasting reaction to the Crucified.[8]

On the left of ·e·, St John supports the fainting Virgin. To her the dying Jesus said: 'Woman, this is your son', to the disciple: 'This is your mother'. Behind stands Mary Magdalene.[9] These three represent grief, obedient shouldering of responsibility, and repentance—all reactions as devotionally relevant as the centurion's acknowledgement of God. Differing devotionally is Longinus, who kneels on the left of ·f·. He opened Christ's side so that blood and water issued from the wound.[10] He points to his sight miraculously restored by blood which ran down the spear. Just as the figures on the right of both *Crucifixions* present contrasting reactions to Christ, so in contrast to the sombre responses of the grief-stricken group on the left of ·e·, Longinus offers gratitude and worship.[11]

According to Genesis ii 22–23, when Adam had gone to sleep, the Lord took a rib from his side and made a woman from it. Now the sleeping Adam signifies Christ dead on the cross, from whose side the sacraments flowed for us when the soldier opened the side of Christ with his lance.

·f·

According to Exodus xvii 1–7, when Moses had led the people across the desert, and the water failed, Moses, because of the shortage of water, struck the rock with the rod he held in his hand, and water gushed out in abundance as if from an inexhaustible source. The rock or stone signifies Christ, who poured out the waters of salvation (that is, the sacraments) from his side when on the cross he allowed it to be pierced by the lance of a soldier.

David, Psalm 68.27
They have added to the anguish of my wounds

Zacharias xiii 6
Why are these wounds in the middle of your hands?

[EVE IS DRAWN FROM ADAM]

The first woman takes her origin from the man's rib

[CHRIST IS PIERCED]
John xix 31–37

[MOSES STRIKES THE ROCK]

The stone giving forth running water is the sacrament of Christ

Lamentations i 12
All you who pass along the road pause and see

Amos viii 9
On that day the sun shall sink and hide its rays

Pure water with blood flows from Christ

Taking ·e·6 first of the four Types related to the Crucifixion, it is clear that the sacrificial implications of ·d·6 are now explicit: Isaac's wood is now cruciform, the ram is in the foreground.[1] Abraham's scabbard on the ground echoes his raised sword, so he stands as if between the justice (blade) and mercy (scabbard),[2] present in the paradox of the Cross. The point of the 'parallel' between divine and human fathers and sons is that Isaac lived, but Christ died.[3]

Jesus referred to 7, prophesying his Crucifixion: 'The Son of Man must be lifted up as Moses lifted up the serpent in the desert, so that everyone who believes may have eternal life in him, for God so loved the world that he gave his only Son'.[4] The serpents (actually a punishment for ingratitude) stand for sins.[5] They attack the head: the senses, the 'doors of sin'.[6] Entangling their victims, they suggest the horror from which the Cross releases us. Faith in God's power to heal their bite *through contemplation of the image of one of them dead*[7] is a model for our response to the Cross:[8] Christ is our flesh 'mortified'.

Two of the Prophecies of ·e· are about suffering: 3 was actually spoken from the Cross;[9] 4 is from the 'Passion Psalm' long related to Christ.[10] The lower two are extraordinary images of paradoxical victory. The 'horns' of 11 literally rays of light emitted by the power of God in majesty but variously interpreted[11] came to mean the Cross[12] or its beam-ends.[13] The monster of primeval chaos (10) not to be snagged like a mere fish is caught by the Cross or the Divinity (a kind of cosmic fish-hook)[14] baited with the Crucified:[15] the fishing-line is the long ancestry of kings in Jesus's family (Matthew i).[16]

The Types in ·f· are about the process of healing mooted in ·e·7. The Gospel relates Moses and the rock (7)[17] to Jesus's: 'If any man thirst, let him come to me'[18] and Paul says: 'Our fathers . . . all drank from the rock . . . and the rock was Christ'.[19] Moses's rod is even compared with the wounding Cross.[20] The page's main message, as 1 and 2 show, is that Christ's death makes the sacraments available: they flow with the blood which restores Longinus,[21] and are equated in 6 with Eve, earthly mother of the Church which makes them accessible, emerging from the Old Adam who in the New Adam will be crucified.[22] Balancing God's gestures of help and blessing stands the fatally fruiting tree of the Fall, itself a Type of the Cross: 'I wyll that my son manhede take, / For reson wyll that ther be thre, / A man, a madyn and a tre; / Man for man, tre for tre, Madyn for madyn; thus shal it be'.[23] Perhaps the three trees on the rock in 7 (reminiscent of Calvary), this one in 6, and the tree in 5, are visually related?

Following the main theme, 3[24] and 4[25] stress the suffering of Christ's piercing, but as in ·e·, the last two Prophecies imply victory. The Good Friday service puts 10 into Christ's mouth on the Cross, while 11 suggests his death and the eclipse which marked it,[26] in both of which the rising of this Son is foreseen.

According to Genesis xxxvii 18–24, when the brothers of Joseph wanted to sell him to the Ismaelites, they robbed him of his coat, and put him in an old well. Joseph signifies Christ, who was put in a well (that is, in the tomb) when friends took him from the cross.

·g·

According to Jonas ii, when Jonas himself had embarked to go to the city of Tharsis, a great tempeſt arose at sea, and when those who were in the ship caſt lots among themselves, the lot fell on Jonas whom they seized and threw into the sea. And at once a great fish swallowed him, in whose belly he was for three days and three nights. Jonas signifies Chriſt, who was three days and three nights in the belly of the earth.

David, Psalm 77.65
The Lord was awakened as if from sleep like a ſtrong man intoxicated with wine

Canticles v 2
I sleep and my heart keeps watch

[JOSEPH PLACED IN THE WELL]

[ENTOMBMENT]
Matthew xxvii 57–60

[JONAS IS SWALLOWED]

He is thruſt down this old well

Jonas is swallowed yet is unhurt

Isaias xi 10
His tomb shall be glorious

Genesis xlix 9
Reſting he shall lie like a lion

Chriſt was embalmed with myrrh and buried by these people

The Types present the Entombment[1] in the light of the coming Resurrection, and underline the literal and metaphorical nakedness of the dead Christ, whose mortal body is stripped of consciousness as well as clothing. This is why *lectio* 1 mentions Joseph's being robbed of his coat,[2] the mark of his father's favour, before being put into the dry well (6),[3] and it explains the nakedness of Jonas (7).

Jesus himself compared Jonas's sojourn in the sea monster with his own time in the tomb.[4] Like Jonas and Joseph, he will emerge from solitude and darkness to complete God's work. Until he does so, the Tomb remains merely a sepulchre, but its later veneration as a shrine may be referred to in Prophecy 10, suggesting also the richness of Joseph of Arimathea's own tomb, given to Christ.[5] The tomb's dignity as gateway to another life may be the reason for the prominence of the large (and iconographically untypical) water-trough in the foreground of 6, recalling the life-giving quality of a well which (unlike this one) is active.[6] Its angle, size, and position echo the fish in 7, which is also life-giving, preserving Jonas from death, and conveying him to a new life. In this context, the well and ship are analogues of the tomb (which shows the same surface decoration as the poop).[7] Like the trough, which recalls water though dry, the fish is double in meaning. It also signifies the 'hell' to which Christ now descends (as the Creed

records) to free souls, emerging from it and the tomb on the third day (·h·, ·i·).[8] The remaining three Prophecies also anticipate conquest and resurrection: 4[9], 3,[10] and 11[11] all refer to sleep soon to be broken, the last two suggesting dormant power.

All this implied activity is absent from the main scene. Christ is suspended in the shroud held by Joseph of Arimathea and Nicodemus[12] (as Jonas is slung between the two sailors, and Joseph is suspended from a rope). He is surrounded by friends. The centrality of his mother anointing his body (as 12 implies),[13] formally flanked by St John and the Magdalene, is marked by the single tree above, which also suggests the garden.[14] The central group mourns undemonstratively.[15] The central vertical takes the eye to the touched body (rather than to the face), on which Jesus's hands are crossed in death. In 6 and 7, verticals also take the eye to bodies being lowered, but they pass through hostile groups who remind us that Jesus's enemies were jealous (like Joseph's brothers) and afraid (like Jonas's shipmates). Gestures in both are strong. Those of and around Joseph suggest a babble of speech: his face is focussed upon by his encirclement, and by the line of the descending rope. Jonas lifts his hands strenuously in prayer;[16] curve of sail, vertical of mast, and surge of advancing fish meet at his face.[17] The passivity of Christ, stressed by contrast, is itself dramatic preparation for the active scenes which follow.

According to 1 Kings xvii 19–51, when David had thrown down the giant Goliath he killed him and cut off his head with the giant's own sword. In the same way, when he freed man from the lower world Christ removed him from the power of the devil, and with his strength weakened the devil himself.

·h·

According to Judges xiv 5–14 concerning Samson, when a lion attacked him he seized and killed it. Samson signifies Christ who when he freed man from the power of the devil killed the lion (that is, the devil).

David, Psalm 106.16
He has broken bronze doors and iron bars

Osee xiii 14
O Death I will be your death, I will devour you, Hell

[DAVID KILLS GOLIATH]

[CHRIST OPENS LIMBO]
1 Peter iii 19

[SAMSON KILLS THE LION]

This man, signifying you O Christ, destroys Goliath

Thus Samson's strength destroys the lion's jaws

Zacharias ix 11
By the blood of your covenant you have freed the prisoners

Genesis xlix 9
You leapt at the spoils, my son

The destruction of the door of the lower world was achieved by the death of Christ

---

The page is about the victory of the seemingly weak over the strong attacker—the theme of **11**.[1] In all three scenes the battle is already won. David (**6**),[2] having killed Goliath with the sling seen empty in the foreground, cuts off the giant's head. David smites him twice (one cut is already visible): before blood has ceased spurting from the wound made by the stone visibly lodged in his forehead, and even before he falls,[3] Goliath folds between his own sword and his fallen club. The design of **7** is in complete contrast. Samson, mastering the lion,[4] bestrides it, forcing its still-resisting jaws, to tear it apart.[5] Lion and man are braced, heads juxtaposed in a compact composition. Sustained struggle is marked by the flourish of Samson's headband and the lion's unhappy tail. The biblical lion is merely torn to pieces: the tearing of its mouth appears in art because of Samson's prefiguration of Christ forcing open Hellmouth (**5**),[6] a relationship pointed by *tituli* **9** and **12**.

The central design is different again,[7] showing apparently effortless victory. In the time between his burial and resurrection, Christ 'descended into Hell'. He simply stands in opposition to the mouth of a hell which is as helpless as a dental patient. Eve and other souls who awaited redemption follow the emerging Adam,[8] whose hand is touched by Christ in a gentle central gesture (contact is unusually delicate, Adam's wrist commonly being grasped). This particular moment of greeting has no biblical foundation at all,[9] but is extraordinarily ancient in literature, appearing in quasi-dramatic form in the third-century *Descent into Hell*.[10] There 'Satan' and 'Hell' discuss their earlier loss of Lazarus, and barricade their gates against Jesus's prophesied coming. But he blinds them with his brightness, overcomes them by his power, and 'holding the right hand of Adam, says: "Peace be to you and all your children" ', and leaves with all those he has freed.[11]

The remaining Prophecies refer to Christ's action: **4** suggests conquest of hell's power to devour;[12] **3**[13] mentions the 'gates of brass and . . . bars of iron', which hell and Satan barricaded (the 'gates of hell' which Christ promised could not resist his Church);[14] **10**[15] reminds us that this release is the result of a ransom.

The whole page recalls the impressive Harrowing of Hell as developed in the medieval drama.[16] Even here it gives a sense of victory after the long suffering of the Passion, a sense of the Fall (**a6**) redeemed in Adam's release to a new relationship with God, a sense of joy which in spite of ·**k**·**5** (the *Three Women at the Tomb*) and ·**s**·**5** (*The Damned Enter Hell*) dominates the remaining pages.

According to Judges xvi 2–3, Samson got up in the middle of the night and by sheer strength tore down both the bronze gates of the city, and carried them out of the city with him. Samson signifies Christ who, rising from the tomb in the middle of the night, threw down the gates of the tomb, and free and strong left the place.

•1•

According to the Book of Jonas the Prophet ii 11, when Jonas had been in the belly of the sea-beast for three days and three nights, the fish threw him up on dry land. Jonas, who came out of the fish after three days, signifies Christ, who after three days left the tomb, that is to say, rose from the dead.

David, Psalm 77.65
The Lord of the house was woken as if from sleep

Genesis xlix 9
Judah is a lion cub; my son

[SAMSON REMOVES THE
GATES OF GAZA]

[RESURRECTION]
Matthew xxviii 1–10

[JONAS IS RELEASED]

Surrounded by many people Samson carries away the gates of the city

This man denotes you rising out of the tomb O Christ

Osee vi 3
On the third day he shall raise us up: we shall know and follow him

Sophonias iii 8
On the day of my resurrection I shall gather the gentiles

Jesus, whom the huge stone covered, leaves the tomb

The major theme is the overcoming of adversity followed by emergence from imprisonment—in a city, a tomb, or a sea monster. The minor theme is ascent to God. Samson (6), as *lectio* 1 and *titulus* 8 show, is a Type of Christ's single-handed power.[1] Both escape from many enemies (Christ's in hell as well as on earth, around his tomb); both move from metaphorical as well as literal darkness into a natural night; both force 'gates' (the gates of hell mentioned in •h•3 and •h•12, as well as the tomb entrance itself, as suggested in *titulus* 12). All these parallels are ancient, as is a fourth, less obvious to the eye: Samson's climbing the mountain, on which we see his feet carefully set, prefigures the Ascension.[2]

Spiritual as well as physical ascent is implied. There is a mountain, too, behind Jonas (7)[3] where we might expect to see Ninive[4] as a kind of visual antithesis to Gaza, in 6. This mountain, traditional retreat for prayer, suggests Jonas's personal goal rather than his immediate destination as a prophet: it complements his gesture of prayer. In the design of the whole page, Samson's ascent and Jonas's gesture lead to Christ. Jonas escapes not by human strength but after prayer, resulting in God's simply 'speaking to the fish' so that it vomits him up.[5] Christ, echoing Samson and Jonas, 'escapes' both by his own power and that of his Father: 4 calls

Christ a lion-cub because, the *Bestiary* tells us, a new-born lion sleeps for three days until woken to full life by the roaring of its sire.[6]

This renewed vigour, the theme also of 3,[7] dominates the central scene.[8] That Jonas is vomited up suggests not only that hell could not contain Christ, but also that his mission does not end with the Resurrection: it continues, bringing us, as Jonas brought the Ninivites, to repentance. Jonas's nakedness[9] even underlines the special nature of Christ's risen body, wounded but unbleeding, newly stripped of human weakness. In telling contrast to the vitality of the victorious Christ, the uncomprehending group of soldiers round the tomb is also a foil for the aspiring solitude and concentration of Samson and Jonas. The soldiers' sleep is one of blindness to Christ, whose brightness they cannot tolerate.

The two lower Prophecies point not the manner but the meaning of the Resurrection. Spiritual death, to which mankind has been subject since the Fall, is conquered: Christ shows us that physical death may be overcome at the general resurrection (10).[10] Such is the power of this double victory that all races will then unite (11).[11]

According to Genesis xxxvii 29–30, Ruben came and looked for his brother Joseph in the well. When he had found it he was extremely troubled. He said to his brothers: 'The boy is not to be seen—and I, where shall I go?' Ruben signifies Mary Magdalene who in sorrow and love looked for Christ in the tomb. However, having received from the angel the reply that he had risen from the dead, she later merited seeing him.

·k·

According to Solomon's Canticles iii 1, the betrothed, seeking her loved one, said: 'I have looked for him whom my soul loves, and have not found him'. This betrothed woman prefigures Mary Magdalene, who looked for her loved one in the tomb, and later found him in the garden.

Isaias lv 6
Look for the Lord while he is to be found: call him while he is near

David, Psalm 104.3
Let the heart of those seeking the Lord rejoice

[RUBEN AT THE WELL]

[THREE WOMEN AT THE TOMB]
Mark xvi 1

[THE BETROTHED SEEKS THE BELOVED]
'I have looked for him and not found him' Canticles iii 1

Ruben fears that the abducted boy has been killed

This holy woman prays while she diligently looks for her lover

Micheas vii 7
I shall look to the Lord and await him

Genesis xlix 18
I shall await your salvation, Lord

The angel tells us it is certain that you are alive, O Christ

This conflation-loving designer could easily have combined the *Three Women at the Tomb* with either the preceding *Resurrection* or the *Mary Magdalene Finds Christ*, which follows.[1] His isolation of the image of the empty tomb is in fact a kind of visual pun. Until the twelfth century it was the usual way of representing the Resurrection.[2] The angel's raised hand indicates his words: 'Do not be afraid: I know you are looking for Jesus who was crucified. He is not here: he is risen, as he said'.[3] There are, thus, two *Resurrections* in the book (·i·, ·k·) balancing two *Crucifixions* (·e·, ·f·).

The context puts unusual emphasis on sorrow (this may indeed explain the alignment of tomb and lid, recalling the Cross).[4] The Types (neither of which has any precedent in relation to the Maries at the tomb) present loss and lamentation with uncompromising force.[5] There is something brutal about the dominating dry well behind which Reuben (6) wrings his hands. He is to receive no comfort.[6] The anguished bride (7),[7] having sought her beloved through the 'streets and squares' of the city in the background, poignantly grieves. Even the scroll bearing her lamentation, emerging centrally and curving down to balance her bowed body, contributes to this. The device was last used in the *Annunciation* (a), where scrolls presented dialogue at Christ's advent. The bride, however, speaks not in dialogue but in isolation. Christ's advent and departure are thus linked and contrasted.

The *lectiones* (1 and 2) stress the sense of loss felt by the Magdalene at the tomb, too, but her touching of the shroud gives the scene a dual emotional charge. The shroud, showing the distressing emptiness of the tomb where the women had thought to find a body for anointing, is itself evidence for the Resurrection, having been left behind (as it would not have been in a body-snatching).[8] It is unlikely to be an accident that this cloth and the lid on which it lies link the otherwise separated groups formed by mourners on one side, and on the other the angel, messenger of joy.

The very sorrow of the bride (7) also implies comfort.[9] She is not merely the lamenting lover (the soul or the Church temporarily separated from Christ). Her place in an erotic love-song[10] powerfully implies the reunion—in the immediate earthly future shown in ·l·7, and in the New Jerusalem which is heaven, suggested in ·v·5. This expectation is the burden of all four Prophecies,[11] the top two particularly stressing the soul's search. Both goals—the immediate and the ultimate—are implied in the enigmatic end to Mary Magdalene's search (mentioned in 1 and 2) shown on the next page.

According to Daniel xiv 30, when the prophet Daniel had been sent into the lions' den so that the lions should kill him, the king came next morning to the lions' den and to Daniel to see if he still lived. When he saw him living he was extremely pleased. Now this king signifies Mary Magdalene when Mary came to the sepulchre: she greatly rejoiced when she saw her Lord, and because he had risen from the dead.

·l·

According to the Canticle of Canticles iii 1–4, when the betrothed woman had found her beloved she said: 'I have found him whom my soul loves' and then: 'I shall hold him again and not let him go'. This betrothed woman signifies Mary Magdalene who, seeing her beloved (that is, Christ) wanted to hold him. He answered her in this way: 'Do not touch me, for I have not yet ascended to my father'.

David, Psalm 9.11
You will not forsake those who seek you O Lord

1 Kings ii 1
My heart has rejoiced in the Lord

[DANIEL IS FOUND AMONG THE LIONS]

[MARY MAGDALENE FINDS CHRIST]
John xx 11–17

[THE BETROTHED FINDS THE BELOVED]

'I held him, I shall not let him go'
Canticles iii 4

The king is delighting in the fact that he sees this man alive

Now the betrothed enjoys the beloved whom she had desired and sought

Isaias lxi 10
With joy I shall rejoice in the Lord: and you, be joyful in God

Osee ii 14
I will lead her into solitude and there speak to her heart

By showing yourself, O Christ, you comfort the loyal Mary

The Types show that the page is about survival and reunion, as well as Christ's strange prohibition ('Do not touch me') illustrated in the central scene.[1] Our attention is directed beyond this world, as in the remainder of the book: full reunion with Christ will be achieved only after death.

The king (6) coming to bewail Daniel's death does rejoice (as *titulus* 8 says) to find him alive. The design, however, emphasises not this reunion but Daniel's remarkable survival: imprisoned for having destroyed the pagans' dragon-god,[2] he is unharmed among seven starved lions, three of which can be seen fawning on him.[3] The 'den' dominates the design, dwarfing the prophet, its strong verticals separating him from his 'mourner'. It recalls the underworld in which Christ survived, destroying not a dragon but the power of the Devil.[4] Daniel's very confinement emphasises Christ's freedom, and with it, ours.

Reunion really is the theme of 7. The comfort promised in ·k·7 is given. There the bride's lament seemed to sink from her in a falling scroll: here it is replaced by a vow of love, set in a scroll exultantly filling the sky.[5] Solitude ends with the return of the bridegroom (depicted as the Christ he traditionally represents). The lovers' formal embrace is central. The simplicity and per-

manence of this comfort ('I shall not let him go', asserts the bride) points the enigmatic quality of the Magdalene's consolation (also promised in ·k·), which is not permanent, but fleeting. The very nature of the risen body she meets is mysterious.[6] Not recognising Jesus at first, she mistakes him for the gardener (hence his spade).[7] When he does identify himself, she who went to the tomb to anoint his body (from the jar in the foreground) is forbidden even to touch him because he is 'not yet ascended to [his] Father'. The prohibition is pointed by the central alignment of her jar, her reaching fingers, and the arresting gesture of Christ.[8] Real reunion with him, foreshadowed by the bride in 7, will take place only in the next world.

The top two Prophecies, 3[9] and 4,[10] underline the ideas of search, reunion, and rejoicing: 10 is strongly eucharistic.[11] Attention is directed by 11 to a new element in the page: the importance of solitude in the soul's search for God[12] (which is why the bride failed to find her lover in the city, the world[13]). Perhaps we are to remember that in his solitary imprisonment Daniel was miraculously fed by Habacuc—an image of the Eucharist, the closest union with Christ offered on this earth.

According to Genesis xlv 1–7, Joseph had seen his brothers ſtunned with fear, afraid of the people and not know- ing that it was Joseph. He said to them: 'I am your brother Joseph; do not be afraid'. And so he comforted them. Joseph signifies Chriſt, who after his resurrection appeared to the disciples when they were together, and by speaking comforted them saying: 'Do not be afraid; it is I'.

•m•

According to Luke xv 11–32, the son of a rich man told his father to give him his inheritance, and when he had handed it over to him he went to a diſtant country and used up all his for- tune in evil living. This done, he went back to his father, and he received him gladly, and comforted him. Now that good father signifies the Father of the heavens who, coming to the disciples, comforted them for his death and made his resurrection plain.

David, Psalm 15.11
You will fill me with joy by showing your face

Wisdom i 3
And he appeared to those who had faith in him

[JOSEPH REVEALS HIMSELF TO HIS BROTHERS]

[CHRIST APPEARS TO HIS DISCIPLES]
Luke xxiv 36

[RETURN OF THE PRODIGAL SON]

He who once angered them is now kind to the brothers

Weeping, the father embraces the son and he is reſtored

Isaias li 1
Look to the rock from which you were cut

Ezechiel xxxiv 11
See, I myself will seek my sheep and go to them

Jesus appears to these men; his risen glory is clear

Familiar stories are used here in new and complex ways. In each, someone thought dead gives comfort, being alive, and receives comfort (**3** may apply to everyone present).[1] Salutary suffering to purge guilt leads to forgiveness, debts are met, fear gives way to trust, a meal is shared by a 'family'. Christ (**5**) comforts the disciples, who, thinking him dead, are alarmed by his sudden appearance in a locked room. Having received forgiveness in the Atonement, as his successors they are to dispense it.[2] Jesus, appear- ing while they are at a 'family' table, will eat with them.[3] We see the domestic scene as if from a street,[4] two separate windows framing the mutual comforters.

Like God, Joseph (**6**) shows that he lives and forgives his brothers —one of whom doffs the very hat he wore when lowering Joseph (·**g**·**6**).[5] He discomfits them to purge their guilt,[6] but is generous to them too, supplying free the grain they came to buy in famine.[7] God does likewise, his Son paying all prices, and more. This is why Benjamin is so prominent in the foreground of **6**. Joseph's motive in making him 'guilty' (hiding the silver cup in his lug- gage) was love for his family and his longed-for youngest brother.[8] Benjamin is both the sought soul and Christ made 'guilty' to

regain it. This stress on family and redemption explains the figure behind Joseph, too. Since Joseph sent away all strangers before identifying himself, this must be Simeon (hostage for Benjamin) or Juda (who offered to be).[9] In this pattern, Joseph is equated with God the Father, hostage-taker, as well as with Christ the comforter.

Indeed, visual symmetry equates Joseph with the old man in **7**, who in the parable is God the Father welcoming the repentant soul[10] (driven, like Joseph's brothers, by famine). In context, he is Christ the comforter too (**2**). But the Prodigal 'who was lost and is found' is also Christ, who, like the brothers in **6**, comforts and is comforted.[11] This extraordinary equation[12] recalls that in **5** Jesus is both Redeemer and redeemed mankind reconciled with the Father.[13] In this pattern the Apostles in **5**, led by Peter, represent the Church.

There is an odd interchange of identities, an interdependence upon which salvation itself depends. This is pointed not by the straightforward **4**[14], or **11**[15], but by **10**[16] (which like **3** is inclusive): the 'rock' to which we must look is the Church[17] built on Peter (*Petrus*),[18] but also Christ[19] and the Father in whose image we are made.[20]

legitur in genesi · v · capitulo de enoch
deo placuit et translatus est in
paradysum enoch et ... cristo placuit
cristum sunt qui summo viro placuit
deo in paradysum celeste · i · in celum
ascendere meruit eum et in die ascensio-
nis super omnes choros angelorum
exaltauit

legitur in · iiii · libro regum · ii · capitulo helyas propheta in curru igneo
tolleretur in celum helyseus clamabat dicens pater mi pater mi currus israel
et auriga eius helyas · xp· signabat
qui vidit eos auli quod helyseus signabat celum ascedentem admirati sunt
eum xp· eius dixit ascedit ad patrem
meum

Ascedit deus in iubilatione et dominus in voce tube   ·O·   Quius est iste qui venit de edom tinctis vestibus &c

vn Enoch translatus
celestibus et sociatus

vn celitus effectus helia
per aera vectus

Deute · xxx · Sicut aquila prouocans
pullos suos ad volandum

michie
·ii·
Ascedit iter pandens
ante eos

vn Scm bru cristus petit astra polore

According to Judges vi 11–14, the Angel of the Lord came to Gideon saying to him: 'The Lord be with you, bravest of men, for you shall free the people yourself'. And so it was. Now Gideno signifies Thomas, to whom came The Angel of Great Wisdom (that is, Christ) and comforting him in his faith, said: 'Put your hand in my side, and see the places made by the nails, and do not be sceptical, but believing'.

•n•

According to Genesis xxxii 23–30, when the Angel of the Lord had come to Jacob he, seizing the Angel, struggled with him and would not let him go until he had blessed him. Jacob denotes the apostle Thomas who, touching the Angel (that is, Christ) earned a blessing, that is, the proof of Christ's resurrection.

Isaias lvii 18
I have seen the way he went, and I have sent him away and led him back

Jeremias xxxi 18
Convert me and I shall return because you are the Lord my God

[GIDEON & THE ANGEL]

[DOUBTING THOMAS]
John xx 24–31

[JACOB WRESTLES WITH THE ANGEL]

The Angel encourages Gideon to fear nothing

Jacob struggling is called Israel and blessed

David, Psalm 85.4
Make the heart of your servant rejoice O Lord

Sophonias iii 7
And yet you will fear me: you will receive correction

You allowed yourself to be touched, O Christ, so that he should yield

---

In each of these confrontations with God the man is uncertain of his visitor's identity, but on learning it takes courage for a great task. The initiative is God's, as 3[1] and 4[2] show. In his doubt, Thomas probes the wound (5), then confidently kneels to say 'My Lord and my God' and receive a blessing.[3] His virtue, privileged treatment and future are implied by the Types.

Gideon (6)[4] and Jacob (7),[5] standard Types of Christ,[6] are here equated with Thomas, whose apostolic future is dominant in the visual impact of 6. Gideon was in fact threshing when so suddenly visited. His armour is a reference to the future, to the angel's: 'The Lord is with you, bravest of men. You will save your people';[7] his sword is significantly central. But Gideon, like Thomas unconvinced of God's presence and power, retorts that the deity does not seem to be 'with' his beleaguered people at all. Not until similarly given signs does he believe that God is God, or that the enemy can be subdued.

For eight days Thomas refused to believe Jesus risen. Only now does Christ make compassionate concession to the human need for proof, gently rebuking Thomas: 'You have seen and believed; they are fortunate who have not seen and yet believe'. But the Gideon parallel suggests that Christ proves not only his own power but also Thomas's worthiness.[8] Doubt is not damning.

Faith is the subject of Jacob's struggle (7). He is slow to recognise his adversary. His bravery earns a blessing, but his temerity (or weakness) earns lifelong lameness. Like Thomas, he is privileged and punished:[9] to be human is 'a proud and yet a wretched thing'.[10] But this enigmatic story is a contrast as well as a parallel. Jacob is determined, not diffident, in the struggle he so unexpectedly wins (an allegory of perseverance in prayer),[11] and his hurt points the fact that under the New Law constancy in contact with Christ results in a welcome, not a wounding. It is not Thomas but Christ who carries the mark of conflict between God and man.[12]

The link between comfort (10)[13] and correction (11)[14] is clear, as it was in •m•. God's gentleness permits Thomas's touch, and shows in the wrestling angel's surprising submission; 'The victor blessed by the vanquished suggests Christ'.[15] Jesus, voluntarily vanquished, raises his hand in blessing, like the angel in 7 who renames Jacob 'Israel' ('seeing God'). Jacob's line will flourish, as the Church will take life even from a doubting Apostle.

According to Genesis v 22–24, Henoch was pleasing to God, and was taken up to paradise. Now Henoch, who was pleasing to Christ, signifies Christ, who was pleasing to the Father above, and therefore deserved to ascend into the celestial paradise (that is, into heaven). Indeed on the day of his ascension he raised him above all the choirs of angels.

•O•

According to 4 Kings ii 9–14, when Elias [Elijah] the prophet was carried up to heaven in a chariot of fire, Eliseus [Elisha] cried out, saying: 'Father, my father! The chariot of Israel and its charioteer!' Elias signified Christ. Seeing him ascending into heaven, the Apostles (whom Eliseus signified) were amazed when Christ said to them: 'I am going up to my Father'.

David, Psalm 46.6
God goes up amid shouts of joy, the Lord goes up to the sound of the trumpet

Isaias lxiii 1
Who is this who comes from Edom with stained clothes etc

[HENOCH ASCENDS]

[ASCENSION]
Luke xxiv 51, Acts i 6–11

[ELISEUS RECEIVES ELIAS' MANTLE]

Taken up, Henoch joins those in heaven

Moved by divine power, Elias is carried through the air

Deuteronomy xxxii 11
Like the eagle persuading her young to fly

Micheas ii 13
He shall go up, opening the way before them

Christ, the holiest of all, seeks the stars of the heavens

Heaven opened at the Lord's descent to Incarnation (a): it opens again for his return. Each design on this page is conventional, but the three relate in a new way. Spectators are as important as what they witness. The dominant effect is of upward-looking awe. This is achieved not only by the ring formed by Mary and the disciples, gazing up in amazement,[1] but also by the three scenes' overall arching shape: strong diagonals in each Type lead the eye inward and up to Christ's disappearing feet. This arch is echoed in the entirely conventional shape of the rock crowned with Christ's footprints:[2] thus there is strong tension between the rising feet and the remaining prints. In a sense, this is what the page is about.

Christ, not seen again on earth, remains with his Church. His disciples will 'receive the Holy Spirit, and . . . be witnesses to me . . . even to the ends of the earth'.[3] The footprints (appearing to complete the circle of onlookers) remind us that the physical reality of Jesus proved to Doubting Thomas (·n·) is as important as the spirituality of his ascent and his gift of the Spirit (·p·). The importance of delegated power is shown in 7. Indeed, the posture of Peter kneeling in the foreground of 5 is echoed in that of Eliseus in 7, kneeling to receive the mantle of Elias and with it his master's authority and responsibility.[4]

But humanity itself takes part in the Ascension. First, it is a triumph on our behalf. That Henoch (6) and Elias (7) escaped death reminds us that Christ did die, his Ascension finally demonstrating divine mastery over fallen flesh:[5] so 3 acclaims a king approaching his throne,[6] 4 identifies a victor stained with the blood of his enemies—a conqueror who has 'trodden the winepress alone'.[7] Second, the Ascension shows what Christ made possible for humanity.[8] The Fathers point out that in contrast to Christ's effortless ascent, Henoch (6) is hauled heavenwards (his clothes hunched round his neck),[9] and Elias (7) has to be carried by a chariot.[10] Great though their virtue is, their as yet unredeemed humanity leaves earth laboriously.[11] Christ's perfected humanity soars unaided—perhaps the sense of 12. The two lower Prophecies show that we can follow. The shepherd preceded his sheep 'opening the way before them' (11).[12] The eagle (10) is doubly relevant, cherishing only those of her young which can bear to look up to the sun, and carrying them on her own back to teach them to fly.[13] We are to look up to Christ the 'sun of justice' and imitate him.

According to Exodus xxxiv 1, the Lord said to Moses: 'Come up to me on the mountain and I shall give you two tablets of the law'. So in this way Moses was given the law, and it was written on ſtone tablets. In the same way the new law was written on the hearts of the faithful on the day of Pentecoſt, when fire appeared over the believers gathered together.

·P·

According to 3 Kings xviii 21–39, while the people were ſtanding round, the prophet Elias [Elijah], when he had placed the burnt offering (that is to say, one ox) on the wood, called on the Lord: and fire descending from heaven consumed everything, and so the people believed in the Lord. This fire from heaven signifies that divine fire which on the day of Pentecoſt came down on the disciples and purified them, consuming all the faults resulting from their sins.

David, Psalm 103.30
Send forth your spirit and they shall be created

Wisdom i 7
The spirit of the Lord has filled the whole world

[MOSES RECEIVES THE LAW]

[PENTECOST]
Acts ii 1–4

[ELIAS' SACRIFICE IS ACCEPTED]

The divine law was given to Moses on the summit of Sinai

Flame came from heaven and softened the hearts of the people

Ezechiel xxxvi 27
I shall set my spirit among you

Joel ii 29
I will pour out over my servants and handmaidens

The life-giving spirit fills the hearts of true men

At the Ascension, Jesus promised: 'you indeed shall be baptized with the Holy Spirit, not many days hence'.[1] Here, the Spirit descends with sound, fire, and the 'gift of tongues'.[2] Mary and all twelve Apostles[3] read the Scriptures which are fulfilled in this confirmation of God's part in history.[4] The Spirit that brooded over the world's creation[5] will henceforth inspire the Church: all four Prophecies (from the Whitsun liturgy) suggest renewal of life.[6]

The descent (Whitsun) took place on the Jewish Feast of Pentecost, celebrating Moses's receiving the law on Mount Sinai (6).[7] Type and Antitype exist not only in the mind but in history: the Spirit came fifty days after the Passion, as God spoke to Moses fifty days after the Passover. Moses's dialogues with God on Sinai were preceded by the people's ritual purification, as Pentecost purified the Apostles. In all three scenes God manifests his power in sound and fire, bringing instruction or inspiration, purification, and evidence of the singleness of the triune God.

The Trinity is implied in the dominant dove, which is cross-nimbed, recalling Christ, who had recently ascended to the right hand of the Father. In addition, both Types stress the uniqueness of God. Moses brought the Ten Commandments down the mountain twice. The first time he found his people worshipping the golden calf and broke the Tablets. Only on the second occasion was he transfigured by light (hence the horns on his head),[8] and able to transmit the law to Aaron and the Israelites[9]—the group visually equated with the Apostles seated around Mary.[10]

Historically, conquest of idolatry is the point of 7. On Mount Carmel devotees of Baal find their sacrifice ignored, but at Elias's summons God consumes the Israelites' offering by sudden fire.[11] As *lectio* 2 implies, there are no gods but God. Purification by fire and water is suggested: Elias soaked the sacrifice the better to demonstrate the power of God's fire. St Ambrose, linking this scene with Whitsun, speaks of baptism with fire and Spirit. The sacrificial animal on the altar is mankind, whose sin will be burned away, his life renewed: 'Do not fear the fire by which you will be illuminated'.[12] This 'illumination', this descent of the third Person, recalls the incarnation of the second Person, as Sinai (6) recalls Moses's earlier mountain-meeting with God in the burning bush, the Type of the Nativity (b6).[13] A chapter ends, a new one begins. The rest of the *Biblia Pauperum* shows the next world.

According to 3 Kings ii 19–20, when Bethsabee the mother of Solomon had come to him in his palace, King Solomon himself had his mother's throne placed next to his throne. Bethsabee signifies the glorious Virgin whose throne was placed next to the throne of the true Solomon, that is, of Jesus Christ.

According to Esther ii 15–23, when Queen Esther had come to King Assuerus in his palace, King Assuerus himself placed her next to him to honour her. Esther the Queen signifies the Virgin Mary, whom Assuerus (that is, Christ) placed next to himself in celestial glory on the day of her assumption.

·q·

David, Psalm 44.13
All the rich among the people will court your favour

Canticles viii 5
Who is this woman coming up through the desert?

[SOLOMON ENTHRONES BETHSABEE]

[CORONATION OF THE VIRGIN]

[ASSUERUS CROWNS ESTHER]

His mother has come in and Solomon places her next to him

When Esther goes in and entreats Assuerus

Isaias xxxv 2
The glory of Lebanon is bestowed on her, the splendour of Carmel and Saron

Wisdom iv 1
How beautiful is the chaste conception in its glory

By lifting her up you have honoured the loving Mary, O Christ

---

We have passed beyond earthly life: the story which began with the Annunciation to Mary of Christ's Incarnation (a)[1] concludes with her coronation by her son.[2] The life on earth of humanity in its most perfect forms—the sinless Virgin, and mankind made divine in Christ—reaches fulfilment. The enthroned Christ elevated mankind in his own person and in that of his mother, an honour celebrated in Prophecy 10.[3]

In the Types, kings acknowledge queens by raising their sceptres to indicate approval. By contrast, the central scene's wholly conventional coronation gesture assumes particular significance,[4] suggesting a relationship even closer than that between mother and son (6) or husband and wife (7).[5] Indeed, the multiplicity of relationships between Christ and Mary is perhaps implied in Prophecy 4, taken from the consummation of the love-song interpreted as a dialogue between Christ and Mary, the Church, or the soul.[6]

King Solomon honours his mother (6).[7] Like the queen in 7, she comes to him with a petition to which he replies: 'Make your request, I shall not refuse you'.[8] The implications in 7 are richer still. King Assuerus receives the petition of his supremely beautiful wife: her looks, her loyalty, and her elaborate four-fold petition in this moving story are highly relevant to our view of the Virgin as Queen of Heaven.[9] Now the Book of Esther is full of petitions and gibbets,[10] so it is not clear which individual occasion is depicted. All are probably conflated: Esther petitions her husband four times, and on the first and last he points his sceptre towards her, as here.[11] The couple by the gibbet are the evil Aman (also seen dismayed behind the throne) and his wife, who plotted the downfall of Esther's people: Aman was finally hanged on the gibbet he had prepared for her uncle. There is no biblical source for their embrace: this standard convention to suggest lechery is probably introduced as a foil to the purity, not only of Esther, but also of the Virgin[12]—a purity celebrated in Prophecy 11.[13]

The implication is that the Virgin will intercede for her people, mankind—a power suggested in Prophecy 3.[14] Her enemies are, like Esther's, destroyed by their own weapon (the Cross),[15] hence the prominence given to the gibbet. Throughout the scenes of suffering we were promised comfort. Throughout the final scenes of triumph we have been reminded of the suffering which was endured and the evil which was overcome.[16]

According to 3 Kings iii 16–28, two harlots came into the presence of Solomon and argued about their sons —about the overlaid and the living son—in front of the judge who, when he could not judge in any other way, said: 'Bring me a sword, and divide the living child'. And the feelings of the mother of the living child were moved, and she said: 'Give her the living child'. And he stopped the judgement. By Solomon the most wise is meant Christ, who judged the honest and dishonest by true standards.

•r•

According to 2 Kings i 1–16, King David remained in Siceleg after the death of Saul, and a man from the land of the Amalecites boasted because he had killed the Lord's anointed (that is, King Saul); and sentence of death was passed on him by David because his own mouth had condemned him, and David said to his guard: 'Attack and kill him'. David signifies Christ, who will reward everyone fairly, each according to his sins, as David judged the Amalecite.

Ecclesiastes iii 17
The Lord will judge the good man and the evil

1 Kings ii 10
The Lord shall judge the ends of the earth

[JUDGEMENT OF SOLOMON]

[LAST JUDGEMENT]
John v 26–28 Apocalypse iv 3, xxi 3–8

[DAVID CONDEMNS THE AMALECITE]

Let him now say: 'The boy is rightly given to his mother'

David judges the man thus because of the Lord's anointed one

Isaias ii 4
He shall judge the gentiles and accuse many people

Ezechiel vii 3
He will judge you according to your ways

I judge frauds and evil men equally worthy of damnation

The four final pages present life after death, as ordinary mortals (not the perfected humanity represented by Christ and the Virgin on the previous page) experience it. Overall, the reader contemplates the Four Last Things—death and judgement, hell and heaven.[1] The general resurrection from physical death,[2] under God's mercy and justice (•r•), is followed by the fate of the damned (•s•), of the blessed (•t•), and finally by the individual soul's reward—the reader's personal goal (•v•)—which is the subject of Prophecy 11.[3]

The first and last of the four are literally apocalyptic, from the last book of the Bible. The central scene here shows Christ enthroned on the rainbow. This sign of God's covenant with Noe, and all living things, meant that there was to be 'no more flood':[4] justice would be tempered by the mercy made accessible by the Redemption, by the wounds Christ displays.[5] He now has total control over his world, central beneath his feet[6] (the subject of Prophecies 4[7] and 10).[8]

Physical death is in the foreground of 6 (the dead child)[9] and of 7 (the Amalecite being executed).[10] But the visual equivalent of these two is the group of bodies rising from graves in 5. There not only physical but also spiritual death and life are in question,[11] symbolised in two ways: the swords on either side of Christ, and the two kneeling intercessors.[12]

The two-edged sword, which in the first chapter of the Apocalypse issues from the mouth of 'one who was dead and is alive', is the Sword of Judgement,[13] here shown as two. The one on Christ's right is associated with Mary's intercession (the New Law) and with the Judgement of Solomon (6), whose sword, the means of his subtle distinction between truth and falsehood (the subject of Prophecy 3[14]), does not kill. In 6 the emphasis is not on the sentence as such, but on the subtle distinguishing of motives in judgement. The unused sword and undivided child are central to picture and meaning, their centrality marked by a background tree. The design presents both the king's wisdom and the true mother's intercession for her son.

In each Type, judge is separated from the judged by strong verticals. In the Antitype, they are separated by the horizontal rainbow: the judged and those interceding for them occupy the lower part. It is significant that in 5 and 6 there are intercessors, while in 7's Old Law execution there is only a spectator behind the throne. The sword on Christ's left is associated with John the Baptist (the Old Law?)[15], and is used on the guilty Amalecite (7).[16] Its spiritual effect is the subject of the next page.

According to Deuteronomy xi 5–8 (and Numbers xvi 12–33), Dathan and Abiron, living in the middle of Israel, were engulfed by the earth together with their homes and tents, because they had not obeyed the law of God. By Dathan and Abiron are meant the sinners who pay no attention to the Catholic law or to the Ten Commandments: and they were sucked down into Hell, which is the place full of sinners in anguish, and fire which shall devour them, and they shall be punished together with the devil.

·S·

According to Genesis xix 24–25, as a result of the sins of the people of Sodom and Gomorrha God sent fire from heaven on to these cities and they were both destroyed. By Sodom and Gomorrha are meant the sinners of the world living according to their bodily desires, which blind their eyes; and when day dawns all the sinners of the earth will appear and will be destined for Hell alive, and damned.

Wisdom xviii 11
The servant shall suffer the same punishment as the master

David, Psalm 74.9
Its dregs are not emptied out: all the sinners of the world shall drink them

[DATHAN & ABIRON ARE ENGULFED]

[THE DAMNED ENTER HELL]
Matthew iii 12, xiii 40–43

[SODOM & GOMORRHA BURN]

These men are given to the earth because they do not obey the anointed one

Thus the Sodomites are thrust out on account of their sinful lives

Jeremias xxv 10
I will take away their sound of happiness from them

Job xvi 11
They are glutted by my sufferings

In this way those who pursue evil are tormented with sufferings

---

It is hard for us to see in this dragging away by demons the ultimate deprivation, the last denial of life.[1] But their self-enslavement is the captivity of the damned; one definition of hell is that self-seeking souls find their goal, themselves alone: another is 'the pain of loss', perpetual remembering of a God made inaccessible by the very limitations the self chooses to place on itself.[2] Here we see the fate of those who abuse the true nature of their bodies and their minds.

A bishop and two monarchs are central to the crowd. The five demons hauling them to hell suggest the five senses by which fleshly sins are conceived and performed. The demons are fallen angels whose pride, preceding all human sin (a6, v7), produced the spiritual disfigurement embodied in deformity such as faces on the chest or back. Sin is not 'natural'.

Sodom and Gomorrha (7) burn because of their inhabitants' unnatural lusts.[3] They also stand for mental arrogance. Twice in the New Testament they are cited with the Fall of the Angels and the Flood to show the fate of those who defy God and, worse, corrupt others. Fall, Flood, and the Sodomites' flame-deluge show how 'the Lord can save the good from the ordeal and reserve until the Day of Judgement the punishment of the wicked, especially those governed by their lusts, and without respect for

authority'.[4] These cataclysms are God's 'cup of wrath'—the theme of Prophecies 4[5] and 10.[6]

The Types are very different in design. Sodom and Gomorrha (7) sit firmly in the landscape, tight little self-contained towns.[7] Indeed, they are a warning against just such complacency: the end of the world 'will be the same as it was in the time of Lot. They ate and drank, bought and sold, planted and built: and on the day Lot left Sodom, fire and brimstone rained from heaven and destroyed them all'.[8] As in 5, death is a leveller, and as 3 observes, damnation is no respecter of persons.[9]

Not false security but the collapse and chaos caused by sin are implied in the dispersed design of 6.[10] Dathan and Abiron rejected and corrupted authority,[11] assuming 'priesthood' against Moses and Aaron (Types of Christ). Evil destroys from all directions, falling from the sky in fire (7), opening below in earthquake (6). The interior effects of which these are analogues are suggested by 11: the lost observe that demons relish torturing, and with dreadful irony they use the words of the suffering Job commonly put into the mouth of Christ crucified.[12] No comparison could more clearly reveal the arrogance, torment, and diminution of the damned.

According to Job i 1–5, his sons used to have feasts in their houses, each one in his own house, sending for their sisters so that they could eat and drink with them. The sons of Job are the holy ones who held feasts daily, sending for those who were to be saved so that they should come to eternal gladness and enjoy God eternally. Amen.

·t·

According to Genesis xxviii 10–16, when Jacob had seen the sun set he found a stone which he placed under his head. In a dream he saw a ladder set up from earth to heaven, and angels descending; and the Lord leaned down over the ladder saying to him: 'I shall give the land on which you sleep to you and your descendants for ever'. By Jacob understand the faithful soul which when it has fallen asleep on the stone (that is, Christ) will gain the land flowing with milk and honey (that is, the kingdom of heaven).

David, Psalm 31.11
Rejoice in the Lord O upright men; and all you of good intent shall be glorified

Tobias xi 11
And they began to weep for joy

[JOB'S FAMILY FEASTS]   [CHRIST GATHERS BLESSED SOULS]   [JACOB'S LADDER]
Luke xvi 22

The children of Job rejoice because they undertake this so happily

The angel appeared to Jacob and he greatly rejoiced in this

Josue i 3
Every place on which the sole of your foot shall step

Isaias lxvi 10
Rejoice with Jerusalem and be glad with her all you who love her

O Father in the heavens, may you wish to feast me in your company

---

Here is not the diminution, indignity and anguish of the damned, but the rich afterlife of the blessed. Contrast with ·s· is implicit in Prophecy 3: we rejoice because 'many torments await the wicked, but grace enfolds the man who trusts in the Lord.'[1] It is hard to find visual or verbal analogues for hell, harder still to find them for heaven. Prophecy 10 uses the image of the promised land, all of which will be inherited by those who walk it. The vision of the New Jerusalem sometimes used is too impersonal to suggest the direct apprehension of God.[2] Instead we have in 5 the curious but common image of God holding 'newborn' souls in a napkin.[3] The holding of a child is implicit also in Prophecy 11:[4] we are to rejoice with Jerusalem, which is presented as a nursing mother, because in his New Jerusalem God will similarly comfort us 'as a mother comforts her son on her lap'. There is tenderness, then, in heaven.

As *titulus* 12 makes clear, this seeming birth image (5) unexpectedly implies family feasting and fulfilment (as in 6). It derives from the parable of the poor man who starved on scraps from a rich man's table, and at death was carried by angels to 'Abraham's bosom',[5] which implied not only great intimacy with God, but also the 'banquet' of the shared joy of heaven (as in the

parable of the wedding feast).[6] Indeed, the point of Prophecy 4 is that Tobias's parents, having wept for joy to see him home again (as God rejoices for his 'family'), celebrate with a seven-day feast. Job (6) has seven sons, each of whom feasts the family—including three sisters, all of whom appear in the picture[7]—one day a week. This implies perpetuity (there are seven souls in 'Abraham's bosom').

Job's feast celebrates family unity, suggesting a heavenly *activity* notoriously difficult to imagine. It also suggests communion with God: *lectio* 1's 'holy ones who held feasts daily' celebrated Masses[8] in the early Church (the design recalls ·m·5, where Christ appears to his disciples before eating with them).

Prophecy and Type have so far indicated the more accessible aspects of the Beatific Vision: entry to promised happiness, sharing joy, completion of eucharistic union. *Jacob's Ladder* (7)[9] implies the still unimaginable. The stick lying by him recalls that he was lamed in his struggle with God, the Type of Thomas's touching of Christ (·n·7). An altogether closer contact with God (who as 2 says leans down from the top of the ladder) is here foreshadowed but not depicted.[10] Though the angels are visible, their home (in deliberate contrast to Job's in 6) remains out of sight.

According to The Canticle of Canticles iv 7–8, the beloved addresses his betrothed, taking her to him, and says: 'You are wholly beautiful, my love, and there is no fault in you: come my love, come, and you shall be crowned'. The true beloved is Christ who, by taking her as his spouse because she is a soul without the stain of any sin, brings her to eternal rest and crowns her with a crown of immortality.

•V•

According to the Apocalypse xxi 9, the Angel of the Lord seized John the Evangelist when he was inspired, and wishing to show him the secret things of God, said to him: 'Come, I shall show you the betrothed, the bride of the lamb'. The angel spoke to everyone in general so that they should come in spirit to attend Christ the innocent lamb crowning the innocent soul.

David, Psalm 18.6
The Lord as bridegroom coming out of their bedroom

Isaias lxi 10
Like a bridegroom he has adorned me with a crown

[THE GROOM CROWNS THE BRIDE]

[CHRIST GIVES THE CROWN OF ETERNAL LIFE]

[THE ANGEL & ST JOHN]

Praise indeed to the soul: be quite confident that you have a husband

The bridegroom loves the bride, and Christ loves the beautiful one exceedingly

Ezechiel xxiv 17
Let your crown be on your head and shoes on your feet

Osee ii 19
I will wed you forever, etc

Then the souls rejoice since everything good is given to them

---

At first this seems a curiously undramatic final page. All the designs are similar, giver on the left, receiver on the right: indeed **6** and **5** differ little.[1] All are rather static: the customary contrasting movements (like those in •t•6, 7) are absent. There are no significant foregrounds,[2] supporting landscapes,[3] or important details.[4] Furthermore, the central scene repeats ideas already raised in the *Coronation of the Virgin* (•q•) and recalled by Prophecy 3's reference to the Incarnation.[5] Lastly, 7 is the only scene in the book which does not illustrate what its *lectio* reveals as a major theme: it merely alludes to it.[6]

The central scene carries two associated but distinct meanings. Its *titulus* (**12**) and its Types show that at one level the woman represents the Church (as did Mary). The Canticle bride (**6**) was often interpreted as the Church,[7] and the New Jerusalem which John (**7**) will see 'coming down from God out of heaven, prepared like a bride adorned for her husband'[8] is the Church Triumphant, or even heaven itself.[9]

But heaven has already been symbolically presented to us in •t•, and the *lectiones* and *titulus* 8 refer to 'the soul' (a possible sense in Prophecies 4, 10, and 11 too,[10] so acknowledgement of the individual soul is clearly also intended). This page may be the last in a group of four asking the reader to contemplate the Last Things, a process essentially a prayer for personal salvation. The grand movements of God's plan, from Creation through the life of Christ to Judgement, have all been offered to the reader so that he may save his soul. The real contrasts are not on the page, but with the three preceding pages about the final relationship between God and all mankind, after which this one has a wholly appropriate stillness and understatement.

Suddenly the 'negative' aspects of the page make sense. Absence of backgrounds gives a bold, timeless quality, an almost abstract power: spaces between figures assume compositional importance, emphasising gestures. Union of the soul and God resists representation, but the very reticence of the page sends the mind back to the great lyrical and visionary expressions of it—the Canticle (**6**)[11] and Apocalypse (**7**)—hence the designer's refusal actually to show the last scene of all. For forty pages we have worked hard on detailed designs, subtle interlocking texts. Now we are sent from the book. It is significant that alone among the 'receivers' John is *not* kneeling.[12] He did try to adore the angel who showed him his vision—who gave him, as it were, his art—but was told: 'Don't do that. I am a servant just like you and . . . like those who treasure what you have written in this book. Adore God'.

NOTES TO COMMENTARY
TRANSCRIPTION OF LATIN TEXT

Notes to Commentary

In the notes which follow, dates and attributions of works in *PL* are those of Migne, except where '*PL*' is preceded by an asterisk, indicating that the date and attribution are those given by Glorieux, *Pour revaloriser Migne*; for example, 's.ix Claudius of Turin ★*PL* L 884' which Migne attributes to s.v Eucherius. Where no date or attribution is given but '*PL*' is asterisked, Glorieux reattributes the work (often without certainty). Simple omission of date or attribution, or both, without asterisk, means that the missing information is the same as that in the immediately preceding reference (except where that information is given in the commentary to which the note directly refers). The *Glossa Ordinaria* once attributed to Walafrid Strabo is referred to throughout as 'the s.xi *Glossa*' (see *ODCC* '*Glossa Ordinaria*').

Pages, columns, and biblical verses are not preceded by 'p.', 'col.', or 'v.', but plates and figures are distinguished by 'pl.' and 'fig.'. Plates in the *Biblia Pauperum* facsimile are indicated by the two alphabets used in the book itself, in bold: **a–v**, **·a·–·v·**. The twelve parts of the *Biblia Pauperum* page are also indicated in bold, as usual. Dates are indicated by 's.' (*saeculo*) followed by small roman numerals; for example, 's.vi' for 'sixth-century'. Names in references not otherwise explained refer to entries in the Bibliography. References to 'the Vienna MS' are to the s.xiv manuscript *Biblia Pauperum* (ed. Unterkircher and Schmidt [q.v.]), which is not to be confused with Vienna Nationalbibliothek MS 2771–2772, a s.xv history Bible. Réau references are to *Iconographie de l'art chrétien* unless otherwise stated. References to 'Schmidt' are to Gerhard Schmidt.

a

1. S.ii Justin *PG* VI 710–11. Compare **k7** and **k5** for a similar causal relationship. Mary's multiple function may be implied in the ambiguous object behind her, suggesting not only the bed often shown (e.g., in the mid-s.xv Book of Hours, Oxford, Bodleian Library MS. E. D. Clarke 30, f. 23ᵛ), but also her still commoner throne, portico, or even the altar to which the Child sometimes descends. Its connotations are thus maternity, royalty, and sacrifice.

2. For *perdit* Cornell (1925) 17 gives *perdet*, but on 13 and 251 he cites Guibert's attribution of this, the only non-Leonine *titulus*, to s.xii Peter de Riga's 'Aurora', which has *perdit* (Petrus de Riga 41, lines 361–62). The s.xiv Viennese MS of the *BP* (Unterkircher and Schmidt) has *vipera vim patitur de inpatiente puella* ('the serpent suffers

violence from the self-discipline of a maiden'). These differences are discussed by Cornell (1925) 156; G. Schmidt 132, 142; and Soltész IX (who misunderstands the MS picture).

3. The Vienna MS, illustrating 'she is to crush your head' (*ipsa conteret capud tuum* quoted in **1**), shows not God but the Virgin, her foot resting on the head of the serpent wound round the tree. Association of the Virgin with the serpent-crusher may derive from or even give rise to error in the Vulgate, whose sources do not present this person as female: cf. *JB* 'I will make you enemies of each other: you and the woman, your offspring and her offspring. *It* will crush your head and you will strike its heel' (my italics). Either Jerome deliberately wrote *ipsa* (*CE* XVI 464e) because association of Eve with Mary was already strong, or *ipsa* is a scribal error—as is likely, since Jerome elsewhere quotes *ipse*. Often (e.g., *PL* L 914) *ipsa* is taken to refer to *humana natura*, but s.xi Fulbert of Chartres *PL* CXLI 320–21 implies that *ipsa* and not merely the 'woman' (*mulier*) is the Virgin; by s.xii Bernard *PL* CLXXXIII 63 this is explicit (his sermon also refers to matter in **1**, **2**, **3**, **4**, **5**, **11**).

4. S.xii Peter Comestor *PL* CXCVIII 1072: *erectus est ut homo*. The serpent is sometimes erect even in Early Christian art (Kirschbaum I 55 and see 57).

5. Mary and Gabriel are traditionally separated by an object such as a lily, corridor, column, or scroll (Schiller I 37–52, pls 66–121), suggesting their different worlds united at the moment of Incarnation. Here, division is made by scrolls. The design is very similar to that in a 1480 Dutch Book of Hours (Byvanck and Hoogewerff II pl. 78); all three designs are similar in the s.xv MS *Schwartze Gebetbuch* (Trenkler pl. 23).

6. The angel's words (and tree?) are not from the occasion of the fleece, but from Judges vi 11–12.

7. Gideon's fleece is linked with the Annunciation and the Psalm (**4**) in ★*PL* XXVI 1090, and with the Annunciation in s.xiii (Mâle *xiiiᵉ siècle* 151–52) and s.xiv art (Kirschbaum II 126). It is linked with the Nativity in art from s.ix (Schiller I 71).

8. As in n. 3 above, typology derives from (or contributes to) an error in the Vulgate, which has *vellus* ('fleece') for a Hebrew word meaning 'grass'. The verse is related both to the birth of Christ—as in the Feast of the Circumcision second antiphon of Lauds, and the Vigil of Epiphany Lauds (*Brev.* 171, 180)—and to his conception, as here (s.iv Ambrose *PL* XVI 734, ★XVII 634; s.xii Bernard *PL* CLXXXIII 64 links the verse with Gideon). *Dominus* ('The

Lord'), not in the Vulgate verse, is in the Response to *Lectio* vi on the third Sunday of Advent (*Brev.* 126).

9. R. T. Davies 155.

10. S.v Jerome *PL* XXII 886; to s.xii Peter de Riga *PL* CCXII 37 the fleece represents the Jews among gentiles.

11. S.xii Honorius of Autun *PL* CLXXII 904.

12. The image is common after 1300. Schiller I 45, pls 99, 102–04. A design typically similar overall is on the early s.xv Lüneburg Altar (Schiller II figs 21–22).

13. The verse is associated with Mary in Matt. i 22–23, also s.ii Justin *PG* VI 381.

14. Associated with Mary in the Office of the Virgin *Lectio* iii (*Brev.* cxiv), and with her virginity (*Brev.* 116, and by s.iv Ambrose *PL* XVI 335, s.ix Rabanus Maurus *PL* CXI 385, s.xii Honorius of Autun *PL* CLXXII 905). See Schiller I 716, and Mâle *xiiie siècle* 149 for its use in sculpture at Laon.

15. This obscure verse is related to the Incarnation by s.iv Athanasius *PG* XXVI 1276, s.v Jerome *PL* XXIV 880, s.xii Bernard *PL* CLXXXIV 109–10. Jeremias's Prophecy is over the Klosterneuburg Altar *Nativity* (Röhrig [1955] 62).

16. The pun is familiar enough to have found its way into the English medieval drama: 'here þis name Eva is turned Aue' (Block 104).

b

1. For a charming late example of the extremes to which defence of the doctrine (*NCE* XIV 692–96) may go, see Franciscus de Retza, who lists wonders in comparison with which the Virgin Birth is unsurprising. Mary's virginity in conceiving Jesus was recognised by s.ii, and in childbirth and thereafter by s.iv: Zeno of Verona *PL* XI 414–15 testifies to all three.

2. The reading of **12** is in doubt. If *maris* is from *mas* ('male'), the *titulus* has typical subtlety relevant to the perpetual virginity: Mary is unhurt either by sexual intercourse or by the birth of her son. *Maris* of a man is unusual: it is normally used of non-human males, as in *cerae opifex sine coitu maris et feminae procreatur* (s.xi Fulbert *PL* CXLI 319). If this sense is, however, correct, the blockbook may preserve an earlier tradition than the physically earlier Vienna MS, in which the difficult *maria maris* has then been corrupted to the familiar *stella maris* ('star of the sea'), one of Mary's ancient titles (cf. the hymn *Ave maris stella*; *Brev.* ciii). But *maria maris* might be a contraction of *maria stella maris*; there is precedent for associating this title with the Nativity: 'as a star emits light without harm to itself, so the Virgin gave birth to her son without damage to herself' (Bernard *PL* CLXXXIII 70). The 'sea' element is, however, irrelevant here. The identical *versus* appears in the scroll of a prophet beginning the text under the *Nativity* in the 'London Passional', BL, MS Add. 18162, f. 19^r.

3. S.iv Gregory of Nyssa *PG* XLIV 332, s.iv Chrysostom *PG* L 794–95, s.ix Rabanus Maurus *PL* CXI 513. In s.ix art Virgin and Child appear in the flames (Underwood [1957] 198, figs 29, 31, 33, 42, 43). Lauds in both the Office of the

Circumcision and of the Virgin (*Brev.* 171, cxiii) use the images of bush and fleece (see **a**) for the Virginity. The *titulus* (**8**) is from s.xii Peter de Riga (Petrus de Riga 94, lines 79–80).

4. S.xii Honorius of Autun, in an influential sermon on the Annunciation (*PL* CLXXII 904–5), uses the images of rod, falling stone, fleece, and closed door which appear in the first two pages of *BP*. Mâle *xiiie siècle* 148–53 shows the sermon's influence on s.xiii sculpture at Laon and Amiens.

5. Art links bush and Nativity implicitly from s.ix, explicitly from s.xiii—Schiller I 71 finds rod, fleece, shut gate, and bush as Types of Annunciation and Nativity from s.ix, common by s.xii. Heimann (1968) Pl. 40c shows a s.xii rod and fleece associated with both.

6. ★*PL* XXXIX 2197–98; Aaron's priesthood, foreshadowing Christ's, helped to bring difficult times to an end.

7. S.xii Bernard *PL* CLXXXIII 63–64.

8. S.iv Gregory of Nyssa *PG* XLIV 332 calls the figure in the bush Christ; its multiple 'personality' is discussed by s.iv/v Augustine *PL* XLII 812, 861. God in the bush is cross-nimbed in the *Bible Moralisée* too (Laborde I pl. 41); in other contexts the crossed nimbus does not necessarily indicate the second Person (F. E. Hulme 67; Wormald pls 4a, b, 5a): in **a5** and **a6**, a similar figure may be God the Father.

9. Play on the shoes is not as far-fetched as it may seem: for association of Mary's removed shoes with those of Moses see Cornell (1924) 38.

10. Joseph applies bellows to a fire in the early s.xv picture in Schiller II fig. 21, but in our picture the brazier's being in the foreground, even overlapping the bottom border, suggests its symbolic importance (cf. the crown at the front of **a5**).

11. Is. i 3: s.iii Origen *PG* XIII 1832, s.iv/v Augustine *PL* XXXVII 1675, s.iv Gregory of Nazianus *PG* XLVI 1142 relate them respectively to the pure and impure, Jews and gentiles, and those yoked to the law and burdened by idolatry. In each case both 'good' and 'evil' recognise Christ. In art from s.iv the animals are part of the scene (Schiller I 59–61, figs 143–206).

12. The Greek equivalent of this influential phrase occurs in two MSS of the Septuagint after the opening sentence of Habacuc iii 2, which forms Prophecy **10**. The Vulgate does not supply the image: *Domine, opus tuum in medio annorum vivifica illud; in medio annorum notum facies* 'O Lord, bring your work to life in our time. In our time thou shalt make it known'. The Latin equivalent of the Septuagint image does occur, however, e.g. in the Dominican Breviary Versicle in the Responsary of *Lectio* v of the Nativity (*Breviarium Sacri Ordinis Praedicatorum* 146: *in medio duorum animalium notum facies*), where it again follows Prophecy **10**; in the crucifixion context of the Mass of the Presanctified (Response after *Lectio* i) in the Dominican (but not the Roman) Missal, and in the s.xiii Dominican Graduale (Oxford, Blackfriars MS 1, 153). The image has been interpreted not only as a reference to the Nativity but also as Christ crucified between thieves (the sense in the Mass), as Christ between Old and New Testaments, between Moses and

Elias (see **m**), cherubim and seraphim, Father and Spirit, Jews and gentiles (★*PL* XLII 1124, linking Isaias and Habacuc, gives the first three).

13. S.iii Origen *PG* XII 632. *RDK* III 94 illustrates a s.xii MS of typology associating rod and Cross.

14. *RDK* III 242: the image may be influenced by Rom. xii 1 ff, in which Paul advises offering the body as 'a living sacrifice' in emulation of Christ; s.v John Chrysostom *PG* LXI 325–26 says the bush represents Christ unconsumed in death.

15. Schiller I 63, 70, 74–75: devotion to the sacrament, generally greater after the Lateran Council of 1215, resulted in increased association of Christ's birth and death, and the development of 'manger-altar' imagery, derived perhaps from s.vii/viii ★*PL* XXX 569.

16. S.xii Honorius of Autun (note 4): just as Nebuchodonosor's statue is crushed by the falling stone, all nations will submit to Christ. The stone is Christ as early as s.v Eucherius *PL* L 743. In a s.xii Chartres Cathedral sculpture, Daniel, beneath the Magi, holds the stone (Heimann [1968] Pl. 39a, where 91–92 give other examples of the story in art). Mâle *xiiie siècle* 150–51 discusses and illustrates the scene in sculpture at Laons and Amiens.

17. ★*PL* XXXIX 1984 relates it to the Incarnation.

18. Micheas actually denigrates Bethlehem as insignificant, but goes on: 'yet out of you shall come a prince to lead my people'. *BP* quotes Matthew's deliberate modification of Micheas, used to tell Herod where Christ would be born: Bethlehem is 'not insignificant'. The verse is used in the Chester play *Magi* as a prophecy of the Nativity (Lumiansky and Mills 169).

19. ★*PL* XLII 1124.

20. S.vii Bede *PL* XCI 1237–38.

21. Schiller I 51 (on s.xv Annunciations): 'utensils of daily life . . . hide their symbolism so successfully behind their commonplaceness that it is only their systematic recurrence which indicates that these objects are not there by chance'. A jug is similarly placed in the Lüneburg Altar 'Golden Panel' Nativity (Schiller II fig. 21).

c

1. **6** has little precedent in art outside MSS of *BP*, and received little patristic attention, suggesting that the designer chose it for just this design potential. The s.xv MS *Schwartze Gebetbuch* shows all three subjects (Trenkler pl. 31). (The *Concordantia Caritatis* shows the Magi prefigured by Sheba as in **7**, and by Solomon and Hiram [2 Paral. ii].)

2. *Lectio* ii of the third Sunday in Advent's fourth feria (*Brev.* 131) preserves the Greek sense 'man' instead of 'sceptre'. The verse is related to the Magi by s.ii Justin *PG* VI 723 and s.iii Origen *PG* XI 770–71, who has the charming theory that the Magi knew the prophecies of Balaam: Gregory of Nyssa *PG* XLIV 6 calls them descendents of Balaam. It is just possible that the phallic position of the sceptres has a traditional basis: the second part of **11** is the beginning of Is. xi 1, the well-known 'a stem

shall spring from the root of Jesse and a flower shall rise up out of his root' (cf. **b7**, *Aaron's Rod*). On this verse is based the familiar Jesse Tree in art, where from the sleeping Jesse rises an often phallic tree (as in the spectacular example in the s.xiv east window of St Mary's, Shrewsbury) in habited not only by the kings of his human ancestry ('and Jesse begot David the king. And David the King begot Solomon . . .'; Matt. i 6, see **6** and **7**) but by the prophets (see Watson [1934]).

3. In antiquity the rising of a star at birth presages a ruler, and in Roman art a star over an emperor indicates his divinity (Schiller I 96).

4. Compare **a5**, where the traditional division between Mary and Gabriel is broken by the cross-carrying Child, uniting heaven and earth. The 'throne' in **c5** may be the 'house' of Matt. ii 11, influenced by the stylised baldachin common in art (Schiller I 105).

5. It is often held by the Virgin as a symbol of her son's kingship (Schiller I 108); cf. **v7**. The basic *Magi* design is common; this particular design has MSS derivatives too (Henry [1983 ii] pl. XVII).

6. The number of Wise Men is implied only in their three gifts.

7. S.iv/v Augustine *PL* XXXIII 1026, where the shepherds represent the Jews.

8. Schiller I 96; perhaps the 'orb' Jesus touches is meant to resemble a typical medieval world map, its three sections signifying the continents (see Destombes pls Bb, Cab, Ea, G, I, X).

9. Tertullian *PL* II 658–59, also Jerome *PL* XXVI 1090, who relates this and the verse in **4** to the honouring of Christ. Epiphany has been celebrated since s.iii, and *Lectio* iii (first Response) in the Office for it cites the verse in **3** (*Brev.* 182). It is quoted in the Chester play *Magi* (Lumiansky and Mills 171). From s.x, psalters often illustrate this Psalm by the Magi. The *Concordantia Caritatis* relates it to them (*RDK* III 838). By s.x they appear in art crowned, from s.xii they are called 'The Three Kings', and from s.xiv the kneeling king removes his crown (Schiller I pls 96, 108, 245–98).

10. Abner may also represent subordination of physical to spiritual life (s.ix Angelom *PL* CXV 339).

11. Her story is also in 2 Paral. ix 1–12. She is equated by Ambrose *PL* XVI 124, s.vii Isidore *PL* LXXXIII 113, 417, s.viii Bede *PL* XCIII 446, s.ix Angelom *PL* CXV 464, s.xii Bernard *PL* CLXXXIII 879–80 with the shepherds; in art from s.xii she prefigures the Church. S.ix Rabanus Maurus *PL* CIX 472 unequivocally equates her with gentiles. She has also been seen as the soul's growing skill in prayer (s.xii Richard of St Victor *PL* CXCVI 181–82). Her association with the Magi, popularised by the *Speculum Humanae Salvationis*, appears in the earlier s.xiii 'Mary Portal' at Amiens (Medding pls 15, 66). Pächt and Jenni Abb. 107 shows a slightly similar design to this in *BP*, by the contemporary Master of the Vederwolken.

12. Matt. xii 42. The gifts she receives have been interpreted as the gifts of the Spirit (Wisdom, Understanding, Counsel, Fortitude, Knowledge, Piety, Fear of the Lord) and as eternal life (s.ix Rabanus Maurus *PL* CIX 473).

In the *Bible Moralisée* (Laborde I pl. 164) the gifts she gives are souls converted to the Church. Matthew may have named myrrh among the Wise Men's gifts to heighten their association with her (*NCE* IX 64): gold and frankincense are mentioned in the Psalm (**4**) as brought by 'those who come from Sheba', but spices are listed only among the gifts brought by the queen.

13. The Latin in **10** might be rendered 'flock to it' (the Temple on a mountain), or 'flock to him' (the Lord whose temple it is). Either way, the sense is that all kinds of people will crowd to Christ: s.v Jerome *PL* XXIV 44 suggests those of heaven, earth, and the underworld. S.vi Paterius *PL* LXXIX 942 suggests that the paradoxical *mons in vertice montem* is the miracle of the Incarnation; ⋆*PL* CXVI 729 says people will gather at the Incarnation which like the mountain 'pierces heaven'.

14. S.iv Jerome *PL* XXIV 595, ⋆*PL* CXVI 1038 respectively.

15. *Lectio* i, first Response in the Office for Epiphany (*Brev.* 182). The meanings occur from s.vi (Schiller I 96) and persist (⋆*PL* CLXXI 1388).

16. John xviii 36.

d

1. A s.xiii tympanum (Schiller I fig. 279) associates *Magi* and *Presentation*. Joseph may be seen behind Mary.

2. If *BP*'s *pro puero* means 'as a result of (her having borne) the boy', the reference to birds is accurate.

3. Mary's Purification merely underlines her independence of it, demonstrated in **b**'s emphasis on her perpetual virginity; see *The Golden Legend* (Jacobus III 20, 24).

4. The same three subjects perhaps appear (the two OT ones are unidentified) in the s.xv MS *Schwartze Gebetbuch* (Trenkler pl. 33). The designer could easily have used another actual event, such as the *Presentation of Isaac* (shown together with that of Samuel in the *Concordantia Caritatis RDK* III 1070). The hanging canopy is present also in the *Presentation* in the late s.xv glass in Exeter Cathedral, once part of the Costessey collection (Drake pl. XIII).

5. The design occurs from s.viii, often (though not here) with a hand of God issuing from heaven to signify acceptance of the 'sacrificed' child (Schiller I 92 and fig. 235). The design is closely related to one by the Master of the Vederwolken (see Introduction Fig. 19).

6. 1 Kings i 20–22.

7. The name Samuel means 'asked of God': Anna asked for her son's conception; Mary did not—she simply accepted it. The song Anna sang when she left her son (1 Kings ii 1–11, in spite of the reference in **2**) is a messianic hymn and a prototype of the *Magnificat* declaimed by Mary when her cousin Elizabeth recognised the unborn Christ (Luke i 39–56).

8. Conflation of priest and Simeon took place early, perhaps because it brought together two kinds of sacrifice, the offering of the child and the prophesied Passion (Shorr 24). The pro-

phecy was followed at once by Simeon's own death. The meeting with Jesus (the 'hypapante') was celebrated as a local feast in Jerusalem until s.xi, when it was accepted by the Greek Church: representations of it are thus rare before this date (Shorr 19).

9. To s.iv/v Augustine *PL* XXXIII 644 the sword represents the Passion, the hatred of the Jews, the weakness of the disciples; s.xii Bernard *PL* CLXXXIII 932–33 implies that it is the love of God. Shorr fig. 25 shows an early s.xiv fresco, resembling **5** in design, where a sword pierces the Virgin's heart. The image became popular in mystical meditation.

10. The handing over or receiving back of Jesus may be depicted. His gesture, indicating a special relationship with Simeon, appears in art from s.xi (Schiller I fig. 226). A late s.xiv relief in Doberan shows it in a *Presentation of Samuel* similar to the design of **5** (Schiller I fig. 23).

11. The feast was established in s.v. S.vii Bede *PL* XC 351 describes the Candlemas procession made with lit candles. Shorr shows clearly how the iconographical evolution and conflation of Presentation, Purification, Simeon, and Candlemas follow the chronological development of the festivals appropriate to them.

12. Matt. xi 10.

13. Both have been seen as references to Christ (s.v Jerome *PL* XXV 1384, 1434).

14. S.xi Fulbert *PL* CXLI 319 explains that at the joint Feast of Candlemas and Purification, candle-light represents Christ's divinity, and the wax 'his pure body'. Prophecies **3** and **4** resemble the Introit and Gradual for the Feast of the Purification: 'we have received thy mercy O God in the midst of the temple' (Ps. xlvii 10).

15. ⋆*PL* XXVI 895–96.

16. After 1 Cor. iii 17, vi 29, for example s.v. Jerome *PL* XXV 1305, s.iv/v Augustine *PL* XXXVI 135. Surprisingly I find no precedent for the association of **3** with the Presentation, but **4** is related to it directly by an anonymous s.xii writer in *PL* CCXIII 779 (a reference for which I am indebted to the Rev. A. H. B. Logan); it is also quoted in the Office for the Purification (*Brev.* 664) and appears in the scroll held by Malachi in A. Lorenzetti's *Presentation* of 1342 (Schiller I 93).

17. S.xii Rupert *PL* CLXVIII 684. Presentation and Crucifixion are equated in the *Bible Moralisée* (Laborde III pl. 481gh).

e

1. Only Matt. ii mentions the Return as well as the Flight. That the grouping of **e–h** is deliberate is suggested by the rarity of the Return in art (Schiller I 124).

2. Schiller I 118 and fig. 56, which is 'presumably not the earliest rendering'.

3. A very similar design is in a Dutch Bible illumination of the period (Hindman [1977] pl. 31c), and on the panel by the 1400 Cologne Master (Kirschbaum III 77); see also Henry (1983 ii) pls XVIII–XIX.

4. Molsdorf 35. The *Concordantia Caritatis* has **7** as a 'holy flight' not related to the Flight (Kirschbaum II 49). Even s.iv Ambrose, who does use

the events shown in **6** and **7** (*PL* XIV 608–9, 612), does not mention the Flight. This paucity of commentary may be connected with the absence of an early official Feast of the Flight (though *CE* I 799b refers to a local one at Beauvais in s.xiii). S.ix Rabanus Maurus *PL* CVII 762 does cite the Flight as an example of avoiding evil.

5. *PL* CVII 591, s.x Remigius *PL* CXXXI 105.

6. ⋆*PL* CLXXV 649.

7. For the frequency with which Jacob appears as Type see Viller VIII 13–15.

8. S.iv/v Augustine *PL* XXXVI 600.

9. In the s.viii/ix *Gospel of the Pseudo-Matthew*, Hennecke I 412–13; also ⋆*PL* CXVI 808 (which explains that Egypt represents the world in the darkness of paganism before the coming of Christ), s.xii Peter Comestor *PL* CXCVIII 1543.

10. S.iv Ambrose *PL* XIV 612 relates it to Christ's retreat to the desert, not to the Flight.

11. S.v Theodoratus *PG* LXXX 1267 and s.xii Euthymius Zigaberus *PG* CXXVIII 573–74, though neither refers specifically to **7**.

12. Perhaps it is not surprising that no precedent is found for the use of Jer. xii 7 (**10**) in this context: it is actually Yahweh's sorrowful admission that he has had to submit his 'house and home' to punishment by their enemies, not that he has had to surrender them (Lapide VI 713).

f

1. *CE* I 615.

2. They appear in s.ix art: Underwood (1967) I 97. The tradition was developed in French medieval drama: see Whittredge 45, 118–19; Schlosser (1892) 327 Nr. 931 quotes the *titulus* of a lost pictorial cycle: *Partibus Aegypti diffetur passio Christi, / Quem simulacra tremunt et cara habitacula linquunt. / Praecipit Herodes natos cruciare recentes, / Milia lactantum tendunt laetantia caelum.* Two idols fall, as here, in the earliest extant s.xii relief representation (Réau II/ii 281; Schiller I fig. 320), and on the s.xiii one at Amiens (Schiller I fig. 319); in s.xiv Karije Djami mosaics many idols fall from city walls (Underwood [1967] II 182–83). A miniature in the Hague Bible shows Flight and Idols conflated: the former very like *BP*'s (Hindman [1977] 55, fig. 21).

3. *Gospel of the Pseudo-Matthew*, Hennecke I 413.

4. But the Fall of the Idols is in s.v Jerome *PL* XXIV 202, and s.xii Peter Comestor *Historia Scholastica PL* CXCVIII 1543.

5. S.xv Denis of Chartreux gives a rare example which may, however, derive from *BP*: 'As Dagon fell before the Holy Ark, so the idols of Egypt fell in the presence of Jesus'; he also relates the Idols to Is. xix 1 (Dionysius f. vii^v). Both Types are in the *Concordantia Caritatis*.

6. S.viii Bede *PL* XCIII 432.

7. ⋆*PL* LXXIX 173–74, s.vii Isidore *PL* LXXXIII 395, s.ix Claudius of Turin *PL* CIV 651, s.ix Angelom *PL* CXV 283, s.ix Rabanus Maurus *PL* CIX 27–28.

8. Because the back is shown in flight.

9. Moses is shown horned after his descent from

the mountain (not while on it): in fact not until he had spoken a third time to God and received the Commandments again (Exod. xxxiv 29) did his face appear radiant (*cornuta*, commonly translated 'horned' instead of 'emitting rays of light'; see Mellinkoff). The same anachronistic use of horns is found in the s.xiii *Psautier de Saint Louis* f. 35^v.

10. The calf is equated with the Devil by s.viii Bede *PL* XCIII 377, s.xi Damian *PL* CXLV 1026–27, s.xii Rupert *PL* CLXVII 727, and the s.xiii Oxford *Bible Moralisée* (Laborde I pl. 55cd). On a s.xiii capital at Vézelay, the Tablets (as in the *Bible Moralisée*) are broken over the calf, from whose shattered body a devil emerges (Porter II pl. 39).

11. *Bible Moralisée* (Laborde I pl. 55gh).

12. Kirschbaum II 478–79; Schiller II 128.

13. *Gospel of the Pseudo-Matthew* (Hennecke I 412–13) and s.xii Peter Comestor *PL* CXCVIII 1543, whose *Cumque ingrederetur Dominus in Aegyptum, corruerunt idola Aegypti* is not unlike **1**. The story also occurs in the Arabian *Gospel of the Infancy*, summarised in James (1966) 80. Earlier interpretations of Is. xix 1 (e.g., s.v Jerome *PL* XXIV 181) do not mention the apocryphal story.

14. Commentators indicate, however, that the idols referred to signify not merely carved images but doctrinal error: on Nahum (**4**) Jerome *PL* XXV 1242, ⋆*PL* CXVII 172; on Zacharias (**10**) Jerome *PL* XXV 1517–18, ⋆*PL* CXVII 267; on Sophonias (**11**) ⋆*PL* CXVII 204.

Possibly *in miserias*, emended in *lectio* **2**, should be retained, and *et simulacra* added: the Vienna MS has *quando arca domini, id est Christus, in Egyptum huius miseriae venit, tunc omnia ydola, id est errores infidelitatis corruerunt.*

g

1. Feasts of the Holy Innocents appear in the early s.v, when the subject also appears in art, becoming common by s.xii (Schiller I 114). Its composition, as opposed to its components, follows no strong scheme (Kirschbaum II 509).

2. ⋆*PL* XXXIX 2150. The 144,000 Blessed of Rev. xiv 3–4 'redeemed from amongst men to be the first fruits for God' were often interpreted as the Innocents.

3. He resembles one in the 1410 Buxtehude Altar (Schiller I pl. 65, 2nd panel, bottom register).

4. The prophecy is Matt. ii 18 recalling Jeremias. Rachel lamented the massacre or deportation of her people by the Assyrians, and was thought to have been buried near Bethlehem (Gen. xxxv 19); see s.v Jerome *PL* XXVI 28.

5. The Psalmist's cry for vengeance (**3**) is in fact not directly from the Vulgate, but from the modified version which forms the tract for the Mass of the Holy Innocents: this implies their sainthood, a prayer being virtually addressed to them. Herod's spurious authority, as a pawn of the Romans lacking Jewish ancestry (as in the Chester play of the *Magi* [Lumiansky and Mills 169]), is doubtless meant by **11**. S.v Jerome *PL* XXV 883 relates it to Saul (though not to the Nobe episode). Regarding **4** as a Prophecy of the Massacre appears to be original, though the

lion has been seen as the tyrant opposing the Church (s.viii Bede *PL* XCI 1020).

6. The murdered priests are compared by Rabanus Maurus *PL* CIX 59 to the suffering Christ. I have found no source apart from *BP* for the assertion (Lapide II 349a, whose sources are patristic, not pictorial) that Saul in this episode is a Type of Herod at the Massacre, not even in the commentaries on 1 Kings ii 20–35, itself a prophecy of 1 Kings xxii 11–18.

7. I find no patristic precedent for Athalia (whose story is also in 2 Chron. xxii 10–12, xxiii 12–15) as Type of Herod: in s.ix she is simply equated with the Synagogue persecuting Christ, whom the dead children foreshadow— suggesting his Passion, not his escape from Herod (s.ix Angelom *PL* CXV 511, Rabanus Maurus *PL* CXI 61). Not until s.xiv did the scene become typological in art (Cornell [1925] 260). In the Chester plays, Herod remarks that no slaughter like the one he plans will have been seen since Athalia reigned (Lumiansky and Mills 171), but this may derive from *BP*.

8. In contrast, for example, to more naturalistic treatments in which the child is concealed (Kirschbaum I 194).

9. S.v Chrysostom *PG* LVII 177–78.

h

1. Kirschbaum II 370–83, I 488; like *BP*, the *Concordantia Caritatis* has Jacob's return as one Type, but instead of David's has Abraham's return from Egypt. The David scene is common in contemporary miniatures; see Delaissé (1968) figs 108, 111.

2. Gen. xxxi 11–13.

3. Gen. xxxi 30.

4. Gen. xxxii 8.

5. Matt. ii 22–23.

6. The s.ix Rabanus Maurus *PL* CVII 761 and 762 observes that the Return, unlike the Flight, was made in daylight, signifying the return of the 'true light' to his people; the apocryphal Arabian *Gospel of the Infancy*, which develops the story of the Return as well as of the Flight, emphasises the Child's new power, revealed in many miracles of healing (Tischendorf 193–209).

7. *In salutari tuo* means both 'on your deliverance' ('when you are freed') and, according to the Fathers, 'in the shape of him who brings your salvation': they explain the phrase by *hoc est, in Filio tuo, quando venerit* (⋆*PL* XXVI 1209, s.xii Bruno *PL* CLXIV 1105, s.xii Oddo *PL* CLXV 1284) and by *hoc est in Christo tuo* (s.vi Cassiodorus *PL* LXX 756, who explains that *in salutari* refers to Christ, as in Simeon's words at the Presentation: *viderunt oculi mei Salutari tuum* ['my eyes have seen your Salvation']). Translation of **3** cannot convey the double meaning.

8. The third Sunday (*Brev.* 125).

9. Compare verse **7** of the Psalm which is quoted in **3**: 'our ancestors in Egypt never grasped the meaning of your marvels': there is perhaps an implicit link between **3** and **4**.

10. S.v Jerome *PL* XXV 1426: see **p** commentary.

i

1. Baptism might be by submersion, immersion, or aspersion. By the early s.xiv the pouring of water had replaced immersion, so it is hard to be certain whether this flagon is for water or oil. In Pisano's s.xiv south doors (Schiller I fig. 381) and Ghiberti's early s.xv north doors to the Florence Baptistry (Krautheimer pl. 22), John probably pours water; in *BP* oil may be implied because then three elements in the sacramental 'form' are present: water, oil, and the laying on of hands—the Baptist's left hand perhaps being laid on Jesus's arm. Christ's Baptism appears in art from s.ii, and until s.xii the Baptist usually lays his hand on Jesus's head (Schiller I figs 349–82), less often on his chest (Schiller I fig. 370) or arm (Schiller I fig. 376).

2. Acts x 38.

3. Mark xvi 1.

4. Matt. iii 11.

5. Baptism removes the guilt but not the effects of the sin committed by Adam, which we inherit with our bodies; in adults, it also remits sins already committed. Not being subject to original or individual sin, Christ had no need of Baptism: he underwent it in humility (s.iv Hilary *PL* IX 795–96), so that the Spirit would show himself, and to fulfil the Baptist's work (ibid. 795; Matt. iii 15, Luke vii 30). See Cornell (1925) 14 for the origin of **12**.

6. The angel performs this duty in scenes from s.v (Kirschbaum IV 251–52, figs 1–4). Similar designs are found in the work of the 1400 Cologne Master (Kirschbaum III 77), and in the *Hours of Turin* (Loo pl. 1); see also Henry (1983 ii) pl. XXI.

7. Matt. iii 16; 'he illumined those same waters with his light' says s.v Epiphanius *PG* XLII 879, as do apocryphal legends (*JB* NT 19 note k). Schiller I 128 cites an early baptismal liturgy suggesting both light and angel: 'You heavenly hosts draw near from Bethlehem . . . to the waters of Jordan'.

8. S.iii Origen *PG* xiii 1871, s.v Jerome *PL* XXVI 31, s.iv Chromatius *PL* XX 330, and s.ix Rabanus Maurus *PL* CVII 775.

9. Luke xii 50.

10. John iii 4–7.

11. S.iv Hilary *PL* IX 927.

12. John vii 37–38 explained by s.v Jerome *PL* XXIV 152–53. *★PL* CXVI 784 sees it as a reference to the gifts of the Spirit received at baptism.

13. I translate *fontibus* as 'from the springs' to clarify the baptismal connotations (*JB* OT 849 note p). S.iv/v Augustine *PL* XXXVI 834 relates the verse to Christ as life-source and to John iv 13–14; more commonly it is allegorised simply, the 'churches' being the Church, the 'springs of Israel' being doctrines spread by the Apostles (s.vi Cassiodorus *PL* LXX 471–72, *★PL* CXVI 419, s.xi Bruno *PL* CXLII 254, s.xii Gerhoh *PL* CXCIV 208).

14. S.v Jerome *PL* XXV 342–43, 1517.

15. The use of the Red Sea as a Type is derived from 1 Cor. x 2, where it is described as a baptism for Moses. Lundberg 116–45 gives its history as baptismal Type. The Klosterneuburg Altar has *Unda rubens mundam baptismi misticat undam* ('The reddish water mystically denotes the pure water of baptism') (Röhrig [1955] 14): the concept is explained and the Red Sea is related to Christ's Baptism directly by s.iv/v Augustine *PL* XXXVIII 1064, *★XXXIX* 1955; they are also related directly on the s.xiii Hildesheim font. Interestingly, the verse of **4** is related to the Red Sea in *★PL* XXVI 1079–80.

After *populum suum* in **1**, a passage in the Vienna MS is absent here, whether by eyeskip or intent.

16. So in the *Bible Moralisée* (Laborde I pl. 48). The failure of his horse is explained by s.v Jerome *PL* XXV 1493: *fallax equus ad salutem* (Ps. 32.17).

17. On the Klosterneuburg Altar it is one Type of the Crucifixion (Röhrig [1955] pl. 28): *Vecte Crucis lignum botro Christi lege signum*. S.vii Isidore *PL* LXXXIII 346 and s.xii Peter de Riga *PL* CCXII 36, echoed in Canterbury Cathedral's s.xiii glass (Fig. 8 above), explain also that the leading figure is the spiritually blind who cannot see Christ, turning their back on him, and the second figure is those with Christ in front of them, as in Matt. xvi 24: 'If anyone wants to come after me let him take up his cross and follow'. In a historiated capital in the *Hours of Turin* it echoes the Carrying of the Cross (Châtelet pl. XVIII). To s.iv/v Augustine *PL* XXXIX 1800 the grapes also represent Christ supported by Old and New Testaments. Another tradition identifies the first figure with Josue (explained as 'saviour'), the second with Caleb ('dog-heart, faithful'): see s.xii Rupert *PL* CLXVII 876. The Bible does not attribute the grape-bearing to them.

18. Schiller I 129–30: see particularly the Hildesheim font, the Klosterneuburg Altar (Röhrig [1955] 14, which is not Josue and Caleb, *pace* Kirschbaum II 701), and the *Speculum Humanae Salvationis* (James and Berenson, Ch. XII; Lutz and Perdrizet II pl. 24; Henry, *The Miroure* 88–89). Lundberg 147 cites Origen's explanation of how the crossing, like the Passion, 'makes a path for us through the waters of death'. The *BP* design is found in Krakow, Muzeum Narodowe, MS 3091, f. 70ʳ: Henry (1983 ii) pl. XXII.

19. See the powerful compositions in which the hand of God, the descending dove, and Christ are on the vertical axis of the design (Schiller I figs 364–68): the Piero della Francesca *Baptism* in the National Gallery is a late echo of this concept.

k

1. The sequence of events suggests that in addition to baptism, the private disciplines are necessary to the soul: see s.iv Ambrose *PL* XV 1697.

2. The *Temptation* is comparatively rare in art, appearing only in s.ix. By the late Middle Ages it was common for gluttony to form the main scene, the others appearing in the background (Schiller I 143–45, pls 389–404); the *BP* designer uses this 'shorthand'.

3. This loss may be indicated by the dry streambed at the foot of the tree: the Tree of Knowledge was early conflated with the Tree of Life, from which flowed the waters of life (see Ameisenowa). The 'device' may be the apple or Satan's disguise. The Vienna MS has in **2**: *quia ea diabolus utebatur tamquam instrumento ad decipiendum primos parentes*. Note the rare reference of **1** to **7** instead of **5**. The *BP* design is echoed in Krakow, Muzeum Narodowe MS 3091, f. 90ʳ (Henry [1983 ii] pl. XXII).

4. The origins of the image are rabbinic (Woolf [1972] 115). S.xii Peter Comestor *PL* CXCVIII 1072 attributes it to Bede in an untraced reference (see Bonnell) also made by Vincent of Beauvais (Vincent f. 388ʳ). Comestor's *Historia Scholastica* had considerable iconographical influence: part of the university curriculum, by late s.xiii it was known throughout Europe in the vernacular (Smalley 178–80). The influential *Bible Moralisée* has an early example of the serpent with Eve's own face and posture—it has arms too (Laborde I 7).

5. For the snake as phallic symbol see *NCE* XIII 123. Adam and Eve's nakedness is concealed before the Fall in a s.ix Bible illustration and on the s.xii Klosterneuburg Altar (Röhrig [1955] 29).

6. *★PL* XVII 682–83, where both Types are related to the Temptation.

7. S.iv Hilary *PL* IX 929–30, s.iv Ambrose *PL* XV 1697, *★PL* XXX 541–42. All three Temptations are related to the Fall in the *Bible Moralisée*. The second clause in **12** is effectively ambiguous: the Devil meant to overcome Christ, but God allowed the Temptation, to overcome him (*JB* NT 19 note 4b).

8. Related to temptation rather than the Temptation, the 'enemies' of **11** are predictably the Devil (s.xii Bruno *PL* CLXIV 608, Rupert *PL* CLXVIII 1033); **10** is not in the Vienna MS, which has *Percussit te inimicus tuus idcirco*.

9. The Psalm verse (**3**), for example, is usually associated not with the Temptation but with the testing and mocking of Christ by the Jews (Matt. xxii 36, Luke xxii 66, John xix 3; see *★PL* XXVI 982–83, s.vi Cassiodorus *PL* LXX 247, *★PL* XCIII 663, *★PL* CXXXI 323, s.xii Bruno *PL* CLII 779, *★PL* CXCIII 1340). The reading *David 34*, with arabic numerals (not found elsewhere in the Prophecies) may be an indication that this is not the first edition cut.

10. Rom. ix 20–21. S.xii Herveus *PL* CLXXXI 279 explains the image in Isaias (**4**) as a comment on the Jews' ill-treatment of Christ, relating it to Is. lxiv 5–6. For the classical origins of the Creator as potter see Curtius 544.

11. S.ix Rabanus Maurus *PL* CVII 583–84 relates the Esau story to loss of the Beatific Vision of God (and to the Fall and Christ's Temptation), and s.ix Angelom *PL* CXV 208 relates the gluttony of Esau to the Fall.

1

1. Three of the eight resurrections recorded in the Bible (*NCE* IV 673) appear on **l**.

2. S.iv/v Augustine *PL* XXXVII 1306, XXXVIII 433.

3. S.v Peter Chrysologus *PL* LII 386.

4. *PL* LII 381–82.

5. John xi 39; the gesture is current in art from late s.vi.

6. Perhaps Martha or Mary. It is unlikely that the latter is the woman who cried over Christ's feet (Luke vii 37–38) in spite of John xi 2 (*JB* NT 105 note h, 171 note a); only tradition identifies her with the Magdalene of Luke viii 2. The design is echoed in at least two Utrecht manuscripts (Henry [1983 ii] pl. XXIII).

7. John xi 46–54.

8. Oddly, not linked by commentators to Lazarus or Christ's Resurrection. S.vi/vii Paterius *PL* LXXIX 782–83, s.ix Rabanus Maurus *PL* CVIII 982, s.xii Rupert *PL* CLXVII 979 regard it as a comment on the purifying effect of suffering; ★*PL* XVII 659 sees a reference to God's destruction of sin by baptism.

9. S.iv/v Augustine *PL* XLI 529 for **11** (which, like **10**, is not in the Vienna MS); for **4** ★*PL* XXVI 957, ★*PL* XXI 747 followed by s.xi Bruno Bishop of Würzburg *PL* CXLII 130 (it is explained in terms of the soul's salvation from evil and concupiscence by s.iv/v Augustine *PL* XXXVI 223, and s.vi Cassiodorus *PL* LXX 203 sees a reference to Christ's return to heaven).

10. S.iv/v Augustine *PL* XLI 529.

11. Respectively, s.iv Ambrose *PL* XIV 846 (but this association is rare), Augustine *PL* XLI 529 and Bruno *PL* CXLII 130. The Psalm in **4** resists certain identification, so its interpretation is naturally in doubt. The Vulgate has *Domine eduxisti ab inferno animam meam*. On at least one occasion it is found as *Domine revocasti ab inferis amimam meam* (★*PL* XXVI 957): this is not only close, it might easily be misread to give the *BP* version. Other possible origins are Ps. 32.19 (Didron) *eruat a morte animas eorum*; Ps. 48.16 *Deus redimet animam de manu inferi*; Ps. 85.13 *eruisti animam meam ex inferno inferiori*.

12. Perhaps deliberately so: Elias's disciple Eliseus imitated him. It is interesting that the equivalent of **6** in the s.xiv Vienna MS of *BP* confuses the two stories, Elias healing the Sunamite instead of the Sarephtan, *in suum cubiculum* (see n. 13): a confusion present, according to Schmidt 5, in all the MSS. Elias is a major Type of Christ, appearing in *BP* at **l**, **·b·**, **·d·**, **·o·**, **·p·**.

13. There is no mention of a mountain in the Vulgate account of Elias's miracle (though Eliseus, in the parallel story, is fetched *from* Mount Carmel). Did the author misread *Tulitque eum de sinu eius et portavit in coenaculum*? If his Vulgate had for the last two words *in cenaculum* ('in the room'), it might have been misread as *in collaculum* ('on the little hill'), paraphrased as *super montem* (**2**). But this assumes that *BP* preserves a better reading than the MSS. Deissmann and Wegener 46–47 suggest that *BP*'s *super montem* is a misreading of a MS *sunamitis*; Koch (1959) suggests *super montem* was an attempt both to correct *sunamitis* and to refer to Mount Carmel, Elias being the 'founder' of the Carmelite order supposedly responsible for *BP*. The design of **6** may, however, be derivative: in the *Bible Moralisée* (Laborde I pl. 168) the child is also on the ground. *BP*'s design is echoed in Krakow, Muzeum Narodowe MS 3091, f. 147ʳ (Henry [1983 ii] pl. XXIV).

14. S.iv/v Augustine *PL* XL 145, s.xii Rupert *PL* CLXVII 1242. The Sunamite is related to it in ★*PL* LI 804–5. The s.xiv *Concordantia Caritatis*

relates it to Lazarus, the *Bible Moralisée* (Laborde I pl. 168) to Christ on the Cross.

15. S.iv Jerome *PL* XXV 1118.

16. For example in s.xiii art such as Bourges stained glass (Künstle I pl. 28).

17. The s.xi *Glossa PL* CXIII 613.

18. His breaths are the gifts of the Spirit: s.vii Isidore *PL* LXXXIII 420.

19. The identical design, perhaps derived from *BP*, is found in a Flemish panel now in the south window of the Exeter Cathedral Lady Chapel (Fig. 21). The allegory explains the detailed presentation of furniture in the pictures.

20. S.ix Claudius *PL* CIV 774–75.

21. Claudius *PL* CIV 774–75; s.ix Rabanus Maurus *PL* CXI 67, s.xii Peter de Riga *PL* CCXII 39. Augustine equates Moses's and Eliseus's rods in this respect: *PL* XXXIX 1830. Moses is not identified by his rod in **n7**, but carries it as identification in **·e·7** as well as in **·f·7**, where his striking of the rock requires it. Unfortunately he does not appear as a quoted prophet elsewhere in *BP*, so we have no norm by which to judge.

22. The tomb shown is in the European tradition commonly followed in Western art (Réau II/ii 386).

m

1. For the doctrine see *NCE* XIV 295.

2. The explanation quoted in **1** and **8**, *tres vidit et unum adoravit* (the idea is in s.iv Hilary *PL* X 115, the words themselves in s.iv Ambrose *PL* XVI 774 and s.iv/v Augustine *PL* XLII 809), is in *Lectio* ii for Quinquagesima Sunday (*Brev.* 246), and is written on the scroll held by the angels in the scene on the Klosterneuburg Altar (Röhrig [1955] 2, where, however, it prefigures the Annunciation). In Byzantine art, these three angels were the usual way of depicting the Trinity from at least s.x (see Heimann Nov. 1934 19).

3. S.iv Zeno *PL* XI 524–25, who says they are in the 'unity of faith' (cf. **2**).

4. The fourth figure, however, is usually interpreted as Christ (s.iii Tertullian *PL* II 409) sent to release souls from limbo (s.v Jerome *PL* XXV 511–12). Lauds for Whit Sunday (*Brev.* 340) refers to the risen Christ who saved the three in the furnace. S.iii Hippolytus *PG* X 679 explains that the fourth figure is unnamed because Christ is not yet incarnate. It appears in a s.xv icon illustrated in *The Connoisseur*, 199, No. 800 (London 1978), xiii, and in the Heidelberg MS *BP* (Berve).

5. Neither Type has precedent for its relation to the Transfiguration except for a s.ix relief perhaps equating Abraham's vision with it (Schiller I 150); the contemporary London, BL, MS Add. 38122, f. 33ᵛ shows Abraham's vision, related by the text to the Transfiguration. The *Concordantia Caritatis* does however equate his vision with a 'Majesty of God'.

6. ★*PL* XCII 81, which also (following s.iv Jerome *PL* XXV 1576) explains Moses and Elias as the law and the prophets fulfilled in Christ, a concept expanded by s.ix Paschasius Radbertus *PL* CXX 584. The Office for the

sixth feria before Quinquagesima Sunday *Lectio* I (*Brev.* 262) is Augustine's account of the same idea, explaining that the prophets accompany Christ because like him they fasted for forty days. (On the next day (*Brev.* 264) the homily explains that the Transfiguration took place to display the Divinity to the disciples.) The usual explanation for their presence is that both were remarkable for having spoken familiarly to God while alive (3 Kings xix, Exod. xxiv–xxxiv), as they did at the Transfiguration (Viller IV/i 566–67). The Transfiguration as an epiphany of the Trinity is found in Jacobus de Voragine I 125: 'when Jesu Christ was baptised, and also when he was clarified, the mystery of the Trinity was showed'; this interpretation persists until s.xiv Gregory Palamas *PG* CLI 426. Pfaff 16 and n. mentions the association, in some rites of the liturgy, of the feasts of the Transfiguration and Trinity: 'The connection between the two . . . is more likely because of the Trinitarian implications of the Gospel story, the verse from the cloud suggesting a parallel to the voice and accompanying dove at the baptism of Christ.'

7. Schiller I 147, figs 405–21; Kitzinger pl. 23. The Trinity was from s.x often depicted as three identical human persons (Heimann Nov. 1934). The design is echoed in two Utrecht MSS, though in Krakow, Muzeum Narodowe, MS 3091, f. 109ᵛ, the figures of Moses and Elias alone appear to be so derived (Henry [1983 ii] pl. XXV).

8. Druthmarus *PL* CVI 1402, Paschasius Radbertus *PL* CXX 584. There is no suggestion that Peter thought the figures he saw were the Trinity: Paschasius accuses him of offensively equating the Lord (Jesus) with the servants (Moses and Elias) by suggesting that they be given similar accommodation. A tendency to regard each group of three (the vision, and its three beholders) as a unity may be seen not only in the disciples' representing the three continents of the world founded by Noah's sons (s.iv Hilary *PL* IX 1014), but also, more relevantly, by the regarding of them as the elect saved and unified by faith in the Trinity (s.ix Rabanus Maurus *PL* CVII 997).

9. Matt. xvii 11–13.

10. S.xii Anselm *PL* CLXII 1400 relates the appearance of Moses and Elias to baptismal resurrection and the shining of the blessed after the general resurrection. The light preoccupied commentators (Schiller I 146–47).

11. In the Greek, the verse from Habacuc is preceded by one meaning 'You will make yourself known between two living creatures', which s.iv/v Augustine *PL* XLI 588 explains as *inter alia* Christ's revelation of his divinity between Moses and Elias—presumably at the Transfiguration. The 'horns' on Christ's hands are the nails of the crucifixion (*PL* XLI 589), the literal sense being 'rays of light'.

12. S.v Jerome *PL* XXV 1574–76 implicitly relates the image to the Transfiguration, the latter is itself a Type of the Ascension and Judgement (Schiller I 150–51).

n

1. For similar conflations in art see Schiller I 157–58, II 16–18; Kirschbaum III 134 treats both scenes together, so difficult is it to distinguish between them.

2. The Bethany occasion is similarly between the *Raising of Lazarus* and the *Entry into Jerusalem* in s.ix and s.xii MS illuminations (Schiller II figs 25, 28) and begins a Passion sequence in a s.xiv Duccio fresco (Schiller II 17).

3. Matt. xxvi 6–13, Mark xiv 3–9, John xi 2, xii 1–8. In Matthew and Mark she anoints his head, in John his feet, wiping them with her hair. The washing of feet signifies humility.

4. Luke vii 37–50. The reading of **3** is in doubt: it should perhaps be *omnes iniquitates non recordabuntur* ('all the sins shall not be recorded'), the verb deriving from Late Latin *recordo*; it might be emended to the Vulgate *recordabor* ('I shall not record'). Its application appears to be original—but the first clause is not Ez. xviii: it may recall xxxiii 12, related to David and Nathan by s.ix Angelom *PL* CXV 364.

5. From s.iv/v. Mary Magdalene was freed of seven devils (Luke viii 1–3); notes in *JB* to Matt. xxvi 6, Luke vii 37, John xi 2 point out that the sinner here is 'most probably not Mary of Magdala . . . still less Mary, sister of Martha'.

6. Bethany scenes are often distinguishable by the presence of nimbed disciples. Neither of the hatted figures is a disciple—not even Judas, the one who complains in John xii 4–6: in *BP* he is always hatless (**q5, r5, s5, ·a·5**). The design of this scene on the s.xiii Hildesheim font-cover is basically similar to that in *BP* (Schiller I fig. 448, see also 450), and there is a close relationship between the *BP* scene and that by the Master of the Vederwolken (Henry [1983 ii] pl. XXVI).

7. *JB* reverses the usual interpretation, suggesting that her love results from the forgiveness of her sins.

8. The Types have little precedent in art or literature for their relation to **5**, though David before Nathan (not in penance) is equated with a similarly conflated scene resembling **5** in the *Speculum Humanae Salvationis* (James and Berenson chap. xiv; Lutz and Perdrizet pl. 28; Henry, *The Mirour* 96). Moses's sister usually represents Synagogue resenting Christ's embracing of the gentiles (s.vii Isidore *PL* LXXXIII 109).

9. The image derives ultimately from Gen. xxviii 12, Jacob's ladder (itself a Type of Christ with the souls of the blessed in **·t·**), and more immediately from the *Rule of St Benedict* (*PL* LXVI 378–410). It is common in literature: for example, s.xiv Deguileville's *Pèlerinage de la vie humaine* (Guillaume, lines 125–42), where Benedict himself supervises the ascent of the souls of his religious up twelve rungs to the celestial city, s.xii Bernard's *De Gradibus Humilitatis PL* CLXXXII 941–58 (which differs in details from the Benedictine series it claims as source) and Raoul de Houdenc's *Le Songe de Paradis*, where the ascent to paradise is by eight rungs (Scheler 222–27). Bernard's Twelve Steps of Pride are in *PL* CLXXXII 957–72.

10. S.ix Rabanus Maurus *PL* CVIII 664, 666

suggests that Moses's intercession for Mary was particularly powerful because of his special relationship with God, evident in the Transfiguration. This may be a link with **·m·**. Moses's wife was a Cushite: Mary probably resented a foreigner's authority over herself and Aaron (*CC* 250). In the *titulus* (**9**), *reacta* as if from *reacto* is Late Latin; the pp. active is unorthodox, so perhaps should be emended (? *peracta*, as in the Vienna MS).

11. The centrality of both suggests their symbolic function; their literal function is more obscure. The Bible does not say where David did penance. The design may be meant to suggest a cellar, in which case the figures in the background, whose feet appear to reach down behind an enclosure, are in fact 'demi-figures', not used elsewhere in *BP* but common enough in the period, for example, in the Master of the Vederwolken's design for a Passion scene (not otherwise similar), in Vienna, Nationalbibliothek MS 2772, f. 65ʳ (Pächt and Jenni Abb. 216).

12. There is similar use of 'barriers crossed' in **a, c, k**.

13. S.v Arnobius *PL* LIII 396.

14. The fulfilment is explained by s.ix Rabanus Maurus *PL* CIX 81, Angelom *PL* CXV 357, s.xi Peter Damian *PL* CXLV 1100, s.xii Rupert *PL* CLXVII 1129, 1131.

15. *ST* 1a2ae.89, 6.

o

1. David is a common Type of Christ, but this scene as Type of Christ's Entry into Jerusalem has no precedent outside MSS of *BP*. It is explained as the Resurrection and Ascension after the conquest of death (s.viii Bede *PL* XCI 629, s.xii Rupert *PL* CLXVII 1102–3) or as the Jews hearing Christ preach (s.ix Rabanus Maurus *PL* CIX 54). The design is echoed in at least two contemporary MSS (Henry [1983 ii] pl. XXIX).

2. David's killing of Goliath has long been equated with Christ conquering evil (s.iv Hilary *PL* IX 844, s.iv/v Augustine *PL* XXXVI 302, s.ix Rabanus Maurus *PL* CXI 53, among many), but the beheading itself (**·h·6**) is referred to, rather than this scene. For two uses of this design—one in a MS ostensibly earlier than *BP*—see Henry (1983 ii) pl. XXIX.

3. Commentators ignore Eliseus's being greeted, though his other experiences are fully allegorised (see **·c·7, ·o·7**). The subject is rare in art, but is under the *Entry into Jerusalem* in the *Milan Hours* (Loo pl. X).

4. The spreading of garments acknowledged a king; the traditional design follows the pattern of a Roman triumphal entry. In s.iv art, when the Entry into Jerusalem is already celebrated as a local Jerusalem feast (reaching the West in s.vii), it is a Type of Christ's own triumph over death (as in the liturgy for Palm Sunday). For a sarcophagus design basically similar to that in *BP* see Schiller II fig. 31 and the s.vi chair in Cecchelli Part i pl. XXXIII; the design is remarkably constant (Loo pl. X).

5. Matt. xxi 4–5, John xii 14–15; on the Klosterneuburg Altar Christ holds a scroll bearing the opening words of **10**.

6. Christ rode 'an ass and a colt, the foal of an ass'. The sense is that his mount came from a long line of patient animals—humility was in its blood (Knox).

7. Luke xix 1–10.

8. Matt. xxi 8 mentions onlookers at the Entry into Jerusalem who cut boughs, and the Entry into Jericho is distinguished by Christ's being on foot. But in simple design where each element carries more than literal meaning, conflation of the two occasions is natural (Pächt and Jenni 69): see the Master of the Vederwolken's designs for both scenes (Pächt and Jenni Abb 200) which show great similarity to the *BP*. Schiller II figs 31–50 show several in which single tree climbers are identified as Zacheus, and several in which many people are in trees. For the use of the *Biblia Pauperum* design in another *Utrecht* MS, see Henry (1983 ii) pl. XXVIII.

9. I have not emended **3**'s *Filiae* to Vulgate *Filii* since, though it may seem more appropriate for **3** and **4** to refer to men and women respectively, some biblical MSS do have *Filiae*, and the reading receives a good deal of commentary (*PL CXVI 691 cites it as evidence against those who deny that women are to be saved).

10. S.iv/v Augustine *PL* XXXVII 1952, carried into the s.xi *Glossa PL* CXIII 1077 and s.xii Peter Lombard *PL* CXCI 1287–88.

11. S.iv Hilary *PL* IX 885–86, s.xi Bruno *PL* CXLII 527, s.xii Gerhoh *PL* CXCIV 989, among many.

12. S.v Jerome *PL* XXVI 1342: Christ's skin is represented by the beaten drums mentioned in the next verse.

13. S.vi Justus *PL* LXVII 976. The Canticle has from the earliest times been seen as an account of the love of Christ for the Church, partly as a result of the Gospels' comparing him to a bridegroom. The crowning mentioned in the verse's continuation may have suggested *BP*'s use of it with the *Entry into Jerusalem*, but it is related by Justus to the Crown of Thorns.

14. Late examples are s.xii Philip de Harveng *PL* CCIII 364, Richard of St Victor *PL* CXCVI 445.

15. *PL LXX 1071, through Gregory the Great and Bede to s.xii Rupert *PL* CLXVIII 881. There are sermons on the verse: s.xii Gillebert de Hoilandia *PL* CLXXXIV 105, like Honorius of Autun *PL* CLXXII 409–10, stresses the coming victory of the Cross.

p

1. xi 15–18: cf. Matt. xxi 12, Luke xix 45, John ii 13–22, the latter providing the detail of the 'whip of cords' shown in the picture.

2. It is found in art as early as s.vi, and by s.xii shows all the major elements apparent in *BP* (Temple, whip, produce, and animals), but it is relatively rare until s.xvi (Kirschbaum IV 261–63). Medieval examples also follow Mark in placing it after the Entry.

3. John ii 18–21; Christ is taunted on the Cross with this claim (Matt. xxvii 39–40).

4. It is almost as if the commoner Types of the Purification (the Expulsion, the killing of Athias) were rejected because of their inherent violence.

5. A common way of showing the scene from s.x (Schiller II figs 35, 51–53).

6. The scene is not common in art until s.xvi, when protestant reformers saw it as a Type of their intentions. The scene by the contemporary Master of the Vederwolken is almost identical (see Fig. 18).

7. This may be accidental: the chronology of 1 Esdras is sufficiently confused to account for error (CC 377 para. 289i–q; JB OT 493).

8. 1 Esdras vi 6–12.

9. Whether the first or second of that name is arguable.

10. JB OT 493–95.

11. 1 Esdras vii 12–28.

12. Neither Darius's action nor the commission to Esdras has received much attention in art or from commentators. S.viii Bede PL XCI 853, however, discussing Darius's action, mentions John ii 18–20, the Jews' reply to Jesus's claim (at the Purification of the Temple) to be able to rebuild the Temple in three days: a link made, however, by Bede only in the context of the Temple's age.

13. He is one of the Nine Worthies, the conquerors who figure in popular plays and pageants (cf. Love's Labours Lost V i). Cycles illustrating his deeds occur from s.x (Stern [1962] figs 7, 9); he appeared in the destroyed s.xiii paintings at Westminster (Borenius 42) and is featured in the Bible Moralisée (Laborde III 447–68). BP appears to be the first to use this scene as a Type of the Purification of the Temple. Commentators have little to say about it. Jerome attributes the two books of Machabees to Esdras (perhaps a link with 6). However, s.ix Rabanus Maurus PL CIX 1163 relates it to the prophecy made by Christ at the Purification of the Temple, and predictably explains the Temple as the Church purified.

14. John ii 17.

15. Jerome PL XXV 10 (followed by s.xii Rupert PL CLXVIII 149) and PL XXV 900 (followed by ★PL CXVII 72) respectively.

16. CC 663 para. 527h.

17. In ★PL CXVII 115 it is a reference to the corrupt will rejecting Christ at the entrance (the senses) of vices to the soul.

q

1. The intention may be penitential, especially if BP is a meditational aid.

2. As Types, 6 and 7 have no precedent outside MSS of BP.

3. Judas is merely promised payment (Matt. xxvi 14; more clearly Mark xiv 10–11 and Luke xxii 5–6, which unlike Matthew do not mention his actual payment). The scene probably conflates the Promise with the occasion known as the Conspiracy, in which Jewish officials, without Judas, plot Christ's downfall (Matt. xxvi 3–5): the Promise is very rare in art, but the Conspiracy is much developed in medieval drama, where it contributes to a sense of political intrigue and a wider sharing of responsibility for the Crucifixion.

4. Schiller III figs 629–89.

5. Joseph in general terms is one of the commonest Types of Christ from the earliest times (s.iii Tertullian PL II 374). The Joseph cycle in the s.xiii Salisbury chapter house (P. Z. Blum) shows Jacob being given the blood-stained coat. The Ghiberti doors at Florence show some of his life: even they do not show this scene (Krautheimer pl. 95).

6. S.iv Ambrose PL XIV 678, followed by s.xii Bruno PL CLXIV 219.

7. It was interpreted as Christ's body by Ambrose PL XIV 679, ★PL XCI 265, s.xi Remigius PL CXXXI 115, s.xii Bruno PL CLXIV 219—its bloodspots made by the enemies who falsely accused him. The last two observe that the coat also points to Joseph's actual escape from death, comparable with the divinity of Christ untouched by suffering and death.

8. S.vi Cassiodorus PL LXX 43, repeated by s.xi Peter Damian PL CXLV 1105; more generally, by s.xii Rupert PL CLXVII 1136.

9. There is little iconographical tradition to assist in interpreting this scene. If the designer's symmetrical habit has been followed here, the young betrayer Absalom is on the left (as in the Vienna MS BP), matching the unmistakably arrogant brother in 6. David being a common Type of Christ, it is not surprising that in general terms Absalom is equated with the Jews from whom Christ fled (s.vii Isidore PL LXXXIII 412, s.ix Angelom PL CXV 369, Rabanus Maurus PL CIX 107, s.xii Richard of St Victor ★PL CLXXVII 1077–78). The French coronation ceremony of the time did use sceptre and crown (Twining 214–15): Charles the Bold had himself crowned by the king in an effort to establish a minor kingdom (Twining 225). For a late s.xiv crown resembling those in BP see Twining pl. 78d.

10. JB OT 75 note c.

11. S.vii Isidore PL LXXXIII 278. The verse is related in general terms to plots against Christ, by s.iv Ambrose PL XIV 710, ★PL XCI 277, s.x Remigius PL CXXXI 126, s.xii Rupert PL CLXVII 551.

12. S.v Theodoratus PG LXXX 1078, s.xii Euthymius PG CXXVIII 347.

13. Non est sapientia neque prudentia, non est consilium contra dominum.

14. The general sense that heretics' plans are vain in the face of divine opposition is expressed by s.viii Bede PL XCI 1001, ★PL CXI 749. According to Lapide III 614 the verse has been applied directly to the selling of Joseph: I cannot trace his source.

15. Et ego quasi agnus mansuetus qui portatur ad victimam et non cognovi quia super me cogitaverunt consilia (s.iii Origen PG XII 358–59).

r

1. Matt. xxvii 3–10; JB NT 61 note d. Judas receiving payment is rare in art, his return of it being much older and more common. Examples from s.xiii and s.xiv show much more emotional treatment of Judas's guilt than does BP, which as usual relies instead on the interaction of the elements on the whole page (Schiller II figs 17c,

54, 55, 83), as does the scene in the Milan Hours (Loo pl. XXV). The BP design is, however, used in a Ghent MS of the period (Henry [1983 ii] pl. XXXI).

2. Exod. xxi 32. Payment was in shekels, not denarii as is commonly said (JB NT 59 note c). The Vulgate and most biblical texts have him sold for twenty silver pieces, but Vetus Latina II 390 lists several readings of thirty, including a variant in a MS of Jerome; s.iii Origen PG XIII 1727 and s.xi Claudius PL L 1012 have triginta argenteis. Ambrose PL XIV 678 remarks on the variety of MSS traditions which mention twenty, twenty-five, or thirty quia non omnibus unius aestimationi pretii valet Christus. Aliis minus, aliis amplius. Joseph's sale is compared directly with that of Christ from s.ii Tertullian PL II 374 to s.xii Bruno PL CLXIV 219.

3. See Seyffert 'denarius' for an account of the relevant devaluation.

4. This is unlikely to be due to the absence of other Old Testament examples of sale into slavery (the author might have used Lev. xxv 44–46).

5. Gen. xxxvii 25. Money and beasts are similarly prominent in the s.xiii Hortus Deliciarum (Herrade pl. XII bis).

6. Little of Putiphar's position as the chief of Pharoah's army is suggested by his dress or hat (which is similar to that worn by the prophet Jeremias in BP) except that it is worn with a coronet indicating his court dignity.

7. S.iv Ambrose PL XIV 680–81 compares Joseph's service under Pharoah with Christ's servitude here for our salvation, a notion repeated in ★PL XCI 264; ★PL XXX 559 compares the sales of Joseph and Christ.

8. Since s.iii Joseph has been treated in literature as a major Type of Christ (s.iii Tertullian PL II 374, s.iv Ambrose PL XIV 662, 721–26, s.v Cyril of Alexandria PG LXIX 283, 375, ★PL XCI 263, s.ix Rabanus Maurus PL CVII 622). See Daniélou (1963) 147–54 for further details of Joseph as Type of Christ, including his life related to Christ's, in a s.viii Missal. The story is illustrated from s.ii.

9. JB OT 59 note a. Six Joseph scenes in BP refer to Christ: q6, r6, r7, ·g·6, ·k·6, ·m·6. The Bible Moralisée has a Joseph cycle relating his life to that of Christ (Laborde I pls 22–35, IV pls 674, 725, 740, 752); The Concordantia Caritatis has sixteen scenes of the same kind (RDK III 835–52); the Chartres glass cycle is in Houvet and Delaporte pls CLXII–CLXVI.

10. Acts i 15–22, followed by s.iv/v Augustine PL XXXIX 1901. S.v Jerome PL XXVI 212 and s.xi Gerhoh PL CXCIV 686 remark that if one so privileged as an Apostle could fall into sin, clergy must be doubly on their guard.

11. S.viii Bede PL XCI 989, ★CXI 735 stresses the importance of the verse's attitude to intention as well as to act, but the commentators do not relate it to Judas.

12. The s.xi Glossa PL CXIII 1100.

13. S.v Jerome PL XXV 1393–94.

14. S.vi/vii Gregory PL LXXIX 1013–14.

S

1. Unambiguously in Matt. xxvi 17 (the only Gospel to mention Judas's actual payment after his being promised it) and possibly Mark xiv 12. *Titulus* **12**, also on the Hildesheim Chalice (Cornell [1925] 13), underlines the irony of Judas's presence.

2. Surprisingly, the Last Supper does not appear in art until s.vi, after the appearance of the crucifixion theme (Schiller II 26–27, fig. 56). Even then there are two main types of image: the paschal meal (as in *BP*) and the Communion, as a liturgical rite, following the s.ii ff. distinction between *agape* and *eukaristia*. The identification of Judas is the commonest of the three Last Supper elements (Schiller II 28, 34), while the Communion is the rarest, but the latter was commoner in Western art after s.xiii (it had appeared earlier and more often in the East) so could easily have found a place in *BP*. See Vloberg.

3. John xiii 36–38, xviii 25–27. The emphasis may also be related to a penitential use of the *BP*.

4. John xiii 26.

5. All are stock elements (Schiller II figs 56–108). The design is very similar, and the Judas identical (except for his having no purse), in two contemporary Utrecht MSS (Henry [1983 ii] pl. XXXIII).

6. 1 Cor. xi 29. John does not mention the Communion of the Apostles; in Matt. xxvi and Mark xiv Judas is identified before, in Luke xxii after, it. Whether or not the wine-sop constituted a communion, on its receipt the Devil (often shown entering his mouth with the wine-sop) entered Judas (John xiii 26–27).

7. Designs so presenting three figures and the lamb occur in the *Milan Hours* (Loo pl. XI, in which, however, Judas does not receive the sop) and possibly in the early s.xv altarpiece by von Soest (Stange 66), where the sop is received. Similar in several respects are late s.xiv and early s.xv paintings (*RDK* VI 181, 182; Kirschbaum III 78; Schiller II fig. 21; Buikstra-de Boer and Schwartz 674, A1491).

8. The lamb is the Gospel's commonest symbol of Christ crucified: 'Look, here is the lamb of God that takes away the sin of the world' (John i 29; *JB* NT 149 note w). At the Crucifixion the bones of Christ remain unbroken in fulfilment of the prophecy which actually describes how to prepare the paschal lamb. John xix 36 fulfilling Exod. xii 46.

9. They are on the Klosterneuburg Altar (Röhrig [1955] 20, 22), where, however, the manna is shown in the golden urn.

10. Ps. 110.4–5, quoted in Heb. v 5–10, vi 20–vii 21. Hebrews does not interpret Melchisedech's use of bread and wine, though its author speaks in the context of Christ's sacrifice. The Fathers clarified the eucharistic implications: s.iii Cyprian *PL* IV 387–88, ⋆*PL* XVI 421, s.iv/v Augustine *PL* XLI 500, s.v Jerome *PL* XXVI 173, s.vii Isidore *PL* LXXXIII 104, and so on. The main point in Hebrews is simply that Christ's priesthood is of an order senior to the Levitical priesthood of the Jews, Levi being a descendant of Abraham.

11. Heb. vii 2. Salem was identified with Jerusalem even in Jewish tradition (*JB* OT 31 note g).

12. The iconography is conventional: cf. a s.xiii sculpture at Rheims (*RDK* VI 174). Melchisedech is a Type of Christ in art from s.vi: for example, in S. Vitale, Ravenna, where the eucharistic sense is clear from the mosaic's relation to the altar and to other eucharistic Types in nearby mosaics (Toesca pls II, IV). Schiller II 25–29 lists other common prefigurations of the Last Supper.

13. John vi 48ff. 1 Cor. x 1–4 calls the manna a Type (*JB* NT 301 note c). It appears in art of the late s.iv, and as eucharistic Type possibly as early as s.v—it is hard to be certain, as the Last Supper is not depicted this early (Kirschbaum III 150).

14. Cf. the Vienna MS, where it appears as rectangular wafers (Unterkircher and Schmidt f. 5ʳ), or the *Bible Moralisée*, where it is snowlike (*RDK* VI 173). On the Klosterneuburg Altar the manna is not falling, but is being placed in the Ark of the Covenant in a scene reminiscent of the Host being placed in the altar tabernacle. The design is echoed in at least two Utrecht MSS (Henry [1983 ii] pl. XXXI).

15. The Klosterneuburg Altar *Last Supper* shows **3** and **4** (Röhrig [1955] pl. 31). The 'food of angels' in the former is so called because they were the agents by which it was made or because it supported life miraculously (*CC* 510). It is related to manna and Eucharist by s.iv/v Augustine *PL* XXXVI 995, ⋆*PL* XXVI 1113; it occurs in the scrolls bearing eucharistic prophecies in a s.vi MS *Communion of the Apostles* (Schiller II 29) and with **4** on scrolls associated with the *Last Supper* on the Klosterneuburg Altar (Schiller II fig. 89).

16. The verse used in **11** forms part of the Versicle and Response after the *Tantum ergo* in the quasi-liturgical service of the Benediction of the Blessed Sacrament instituted in s.xiv: *panem de caelo praestitisti eis omne delectamentum in se habentem*. The next verse (literally 'and your substance demonstrated your sweetness'), describing manna's taste and the goodness of God in giving it, was applied to the Eucharist by s.iv Gregory *PL* LXXIX 920, s.ix Rabanus Maurus *PL* CIX 748–49. The whole context is the miraculous power and behaviour of manna and Host.

17. S.iii Cyprian *PL* IV 389.

18. S.v Jerome *PL* XXIV 528–29, ⋆*PL* CXVI 1000–2.

t

1. It appears with surprising consistency of design (Schiller II figs 13, 17ad, 18a, 144, 146–48 illustrating works from s.x–xiv).

2. Matt. xxvi 36–37, Mark xiv 32–33, Luke xxii 41–42.

3. John xiii 33, my italics. Prophecy **11** goes on: *vos autem benedicite Deum, et narrate omnia mirabilia eius*—suggesting the Apostles' commission.

4. John viii 12–24.

5. Quoting 3 Kings xxii 17.

6. Like **7**, this scene receives little attention in art or in commentaries: the designer chose both very deliberately, therefore. The background scenes in **6** and **7** have interesting parallels in a Utrecht MS apparently earlier than *BP* (Henry [1983 ii] pl. XXXII).

7. Matt. xxvi 31, Mark xiv 27, quoting Zach. xiii 7. In the *Milan Hours* the verse is illustrated, under Judas receiving payment (Loo pl. XXV).

8. The scene is rare (Kirschbaum I 617 item 20), and receives only commonplace patristic interpretation: the unbelieving compared with pagans and heretics, famine with absence of enlightenment, flour with Christ (s.ix Rabanus Maurus *PL* CIX 236–37 followed by Angelom *PL* CXV 509 and the s.xi *Glossa PL* CXIII 615); in the *Bible Moralisée* the woman who ate her son is the Synagogue, and interpretation is commonplace (Laborde I pl. 181ᵛ).

9. John xiii 4–16; Schiller II figs 64, 69, 84, 86, 87, 92, also 117–38.

10. Some regarded it as abolishing sin in a manner similar to baptism (s.iii Origen *PG* XII 185, XIV 742–43, s.iv/v Augustine *PL* XXXV 1787–89).

11. Schiller II 42–45.

12. Only **10** has received any relevant patristic attention: ⋆*PL* CXVII 139, elaborating the commonplace association of Jonas and Christ, seems to put these words in Christ's mouth. Jonas, of course, merely desired to die out of pique.

13. John xiii 34–xviii 1.

V

1. Matt. xxvi 39, Mark xiv 34–42, Luke xxii 40–46. The Agony is not in John, which the designer followed in **s** and **t**.

2. Compare the *Presentation* (**d**).

3. The *Agony* appears in art in s.iv, but not until s.vii is the hand of God shown. Curiously, the *Agony* is comparatively rare (it is not on the Klosterneuburg Altar, for example) until s.xiv, becoming more common in s.xv Passion cycles (Schiller II 48ff; figs 22, 141–55 show the traditional elements deployed in *BP*).

4. The Purification of the Temple (**p**) was the last demonstration of divine power (as opposed to divine knowledge, apparent in the Last Supper).

5. The scene is rare in art, so its inclusion here is not merely conventional. Schiller II 56 and figs 166, 181, 182 mention it as s.ix, illustrating examples from ss.x, xii, xv. Kirschbaum IV 440 does not even mention *BP*. It was developed in medieval drama, which may be an influence here—for example, the York *Betrayal* presents dazzled guards (Toulmin Smith 251); in the N-Town *Betrayal* they fall down (Block 265).

6. *Quid judicaturus faciet, qui judicandus hoc fecit?* (s.iv/v Augustine *PL* XXXV 1931, followed by s.vi/vii Gregory *PL* LXXIX 1260, ⋆*PL* XCII 896, s.ix Alcuin *PL* C 969–70).

7. S.xii Rupert *PL* CLXIX 767 relates the Falling Back to Paul's words, quoting Rom. ii 5–11 and then Exod. iii 14 (see *JB* OT 81 note h).

8. It is the second of three parables about the fate of those inactive in God's service, followed by an account of the Last Judgement. Every

detail receives predictable interpretation: the lamps are the soul's light, the oil is good deeds or grace, the noise that wakes the girls is the Last Trump (s.iv Hilary *PL* IX 1060, ★*PL* XXX 558, s.iv/v Augustine *PL* XXXVIII 574 to s.xii Richard St Victor ★*PL* CLXXV 799). In art the foolish girls are often associated with the *Last Judgement*: Künstle I 398 cites a late s.xii tympanum, Schiller I 158 a s.xiv predella; see also Schmitt (1926) I 49–51, pls 111, 112, 114–16. The design may be influenced by drama: in the late s.xi play *The Wise and Foolish Virgins*, devils thrust the latter to hell (L.-P. Thomas 186–87, who gives the patristic tradition 33–37). It is utterly unlike the design used, for example, by the Master of the Vederwolken, often so close to *BP* (Pächt and Jenni Abb. 207). Perhaps there is some relation to the 'Ladder of Charity' from which devils shoot the wicked, as in the *Hortus Deliciarum* (Herrade pl. LVI).

9. The Fall of the Angels is implied in Matt. xxv 41; Rev. xx 1–3 gives the binding of Satan in the bottomless pit; 2 Peter ii 4 has: 'God did not spare the angels that sinned, but sent them down to the underworld and consigned them there to dark underground caves to be held there until the day of Judgement'. The scene is rarely shown alone: the first example in Kirschbaum I 642 is s.xii.

10. The page therefore looks back to **a** and on to **·r·**, **·v·**.

11. S.iii Origen *PG* XI 163 on the fall of Lucifer, citing Luke x 18.

12. Rev. xii 7–9: 'And there was a great battle in heaven. Michael and his angels fought with the dragon, and the dragon and his angels fought . . . and the great dragon was cast out, that old serpent, who is called the devil and Satan, who seduces the whole world'. Origen *PG* XI 163 describes the decay of Lucifer's glory —often shown in late medieval art.

13. S.ix Paschasius *PL* CXX 1133.

14. S.xii Herveus *PL* CLXXXI 49.

15. Neither **10** nor **11** is related to Types or Antitype by commentators.

·a·

1. The *Betrayal* is among the earliest Passion scenes to appear in art, in s.iv. By s.x the various elements had already formed the basic design used in *BP* (Schiller II fig. 169: other designs are shown in Schiller II figs 4, 11, 16, 78, 158, 160, 164–66, 168–79; Byvanck [1943] fig. 22 and Oxford, Bodleian Library MSS D.inf.2.13 f. 62ᵛ and Douce 93 f. 80ʳ represent typical s.xv Netherlands illuminations similar in design to *BP*. The *BP* design itself is used in at least one Utrecht MS (Henry [1983 ii] pl. XXXIV). Peter and Malchus are named only in John xviii 2–11, an account which omits the kiss mentioned in Matt. xxvi 47–56, Mark xiv 43–51, Luke xxii 47–53.

2. The Vulgate says he was stabbed in the belly. In art he is stabbed in belly or back, the latter action doubtless a metaphor of his betrayal. The scene is rather rare, but appears as a Type of the *Betrayal* on the Klosterneuburg Altar (Fig. 7B, the lower register): indeed, the *versus* (**8**) is on the Altar too. The design is echoed in the work of the Master of the Vederwolken, in the *Hours of Mary van Vronensteyn* (Smeyers [1975] 313). The *Speculum Humanae Salvationis* gives Joab's murder of Amasa (Neumuller f. 23ᵛ): the s.xv Flemish stained-glass panel now in Exeter Cathedral Lady Chapel (Drake pl. XXII) was probably once a Type of the *Betrayal*. The Fathers do not relate the incident to the Betrayal, but make predictable comparisons between Joab and the devils or the Jews, and between Abner and the deluded faithful or the prophets (s.ix Rabanus Maurus *PL* CIX 77–78, Angelom *PL* CXV 341).

3. Tryphon's action has received little attention in art or commentary. He is predictably equated with the heretic and hypocrite (Rabanus Maurus *PL* CIX 1199).

4. Both lack patristic precedent for their association with the Betrayal, but **10** has been linked with the Arrest (s.v Cyril *PG* LXX 107) as has the verse preceding it (s.iv Basil *PG* XXX 303 and s.vi Procopius *PG* LXXXVII 1903).

5. John xiii 17–18.

6. S.iv Eusebius *PG* XXIII 366, s.iv/v Augustine *PL* XXXVI 461, ★*PL* XXI 802, ★*PL* XXVI 1005.

·b·

1. It belongs to a very corrupt passage, and has received little attention from commentators; s.vii Olympiodorus *PG* XCIII 378 observes that the victim will be avenged.

2. S.v Jerome *PL* XXIV 86, s.vi Procopius *PG* LXXXVII 1919, ★*PL* CXVI 750–51, s.xi *Glossa PL* CXIII 1242, s.xii Herveus *PL* CLXXXI 80.

3. The hand-washing was used to show the innocence of those associated with a man being found dead (Deut. xxi 6).

4. Herod Antipas, son of the Herod responsible for the Massacre of the Innocents. The event, recorded only by Luke xxiii 6–12, is not in Matt. xxvi–vii, Mark xiv–v, John xviii.

5. Evidence for the familiarity of this superficially tedious sequence is found in its development in medieval drama, which instead of contracting it, develops it to show the unwillingness of officialdom to incur the very guilt Pilate tries to avoid. The trials before Annas and Caiaphas, and the Buffeting which Christ took at the latter's house (with Peter's triple denial of Christ), are also found in art, especially in the great passion cycles of the late medieval period. However, all phases of the Trial might be indicated from s.iv by just the *Washing of Pilate's Hands* (the *Judgement of Christ*): see Schiller II figs 204–10, 220, 222, 227.

6. It is related directly to the condemnation of Christ by s.xii Rupert *PL* CLXVIII 318 (interestingly, he also relates **7** to **5**).

7. Pilate appears on early sarcophagi (Pfeiffenberger figs 4, 5). The wife's messenger appears in art in s.vi, and is present still in s.xii and s.xiii (Kirschbaum III 436–38). The s.iv/v apocryphal *Acta Pilati* develops the whole episode, naming her Claudia Procula, whom the Devil warned in an attempt to prevent the Redemption. The *Acta* remained highly popular, appearing, for example, in Old English and in s.xv Middle English (see W. H. Hulme).

8. Christ himself draws attention to the distribution of guilt (John xix 11).

9. The design is very similar, in mirror image, to that on the *Roermond Passion* (Buikstra-de Boer and Schwartz 674). It is used in at least three contemporary Utrecht MSS (Henry [1983 ii] pl. XXXV).

10. Christ himself used this abuse of Elias as an example of the treatment John the Baptist received from the Jews (Matt. xvii 12–13). The same design occurs in the work of the Master of the Vederwolken, in the *Hours of Mary von Vronensteyn* (Smeyers [1975] 316).

11. S.vi/vii Gregory *PL* LXXIX 810 followed by s.ix Claudius *PL* CIV 759, Rabanus Maurus *PL* CIX 210, Angelom *PL* CXV 482, the s.xi *Glossa PL* CXIII 607, s.xii Rupert *PL* CLXVII 1245.

12. Rupert *PL* CLXVII 1511, commenting on Dan. vi, equates Daniel with Christ condemned by an unwilling judge put under pressure by the envious.

13. The text of **2** calls him Nebuchadonosor. The king in Dan. xiv is Cyrus, and should be Cyrus in vi, but is given as Darius, a man unknown to history. Either we have real error (*JB* OT 1131–32 explains the textual confusion of the book) or the author is conflating Dan. xiv and vi with iii, where Nebuchodonosor threw the three youths into the fiery furnace; it is interesting that Jerome *PL* XXV 527 equates Nebuchodonosor and Darius in their conversion by their victims and issue of proclamations ordering worship of God.

The Vienna MS has after *danielem*: *qui devictus timore eis Danyelem innocentem tradidit*: the blockbook, by either eyeskip or intent, omits this reference to the king's cowardice.

14. See **·h·** (and **·h·** n. 8) for a lion as limbo, and **·1·** for Daniel certainly in the lions' lair. S.v John Chrysostom *PG* LXI 326 compares the bursting of the dragon in Dan. xiv with the resurrection of Christ from the underworld.

15. 'Then Daniel took pitch and fat and hair, boiled them up together, rolled the mixture into balls and fed them to the dragon. The dragon burst' (Dan. xiv 26).

·C·

1. Mark xiv 65, Luke xxii 64 mention the blindfold; Matt. xxvi 67 does not. The *Buffeting* appears in art in s.vi but is rare until s.xii (Schiller II 58, figs 11, 15, 200).

2. Two sticks crossed *in modum crucis* are commonly shown (Schiller II figs 245, 251–52), but sometimes one is shown, as here: for example, on the early s.xv *Roermond Passion*, which also shows the Crown and homage-giver associated with the Second Mocking (Buikstra-de Boer and Schwartz 674).

Translation of **12** is doubtful: *pie* might be adverbial: 'dutifully'.

3. The *Crowning* is commoner than the *Buffeting*, appearing in art in s.iv, popular by s.xiv. It did sometimes show Christ blindfold—a feature borrowed from the *Buffeting* (Schiller II fig. 249, but this is the only detail traditionally conflated: Schiller II figs 193, 237–53, 256). The *BP* design again resembles one by the Cologne Master of

1400 (Kirschbaum III 78), and is echoed in at least two Utrecht MSS (Henry [1983 ii] pl. XXXVI).

4. S.vii Olympiodorus *PG* XCIII 746, s.ix Radbertus *PL* CXX 1157, who even relates this verse to that used in **3**.

5. S.iv Eusebius *PG* XXIII 207, s.iv/v Augustine *PL* XXXVI 174, *PL XXVI 933, *PL XXI 721, s.xii Peter Lombard *PL* CXCI 230, Gerhoh *PL* CXCIII 1007, referring to Matt. xxvii 39–44.

6. S.v Jerome *PL* XXIV 28, *PL CXVI 719, the s.xi *Glossa PL* CXIII 1233, s.xii Herveus *PL* CLXXXI 24. The other insults are in Matt. xiii 55, John viii 48.

7. Baldness was a stigma among Jews, hence the tonsure as a sign of Christian humility.

8. *PL XXXIX 1826–27, s.vii Isidore *PL* LXXXIII 113, 420, s.ix Claudius *PL* CIV 773, Rabanus Maurus *PL* CXI 67, s.xii Peter de Riga *PL* CCXII 39. The two bears are interpreted as the emperors Titus and Vespasian, as illustrated in the *Bible Moralisée* (Laborde I pl. 176)!

9. Prophecy **4** is not related by commentators to Christ: s.vi Procopius *PG* LXXXVII 1422, s.viii Bede *PL* XCI 995, *PL CXI 742.

10. Kirschbaum I 614–16 and Réau II/i 361 suggest that it does not appear in art as a Type until s.xiii (*Bible Moralisée* [Laborde I pl. 175] where the boys' mockery foreshadows the *Crucifixion*), though alone it may appear on an early sarcophagus and in s.xii. By the late Middle Ages it is very popular in the Netherlands, appearing, for example, in the s.xv Costessey glass now in Exeter Cathedral (Drake 9 no plate). The animals in ·**c**·**7** appear to include a lion.

11. He cursed Cham's son Chaanan in fact: the curse affects the entire line.

12. Compare Ghiberti's clear presentation of the biblical account (Krautheimer pl. 83), or the *Speculum Humanae Salvationis* (Lutz and Perdrizet I pl. 38; Henry) where two cover Noe; in the *Hours of Turin* (Châtelet pl. xvii) one uncovers Noe and two are modest; commonly one uncovers Noe and two are shocked (Durrieu [1902] pl. xxv). In the *Bible Moralisée*, the covering of Noe is related to the stripping of Christ (Laborde I pl. 10).

13. Noe and his vines appear in art in s.x and persist (Kirschbaum IV 611–18, Réau II/i 112): they occur in the Salisbury Cathedral chapter house reliefs, for example. His drunkenness appears in s.vi but becomes a Type of the Passion only in s.xiv, in the *Hours of Turin* where it is under the *Flagellation* (Châtelet pl. xvii), and in the *Concordantia Caritatis* and *Speculum Humanae Salvationis* (Lutz and Perdrizet I pl. 38). The design is in the work of the Master of the Vederwolken (Smeyers [1975] 318).

14. 'The vineyard of the Lord of Hosts is the house of Israel' (Is. v 7); the Tract Versicle in the Mass for Holy Saturday.

15. See **v5** for this wine-chalice as symbol of Christ's sufferings.

16. S.iii Cyprian *PL* IV 386–87, s.iv/v Augustine *PL* XLI 478–79, s.v Paulinus *PL* LXI 359, s.vii Isidore *PL* LXXXIII 102–3, s.ix Rabanus Maurus *PL* CVII 320, s.xii Bruno *PL* CLXIV 185, who gives one of the longest comparisons between Noe and the Passion, and Rupert *PL*

CLXVII 362, CLXX 151.

17. The imagery suggests the play on blasphemy, dismemberment, and the sacrament which underlies the *Pardoner's Tale*.

18. Christ 'who humbled himself to share in our humanity' is commemorated at the mingling of the water and wine before the offertory in the Mass.

·d·

1. Matt. xxvii 31, Mark xv 20.

2. Until s.v Christ is not shown carrying his own Cross: Simon of Cyrene bears it for him. Then Christ carries it effortlessly as if in conquest; even by s.xiv the Cross rarely appears as a very heavy burden (Schiller II 78–82, figs 206, 285, 288–89). By the late Middle Ages though, the image is one of deep suffering: *BP* is not as extreme here as its late date would allow.

3. The 'sacrificial animal' image predominates, other possible elements in the traditional scene having been deliberately omitted: Simon, the weeping women of Jerusalem, Veronica wiping Christ's face. The basic design resembles that by a s.xv Cologne Master (Kirschbaum III 78), and the *BP* version is in two Utrecht MSS (Henry [1983 ii] pl. XXXVII).

4. The verse is quoted in Acts viii 32, where it is implicitly related to Christ, Philip telling an Ethiopian he finds trying to understand the passage, how it relates to Jesus. It is related to Christ's Passion (but not specifically to the carrying of the Cross) by s.iv Eusebius *PG* XXIV 458, who quotes Symmachus's stress on Christ's silence in affliction, by Theodorus *PG* XVIII 1358, s.v Cyril *PG* LXX 1178, Jerome *PL* XXIV 508. S.ix Haymo *PL* CXVI 990 followed by the s.xi *Glossa PL* CXIII 1296 and s.xii Rupert *PL* CLXVII 1338 extends the image of the lamb: it feeds and clothes us, and is silent as if *sheared and whipped* by the shepherd. This recalls the stripping and whipping implicit in ·**c**·. The verse is used in the Office for Holy Saturday, *lectio* 1 (*Brev.* 323).

5. The verse is interpreted as a reference to Christ's innocence by s.iii Origen *PG* XIII 358, and more generally by s.v Jerome *PL* XXIV 756, John Chrysostom *PG* LXIV 870, s.vii Olympiodorus *PG* XCIII 651, who like Origen links it to the verse used in **3**.

6. This verse and its continuation (**4**, related to the Cross by s.iii Tertullian [translated in Auerbach, 1959, 31] and s.ix Claudius *PL* L 744) are used in the seventh reading of Matins for Maundy Thursday (*Brev.* 316). Tertullian interprets the 'wood' as 'on the bread'—that is, the Cross is laid on the body of Christ.

7. Isaac's carrying of the wood is explained as the carrying of the Cross, implicitly in s.ii Melito *PG* V 1218, clearly in s.iii Origen *PG* XIII 359, Tertullian *PL* II 374, s.ix Rufinus *PL* XXI 361, s.v Jerome *PL* XXIV 756, John Chrysostom *PG* LXIV 870, s.vii Olympiodorus *PG* XCIII 651 (who also sees Christ as the 'bread of life' fixed to the Cross); the scene appears in s.xii art (Schiller II fig. 428). The *BP* design is used by the Master of the Vederwolken in the *Hours of Mary van Vronensteyn* (Smeyers [1975] 319).

8. See **d5**.

9. The ram of Gen. xxii 13 often becomes a lamb in the commentaries, by association with the Lamb of God.

10. S.iv/v Augustine *PL* XLI 510–11, see also XXXV 1464.

11. S.ii Melito *PG* V 1215, who also equates the silence of Christ with that of the ram.

12. Luke iv 26.

13. S.iii Cyprian *PL* IV 638–39; s.iii John Chrysostom also discusses the event: neither relates it to the Cross.

14. Augustine *PL* XXXIX 1824–25. Like the image of Isaac carrying his wood, the widow's crossed sticks first appear in s.xii typological art (Schiller II figs 429, 430–31, 434; Loo pl. 38), though the scene itself appears in Jewish art even in s.iii (Kirschbaum IV 45).

15. Augustine *PL* XXXIX 1824–25: *Nam quicumque corpus Christi digne manducare voluerit necesse est ut moriatur praeteritis.*

16. In marked contrast to the other Prophecies, **10** is not liturgical, and receives no relevant attention from commentators, for example, *PL XVII 1013.

17. It is not clear why the author of *BP* should attribute a verse from Ezechiel (or Revelation where it is quoted) to 'David', who is certainly the prophet drawn: neither forms part of the seven books (Job–Ecclesiasticus) sometimes referred to as 'Psalms'.

18. Rev. vii 16–17.

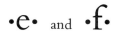

·e· and ·f·

Notes to Central Scenes

1. Surprisingly, the *Crucifixion* (unlike most Passion themes) does not appear in the art of the early Church: the reason for this is debated. It first appears unequivocally in s.v (Schiller II 82–102, figs 321, 323, 326). The dead, as opposed to the triumphal, Christ appears in s.vii. The *BP* images resemble those by Jan van Eyck and Roger van der Weyden (Kirschbaum II 625–26, figs 16, 17). The first image is used in a contemporary Utrecht MS (Henry [1983 ii] pl. XXXVIII).

2. Conflation is common in *Crucifixion* images: see Schiller II 92.

3. The origin of this name is not known: it appears in illuminations of s.ix and x (Schiller II figs 389, 390, 392).

4. As early as s.vi/vii he appears in the act of offering the sponge to Christ (Schiller II figs 322, 327–29, 345, 347, 349, 353, 358, 359, 361, 365, 368, 370, 372–75, 378, 381, 389–92). The bucket is shown on the ss.vi–xiv objects illustrated in Schiller II figs 327, 368, 370, 375, 378, 381, 389, 505, 510, 516, and on a s.x book-cover (Metz, colour pl. xiii).

5. *JB* NT 63 note u.

6. Matt. xxvii 39–44, Mark xv 29–33, Luke xxiii 35–37; the concept is illustrated in Schiller II fig. 355. A similar conflation of the functions of St John and the centurion is suggested (Schiller II 90) from s.ix, and possibly (Schiller II fig. 376) from s.xi, in which Stephaton is untypically on the left of the Cross, and the mocker

is on the right (but see note below). The *Hours of Turin* (Durrieu [1902] pl. xx) show the centurion making this 'mocking' gesture—possibly a different conflation.

7. *iesu nazarenus rex iudaeorum*; each word is 'etymologically' interpreted in *★PL* CLXXXIV 727, giving 'salvation, flowering, wealth, glory'.

8. Perhaps this gesture of witness appears in Schiller II fig. 376: where only one figure makes a pointing gesture it is hard to be certain whether a mocker or the centurion is intended (unless the figure is in armour).

9. Less likely (because less relevant) identifications might be Salome, or the wife of Cleophas (*JB* NT 187 notes j, k).

10. Separation of blood from plasma indicates death. The soldier of John xix 34 (not in Matt. xxvii 33–50, Mark xv 22–41, Luke xxiii 33–49) had been sent to break the legs of the crucified to ensure their death before the sabbath (their unsupported body-weight would cause asphyxia by closing the lungs), but he found Jesus already dead. He is named and his legend told in the s.iv *Acta Pilati* (Hennecke I 449–70), and he is named in illuminations of s.vi and s.viii (Schiller II figs 327–28).

11. The complexity of response which the double image (·**e**· and ·**f**·) creates is typical of late medieval literature and art influenced by meditational techniques centred on personal participation in the Passion, as developed by s.xii Bernard of Clairvaux, the Franciscan movement and its *Meditationes Vitae Christi* (Ragusa), s.xiv/xv Thomas à Kempis, and the drama.

·e· and ·f·

Notes to Types and Prophecies

1. The scene is probably a substitution for the Cross by s.iv: it is combined with the Cross from s.x (Kirschbaum I 20).

2. *★PL* CXII 1072 interpreting John xviii 11: 'Sheath your sword'.

3. S.ii Melito *PG* V 1218. Paul may have had the Isaac story in mind when he said 'God did not spare his own son'; it is mentioned in Heb. xi 17–19 but only as the example of great faith, as in Jewish art (Kirschbaum I 20).

4. John iii 14–16.

5. Sins of mind and body: 1 Cor. x 9 explains the literal sense, *★PL* CLXXXIV 729 the allegorical.

6. The image of the senses as openings admitting pollution to the soul (s.vii Isidore *PL* LXXXIII 628, *★PL* XCIII 535, s.xii Hugh of St Victor *PL* CLXXVI 899, among many) may derive from Jeremias ix 21: *ascendit mors per fenestras nostras* ('death' being sin). The treatment of the serpents is unusually vivid: cf. Schiller II fig. 488. The design is used by the Master of the Vederwolken in Brussels, Bibliothèque Royale Albert Ier MS II 7619, f. 131ᵛ: (Koch [1977] 285 n.13).

7. The scene appears as early as s.v; even when clearly typological it often shows not a dead snake but an active one (or a dragon) on a column (Loo pl. 38; Schiller II figs 422, 428–30 show s.xii examples). The image-type here appears

in s.xii (Schiller II figs 429–30).

8. S.iv/v Gregory *PG* XLIV 414–15, *★PL* XVII 35. A sermon on the subject in *★PL* XXXIX 1807–8 explains that the model is brass to signify the eternity and 'clear sounding voice' of the message of the Cross. The early patristic history of the image is discussed by Daniélou (1950) 144–45.

9. 'My God, my God, why have you forsaken me?' begins the Psalm probably recited in full on the Cross (Matt. xxvii 46), and said at Prime on Friday in the weekly Office (*Brev.* 25). The next verse—'They divided my garments among them'—is related in the Gospel to the dicing for Christ's clothes, hence the recital of the Psalm at the Stripping of the Altar before Good Friday. Prophecy **3** with the first part of Prophecy **4** appears on the late s.xii Bury St Edmunds ivory cross. It is related to the Crucifixion by s.iii Tertullian *PL* II 376. S.vi Cassiodorus *PL* LXX 160 and s.xii Peter Lombard *PL* CXCI 234 say that *foderunt* ('they dug', here translated 'they pierced') is used to suggest the 'fruit of life' yielded in Christ (note the visual parallel in ·**f·1** with the fruit on the tree in ·**f·6**).

10. S.iv Eusebius *PG* XXIV 458, Theodorus *PG* XVIII 1358, s.v Cyril *PG* LXX 1178, Jerome *PL* XXIV 508, and cited in *★PL* CXVI 989 with the verse forming ·**e·3**. Is. liii 7 directly precedes the verse forming ·**d·3**; Is. liii 11 has *iniquitates eorum ipse portabit*; our reading is from the Office for Maundy Thursday (*Brev.* 316).

11. As symbols of kingdom, power, or pride in s.v Cyril *PG* LXXI 907, Jerome *PL* XXV 1314, of animal-like fighting strength in Theodorus *PG* LXVI 443, Theodoratus *PG* LXXXI 1827, s.xii Theophylactus *PG* CXXVI 882.

12. S.iv/v Augustine *PL* XLI 588, *★PL* CXVII 189; see **m**. The nails may even be seen in art as these horns: Schiller II fig. 485 shows a s.xiv crucifix in which Christ's hands *held in front of him* have horn-like nails projecting from them.

13. S.iii Tertullian *PL* II 374 (who does not mention this verse), s.xii Rupert *PL* CLXVIII 631. The Canticle from which it comes is said at Lauds on Friday in the weekly Office (*Brev.* 76).

14. S.ix Rabanus Maurus *PL* CXI 240. The s.xiii *Legenda Aurea* (Jacobus I 79) has: 'Jesu Christ hath hid the hook of his divinity under the meat of our humanity, and the fiend would take the meat of the flesh and was taken with the hook of the Godhead . . . He laid out his bait to our deceiver and adversary; he hath set forth his cross'. S.xiii *Hortus Deliciarum* has the best-known image of this (Herrade pls XIV, XXIV).

15. S.v Jerome *PL* XXIII 1532, XXVI 833.

16. S.xii Rupert *PL* CLXVIII 1184.

17. The water of the rock usually signifies baptism or the Eucharist 'flowing from the wound in Christ's side' (Daniélou [1950] 170–71): s.iii Tertullian *PL* I 1318–19, s.iv Ambrose *PL* XIV 983, s.v Augustine *PL* XXXIX 1553–54, s.ix Rabanus Maurus *PL* CVIII 83–84, the s.xi *Glossa PL* CXIII 241, s.xii Bruno *PL* CLXIV 271; *Bible Moralisée* (Laborde I pl. 50).

18. 'As scripture says: "from his breast shall flow fountains of living water" ' (John vii 37–38; *JB* NT 163 note r).

19. 1 Cor. x 3–4: *JB* NT note d explains that in

Jewish tradition the rock was already equated with Yahweh. The subject, found even in the catacombs of Rome (Kirschbaum III 288), emerges in typological art in s.xii (e.g., Schiller II fig. 421).

20. Augustine *PL* XXXIX 1553–54.

21. Like Adam's (·**f·6**) this wound has been seen as the Church's origin: in a general sense by s.v Chrysostom *PG* LVIII 776, *Bible Moralisée* (Laborde I pl. 6). Sacraments flow from the wound in s.iv/v Augustine *PL* XXXV 1513, a concept common in art by s.xv (Rushforth [1929]).

22. Eve emerging is equated with the Church and sacraments flowing from Christ, by Augustine *PL* XXXV 1513, s.vi Gregory *PL* LXXI 163, s.ix Rabanus Maurus *PL* CVII 484, s.xi Peter Lombard *PL* CXCII 216. The sacramental implications are less obvious in early forms where God removes the rib from Adam, or Eve merely stands by. In s.v/vi designs (perhaps influenced by Augustine) she emerges—commonly so by s.xi/xii (Kirschbaum I 51–58). The basic design is common (Pächt and Jenni pl. V).

23. England and Pollard 86–87. Equally, ·**f·6** might show the Tree of Life rather than of the Knowledge of Good and Evil, but it too is a Type of the Cross (Schiller II 134).

24. From a messianic Psalm frequently quoted in NT. The additional pain Christ suffers is non-physical (s.iv Eusebius *PG* XXIII 755–58, s.iv/v Augustine *PL* XXXVI 861, *★PL* XCIII 850, *★PL* CXVI 426, *★PL* CXXXI 499, s.xi Bruno *PL* CXLII 262, s.xii Peter Lombard *PL* CXCI 638, Euthymius *PG* CXXVIII 702).

25. The application of this verse to Christ (rare, but see s.xii Rupert *PL* CLXVIII 802) is ironic, as it refers literally to a man accused of bearing the self-inflicted gashes of a prophet, but one who denies his power, in fear.

26. Christ is *sol justiciae* (*★PL* XXVI 1050). The verse is related to his death in *★PL* XXV 1082 and by s.xii Rupert *PL* CLXVIII 361.

·g·

1. The Eastern image shows the burial in a cave, the Western in a sarcophagus as used since antiquity. It appears in art in s.ix (s.x in the West): emphasis on death came into Christian art late.

2. The scene is more commonly related by the Fathers to Christ's descent into limbo (the Harrowing of Hell), which forms the main scene in ·**h**· (s.xi Claudius *★PL* L 1013–14, who like s.iv Ambrose *PL* XIV 679 also regards Joseph's coat as the flesh of which Christ is 'stripped' on death: the *tunica corporalis*).

3. Joseph was meant to die in the dry well, but without the shedding of blood which would 'cry for vengeance' thereafter. The scene appears as early as the well-known s.vi Ivory Chair (Cecchelli 50) and the mosaics of St Mark's, Venice (Weitzmann figs 24, 25). It is on the Klosterneuburg Altar (Röhrig [1955] 32) with the swallowing of Jonas (Röhrig [1955] 34), prefiguring the Entombment. The design occurs in the work of the Master of the Vederwolken in the *Hours of Mary van Vronensteyn* (Smeyers [1975] 120). The well in the *Bible Moralisée* is the Jews who would like to kill Christ.

4. Matt. xii 40 explains the scene's early appearance on sepulchres (in substitution for the implied *Resurrection*) and in other s.iv art not overtly typological. For an analysis of the s.xiv English poem *Patience* in the light of Jonas as a Type of Christ, see Andrew. Jonas's contrasts with Christ are often as instructive as his similarities.

5. The Hebrew has a verse meaning 'and his rest will be a glory', the version commented on by s.v Eusebius *PG* XXIV 174, s.v Jerome *PL* XXIV 149, Cyril *PG* LXX 327, who see it as a reference to the glorification of Christ when he died. The verse appears on the Klosterneuburg Altar with the *Lamentation* (Röhrig [1955] 30), which before the 1331 restoration was the *Deposition from the Cross*.

6. The well was dry to signify lifelessness (s.v Cyril *PG* LXIX 306). Is the trough a deliberate echo of the tomb-shape? See ·h· note 15.

7. The shroud is a 'vehicle' to death; cf. George Herbert's 'Mortification': swaddling-clothes are 'little winding-sheets, which do consign and send them unto death'. Circles decorating the tomb are common in s.xii and s.xiii art (Schiller II 172).

8. When Jonas was cast out of the ship the sea quietened, as death was subdued by Christ's burial (s.iv Hilary *PL* IX 473); Jonas went to the fish as Christ went to the tomb (s.iv/v Augustine *PL* XXXIII 384); *PL* XXV 1130 may explain the prayerful attitude of Jonas in **7**: the sailors took hold of Jonas as if with honour, and he willingly complied, going down to the sea and sea monster as Christ went to death and the underworld.

9. Also with the *Entombment* on the Klosterneuburg Altar (Röhrig [1955] 33). The verse is frequently interpreted by the Fathers: the development of spiritual peace in the midst of worldly cares increases the love of God (*PL* LXXIX 517, s.vii Isidore *PL* LXXXIII 1125, s.ix Angelom *PL* CXV 612); the voice of the Church is heard even in times of peace (*PL* CXVII 327, *PL* CLXII 1211). Surprisingly, connection with the Entombment is rare. Christ's heart kept watch since, though dead in the flesh, the divinity cannot sleep (s.xii Bruno *PL* CLXIV 1263). It is just possible that there is precedent for this as early as s.vi: the speaker is prepared to die for Christ but trusts in eternal life (Justus *PL* LXVII 979).

10. The Fathers commonly interpret this as God's being roused by repentance (*PL* XXVI 1117) or prayer (Arnobius *PL* LIII 438, s.xii Gerhoh *PL* CXCIV 476); s.iv/v Augustine subtly observes that the 'intoxication' refers to God's occasional appearance of slowness in answering prayer (*PL* XXXVI 1005).

11. The *Physiologus* on which the medieval *Bestiary* is based describes the lion-cub sleeping for three days and nights after its birth, when it is roused by the roaring of its sire (quoted by s.iii Origen *PG* XII 257–58: Christ is similarly 'roused' by his Father).

12. From s.x, Joseph of Arimathea and Nicodemus appear thus (Kirschbaum II 192; Schiller II 168–69). By s.xiv the basic design is common.

13. The *titulus* (**12**) is evidence that the central scene conflates two iconographical concepts: the *Anointing of Christ's Body* (usually by his mother) typically shows the gesture made here by Mary

(Schiller II 171 cites, and III fig. 176 illustrates, a comparable conflation).

14. The central tree in the otherwise dissimilar Klosterneuburg Altar *Entombment* (Röhrig [1955] 33) is similarly explained by Schiller II 170.

15. As is typical of the Northern image (Schiller II 171).

16. The sail's function is clearly compositional, not realistic: the ship is apparently sailing backwards, towards the rudder.

17. The design is used by the Master of the Vederwolken in Brussels, Bibliothèque Royale Albert Iᵉʳ, MS II 7619, f. 135ʳ (Koch [1977] 99).

·h·

1. The opening of this verse is Prophecy ·i·4 referring to Christ's Resurrection: 'Juda is a lion's cub: you "leapt at the spoils" [? "went up to the prey"] my son. Resting you lay like a lion or a lioness. Who shall rouse him?' This is a splendid example of the flexibility of medieval symbols: the lion is the Devil in **7**, Christ in ·i·4. The Fathers comment on the Septuagint version *Ex germine, fili, ascendisti*, relating it to the Resurrection after the Entombment and Harrowing of Hell (s.iv Ambrose *PL* XIV 712–13, s.ix Rabanus Maurus *PL* CVII 656, Angelom *PL* CXV 233, s.xii Rupert *PL* CLXVII 553, for example).

2. He wears the 'royal hat' he has as Psalmist in **3**.

3. The *Bible Moralisée* (Laborde I 137) relates the actual beheading to Christ's general victory over the Devil. *BP*'s application of the scene is rare. The Fathers do not offer any unequivocal parallel with the Harrowing of Hell, though s.xii Rupert comes near it, comparing David's victory with Christ's conquest and crushing of the Devil, and destroying of death (*PL* CLXVII 1103–4), Goliath's beheading signifying the Devil robbed of power by him who, rising from the dead, ascended victorious. Every detail has, however, long been allegorised in terms of general victory: to s.iv/v Augustine *PL* XXXVIII 198 and in *PL* XXXIX 1820 the stone is Christ, and Goliath's forehead represents the wicked, unprotected by the baptismal sign of the Cross; the giant dies by his own sword because the Devil was destroyed by the very harm he did Christ, who carried his Cross against him. These ideas are developed with minor variations in *PL* LVII 450, s.vii Isidore *PL* LXXXIII 113, s.viii Bede *PL* XCI 621 (who compares the bringing of the sword out of its sheath to the bringing of sinners out of darkness), s.ix Rabanus Maurus *PL* CIX 42, CXI 58 (who also points out that in 1 Kings xvii 34 David kills lions, seizing their jaws to free sheep from them), s.xi Claudius *PL* L 1069.

4. 1 Pet. v 8: 'the devil walks about like a roaring lion, looking for someone to devour'.

5. The Bible describes the lion torn 'as a man tears a kid': it was probably torn ritually by ripping apart its hind legs (Burney 357, n. 6)—the likely sense of the Hebrew word (pace Kirschbaum IV 31) which gave the more general Latin *delaceravit*. The oldest representations show Samson strangling it (Kirschbaum IV 33,

fig. 1), as in s.iv Ambrose *PL* XVI 1028.

6. The scene first prefigures the *Harrowing of Hell* on the Klosterneuburg Altar (Röhrig [1955] 37), where, however, the souls emerge not from Hellmouth but from broken gates. Treatment of the event by the Fathers is surprising: not the wrenching open of the animal's jaws but Samson's returning to find a honeycomb built in the jaws of the lion's carcase, is compared with the Harrowing of Hell; honey (or a swarm of bees) comes out like souls saved from the Devil's gullet (*PL* XXXIX 1641, s.vii Isidore *PL* LXXXIII 111, s.ix Rabanus Maurus *PL* CXI 57, *PL* CLXXV 680). But variations abound: s.xii Rupert *PL* CLXVII 1043 relates the struggle to the Temptation of Christ, and Augustine himself says that bees, that is the saved, come from its mouth, that is from the death of Christ, who 'resting slept like a lion'. Samon's general prefiguration of Christ is common (s.viii Bede *PL* XCIII 428–29, Isidore *PL* LXXXIII 389–90, the s.xi *Glossa PL* CXIII 531).

Even when not overtly typological, Samson is commonly shown wrenching open the lion's jaws; for example, in s.xii designs forming a candlestick and jug (*L'Europe Gothique* pls 140–41), in designs shown in Porter II pls 18, 68, and in three Exeter vault bosses (Prideaux and Shafto nos 67, 185, 219).

7. With Hades as a monster trodden underfoot by Christ, the subject appears in art in s.vi; by s.xi the souls often emerge from a Hellmouth, perhaps under the influence of Is. v 14 (Villette 99–162, 291). The *BP* design appears in London, BL, Add. MS 29887 (Henry [1983 ii] pl. XXXIX).

8. The Descent into Hell is explained in *NCE* IV 788–89, with patristic references as early as s.ii. Until man's redemption from the effects of original sin, even the innocent had no access to the vision of God. They occupied 'limbo', not in the divine presence but not forever barred from it (the s.xi *Glossa PL* CIV 686; s.xii Godefridus *PL* CLXXIV 279, 284, s.xiii Alan of Lille *PL* CCX 344).

9. The Bible has little to say on the whole event. Christ 'put to death indeed in the flesh . . . rose in the spirit, and went to preach to the souls in prison': 1 Peter iii 19, *JB* NT 405 note h; cf. 1 Peter iv 6; Heb. xi 39–40. The Creed's 'he descended into hell' is still more cryptic.

10. James (1966) 117.

11. James (1966) 138–39. Descriptions resembling the 'Descent into Hell' are in s.iv Cyril of Jerusalem *PG* XXXIII 847 and s.vi Fortunatus *PL* LXXXVIII 132–33 who visualises a Hellmouth as 'prey' (cf. **5, 7, 11**): *Inferus insaturabiliter cava guttura pandens, / Qui rapuit semper, fit tua praeda, Deus.*

12. S.v Jerome *PL* XXV 937 sees this as a reference to Christ overcoming hell, which devours with its jaws. On the Klosterneuburg Altar the verse applies to the *Harrowing* (Röhrig [1955] 36).

13. Related to the Harrowing by ·s.xii Euthymius *PG* CXXVIII 1062, earlier Fathers surprisingly relate it only to general release from captivity, through repentance.

14. Matt. xvi 18.

15. Related to the Harrowings by ·v Jerome

PL XXV 1485, ★*PL* CXVII 251, s.xii Rupert *PL* CLXVIII 773, who adds an explanation of the rest, *de lacu in quo non est aqua*: the *lacus* was filled with the blood of Christ to wash away sins. (Cf. the imagery of ·**g**·**6**, Joseph lowered into the dry well.)

16. The plays are in England and Pollard 293; Toulmin Smith 372; Lumiansky and Mills 325; Block 318.

·i·

1. The scene often prefigures not the *Resurrection* but the *Harrowing of Hell*, where the parallel of broken gates is stronger. Its first typological appearance in art is on a s.xii enamel (Kirschbaum IV 36; Falke and Frauberger pl. 79) where Samson, as here, climbs the mountain; and it is in the *Bible Moralisée* (Laborde I 117). It prefigures the *Resurrection*, however, on the Klosterneuburg Altar (Röhrig [1955] 40); on the s.xii Stavelot portable Altar, where with Jonas emerging from the whale it flanks a Relic (Lejeune and Steinnon pl. 32). A basically similar design occurs in the stained glass formerly part of the Costessey collection, and now in the Lady Chapel of Exeter Cathedral (Henry 'Eliseus Raises the Sunamite' [1983, 1984], fig. 3: the panel unrestored is in Drake pl. XVII).

It is notable that the *BP* designer did not use the *Raising of Joseph from the Well* here, which would have completed the pattern begun in ·**g**·, where Joseph enters the well, and Jonas the fish. The empty well is used instead in ·**k**·**6**. The break in expectation suggests conscious rather than unthinking use of the Samson prefiguration.

2. ★*PL* XXXIX 1642 followed by s.vi/vii Gregory *PL* LXXVI 1173, s.ix Rabanus Maurus *PL* CVIII 1194, s.xii Rupert *PL* CLXVII 1049. Samson's life is elaborately interpreted in terms of Christ even in s.v Jerome *PL* XXVI 645. The *Ascension* often appears in early art *with the Resurrection* (Schiller III 21–26).

3. The scene may be typological even when it appears alone, as on s.iii sarcophagi (Gough pls 29–30) or in catacomb paintings (Kirschbaum II 414). It is overtly typological by s.xii (Schiller II fig. 428 shows an enamel where it is opposite *Samson and the Gates of Gaza*, as here, and Boeckler fig. 36 shows it in a s.xii MS in praise of the Cross). It prefigures the *Resurrection* in s.xiii stained glass (Mâle *xiiie siècle* fig. 78), and in the early s.xv *Milan Hours* it appears *bas de page* under the *Resurrection* (Loo pl. XVIII).

4. Ninive is some four hundred miles inland, but Jonas is sometimes shown landing there and is so described in some early Fathers (Lapide VII 388).

5. As is to be expected with a Type used by Jesus himself, Jonas's emergence is related to the Resurrection by many Fathers, including ★*PL* LVII 814, s.viii Isidore *PL* LXXXIII 115, ★*PL* CXVII 136, s.xiii Peter de Riga *PL* CCXII 41. In addition, every detail of his life is, like Samson's, interpreted in terms of Christ: both are sent on a mission; the ship in which Jonas sleeps on the 'sea of the world' is the Cross; the storm is betrayal by the Jews; the lots cast to identify the man forfeit to the sea are the lots cast for Christ's garments; the fish saves Jonas from the

sea, as Christ is preserved from final death; the fish is also the underworld, Jonas's emergence, the Resurrection. These ideas are already in s.iv Zeno *PL* XI 447–48 (but the lots are the prophecies of Christ), and then in ★*PL* XL 666, ★*PL* LII 303–6, up to s.xii Rupert *PL* CLXX 125, CLXVIII 401. S.v John Chrysostom *PG* XLIX 77–78, XLIX 309–10 explains the whole tale in terms of the impossibility of escaping from God. For further explanations see Bowers.

6. We have already seen how the continuation of this verse forms ·**h**·**11**. (·**h**· note 1). The *Bestiary* is cited by s.v Paulinus *PL* XX 721, Rufinus *PL* XXI 301–3, s.vii Isidore *PL* LXXXIII 106, s.ix Rabanus Maurus *PL* CXI 43.

7. The Fathers usually comment on this verse's literal meaning, God seeming to sleep in temporarily allowing his enemies victory; but the s.xi *Glossa PL* CXIII 973–74 followed by s.xii Bruno *PL* CXLII 300 speaks of the 'sleep' of the Passion, and the awakening at the Resurrection.

8. Surprisingly, the subject is rare in Early Christian art, where it is treated symbolically (Kirschbaum I 201; *RDK* I 1230–40; Schiller III 18–28). It appears by s.x (Schiller III fig. 178, for example, where Christ emerges, as often even later, from a monument). By s.xi the tomb is commonly a sarcophagus (Schiller III fig. 187, where a lion—cf. **4**—with the legend *Ecce leo fortis transit discrimina mortis* looks on); Schiller III figs 175–235 illustrate the development to the typical High Gothic design shown here, with three sleepers. The identical design (perhaps pounced from *BP*) is found in a Book of Hours of 1468 (Byvanck and Hoogewerff pl. 73b), and see Henry [1983 ii] pl. XXXIX, for a borrowing in Krakow, Muzeum Narodowe MS 3091.

9. The Bible does not mention whether he is clothed or not, but in art he is usually naked: contrast the s.xiv English poem *Patience*, where he emerges to clean his soiled cloak (Andrew and Waldron 199).

10. ★*PL* XL 666 cites this verse in the context of Christ's Resurrection; to s.v Jerome *PL* XXV 867 followed by ★*PL* CXVII 47–48 and s.xii Rupert *PL* CLXVIII 91–92 the 'third day' means also the general resurrection—the third advent of Christ (the first being his incarnation in humility, the second his rising in glory, the third his coming in Judgement).

11. The verse receives little comment from the Fathers: s.v Jerome *PL* XXV 137–38, ★*PL* CXVII 207–8, s.xii Rupert *PL* CLXVIII 675 relate it to the Last Judgement.

·k·

1. By s.x such conflations are common (Schiller III figs 271–94).

2. Schiller III 18–28 and figs 1–54. The three traditional elements shown here are ancient: the empty grave, the lamentation of the spice-bearing women, the message of the angel. The subject appears in a s.iii mural (of AD 250 according to Schiller III fig. 1, before AD 235 according to Kirschbaum II 56); from s.ix three women are commonly shown (following Matthew rather than Mark or Luke).

3. The comfort implicit in the loss explains the liturgical use of the scene (the earliest to receive

dramatic treatment) in the Easter liturgical tropes based on the words of the angel: *Quem quaeritis . . . ?* (Woolf [1972] 1–6).

4. Schiller III fig. 45 shows a s.xiii example and Winkler (1925) pl. 105 a s.xv Cologne miniature with the same possibly symbolic configuration. After AD 1000 the sarcophagus replaces other grave-types (cave, sepulchre): the lid often figures because of its theological significance as the stone rolled from the tomb.

5. The effective restraint in **6** and **7** is discussed by Soltész XX.

6. Reuben's lamentation appears as a Type for the first time in *BP* (Kirschbaum II 424, III 572). Though the Joseph story receives elaborate exegesis the Fathers make no relevant comment on this scene: s.xii Bruno *PL* CLXIV 219, for example, simply explains Reuben as the Type of those who do not condone the killing of Christ.

7. *RDK* II under 'Braut' analyses the lengthy treatment of the Canticle in the Fathers, and in art. The bride is understood as the soul as early as s.iv Methodius *PG* XVIII 126–27, Ambrose *PL* XVI 210, and on to s.xii Bernard *PL* CLXXXIII 1163, ★CLXXXIV 643. She is the Church to Ambrose *PL* XVI 341, s.v Jerome *PL* XXIII 263 (where the Canticle is itself the Church and Christ in dialogue after the Resurrection), s.vi Justus *PL* LXVII 978, at least up to s.xii Anselm of Laon *PL* CLXII 1187. By s.xii the bride is the soul, the Church, the Virgin, and even the soul's final reward (s.xii Honorius of Autun *PL* CLXXII 359); she is the Virgin also to s.xii Rupert *PL* CLXVIII 839, ★*PL* CLXXVII 1210.

In art she appears in s.xii as the Church (Kirschbaum I 320, fig. 2; *RDK* II 115–17), as the Virgin in s.xiii, and as the soul, surprisingly, only in s.xv (Kirschbaum II 308–12).

8. The bride in the Canticle was even in rabbinic times understood as Israel seeking God (*JB* OT 993, 996). Her Christian identification with the Church and the individual soul is particularly relevant here and to her comforting at ·**l**·**7**; her identification with both and with the Virgin is important when she takes the central place in the final main scene of the book (·**v**·**5**). The particular scene in ·**k**·**7** is related by s.xii Bernard *PL* CLXXXIII 1150 not only to the Resurrection but also to the need to seek Christ in the next world; s.xiii Alan of Lille *PL* CCX 72 is rare in relating it directly to the visits of the Magdalene and the Virgin to the tomb, and their subsequent meetings with Christ on earth: to him, the bed from which the bride misses her lover is the empty tomb. (Immediately before her lover's disappearance, the bride rose to admit him, her hands dripping oil and myrrh: Magdalene approached the empty tomb bearing myrrh, as in ·**k**·**5**, ·**l**·**5**.) In no. 43 of his eighty-six sermons on the Canticle, s.xii Bernard *PL* CLXXXIII 994 related the myrrh of Canticle i 12 to that which Christ was offered on the Cross, and that which the women brought to the tomb.

9. The grave-clothes feature prominently in designs from s.x (Schiller III figs 14, 19, 24, 27, 28), where they are still rolled, to indicate the passage through them of a glorified body; from s.xii they appear draped (Schiller III fig. 29), and

by s.xiii are the object of the Magdalene's attention, as here (Schiller III fig. 45; Kirschbaum II 60, fig. 3).

10. *JB* OT 991–92.

11. Prophecy **3** is related directly to the bride of **7**; s.xii Bernard *PL* CLXXXIII 1145, 1148 compares the bride, who missed her lover in her bed, to the Apostles who failed to find Christ in the tomb.

Prophecy **4** is related in general terms to the soul's joy in Christ, by s.iv/v Augustine *PL* XXXVII 1391, ⋆*PL* XXVI 1204, Arnobius *PL* LIII 479–80 (who recalls all Christ's life, from Birth to Ascension), through Bede, Haymo, to ⋆*PL* CXXXI 683, which mentions hope of the sight of Christ, and s.xii Bruno *PL* CLII 1191, who relates the verse following to the Nativity and the Resurrection.

Prophecy **10** is related to the Last Judgement by s.v Jerome *PL* XXV 1218, receiving little other relevant comment. Though **11** receives a great deal of attention from the Fathers, none is in this context. To s.iv Ambrose *PL* XIV 718 it is a reference to salvation from sin, and the final resurrection; more commonly it is an expression of confidence in Christ (as opposed to Antichrist or the world, whose attacks the preceding passage was thought to describe). It is an expression of confidence at the centre of Jacob's blessing of his twelve sons (the Twelve Tribes [*JB* OT 75 note m]), so may also be relevant to **6** (Reuben's lamentation over Jacob's son Joseph).

·l·

1. This is the first of the three post-Resurrection appearances of Christ in *BP* (·l·, ·m·, ·n·); there are seven in the Bible (Kirschbaum I 671—counting the appearance to the Apostles and to Thomas as two); see *RDK* V 1294–1307, figs 1–7. The Vulgate reading, which determined medieval exegesis and iconography, derives from mistranslation of the Greek, which means 'Do not cling to me': the Magdalene perhaps grasped Jesus's feet, and did not understand that his physical return to earth was temporary (*JB* NT 189, notes on John, the only evangelist to describe this event).

2. Daniel is thrown to lions in Dan. vi and xiv (see ·b·). The context and *lectio* **1** suggest the latter occasion here. The offence for which he was imprisoned is illustrated in a s.xiv MS (*RDK* III 1042) where he prises open the dragon's mouth to administer the fatal fur-balls: the association of this with Hellmouth and Samson, as in ·h·, is clear.

3. The lions are predictably interpreted as the seven deadly sins (Réau II/i 402). Their fawning represents the subjugation of evil by Christ (in a s.xii relief illustrated in *RDK* III 1038 they lick Daniel's limbs): s.v Augustine *PL* XXXV 2039 observes that they submitted to Daniel as he to God.

4. *Daniel in the Lions' Den* appears in art as early as s.iii, its context in the catacombs and on sarcophagi of s.iv implying that it is already typological (Réau II/i 404–6). The scene and its typological function are not standardised in art: in the *Bible Moralisée* the scene prefigures Christ's being tended by angels during the

Agony (Laborde III 432). Daniel appears in similar 'dens' in illuminations to contemporary Dutch picture-Bibles (e.g., one of *c.* 1440 [Byvank and Hoogewerff pl. 89D]), where he is often shown being fed by Habacuc in spite of the locked doors round him. The latter miracle is sometimes a Type of the inviolate virginity of Mary at the Nativity (s.xii Honorius of Autun *PL* CLXXII 905). The sealed door in the *BP* picture may carry this connotation, as at Christ's emergence from the tomb we may be intended to recall his entry to the womb and then the world.

⋆*PL* LI 812 relates Daniel's escape from the lions to Christ's escape from enemies in general and from the Devil, but does not mention the Harrowing of Hell; s.xii Rupert *PL* CLXVII 1512 is rare in relating it (as described in Dan. vi) to the Harrowing. Otherwise, the Fathers concentrate on Daniel's purity and his trust in obedience to God (s.v Augustine *PL* XXXVII 1731, s.vii Isidore *PL* LXXXIII 114).

5. S.xii Bernard *PL* CLXXXIII 1165 relates this vow to the soul's determination to keep faith in Christ.

6. S.xii Bernard *PL* CLXXXIII 925–26 explains in a sermon on the Canticle how the truth is beyond the experience of the Magdalene's reaching hands, and a sermon on the Magdalene ⋆*PL* CLXXXIV 766 gives Christ a long speech: he is the second Adam, gardener of his paradise, and he will be accessible to the mind, not the body—*mens tua hortus meus est*.

7. The spade marks this as the scene described by John. In other post-Resurrection appearances Christ may carry a banner or a scroll.

8. The 'keep back' gesture appears in the image from the beginning (Kirschbaum III 332; Réau II/ii 556). The basic elements of this design are common (for example, a French Breviary of 1467 [Pächt and Thoss I fig. 361]), but it bears an unusual resemblance to one by the s.xv Master of the Golden Retable (Pächt and Thoss I 334, fig. 2) which, though in mirror image (perhaps because the blockbook designer copied this, a copy, or a common source, printing reversing the image), shows the same alignment of jar and hands, and a similar garden fence. See also the relation between the *BP* design and two by the Master of the Vederwolken as well as one in a third Utrecht MS (Henry [1983 ii] pl. XL).

9. Prophecy **3** receives no very relevant exegesis; it has been seen as a reference to God's continued support of those in physical adversity (⋆*PL* XXVI 891), and the 'gates of death' from which the Psalmist is preserved in verses 15ff. are related to Christ's emergence from hell (⋆*PL* XCIII 536).

10. Prophecy **4** is more resonant: it is from the 'Old Testament *Magnificat*' spoken by Anna at Samuel's Presentation at the Temple, and so recalls the Virgin's *Magnificat* when at the Visitation her unborn son was recognised. The reappearance of Christ from the tomb is thus again related to his birth. Anna is also seen as the Church rejoicing in the advent of Christ (s.vii Isidore *PL* LXXXIII 392, through s.ix Claudius of Turin ⋆*PL* CIV 639, Rabanus Maurus *PL* CIX 16, Angelom *PL* CXV 261, to s.xii Rupert *PL* CLXVII 1062–63). The verse is, interestingly, related to the bride in the Canticle too

(s.vi/vii Gregory *PL* LXXXIX 77, Angelom *PL* CXV 261).

11. The prophet in **10** also goes on 'as a bridegroom he has decked me with a crown and as a bride adorned with her jewels'—words attributed to the Jewish community but traditionally given eucharistic meaning, together with the rest of the chapter (Lapide VI 572).

12. In view of the connotations of the bride in **7**, it is interesting that Prophecy **11** is explained as the Church addressing Christ the bridegroom (s.v Jerome *PL* XXIV 603, s.xii Rupert *PL* CLXVII 1352).

13. The verse (**11**) presents God as a jilted lover who, having tested his bride's repentance for adultery, forgives her and leads her into the desert to speak to her in the surroundings where, during the Exodus, she used to be innocent. It goes on 'I will wed you forever ... with tenderness and love': part of which is used in Prophecy **11** in ·v·. Here it thus relates not only to the bride of **7**, but also to Christ's having made a new covenant with his people. The Fathers present no consistent interpretation. S.v Jerome *PL* XXV 835 sees the desolation of Jerusalem; s.xii Rupert *PL* CLXVIII 46–47 relates the 'solitude' to Pentecost and the gifts of the Spirit.

·m·

1. The Fathers generally put this messianic Psalm into the mouth of Christ, who in the previous verse has observed that his Father will not leave him in the underworld. Here he looks forward to reunion with the Father (s.iv/v Augustine *PL* XXXVI 145, ⋆*PL* CXVI 240, ⋆*PL* CXXXI 217, s.xi Bruno *PL* CXLII 87, Oddo *PL* CLXV 1177, Peter Lombard *PL* CXCI 17). It may be, therefore, that the author of *BP* intends a reference to the greatest of all 'reunions'. Relevantly but idiosyncratically, s.xii Gerho *PL* CXCIII 840 interprets the 'joy' as the Holy Spirit conveyed by Christ.

2. John xx 19–23. Christ gave the Spirit to the Apostles present, and said: 'Those whose sins you forgive, they are forgiven; for those whose sins you retain, they are retained'.

3. Apparently a deliberate contrast with the miraculous manner of his entry, and even with the traditional explanation for the *Noli Me Tangere* to Mary Magdalene. The glorified body can behave as is appropriate, passing through doors or eating fish and honeycomb.

4. The design here is unusual; as a rule we are in the room, and the closed door is seen from the inside; the Apostles are often at table. The subject appears in art in s.v (Kirschbaum I 671); *RDK* V 1327–43, figs 20–30 show designs from s.ix–xv. The design is used by the Master of the Vederwolken in Vienna, Nationalbibliothek, MS 2772 f. 70ᵛ (Henry [1983 ii] pl. XLI).

5. The revealing of Joseph's identity is related to Christ's appearance to his Apostles by s.iv Ambrose *PL* XIV 700, and the brothers telling Jacob that Joseph is alive is related to Christ's survival through his Apostles (s.v Rufinus *PL* XXI 328). Neither precedent is followed by the Fathers, even in the long interpretations of the Joseph story by Rabanus Maurus and Rupert (*PL* CVII, CLXVII respectively).

See *RDK* II 492, fig. 8; Schiller III figs 320–37; Réau II/i 168 for examples in art (none resembling ·**m**·**6**): the latter mentions a s.xiv window in which the scene is the Type not of this central scene but of the next, *Doubting Thomas*.

6. S.vi/vii Gregory *PL* LXXVI 1055, s.ix Alcuin *PL* C 556; as he reveals his identity he says: 'I am your brother Joseph, whom you sold into Egypt. But now, do not grieve, do not reproach yourselves for having sold me here, since God sent me before you to save your lives' (Gen. xlv 4–5).

7. The famine is interpreted as want of the word of God, the grain as the preached Gospel (s.vii Isidore *PL* LXXXIII 274, s.xiii Alan of Lille *PL* CCX 236).

8. Benjamin would actually have been adult by this time (he was old enough to weep on Joseph's shoulder): perhaps he and the Prodigal in **7** appear juvenile to identify them, and to suggest their symbolic relationship as the 'much-loved member of the family' in each story.

9. Gen. xlii 34, xliv 32.

10. Luke xv begins with three parables about God's love for the repentant soul; this is the third. The standard interpretation of all three parables is found from s.ii Tertullian *PL* I 1353; the father may be God the Father moved to pity so that he runs to his son (Adam and his descendants) as Christ becomes man (★*PL* XXX 574), or because he has foreknowledge of repentance (s.v Prosperus *PL* LI 395); but he may be the Church and confession (s.viii Bede *PL* XCII 524, Paul *PL* XCV 1259, ★*PL* CXVIII 249), while the fattened calf is Christ (s.v Maximus *PL* LVII 825, s.vii Isidore *PL* LXXXIII 126, Bede *PL* XCII 525, ★*PL* CXVIII 249). Gestures from father to son are commonly important, as in *BP* (Kirschbaum IV 171, fig. I, from a s.xi MS).

11. There may be a hint of the *BP*'s equating the son with Christ, and of the dual role played by the Prodigal's father, in explanations of the father as God the Father *always with* Christ: *Revertenti filio pater occurrit, quia Deus semper fuit cum unigenito Filio. Et licet solus Filius pro nostra salute carnem assumpserit, tamen in eo Deus Pater semper mansit, et cum eo ad hanc nostram peregrinationem descendit* (s.viii Paul *PL* XCV 1259, similarly in ★*PL* CXVIII 249, where it is related to 2 Cor. v 19–21).

12. Use of parables in new contexts has plenty of parallels in literature—for example, in the parable of the Vineyard in the s.xiv *Pearl* and of the Samaritan in *Piers Plowman*.

13. If deliberate, the echo of Benjamin's gesture of surprise (**6**) in that of the Prodigal's father (**7**) links them as *givers* of comfort, and plays interestingly across the relationships of children and adults on the page.

14. 'He is to be found by those who do not put him to the test, and he appeared to those who had faith in him'. This draws attention to the absence of Thomas, who is present in ·**n**· (s.v Gaudentius *PL* XX 962).

15. The messianic passage in Ezechiel is naturally associated with Christ: *JB* OT 1403 observes that in it there is 'an outline of the lost sheep parable' (associated with the Prodigal). The verse has no strong exegetical tradition.

16. 'Look to the rock from which you were cut, and the quarry from which you were hewn'.

17. Also the tomb from which the Church emerges with Christ: both are in s.v Jerome *PL* XXIV 483, ? s.ix Remigius ★*PL* CXVI 975.

18. Matt. xvi 18–19.

19. Jerome *PL* XXIV 483, ★*PL* CXVI 975 after I Cor. x 4 (Christ as the rock in the desert, ·**f**·**7**); he is also the 'rock cut from the mountain' (**b3**).

20. Historically, the verse refers not to our Father but to our fathers, adjuring the Jews to recall their descent from Abraham and Sara, their 'stone and quarry'.

·n·

1. The context suggests God's loving watch over the doubting or erring soul, but s.v Jerome *PL* XXIV 560 relates it to God the Father's watch over Christ, wounded and then healed in the Resurrection.

2. The verse is predictably seen by s.v Jerome *PL* XXIV 878 (echoed by s.ix Rabanus Maurus *PL* CXI 1036) as a comment on God's initiative in our repentance.

3. The subject appears in art in s.v (Réau II/ii 568–70; Schiller III 108–14, figs 340–63; *RDK* V 1294 fig. 1, 1307 fig. 5, 1326 fig. 19). In earlier examples Christ displays his wounds or raises his hand in blessing, or seizes Thomas's hand to thrust it into the wound. The simple touching is rare until s.xiii. The basic design is common (s.xii examples are in Kirschbaum IV 301, fig. 1). As often, there is a very similar one among the paintings of the Cologne school of the s.xv (Schiller III pl. 338). The *BP* design is used in Ghent, Bibliotheek van de Rijksuniversiteit, MS. 632 (Henry [1983 ii] pl. XLI).

4. Kirschbaum II 125 gives only *BP* as an example of this scene's use as a Type of *Doubting Thomas*. The city in the background may represent those he is to save, as the not uncommon church (?) in **7** may suggest the Church said to descend from Jacob (Viller VIII 16, in a splendid article on Jacob).

5. *JB* OT 53 note d. The angel is equated with God and the word of God by s.ii Justin *PG* VI 599 and s.iii Origen *PG* XII 127 respectively, and to s.v John Chrysostom *PG* LIV 510 the angel prefigures the Incarnation.
  The scene appears in art in s.v, God not being disguised (Kollwitz 7); by s.viii the angel is shown (Réau II/i 150; Kirschbaum II 378). By s.xiv the subject is common.

6. Gideon represents Christ battling against evil; the threshing he is engaged in signifies mortification of the body; the tree he is under when greeted is the Cross (s.vi/vii Gregory *PL* LXXIX 785, s.vii Isidore *PL* LXXXIII 381, s.viii Bede *PL* XCIII 424, ★*PL* CLXXVII 1095, Rupert *PL* CLXVII 1035). For Jacob as Type of Christ see note 4.

7. Conceivably we are meant to recall the inaccurate use of this greeting in a scroll in **a7**, where the angel addresses Gideon, on the later occasion of the miraculous filling of the fleece with the dew (and its subsequent protection from the dew). The effect is to link the advent of Christ's mortal body with its glorification. But it is unlike the designer to have failed to dress Gideon identically in **a** and ·**n**·, so perhaps the connection is not intended.

8. Thomas was absent from the Lord's first appearance to the disciples (·**m**·); whether because of Thomas's doubt or not, Christ's action here proves the Apostle's worthiness.

9. Interpretations vary widely (Jacob is Synagogue, the angel the Church; Jacob is the good soul struggling with vices), but the Fathers' frequent insistence that Jacob represents *both* faith and doubt, as revealed by his victory and his hurt, is most relevant to the Antitype: s.vii Isidore *PL* LXXXIII 266, ★*PL* XCI 259, s.ix Alcuin *PL* C 552, Rabanus Maurus *PL* CVII 610, s.x Remigius *PL* CXXXI 110, s.xii Bruno *PL* CLXIV 213–14, who also relevantly explains the angel's desire to leave at dawn, in terms of Christ's desire for the Ascension, without which there can be no descent of the Spirit (·**o**·).

10. Sir John Davies, 'Nosce Teipsum'.

11. S.ix Rabanus Maurus *PL* CVII 611, s.x Remigius *PL* CVII 611, *JB* OT 53 note d.

12. The wounds of Jacob and Jesus are equated by s.iv Ambrose *PL* XIV 656.

13. The next verse means 'For I have lifted up my heart to you O Lord', which ★*PL* XXVI 1143 interprets as a reference to the Resurrection, and is from a Psalm of prayer in ordeal. Beyond that there is no steady, relevant tradition of interpretation.

14. Verse **8** means 'so the Lord said "Look for me on the day of my coming resurrection" '. No directly relevant commentaries are found, most Fathers simply regarding it as a prophet's exhortation to repentance (e.g., s.v Theodorus *PG* LXVI 470, ★*PL* CXVII 207–8, s.xii Rupert *PL* CLXVIII 674–75).

15. *Quando victor a victo benedicebatur Christus figurabatur* (s.iv/v Augustine *PL* XXXVIII 682, who also explains the name 'Israel', as does s.v John Chrysostom *PG* LIV 509. The tale has the enigmatic impact of folk-tale: the struggle is sudden and unexplained, the adversary fears day and gives a wound, yet allows itself to be conquered with good grace, and an 'etymological' explanation is given.

·O·

1. The Virgin, not recorded as present on this occasion, is commonly shown, perhaps because in the early Church the Ascension and Pentecost (when her presence was implied by preceding events in Acts i 13–14) were celebrated at the same time, resulting in conflation. There are usually eleven Apostles, as here: Matthias is not elected to take Judas's place until later.

2. This type of *Ascension* is midway between those in which Christ is helped by God to climb to heaven, or is raised by angels, and those in which he is already enthroned in majesty. This ancient dogma, mentioned in the earliest Creeds, has a long art history, appearing first in s.v (Schiller III 141, figs 21–26, 443–515; Réau II/ii 582–90; Kirschbaum II 268). This design appears in s.xi and is commonplace by s.xiv (e.g., Byvanck [1943] fig. 15; Kirschbaum III 77 showing a design by a Cologne Master); it occurs repeatedly in Dutch history-Bibles of s.xv: for use of the *BP* version see Henry (1983 ii) pl. XLII.

3. Acts i 9 goes on: 'And when he had said these

things, he was carried up as they looked on, and a cloud received him out of their sight'. See also Heb. iv 14, and John xvi 7: 'If I do not go, the Paraclete will not come to you'.

4. The subject appears in art in s.iv (Schiller III figs 448, 450–52, 455, 499; Kirschbaum I 607, 613–14). By s.xii it is a Type of the *Ascension*, appearing, for example, on the Klosterneuburg Altar, together with Henoch (Röhrig [1955] 41–43), and in *Concordantia Caritatis* (*RDK* III 845, fig. 5). See also Réau II/i 359–64; *RDK* I 175, IV 1406–25. Elias's mantle is compared with the apostolic grace Christ leaves with the disciples by s.v John Chrysostom *PG* L 449, ★*PL* LI 804.

5. They are discussed in this context by s.iii Tertullian *PL* II 780, 928, and identified with the two 'witnesses' of Apoc. xi 3–10, whose death was delayed until the end of the world. The nature of the 'heaven' to which they had access before the Redemption is discussed (e.g., by s.xii Rupert *PL* CLXVII 321).

6. The offertory of the Mass for Ascension Day, the verse is commonly associated with the Ascension (★*PL* XXI 833, ★*PL* XXVI 1019, s.iv/v Augustine *PL* XXXVI 528, s.vi Cassiodorus *PL* LXX 334, s.viii Bede *PL* XCIII 728, s.xi Gerho *PL* CXCIII 1579, s.xii Bruno *PL* CLII 948, Bishop Bruno *PL* CLXIV 863, Peter Lombard *PL* CXCI 453).

7. The verse is associated with the Ascension early (s.iv Theodorus *PG* XVIII 1367, s.v Cyril *PG* LXX 1382, Theodoretus *PG* LXXXI 475). The 'stained clothes' are the flesh (s.v Jerome *PL* XXIV 609, ★*PL* CXVI 1051 and the s.xi *Glossa PL* CXIII 1306 which explain that the angels do not at first recognise the second Person of the Trinity in human flesh, ascending without their assistance).

8. Christ ascending as victor, initiating acceptance at the throne of God of the humanity he bears to his father as a prize of battle, is a major concept in the important account by s.xii Honorius of Autun *PL* CLXXII 955–58 (in which Elias and Henoch are Types of the Ascension too).

9. There is no strong tradition in art governing the design of this scene (Kirschbaum I 644–45), and the Bible says hardly anything about Henoch except that he lived three hundred and sixty-five years (a solar year, giving him another affinity with Christ as 'sun'). His name is interpreted as 'dedication to God', and that he 'walked with God' is explained as his imitating God's goodness (s.ix Angelom *PL* CXV 153, and ★*PL* XCI 221, s.x Remigius *PL* CXXXI 72 respectively).

10. Elias in the chariot is sometimes compared with Christ, driving his elect and raising them up (s.ix Claudius ★*PL* L 1182–83, who also compares the received cloak with the gift of accepting the word of God. Ambrose *PL* XV 1668 sees Elias as a foreshadowing of the exaltation of the Church. Most relevantly, the chariot is interpreted by s.xii Rupert *PL* CLXX 248 as the Church, controlled and raised by Christ, whose departure must precede the gift of the cloak (Spirit). The event's varied treatment is discussed by Daniélou (1964) chap. 5.

11. The contrast between Christ's light ascent and the journeys of Henoch and Elias, assisted because of their unavoidably unredeemed

physicality, is explained by s.vi/vii Gregory *PL* LXXVI 1217: Henoch, the Type *ante legem*, is *translatus, per coitum genitus et per coitum generans* (he had many children in his three hundred and sixty-five years); Elias, the Type *sub lege*, is *raptus, per coitum genitus*, but Christ is *assumptus, neque per coitum generans neque per coitum generatus*. These ideas are repeated in s.ix Rabanus Maurus *PL* CIX 222–23.

12. S.xii Rupert *PL* CLXVIII 464. The preceding verse has begun the metaphor of the shepherd gathering his sheep, and this verse goes on: 'They shall divide and pass through the gate and come in by it; and their king shall pass before them, the Lord at the head of them'. The verse has not received much exegetical attention: Christ leads the way out of the prison of this world at his Ascension, s.xi Theophylactus *PG* CXXVI 1049–1190.

13. The eagle metaphor from the *Bestiary* is developed in relation to the Ascension by s.ix Rabanus Maurus *PL* CVIII 974, God snatching the prize (human nature in Christ) from the enemy and taking it to heaven, as the eagle snatches its prize from the 'sea of this world' and carries it to the shore. S.vi Gregory *PL* LXXVI 625 relates the eagle's behaviour to that of Christ at the Ascension, explaining in a sequence of images all familiar in *BP* that Christ is *homo nascendo, vitulus moriendo, leo resurgendo, aquila ascendendo*.

·P·

1. Acts i 5; see also the Baptist's words at Luke iii 16: 'I indeed baptize you with water . . . He shall baptize you with the Holy Spirit and with fire'.

2. The basic design is commonplace (Kirschbaum III 415–20, figs 1–6; Réau II/ii 591–96) particularly in manuscripts (Oxford, Bodleian Library, MS Buchanan f.1, f. 76ᵛ is typical). The identical design (perhaps pounced from *BP*) appears in The Hague, MS 133 E 22, f. 67ᵛ and in at least one other Utrecht MS (Henry [1983 ii] pl. XLII). Mary's presence derives from Acts i 13–14, ii 1 (*JB* NT 203 note 2a): she appears in the scene in s.vi, and after s.xii is usually present (Schiller IV i pls 1–75). The dove (instead of the tongues of fire described in Acts) derives from the Spirit's appearance at the Baptism of Christ, emphasising that Whitsun is a *'baptism' by fire*. Here it is unusually large, to dominate the page.

3. Acts i 26. Only eleven Apostles appear in ·n·, but Matthias has now been elected to take Judas's place. However, it is possible that the bald, bearded figure prominent on the right is Paul, balancing Peter on the left: he can appear in the scene from s.x, and his presence would add weight to the theme of preaching, which is important on the page.

4. The Spirit descends on the individual in the sacrament of Confirmation (*NCE* IV 145–51).

5. 'And the earth was void and empty, and darkness was over the face of the deep. And the spirit of God moved over the waters, and God said "Let there be light" ' (Gen. i 1–2). Significantly, Prophecy 3 comes from the Psalm which follows the sequence of Creation described in Gen. i.

6. The two top Prophecies, **3** and **4**, are the Versicle and Introit for the Mass on Whitsunday respectively: **3**'s *Emitte* echoes this, not Vulgate *Emittes*. In context, **3** runs: 'If you turn away your face, they shall suffer; you take away their breath, and they die, and return to dust. Send forth your spirit, and they shall be created: you will renew the face of the earth'. The Fathers speak of the Spirit's gifts (1 Cor. xii), and of the life he promises in the next world—the subject of the rest of *BP* (s.iv Eusebius *PG* XXIII 1286, s.iv/v Augustine *PL* XXXVII 1388, ★*PL* XXVI 1199–1203, Prosperus *PL* LI 296, Arnobius *PL* LIII 478 through to s.xii Bruno *PL* CLXIV 1097).

S.ix Rabanus Maurus *PL* CIX 674–75 and the s.xi *Glossa PL* CXIII 1167 relate Prophecy **4** to 1 Cor. xii too.

Prophecy **10**'s context suggests idolatry overcome (cf. **7**, and its *titulus* **9**): 'I will pour clean water on you, and you will be cleansed: I will cleanse you of your defilement and all your idols. I shall set my spirit among you, give you a new heart and put a new spirit in you, take away your stony heart and give you a heart of flesh. I shall set my spirit among you'. The preceding verse is the Introit to the Low Mass for the Vigil of Whitsunday.

St Peter quotes Prophecy **11** in Acts ii 17's account of the Spirit's Descent: 'your sons and daughters shall prophesy, your old men shall dream dreams, and your young men shall see visions: I will pour out [my spirit] over my servants and handmaidens . . .'. Related by s.v Jerome *PL* XXV 974–75 to 1 Cor. xii, it is in the first lesson of the Mass for Ember Saturday in Whitsun week.

7. *CC* 1024.

8. It is not clear which occasion is illustrated in **6**. *Lectio* **1** refers to Exod. xxxii: the scene must be Exod. xix 16–17 (xxxi 18), or xxxiv. The *lectio* suggests the former, in which case the group in the foreground plotting idolatry is parallel with the priests of Baal implicit in Elias's miracle in **7**. But that Moses is horned suggests Exod. xxxiv, in which case Aaron's group is related to the Apostles. True, Moses may be anachronistically horned (**f6** note 9), but the fact that his first ascent to Sinai is shown there suggests that in ·**p·6** we have the second ascent. The *BP* design is used in Krakow, Muzeum Narodowe, MS. 3091 (Henry [1983 ii] pl. XLV).

9. Moses, the ancient Type of Christ, is perhaps equated here with St Peter (who in Acts ii describes Pentecost, and leads the Apostles). The recipients of the law at Sinai are equated with the Apostles by s.iii Clement *PG* VIII 674. The finger with which God wrote on the Tablets (Exod. xxxi 18) is interpreted as the Holy Spirit (s.v Eucherius *PL* L 780), Mount Sinai is the contemplation which (as in the central scene) precedes the advent of the Spirit (s.vi/vii Gregory *PL* LXXIX 735, s.vii Isidore *PL* LXXXIII 300, s.viii Bede *PL* XCIII 373, to whom the thunder on the mountain is the preaching of the Apostles with the 'gift of tongues', s.ix Rabanus Maurus *PL* CVIII 91, s.xi *Glossa PL* CXIII 247, s.xii Rupert *PL* CLXVII 672).

10. The subject is common, appearing in s.iii Jewish art, but it is often hard to know which giving of the law is depicted. Moses appears horned from s.xii (Kirschbaum III 287, fig. 4;

Réau II/i 177, 203–4). On the Klosterneuburg Altar a similar scene prefigures *Pentecost* (as it often does), the emphasis on the singleness of God being explicit in the scroll he hands to (unhorned) Moses: *Devs tvvs devs vnvs est* (Röhrig [1955] 46). But absence of the Tablets, and the trumpets and fire depicted, suggest Exod. xx.

11. The subject is rare in art (Kirschbaum I 607; Réau II/i 354–55). In s.xiii *Bible Moralisée* it is interpreted as Christ's sacrifice on the Cross (Laborde I pl. 169). It is a Type of *Pentecost* in the s.xiii frescoes in Cologne's St M. Lyskirchen (Goldkühle figs 49–50) and in MSS of the *BP*. The design is used by the Master of the Vederwolken in Brussels, Bibliothèque Royale Albert Ier, MS II 7619 f. 74^r (Koch [1977] 285 n.13). Presumably the figure on the left is Elias, beardless as in ·d·7 rather than bearded as in 16, ·b·6, ·o·7.

12. *PL* XIV 762; the purgative effect of the Spirit is explained also by s.xii Honorius of Autun: he descended as a dove to show his purity, and as fire to show his power to cleanse of sin—*per sanctum spiritum datur remissio peccatorum* (*PL* CLXXII 964–65). S.ix Claudius of Turin ★*PL* L 1173 explains the miracle differently: the sacrificial bull is the Old Testament, the altar signifies acceptance of the Trinity revealed in the New Testament, the wood is the Cross, the fire the Spirit at Pentecost and at our baptisms. To s.ix Rabanus Maurus *PL* CIX 209 (followed by s.ix Angelom *PL* CXV 481 and the s.xi *Glossa PL* CXIII 607) the altar of twelve selected stones signifies those who believe in the apostolic faith. The scene is compared with Pentecost by s.xiii Joinville (Friedman 76, pls XIX, XX).

13. The comparison is made by s.viii Bede *PL* XCIII 373.

·q·

1. Association of Annunciation and Coronation is common: s.ix Rabanus Maurus *PL* CX 55 epitomizes the idea 'he to whom she gave the hospitality of her womb crowns her queen of his heavenly home'. Dante *Paradiso* Canto 23 fuses the images.

2. Not in the Bible, the Coronation is implicit in the earliest accounts of the Assumption (e.g., s.ii Melito *PG* V 1238–39 followed by s.vi Gregory *PL* LXXI 708). It is described by s.xii Amadeus *PL* CLXXXVIII 1341, Peter *PL* CCVII 661, Bernard *PL* CLXXXIII 416, who emphasises the bridal associations of her ascent to the throne. It is celebrated in the liturgy in the use of the s.xi *Salve Regina* and s.xii *Regina Coeli* (q.v. in *ODCC*). S.xiii *Legenda Aurea* describes the Assumption at length—the Coronation is implicit (Jacobus IV 237–38, 245–46). The Coronation is the fifth Mystery of the Rosary.

3. The verse describes a landscape burgeoning after winter (the earthly life). Originally an image of New Sion, it was usually interpreted as an image of the glories of the Synagogue transferred to the Church (s.iv Eusebius *PG* XXIV 339, s.v Cyril *PG* LXX 754, Jerome *PL* XXIV 374, ★*PL* CXVI 894, the s.xi *Glossa PL* CXIII 1277). Here it suggests the New Jerusalem of heaven.

4. The subject may be confused with the *Crown-*

---

ing of the Church (Cames pl. XXIX) or the *Triumph of the Virgin* Réau II/ii pl. 42). Her *Coronation* (by her son) appears in s.xii: by s.xiv it is common (Kirschbaum II 671–72; Réau II/ii 597–99, 621–25; Katzenellenbogen figs 46–47; Loo pl. XII; Mâle *xiiie siècle* figs 124, 131).

5. Interpretation of Canticle iii 9–11 (Solomon enthroned, wearing the crown his mother gave him) as Christ 'crowned' by the flesh Mary gave him, adds to the image's meaning (perhaps included also in the last central image of the blockbook). Mary is surrogate for so many aspects of humanity (s.xii Peter Comestor *PL* CXCVIII 1772) that 4's questioning of identity takes on new significance.

6. Cf. ·k· note 8. Prophecy 4, referring to a bridal cortège, is very variously explained; for example, it is Synagogue amazed at the Church emerging from the desert (gentiles) (s.vi Cassiodorus *PL* XXVII 963), or the Church or soul ascending from the desert of this world to heaven (Gregory *PL* LXXIX 540): s.ix Alcuin *PL* C 662, Angelom *PL* CXV 624, Haymo *PL* CXVII 352, s.xii Honorius *PL* CLXXII 540 follow Cassiodorus. By s.xii it is related to the Assumption, the Virgin leaving earth to be received by her 'bridegroom' (Godefridus *PL* CLXXIV 985, Amadeus *PL* CLXXXVIII 1336, 1341, Thomas the Cistercian *PL* CCVI 804, Alan of Lille *PL* CCX 105, Peter *PL* CCVII 662).

7. Unlike 7, this is rare in art (Kirschbaum I 253; Réau II/i 273–76; *RDK* I 1517). It appears to be first used as a Type in *BP*.

8. Lapide II 484, perhaps influenced by *BP*, relates Bethsabee (mentioned in Jesus's genealogy [Matt. i 6]) to the Crowned Virgin. Surprisingly, commentators do not. S.xii Godefridus *PL* CLXXIV 1026–27 does relate her to the Virgin, but only because both were inseminated by someone other than their husband, and because their sons are traditionally equated. S.ix Rabanus Maurus *PL* CIX 126 and Angelom *PL* CXV 394 relate Solomon's subsequent judgement between the Jews and their persecutors to the Last Judgement (·r·).

9. As in 6, the queen has often been interpreted as the Church acknowledged by Christ and successfully pleading for her 'family' (s.v Jerome *PL* XXV 1337, s.vii Isidore *PL* LXXXIII 116, s.ix Alcuin *PL* CI 1127, Rabanus Maurus *PL* CIX 464, the s.xi *Glossa PL* CXIII 739). Esther is related to the Coronation by s.xiii Vincent of Beauvais *Speculum Naturale* XX chap. lxvi (Vincent f. 388^r), and her going before Assuerus is compared with the Virgin's Assumption by s.xiii Bonaventura (q.v., f. 16^r). According to Lapide II 927 the parallel is also in s.xii Bernard's *de Assumptione*, but I cannot trace the source; Esther's coronation as a Type of the Coronation of the Virgin in a nineteenth-century devotional work (Formby 137) may be derived from Lapide. It is interesting that the scene is related to the Last Judgement (·r·) by s.xii Richard of St Victor *PL* CXCVI 710.

10. For example, Esther ii 21, but that story is inappropriate here, where the plotters are clearly male and female, and it is rare in art; the *Hanging of Aman* (Esther iii 5–vii 17) often occurs (e.g., Herrade pl. XVIII). *Lectio* 2 refers to Esther ii—her coronation—but 7 clearly conflates this with later events.

---

11. The earliest known appearance of Esther (in Jewish art) does show her enthroned (Kirschbaum I 684–87), and the scene persists (*RDK* VI 50–59, figs 1, 3, 8): the king often holds out his sceptre to the queen, who is commonly a Type of the Church, as in the *Bible Moralisée* (Laborde II pl. 201). But *Esther Before Assuerus* is commoner (*RDK* VI figs 1–4, 7–11, 14, 16; Kirschbaum I 685, fig. 1; Cames pl. XLII, fig. 72). *BP* first shows it as a Type of the *Coronation*: all three scenes appear, doubtless under *BP*'s influence, on a s.xv altar tapestry at Sens (Réau [1929] pls 1–3).

12. Deliberate modification of the pictorial tradition is suggested: Aman's wife does not appear in any of the cited illustrations of the scene. Just possibly the couple's presence is related to s.ix Rabanus Maurus *PL* CIX 652 (followed by the s.xi *Glossa PL* CXIII 743), comparing Aman with those powerful people who will not share with their fellows the privileges they enjoy (*quos consortes habent naturae, socios gratiae habere despiciunt*), which glosses Esther iii, and seems to refer to Aman's 'embracing of evil' in rejecting the Jews in his country.

13. The verse's context is relevant: the 'chaste conception' is 'crowned triumphant through all eternity'. In the page's context the reference is to Mary as the Immaculate Conception (she being conceived untainted by original sin), to the Virgin Birth, and perhaps to Christ himself. The standard commentaries on Wisdom offer no precedent.

14. The Introit to the Mass of the Vigil of the Assumption (*Brev.* 1136), literally '. . . will beg to see your face'. Context is relevant: the verse (3) is preceded by 'the king will fall in love with your beauty'. This marriage song (perhaps of Solomon himself) is related to the marriage of the Messiah—with Israel, the Church, and then the Virgin (so Thomas Aquinas, quoted *CC* 456). S.xii Bernard *PL* CLII 832 and Peter Lombard *PL* CXCI 444 relate it to the Church; Bishop Bruno *PL* CLXIV 695 to the Virgin.

15. Aman *suspensus est . . . in patibulo* (Esther vii 10), but Assuerus also says *affigi cruci* (viii 7). S.xii Rupert *PL* CLXIX 169 understood a reference to the Cross: Aman, flattered by Esther's invitations to feasts (after which she denounced him), is like Leviathan (the Devil), who took the hook of the Cross hidden in bait (cf. ·e·10 and n. 14 to ·e· and ·f·); in *PL* CLXX 106 he compares Aman dying on his own cross to the Devil, who died by the Cross he prepared for Christ. Kirschbaum I 685, fig. 1, shows a s.xi MS in which Aman appears hanged in the fork of a tree.

16. Rupert *PL* CLXIX 169 compares Assuerus, Mardochai the uncle, and Esther, to Father, Son, and Spirit conquering Aman, the Devil. This places significant emphasis on the part played by all three Persons of the Trinity in mankind's salvation—a fitting close to this sequence of *BP*.

·r·

1. See *ODCC* 'Eschatology'; *NCE* V 524, 532.

2. John v 26–29: 'the dead will leave their graves at the sound of his voice: those who do good will rise again to life, and those who did evil, to con-

demnation'. Apoc. i 17–18, where Christ with the two-edged sword issuing from his mouth says: 'I am the First and the Last, am alive, and was dead . . . and have the keys of death and of hell', and xx 12–13: 'I saw the dead, great and small . . . and the dead were judged . . . according to their works'.

3. The prophet's vision is of divine retribution, but s.v Jerome *PL* XXV 63–64, Theodoratus *PG* LXXXI 874, followed by s.ix Rabanus Maurus *PL* CX 609 see a reference to reward as well as punishment at the Judgement.

4. Gen. ix 12–17, to which ★*PL* XXXV 2430 may implicitly refer: the rainbow represents Judgement and the 'continuing promise to the Church'. The immediate image is Apoc. iv 3: 'there was a throne set in heaven, and someone sitting on it . . . and there was a rainbow round the throne'. Like the judgement, the rainbow extends to the good on the right, and the wicked on the left (s.xii Richard of St Victor *PL* CXCVI 747).

5. The image of Christ wounded, not from the Apocalypse, appears in Judgements in late s.xi art, perhaps under the influence of Job xix 25: 'I know that my redeemer lives, and that in my flesh I shall see God'. Christ will be recognised by his wounds (s.iv Hilary *PL* X 85), coming to judge in the form in which he himself was judged (s.iv/v Augustine *PL* XXXVII 1096).

6. Like the wide cloak held by one clasp, the orb is a classical symbol of a ruler (in s.v Christ is shown standing on one [Schiller III fig. 579]). Not Apocalypse, but Is. lxvi 1: God has 'heaven my throne, and earth my footstool'. Rainbow and orb are in the early *Maiestas Domini* image following Apocalypse iv: Christ in glory, surrounded by Four Beasts.

7. From the 'proto-*Magnificat*' sung by Anna, this may recall the infant Christ (**d** note 7). The Fathers concentrate on 'the ends of the earth' (★*PL* L 1052, ★*PL* LXXXIX 76, s.viii Bede *PL* XCI 512 who states that not only remote but also familiar regions will be judged). The orb under Christ's feet shows the conventional 'T-in-O' world map division into Africa, Asia, and Europe (Bagrow 42–43, figs 1–3).

8. Like the rainbow on which Christ is enthroned in **5**, Prophecy **10** is a portent of peace; it is followed by the familiar image of the end of war: swords hammered into ploughshares and spears into sickles. Gentiles will be judged on their merits, Jews who rejected Christ condemned (s.v Jerome *PL* XXIV 45, followed by ★*PL* CXVI 730).

9. The scene occurs as early as s.iv. On later cathedral portals it is usually an example of justice, not directly associated with the Judgements so common there (Réau II/i 289). The Master of the Vederwolken has the identical design, and all three *BP* designs are echoed in the s.xv *Schwartze Gebetbuch* (Henry [1983 ii] pls XLVI, XLVII).

S.iv/v Tichonius *PL* XVIII 27 cryptically explains Solomon's judgement 'all are justified by Grace rather than deeds'. The two women commonly represent heretics and believers, false and true teachers, Synagogue and Ecclesia (s.iv/v Augustine *PL* XXXVIII 92, who reminds us that Christ came not to bring peace but the sword; s.ix Claudius of Turin ★*PL* L 1103, who

explains that the sword is Christ's teaching, revealing the true mother, the Church; s.vii Isidore *PL* LXXXIII 417; s.ix Rabanus Maurus *PL* CIX 127; the s.xi *Glossa PL* CXIII 416). The Last Judgement is not mentioned explicitly (Lapide II 492–94), but s.v Jerome *PL* XXII 682–85 says Solomon is a warning to those living at the end of the age (1 Cor. x 11), and compares the division of the child (souls?) to the division of law and grace; s.ix Angelom *PL* CXV 397–401 compares the true mother with good governors or magistrates to be rewarded 'at the final trial'.

10. Lapide II 378–79 seems to be correct in finding no precedent for association of this with Judgement. It is rare in art: Réau II/i 254–86; Kirschbaum I 483–85 lists David cycles from s.iii, but makes no mention of this scene; the *Bible Moralisée* (Laborde I pl. 148) explains it as the fate of those who wish their fellows ill.

11. In s.iv art the *Last Judgement* is represented by sheep and goats (Matt. xxv 31–46). The more literal form appears in s.viii/ix (Kirschbaum IV 517, fig. 1). The design-type in **5** is a conventional fusion of traditions, common by s.xv: the *Maiestas Domini* from Apoc. iv (Mâle *xii*ᵉ *siècle* figs 218–23), the judgement scene in which Christ displays his wounds (from s.xii) with Mary and John interceding on either side (from s.x), and the general resurrection (Schiller III 233–49). The s.xii/xiii images are in Mâle *xii*ᵉ and *xiii*ᵉ *siècle* figs 136, 137 and 166, 169, 173–79 respectively.

The identical design, perhaps pounced from *BP*, is in The Hague, MS 133 E 22, f. 85ᵛ; it is also used in Krakow, Muzeum Narodowe, MS 3091 and by the Master of the Vederwolken (Henry [1983 ii] pl. XLV). See also a s.xiv Cologne master (Kirschbaum III 77); s.xv images in Konrad, pls 2–7; Dutch MSS in Byvanck and Hoogewerff III pl. 233A; Byvanck (1937) pls LVIII, LXVI, fig. 184, LXXIII fig. 206, LXXIV fig. 208, LXXV fig. 211; Delaissé (1968) figs 83, 101; Oxford, Bodleian Library MSS Buchanan f 1, f. 109ᵛ; Douce 93, f. 46ʳ; and Zehnder and Smith 82 pl. 28.

12. By s.xii Mary and John the Evangelist as intercessors are commonplace on Judgement portals, because both were at the Cross, because the Evangelist was regarded as the author of the Apocalypse, and because legend based on John xxi 22 describes him as having (like the Virgin) never corrupted in death, the earth over his grave having been seen to move as he breathed long after his burial (s.ii Acts of St John, in James [1966] 270, and a sceptical s.iv/v Augustine *PL* XXXV 1971).

13. S.viii Bede *PL* XCIII 156, doubtless following Heb. iv 12: 'the word of God is living and powerful and more effective than any two-edged sword, reaching even into the place where soul is divided from spirit, or the joints from the marrow; it is a discerner of thoughts and emotions'.

S.x Aretha *PG* CVI 522 explains that it is in the mouth rather than scabbarded, because God's Judgement is swift; s.xii Rupert *PL* CLXIX 859 explains that it is justice effective to both 'left and right', according to merit. In art even to s.xiv it is represented literally. Later it commonly becomes a sword on the side of the damned, and a lily (Virgin?) on the side of the

Blessed (Réau II/ii 687; Kirschbaum IV 513–23, fig. 6), or two swords: 'the love and the fear of God is not without reason called "swords" ' (s.xii Godefridus *PL* CLXXIV 1190). S.vii Isidore *PL* LXXXII 644 explains *gladius* ('sword') in terms of its 'opening of throats': *quod gulam dividit, id est, cervicem secat*—GuLAmDIVidit. This meaning is developed in s.xiv Deguileville's *Pèlerinage de la vie humaine*, where the sword of justice gives skill in discerning spoken (throat-produced) truth from falsehood (Guillaume, lines 1105–12)—a sense relevant in **5** and **6**.

14. All the Prophecies contain *iudicabit*, but stress different aspects of judgement. Prophecy **3** has long been related to the Judgement, at which all behaviour will be properly assessed (s.v Jerome *PL* XXIII 1093–94, s.ix Alcuin *PL* C 682); s.xii Rupert *PL* CLXVIII 1233 stresses that it is the whole world (*orbem*) that will be judged (notes 6, 7).

15. Sometimes the second figure is John the Baptist (James [1931] 43 derives this tradition from the East): he wears the Baptist's identifying fur garment (*RDK* III 1199–1206, figs 1–3; Mâle *la fin* fig. 253), seen for example in Stephen Lochner's *Judgement* in the Wallraf-Richartz Museum, Cologne. The Baptist represents the end of the Old Law (the two-edged sword is related to New and Old Testaments by s.v St Victorine *PL* V 319 and ★*PL* C 1099). Perhaps our design conflates Evangelist and Baptist.

16. The Amalecite who boasted of having killed King Saul at his own request was lying (*CC* 317); but the Amalecites were often regarded as generally condemned by God (s.v Theodoretus *PG* LXXX 598, s.vi Procopius *PG* LXXXVII 1119); s.xii Rupert *PL* CLXVII 1212 equates them with the wicked destined for damnation.

•S•

1. The scene is a commonplace in art from s.xii, usually forming part of a full-scale *Last Judgement* (Kirschbaum II 313–21; Mâle *xiii*ᵉ *siècle* figs 179, 180, 183, 185; see Hughes pt. 3).

2. The theology is explained in *NCE* IV 627, VI 1005–7.

3. Jude 7 and *JB* NT 423 note i.

4. Jude 7 and 2 Peter ii 6. The s.xiv poem *Purity* uses the same three exempla to illustrate not only corruption but also God's power to preserve the good from it.

5. Psalm 74, about God as judge, is full of imagery relevant to this page: arrogance will be punished by earthquake, and the wicked will find themselves forced to drink the very dregs of God's anger (s.iii Origen *PG* XII 1535, who first explains that the 'cup of wrath is of mixed wine, the dregs for the damned', s.iv Eusebius *PG* XXIII 871, Athanasius *PG* XXVII 339, s.v Theodoretus *PG* LXXX 1471, s.vi Cassiodorus *PL* LXX 539, ★*PL* XCIII 884, ★*PL* CXVI, ★*PL* CXXXI 535, s.xi Bruno of Würzburg *PL* CXLII 284, s.xii Bruno of Siena *PL* CLXIV 987, Gerho *PL* CXCIV 387, Richard of St Victor *PL* CXCVI 323, Euthymius *PG* CXXVIII 767, s.xiii Nicephorus *PG* CXLII 1508).

6. The verse refers to the sudden cessation of the

material pleasures of life: the chapter ends with a reference to the shepherds whose land will become waste under the destroying sword. In the page's context, which so emphasises the duties of responsibility, this may glance at the fate of irresponsible clerics, among whom the reader the book was designed for may well have feared to be. In complete contrast to Prophecy **4** it receives no relevant comment from the Fathers.

7. The subject appears in s.iv Eastern art (Kirschbaum III 107–9). The basic design is commonplace: Réau II/i 117 cites s.xii–xv examples.

8. Luke xvii 28, after describing the suddenness of the Flood overwhelming those occupied with their own business. Matt. x 14–15, xi 23–24 say that the fate of towns that reject the disciples will be even worse than that of the two cities. S.vii Isidore *PL* LXXXIII 105, 245 compares it to the punishment of the damned. ★*PL* XCI 239 follows 2 Peter ii in comparing Lot with those who must suffer among the wicked until released at the end of the world; s.ix Rabanus Maurus *PL* CVII 556 also compares the cities' fate to that of the damned, and Lot to the body of Christ (? the Church). Interestingly, in view of the demons in the central scene, he also compares the five cities destroyed in all (*JB* OT 37 note g) to the five senses, which used libidinously bring the sinner to eternal fire.

9. The application of the verse appears to be original. It receives little comment (s.ix Rabanus Maurus *PL* CIX 766 and the s.xi *Glossa PL* CXIII 1182 merely relate it to the slaughter of the first-born of Egypt).

10. The subject is rare in art (Kirschbaum III 295).

11. The event receives little comment, too. S.vii Isidore *PL* LXXXIII 347 compares Dathan and Abiron to heretics, s.viii Bede *PL* XCI 365 to heretics who contradict the clergy and infect others with their errors, so deserving to be 'food for the eternal fire'; see also s.xii Peter de Riga *PL* CCXII 36. This is presumably the point of **8**'s *christo non famulantur*.

12. In **k11**, the preceding verse describing how the enemies of Job (Christ) stare at him with terrible eyes is related directly to Satan in **k5**. The fundamental irony of its use here is that Job's appalling sufferings were endured for the love of God and finally alleviated: these are permanent, the damned being past purgation. ★*PL* XXIII 1497, s.vi Gregory *PL* LXXV 1025, followed by s.x Odo *PL* CXXXIII 249 see a reference to the delight taken in persecuting the Church, but the verse otherwise receives little comment.

·t·

1. Ps. 31.10: Prophecy **3** is a loose amalgam of Ps. 32.1 *Exsultate, justi, in Domino* and Ps. 31.11. The application of all four Prophecies (and **6**) appears to be original (though the Fathers predictably equate 'Jerusalem' in **11** with the Church).

2. See, for example, the facsimile Apocalypses by Brieger, and Hassall and Hassall; see Stucky for the great Angers tapestries. James (1931) lists other manuscript Apocalypses.

3. The central design was probably pounced for

The Hague, MS 133 E.22 f. 101ᵛ (**·p·5**, **·r·5** were similarly used in this MS). It is also used by the Master of the Vederwolken in Utrecht, Catharijneconvent MS 22 f. 89ᵛ (see Henry [1983 ii] pl. XLVIII for both). The napkin (see note 5 below) may be influenced by the cloths on which babies were lifted, or 'devotional cloths' used for handling holy objects (Schiller III 163). Both notions may be present in a s.xii relief at Arles in which angels pass souls, each on a cloth, to Partriarchs' laps, while the general resurrection takes place below (Kirschbaum I 26, fig. 6). The image appears in s.xi in developed Last Judgements (as do all the elements in the central scenes of our book's last four pages). God is more usually seated (Réau II/i pl. 12 opposite 161; Mâle *xiiiᵉ siècle* figs 186, 187; illuminations in Byvanck and Hoogewerff III pl. 232A, and Oxford, Bodleian Library MS E.D.Clarke 30, f. 105ᵛ, typical of many contemporary illuminations). It is found as late as the s.xvi glass of St Neot's, Cornwall (Hedgeland pl. II, where it is described as St Brechan holding his children—correctly interpreted by Bourke 66).

4. From the chapter describing the world as footstool to God (**·r·5**). The image of *Ecclesia lactans* may be relevant (Schiller IV, i pls 211–16).

5. Luke xvi 22. The poor man's soul is carried by angels *in sinum Abrahae*: the primary meaning of *sinus* is a fold in the cloth of a toga; a relief at Moissac shows the poor man's soul held in just such a fold (Mâle *xiiᵉ siècle* fig. 17). To the Jews, to 'go to Abraham's bosom' was the equivalent of being 'gathered to one's fathers'. In a Christian context it may refer to limbo (**·h·5**) or as here to heaven itself (s.iv/v Augustine *PL* XLIV 499).

6. Matt. xxii 1–14.

7. The scene is rare in art. Its use as a Type of *Abraham's Bosom* appears to be original. Réau II/i 310–18; Kirschbaum II 407. Could it be relevant that s.x Odo of Cluny compares the three sisters to Faith, Hope, and Charity? Commentators do not relate the feast to paradise.

8. Perhaps the *agape* or 'love-feast' (q.v. in *ODCC*).

9. In contrast to **6**, the scene is ancient and common in art, dating from s.iii (Kirschbaum II 283, 370; Réau II/i 142–55; Underwood [1957] 194–97). Indeed, 'soul-ladders' are of oriental origin (J. R. Martin). The s.xii *Hortus Deliciarum* image shows two angels on the ladder, and Christ at the top (Cames pl. XLIX fig. 82). The image is common in literature; for example, in Raoul de Houdenc's *Le Songe de Paradis* a pilgrim ascends to paradise by an eight-rung ladder; in s.xiv de (Henry [1985] lines 68–70) souls ascend the twelve rungs of humility to the celestial city (see next note).

10. The steps of the ladder are the virtues to s.iv Zeno *PL* XI 428. The sleep of Jacob is the death of Christ, and the ladder Christ himself, to s.ix Claudius ★*PL* L 991, s.ix Rabanus Maurus *PL* CVII 591. Ladder-imagery was affected by s.vi Benedict's *Rule* (*PL* LXVI 378, 410) and s.xii Bernard *PL* CLXXXII 943–44, where twelve steps of humility (as perhaps here) are mounted to the vision of God (see also variants in s.xii Guibert *PL* CLVI 215, Honorius of Autun *PL* CLXXII 869). The stone as Christ, mentioned in *lectio* **2**, is in s.v Prosper *PL* LI 751, s.ix Ange-

lom *PL* CXV 211, s.xii Bruno *PL* CLXIV 209. None of these equates the ladder with paradise itself.

·V·

1. It is often impossible certainly to distinguish the Canticle's *Crowning of the Bride* from *Christ Crowning the Church* or *Christ Crowning the Soul*. In addition, christological interpretation of the Canticle is as we have seen (**·q·**) so early and varied that it is hard to distinguish mere illustrations of the *sponsa* and *sponsus* from their typological use (*RDK* II 1110–24; Kirschbaum I 318, IV 138.) It is particularly hard to distinguish the *Crowning of the Church* from the *Crowning of the Soul* (in a s.xiii Bible the *Ecclesia* figure is transformed into the soul [Kirschbaum I 325]). The image naturally blends into that of the New Jerusalem bride of Christ (note 6).

We have already seen that the Canticle's bride often represents the Virgin (**·q·**—as in s.xii Thomas the Cistercian *PL* CCVI 449, for example). The *sponsa* is the Church in s.vi Justus *PL* LXVII 977, ★*PL* LXX 1073 (the simple as well as the learned are lovely in the eyes of Christ), s.xii Honorius *PL* CLXXII 417 (an extended account of the Coronation, and the meaning of the crown's jewels). To Bernard *PL* CLXXXIII 796 she is the soul.

2. **a5**; **b5**; **f6, 7**; **p5**; **s5**; **·m·6**; **·q·7**; **·r·6, 7**; and so on.

3. **f6**; **h5, 6, 7**; **i7**; **l5, 6**; **n7**; **o6, 7**; **p6, 7**; **q6, 7**; and so on.

4. **a5, 7**; **b5**; **i6**; **k5, 6**; **m7**; **t5, 6, 7**; **·l·6**.

5. **3**, which in the Psalm is a reference to the rising sun, is seen as a reference to Christ linked to human nature as the groom is to the bride, the marriage-bed being the Virgin's womb (★*PL* XXI 712–13, ★*PL* XXVI 925, s.iv/v Augustine *PL* XXXVI 161, s.vi Cassiodorus *PL* LXX 139, Gregory *PL* LXXIX 830, s.viii Bede *PL* XCIII 581, s.ix Haymo *PL* CXVI 255, ★*PL* CXXXI 239, s.xi *Glossa PL* CXIII 871, Bruno of Würzburg *PL* CXLII 100, s.xii Bruno *PL* CLII 709, Bruno of Siena *PL* CLXIV 758, Peter Damian *PL* CXCI 209, Gerhoh *PL* CXCIII 904–5).

6. Two images are relevant here. First is one in the mind's eye, a group resembling **6** and **5**: the *New Jerusalem as the Bride*, which John is to see. Second is *The Angel and John*, which we actually see. The first has multiple associations (Virgin, Church, heaven): this bride is also interpreted as the soul loving God (s.v Methodius *PG* XVIII 122) and as Church (Augustine *PL* XLII 304–5).

The scene showing John and the angel is probably included in the earliest Apocalypses in art, from s.vi (perhaps there was one in the Wearmouth–Jarrow cycle tantalisingly mentioned by s.viii Bede *PL* XCIV 718: James [1931] 34 refers to it in an *Apocalypse* of s.vii/viii). It is enough to conjure up the whole Book of the Apocalypse, since the angel leads John into his vision, as well as introducing closing images of the New Jerusalem (Kirschbaum I 124–42; *RDK* I 751–58; Réau II/ii 663–726). Illustrated Apocalypses became very popular in s.xiii, and by s.xv the blockbook *Apocalypse* was in circulation (Musper [1961]; James [1931]; Bing).

7. See ·**q**· notes 3, 5.

8. Apoc. xxi: John has already seen this vision of the bride when the angel shows it to him at **xxi** 9: Berengaudius *PL* XVII 1032 explains this in terms of the efforts made by preachers to convey the almost incommunicable blessedness of those in heaven.

9. ★*PL* XXXV 2450, s.viii Bede *PL* XCIII 195, who explains that this bride remains always chaste, bearing spiritual sons to God, ★*PL* CXVII 1197, s.xii Bruno *PL* CLXV 719, Richard of St Victor *PL* CXCVI 864, who echoes Bede.

10. The soul speaks in Prophecy **4**, which to match **5** may deliberately have the bridegroom crowning instead of (as in the Vulgate) being crowned.

Prophecy **10** is part of God's admonition to Ezechiel to eschew signs of mourning (shorn hair and bare feet) when his wife dies: he is to preserve an outwardly normal manner. This is an extraordinary application of the verse, which seems to operate by contrast, suggesting not the loss of a spouse but the embracing of one.

Prophecy **11** is from God's promise to take back his unfaithful 'wife'— his 'chosen people' (s.iv Rufinus *PL* XXI 979; s.v Jerome *PL* XXV 840 explains that while a man in marrying makes a woman of a virgin, God makes a virgin of a woman; s.v Cyril *PG* LXXI 94 explains that God's marriage with Synagogue was replaced by another in which 'we are united to God in spirit, and are enriched by the experience of his divine nature'.

11. See Bouvet for a contemporary picturebook version.

12. In spite of the fact that the angel has been interpreted as Christ himself, the 'angel of good counsel', and the messenger of the Father's will (★*PL* CXVII 1197).

Transcription of Latin Text

See introduction, p. 24.

a

1 Legitur in genesi iij capitulo quod dixit dominus serpenti super pectus tuum gradieris et postea ibidem legitur de serpente et muliere: ipsa conteret capud tuum et tu insidiaberis calcaneo eius: Nam istud in annunciatione beatae marie gloriose virginis adimpletum est **2** Legitur in libro iudicum vi° capitulo quod Gedeon petiit signum victorie in vellere per rorationem irrigandam: quod figurabat virginem mariam gloriosam sine corruptione impregnandam ex spiritus sancti infusione **3** Isayas vij Ecce virgo concipiet et pariet filium **4** Dauid: Descendet dominus sicut pluuia in vellus **5** ANNUNCIATION ave gracia plena dominus tecum Ecce ancilla domini fiat mihi **6** EVE & THE SERPENT **7** GIDEON'S FLEECE dominus tecum virorum fortissime **8** Versus vipera vim perdit: sine vi pariente puella **9** Versus Rore madet vellus: permansit arida tellus **10** Ezeciel xliiij Porta haec clausa erit et non aperietur **11** Jheremias xxxi Creauit dominus nouum super terram femina circumdabit virum **12** Versus virgo salutatur: innupta manens grauidatur

4 dominus] *not in* V. **10** Ezeciel xliiij] *missing*: *Dresden copy damaged.*

b

1 Legitur in libro Exodi iij° capitulo quod moyses vidit rubum ardentem et non ardebat et dominum audiuit de rubo sibi loquentem: Rubus ardens qui non consumitur significat beatam virginem mariam parientem sine corruptione integritatis corporis quae virgo peperit et incorrupta permansit **2** Legitur in libro Numerorum xvij° capitulo quod virga aaron vna nocte fronduit et floruit: quae virga figurabat virginem mariam sterilem sine virili semine parituram filium scilicet ihesum cristum semper benedictum **3** Daniel ij lapis angularis sine manibus abscissus est a monte **4** Ysaias ix parvulus natus est nobis filius datus est nobis **5** NATIVITY **6** MOSES & THE BURNING BUSH **7** AARON'S ROD **8** Versus Lucet et ignescit: sed non rubus igne calescit **9** Versus Hic contra morem: producit virgula florem **10** Abacuc iij domine audiui auditionem tuum et timui **11** Micheas v Tu bethlehem terra iuda non eris minima in principibus iuda **12** Versus Absque dolore paris [o] virgo maria maris

12 o] *supplied to give hexameter*

c

1 Legitur in 2° libro Regum 3° capitulo quod Abner princeps militiae saul venit ad dauid in iherusalem vt ad eum reduceret totum populum israel qui tunc sequebatur domum saul Quae figurabat aduentum magorum ad christum qui eum misticis muneribus christum adorabant **2** Legitur in 3° libro regum x° capitulo quod regina Saba audita fama Salomonis venit in iherusalem cum magnis muneribus eum adorando quae regina gentilis erat Quod bene figurabat gentes quae dominum de longinquo muneribus veniebant adorare **3** Dauid Reges tharsis et insulae munera offerent **4** Ysaie lx Et adorabunt vestigia pedum tuorum **5** ADORATION OF THE MAGI **6** ABNER BEFORE DAVID **7** SHEBA BEFORE SOLOMON **8** Versus Plebs notat haec gentes cristo iu[n]gi cupientes **9** Versus Hec typ[ic]e gentem: notat ad cristum venientem **10** Ysaie ij Fluent ad eum omnes gentes & ibunt populi multi **11** Balaam Numer[i] xxiiij Orietur stella ex iacob & surget virga de radice **12** Versus Cristus adoratur aurum th[u]s mirra locatur

1 israel] isl'r. **8** iungi] iugi. **9** typice] typate. **11** Numeri] Numere; surget] consurget V. **12** thus] thijs.

d

1 Legitur in libro leuitici xij capitulo quod omnis mulier pariens primogenitum ipsum redimere cum oue deberet: pauperes autem qui ouem non habere poterant: turtures aut duos pullos columbarum pro puero offerre debebant et hoc pro sua purificatione quod virgo gloriosa impleuit quamuis purificari non indiguit **2** Legitur in primo libro regum i capitulo quod cum anna mater samuelis ipsum samuelem ablactans obtulit eum hely sacerdoti in tabernaculo dei quae oblatio praefigurabat oblationem dei in templo symoni factam **3** Dauid Dominus in templo sancto suo **4** Malachias iij veniet ad templum sanctum suum dominator quem vos quaeritis **5** PRESENTATION **6** LAW OF PRESENTATION **7** ANNA PRESENTS SAMUEL **8** Versus Hic presentatur partus prior vt redimatur **9** Versus oblatum christ[e] samuel te denotat ist[e] **10** Sacharias ij Ecce ego venio & habitabo in medio vestri **11** Sophonias iij Rex israel dominus in medio tui **12** Versus Virgo liban[s] christům symeon[i] recipit istum

3 sanctum] *not in* V. **9** christe] christum; iste] istum. **10** vestri] tui V. **12** libans] libana; symeoni] symeonis.

e

1 Legitur in genesi xxvij capitulo quod cum rebecca mater esau & jacob audisset quod aliquando tempore euenire posset quod jacob interficeretur ipsa filium suum jacob de terra sua misit ad terram alienam vt necem subterfugeret Quod bene figurabat fugam christi in terra egipti quando herodes ipsum iam natum quaesiuit ad perdendum **2** Legitur in primo libro regum capitulo xix quod rex saul misit apparitores vt quaererent dauid ad interficiendum: vxor autem dauid nomine mycol submisit ipsum per unam fenestram cum fune et sic euasit quaerentes eum: Rex autem saul herodem significat qui cristum quaesiuit ad perdendum quando Joseph eum cum maria in egyptum duxit & sic manus quaerentium eum euasit **3** ysaye xix Ecce dominus ingredietur egyptum & mouebuntur symu[l]acra **4** Dauid Ecce elongaui fugiens et mansi in solitudine **5** FLIGHT INTO EGYPT **6** ESAU FLEES JACOB **7** DAVID FLEES SAUL **8** Versus Liquit tecta patris Jacob formidine fratris **9** Versus Per mycol dauid saul insidias sibi cauit **10** jheremias xij Reliqui domum meam & dimisi habitacionem meam **11** Osee v vadent ad quaerendum dominum et non inuenient eum **12** Versus Herodis diram christus puer effugit iram

3 mouebuntur] commovebuntur V; symulacra] symullacra. **10** &] not in V; habitacionem] haereditatem V. **11** eum] not in V.

f

1 Legitur in exodi xxxi & xxxij capitulo quod cum moyses venisset ad radicem montis synay ipse solus ascendit in montem ad recipiendum legem quo facto ipso descendente vidit vitulum conflatulem quem aaron fecerat de auro ipse moyses tabulis projectis: vitulum destruxit & fregit quod bene figurabat corruen[d]a ydola christo ingrediente in egyptum **2** Legitur in primo libro regum v capitulo quod phylistinj archam domini quam rapuerant in bello: posuissent iuxta dagon deum eorum de mane intrantes templum: inuenerunt dagon iacentem in terra & vtrasque manus praecisas: quae figura vere completa est quando beata virgo cum christo puero suo venit in egyptum tunc ydola egypti corruerunt & bene figurat hoc quod cum christus venit [simulacra] id est errores infidelium corruerunt **3** Osee x Ipse confringet symulachra eorum depopulabitur **4** Nahum primo De domo dei tui interficiam omne symulachrum **5** EGYPTIAN IDOLS FALL **6** GOLDEN CALF **7** DAGON FALLS **8** Versus Per moysem sacrum t[e]ritur vituli simulacrum **9** Versus Archa repentine Fit dagon causa ruine **10** Zacharias xiij In die illa di[sperd]am nomina ydolorum de terra **11** Sophonias ii Attenuabit dominus omnes deos [terre] **12** Versus ydola praesente christo cecidere repente

1 corruenda] corruencia (? nonce-noun). **2** simulacra] in miserias. **4** omne symulachrum] sculptile et conflatile V. **8** teritur] tritur. **10** disperdam] V, dipergam. **11** terre] for terrae V, de terra.

g

1 Legitur in primo libro regum xxii capitulo quod rex saul fecit occid[i] omnes sacerdotes domini in nobe quia dauid fugientem receperant et ei panem sacrum ad comedendum dederant: Saul significat herodem Dauid enim christum significat: sacerdotes vero pueros: quos herodes innocente[s] fecit occidi propter cristum **2** Legitur in quarto libro regum xi capitulo quod athalia regina videns filium suum o[b]mortuum fecit occ[i]di omnes filios regis ne regnarent pro patre suo: tunc autem soror regis subtraxit filium suum iuniorem qui postea factus est rex: Regina crudelis herodem significat qui propter cristum pueros fecit occidi puer autem subtractus morti significat christum qui occisione regis herodis furti[m] subductum **3** Dauid Vindica domine sanguinem sanctorum tuorum qui effusus est **4** prouerbia xxviii Leo rugiens & ursus esuriens princeps impius super populum pauperem **5** MASSACRE OF THE INNOCENTS **6** SAUL HAS PRIESTS SLAIN **7** ATHALIA HAS PRINCES SLAIN **8** Versus Saul propter dauid: christos domini nece strauit **9** Versus vno sublato stirps est: data regia furto **10** Jheremias xxxi Vox in rama audita est ploratus et ullulatus **11** Osee viii Ipsi regnauerunt et non ex me **12** Versus isti pro cristo mundo tol[l]untur ab isto

1 occidi] occidere; innocentes] innocenter. **2** obmortuum] omortuum; occidi] occedi furtim] furti. **12** tolluntur] tolbuntur.

h

1 Legitur in 2° libro regum ii capitulo quod mortuo rege saul Dauid consuluit dominum qui respondit sibi vt reuerteretur in terram iuda Dauid enim significat christum qui post mortem herodis rediit in terram iuda: sicut enim evangelium testatur dicens: angelus domini apparuit Attolle puerum & matrem eius & vade &c defuncti sunt enim qui querebant animam pueri **2** Legitur in genesi xxxi & xxxii capitulo quod jacob reuertens in terram suam de qua fugerat propter timorem esau fratris sui praemisit oues et boues camelos & asinos & ipse sequebatur cum vxoribus & pueris: Jacob qui fugit fratrem suum cristum significat qui herodem regem fugit quem esau significat quo vero herode mortuo christus in terram iuda reuertitur **3** Dauid Vi-[sit]a nos domine in salutari tuo **4** Osee Egipte noli flere quoniam dominus doluit super te **5** RETURN FROM EGYPT **6** DAVID RETURNS **7** JACOB RETURNS **8** Versus Ad patriam dauid defuncto saul remeauit **9** Versus Formidat fratrem Jacob ardet visere patrem **10** Osee xi Ex egipto vocaui filium meum **11** Sacharias primo Reuertar ad jherusalem in misericordjis **12** Versus Ad loca sancta re[d]it Jhesus egiptoque recedit

3 Visita nos domine] Domine . . . visita nos V, Vindica nos domine. **12** redit] regit.

i

1 Legitur in exodo xiiij° capitulo quod pharao cum persequeretur filios israel cum corribus & equitibus intrauit mare rubrum post filios israel & dominus reduxit aquas maris super eos: et ita liberauit populum suum de manu inimici persequentis ita & nunc per aquas baptismi a christo consecretas populum christianum a vinculis originalis peccati liberauit **2** Legitur in libro numerorum xiij capitulo quod nuncii qui missi erant ad explorandum terram promissionis cum redirent praeciderunt botrum & portauerunt in vecte & transito iordane adduxerunt in testimonium bonitatis terre illius quod significat si volumus intrare regnum celorum oportet nos primo transire per aquas baptismi **3** ysaias xii Haurietis aquas in gaudio de fontibus saluatoris **4** Dauid In ecclesiis benedicite deo domino de fontibus israel **5** BAPTISM OF CHRIST **6** CROSSING THE RED SEA **7** JOSUE & CALEB RETURN FROM JORDAN **8** Versus Hostes merguntur per maris iter gradiuntur **9** Versus Flumen transitur et patria mellis aditur **10** Ezechiel xxxvj Effundam super vos aquam mundam **11** Zacharias xiij In die illa erit fons patens dom[ui] dauid **12** Versus Dum baptisatur christus baptisma sacratur

2 praeciderunt] inserted at end of 2. **11** domui] V, domus.

k

1 Legitur in gen[e]si xxv capitulo quod esau pro decoctione quam fecerat frater eius jacob vendidit sibi primogenita id est honorem qui debetur primogenito & benedictionem paternam perdidit: sic dyabolus primos parentes propter gulam & superbiam decepit dicens quacumque hora comederitis eritis sicut dij scientes bonum & malum **2** Legitur in gen[e]si iij capitulo quod adam & eva decepti fuerunt per serpentem qui eos de gula temptaba[t] quia nos dyabolus tamquam instrumentum seducit decipiendo quod bene figurabat temptacionem quam dyabolus christo adhibuit quando cristum temptauit dicens si filius dei es dic vt lapides isti panes fiant quae temptacio gulam inferebat **3** David 34 Temptauerunt me subsan[n]auerunt me subsan[n]acione **4** ysaie xxix Peruersa [c]ogitacio quasi lutum contra figulum **5** TEMPTATION **6** ESAU SELLS HIS BIRTHRIGHT **7** THE FALL **8** Versus Lentis ob ardorem proprium male perdit honorem **9** Versus Serpens vicit adam vetitam sibi sugeret escam **10** 2° regum vij Interfeci vniuersos inimicos tuos **11** Job xvi Hostis meus terribilibus oculis intuitus est me **12** Versus Cristum temptauit sathanas vt eum superaret

1, 2 genesi] genisi. **2** temptabat] temptabant. **3** Temptaverunt] Tentaverunt V; subsannauerunt] subsanauerunt; subsannacione] subsanacione. **4** cogitacio] gogitacio. **11** oculis . . . me] oculis me intuitus est V.

l

1 Legitur in iij° libro regum xvij capitulo quod helyas propheta tulit puerum mortuum super montem orans et dicens obsecro reuertatur anim[a] pueri & factum est ita & reddidit puerum matri sue viuum: quod bene figurabat lasari resuscitacionem quem dominus a mortuis resuscitauit & eum suis sororibus id est marie madalene et martha restituit **2** Legitur in iiij° libro regum iiij° capitulo quod helizeus propheta vidit puerum vidue qua[cum] hospitar[i] solebat defunctum & prostrauit se super puerum & calefacta est caro pueri & reuixit puer Helizeus christum figurat puer vero quem a mortuis resuscitauit lazarum representat quem videntibus iudaeis ad vitam renouuit **3** Deuteronomium [xxxii] Ego occidam & viu[er]e faciam percuciam & ego sanabo **4** Dauid Domine liberasti animam meam ab inferis **5** RAISING OF LAZARUS **6** ELIAS RAISES THE SAREPHTAN **7** ELISEUS RAISES THE SUNAMITE **8** Versus Est vidue natus per helyam viuificatus **9** Versus Per tua dona deus vitam dedit huic heliseus **10** Job xiiii Putasne mortuus homo rursum viuat **11** j° regum ij Dominus mortificat et viuificat **12** Versus Per te fit christe rediuiuus lazarus iste

1 anima] animam. **2** cum] eum; hospitari] hospitare. **3** xxxii] xxxi; &] et ego V; viuere] viue.

m

1 Legitur in genesi xviij° capitulo quod abraham vidit tres pueros scilicet angelos qui ad hospicium suum venerant tres vidit et vnum adorauit tres angeli significabant trinitatem personarum sed in hoc quod vnum adorauit ipse dedit intelligi vnitatem essenciae ita christus in sua transfiguratione se ostendit verum deum in essencia vnum: et in personis trinum **2** In daniele legitur iij° capitulo quod nabugodonosor Rex babylonis misit tres pueros in caminum ignis et cum ad caminum accederet vt eos in igne prospiceret vidit cum eis quartum similem filio dei: Tres pueri personarum trinitatem dabant intelligi quartus vnitatem essencie christus in transfiguratione sua se ostendit verum in essencia vnum in personis trinum **3** Dauid Speciosus forma prae filijs hominum **4** Ysaias lx Iherusalem venit umen tuum & gloria domini super te orta est **5** TRANSFIGURATION **6** ABRAHAM & THE THREE ANGELS **7** THREE YOUTHS IN THE FURNACE **8** Versus Tres contemplatur abraham solum veneratur **9** Versus Panditur en isti gentili gloria christi **10** Malachias vltimo Orietur vobis timentibus nomen meum sol iusticie **11** Abacuc iiij Splendor eius ut lux erit & cornua in manibus eius **12** Versus Ecce dei natum cernunt tres glorificatum

4 Iherusalem venit] Surge, illuminare, Ierusalem, quia venit V. **11** &] not in V.

n

1 Legitur in ij° libro regum xij capitulo quod nathan propheta missus fuerat ad dauid vt eum corriperet ipse vero rex dauid penitentia ductus misericordiam est a deo consecutus Dauid enim penitens mariam magdalenam penitentem designat quae meruit omnium peccatorum suorum veniam **2** Legitur in libro numerorum xij capitulo quod maria soror moysi et aaron propter suum peccatum leprosa facta fuit et a sua inmundicia per moysem curata est Moyses enim christum significabat qui mariam magdalenam ab omnibus inmundiciis suorum peccatorum mundauit sicut ipse in luca testatur dicens remittuntur tibi peccata tua &c **3** Ezechiel xviij Quacumque hora homo ingemuerit omnium iniquitat[u]m non recordabuntur **4** Dauid Cor contritum & humiliatum deus non d[e]spicies **5** MARY MAGDALENE REPENTS **6** NATHAN BRINGS DAVID TO REPENTANCE **7** MOSES' & AARON'S SISTER MARY REPENTS **8** Versus Voce nathan tactus rex prauos corrigit actus **9** Versus Hec lepra facta: pena fit munda reacta **10** Zacharias primo Conuertimini ad me et conuertar ad vos **11** Dauid Non est similis tu[i] in dijs domine **12** Versus Hanc a peccatis: absoluit fons bonitatis

3 iniquitatum] V, iniquitatem; recordabuntur] recordabor V. **4** despicies] V, dispicies. **10** Conuertimini ad me] ait Dominus exercitum *added* V. **11** tui] tuis.

o

1 Legitur in i° libro regum xvij capitulo quod cum Dauid percussisset golyam praescidit caput eius & tulit illud in manu sua cui venienti de praelio occurrerunt mulieres cum tympanis & choris ipsum gaudentes receper[u]nt in iherusalem cum magna gloria Dauid enim christum significat quem pueri hebreorum receperunt in iherusalem voce magna clamantes et dicentes benedictus qui venit in nomine domini **2** Legitur in iiij° libro regum ij° capitulo quod cum helyseus reuerteretur ad ciuitatem occurrerunt ei pueri prophetarum ipsum cum magna gloria & honore recipientes et laudantes Helyseus cristum significat quem venientem in iherusalem pueri hebreorum cum magna gloria et honore receperunt **3** Dauid Filie syon exulte[n]t in rege suo **4** Canticorum iij Egred[i]mini fili syon et videte regem salomonem **5** ENTRY INTO JERUSALEM **6** DAVID IS GREETED **7** ELISEUS IS GREETED **8** Versus Hostem qui strauit: laudatur carmine dauid **9** Versus Gloria nate dei tibi conuenit haec helysei **10** Sacharias ix Dicite filie syon ecce rex tuus venit tibi mansuetus **11** Sacharias ix Ipse tanquam pauper ascendens super pullum asine **12** Versus Carmen hebreorum te laudat christe bonorum

1 receperunt] receperent. **3** Filie] Filii V; exultent] V, exultet. **4** egredimini et videte, filiae Sion, Regem Salomonem V; Egredimini] Egredemini. **10** mansuetus] iustus V. **11** Ipse pauper et ascendens super asinam Et super pullum filium asinae V.

p

1 Legitur in primo libro esdre scribe capitulo uj° quod Rex darius praecepit esdre scribe vt iret in iherusalem & qui ipse templum mundaret rex enim darius cristum significabat qui ementes & vendentes de templo expulsit sic templum domini mundauit ab illicitis dans per hec intelligere quod templum domini domus orationis et non emptionis neque venditionis **2** Legitur in [j]° libro machabeorum [iv]° capitulo quod iudas machabeus precepit iudeis vt templum de illicitis mundarent et sanctificarent quia contra legem pollutum erat iste machabeus cristum significat qui facto flagello de funiculis ementes et vendentes in templo de ipso expulsit et excussit dicens nolite facere domum patris mei domum neg[oti]ationis **3** Ozee [ix] Eiciam omnes de domo mea **4** Dauid Zelus domus tue comedit me **5** CHRIST PURIFIES THE TEMPLE **6** DARIUS PURIFIES THE TEMPLE **7** JUDAS MACHABEUS PURIFIES THE TEMPLE **8** Versus Templum mundari iubet hic et festa vocari **9** Versus Et tua sancta deus mundare studet machabeus **10** Amos v Odio habuerunt in porta corripientem **11** Zacharie vltimo Non er[i]t vltra mercator in domo domini **12** Versus Cristus vendentes templo repellit ementes

2 j°] iiij°; iv] x; negotiationis] negationis. **3** ix] xi; Eiciam . . . mea] De domo mea eiiciam eos V. **10** in porta corripientem] corripientem in porta V. **11** erit] erat; vltra mercator] *trs.* V.

q

1 Legitur in genesi xxxvij° capitulo quod fratres ioseph miserunt ad patrem suum iacôb nuncium quemdam dicentem quod fera pessima deuorauit filium suum ioseph hoc enim facerent dolose conspirantes in mortem fratris sui: Joseph dolose venditus a fratribus suis cristum significat qui a iuda dolose venditus fuit in mortem sine culpa **2** Legitur in ij° libro regum xv capitulo quod absolom filius dauid stetit ad introitum porte ciuitatis iherusalem et populo ingrediente loquabatur quis me constituet iudicem: et inclinauit corda virorum qui secum conspirantes erant contra patrem suum dauid ipsum in regem constituerunt & postea patrem persequentes ipsum occidere intendeba[n]t: isti absolon iudam proditorem significat qui in mortem cristi cum iudeis conspirauit **3** genesi Jacob xlix In consilium eorum non veniet anima [mea] **4** Dauid Iniquitati dum convenirent consiliati sunt accipere animam **5** CONSPIRACY **6** CONSPIRACY AGAINST JOSEPH **7** ABSOLOM CONSPIRES AGAINST DAVID **8** Versus Turba malignatur fratrum puer nominatur **9** Versus Nititur in facta patris proles scelerata **10** Prouerbiorum xxi Non est sapientia neque prudencia **11** Jheremie xi Super me cogitauerunt concilia **12** Versus In mortem cristi conspirant insimul isti

2 constituet] constituat V; intendebant] intendebat. **3** veniet] veniat V; mea] meam. **4** In eo dum convenirent simul adversum me, Accipere animam meam consiliati sunt V. **10** neque] non est V. **11** cogitaverunt super me consilia V.

r

1 Legitur in gen[e]si xxxvij° capitulo quod fratres ioseph eum hy[s]maheliris vendiderunt pro xxx argenteis ioseph iste iustus a fratribus suis venditus innocent[e]r cristum innocentem a iuda dolose venditum designat qui iudas ipsum cristum iudeis pro xxx argenteis vendidit & hij xxx d[e]narij fuerunt pro quibus ioseph venditus fuit quorum vnus valebat decem pluralium d[e]nariorum **2** Legitur in genesi xxxix capitulo quod cum hysmaheliti qui emer[a]nt ioseph in suam terram venissent et ipsum ioseph secum duxissent · vendiderunt eum in egypto principi milicie regis egyptiorum nomine putifari puer isti ioseph cristum venditum significat qui ab impio iuda vendebatur **3** Dauid Fiant dies eius pauci & episcopatum eius &c **4** Salomon prouerbia xvj Qui attonitis oculis cogitat praua **5** JUDAS IS PAID **6** JOSEPH IS SOLD TO THE ISMAELITES **7** JOSEPH IS SOLD TO PUTIPHAR **8** Versus Te significat crist[e]: iuuenis venumdatus iste **9** Versus Conuenit hoc christo quidquid puero fit in isto **10** aggeus i Qui mercedes congregauit misit eas in sacculum pertusum **11** Sacharias xi Et appenderunt mercede[m] treginta argentis **12** Versus Qui cristum vendis iudas ad tartara tendis

1 genesi] genisi; hysmahelitis] hymahelitis; xxx] viginti V; innocenter] innocentur; denarij] donarij; denariorum] donariorum. **2** emerant] emerent. **3** &c] accipiat alter V. **8** criste] cristum. **11** mercedem] mercede; argentis] argenteos V.

t

1 Legitur in iij° libro regum xxij capitulo quod rex samarie & rex josaphat parati ad bellum consuluerunt prophetas circiter quadringentos et spiritus mendax est locutus in ore omnium prophetarum illorum scilicet placida Et mycheas verus propheta domini prophetauit regem in bello mansurum sicut sibi contigit praecepit ergo rex sibi dari panem tribulationis &c Iste mycheas cristum significat cui propter veritatem est datus panis tribulationis scilicet passio usque ad mortem **2** Legitur in iiij° libro regum vj capitulo quod in samaria erat tanta fames quod mulier coxit filium suum & comedit voluit ergo rex occidere helyzeum prophetam domini dixit ei heliseus cras erit modius siliginis pro statere vno & noluit credere sicut propheta dixerat et dixit helizeus videbis et non gustabis ex eo \et/ altera die conculcatus est in porta samarie a portantibus siliginem iste helizeus cristum significat qui dixit iudeis veritatem qui non crediderunt et interfecerunt pium ihesum innocentem **3** mychee ij Surgite & ite quia non habetis hic requiem **4** Baruch iiij Filij paciencer sustinete iram quae superven[it] vobis **5** CHRIST PREDICTS HIS PASSION **6** MICHEAS IS PUNISHED FOR PREDICTING DEFEAT **7** CONDEMNED ELISEUS PREDICTS THE TRUTH **8** Versus Mycheam cedunt: prophete qui male credunt **9** Versus premitur a populo: non credens hic helyseo **10** Jone iiij Melius est mihi mori quam viuere **11** Tobie xij Tempus est vt reuertar ad eum qui misit me &c **12** Versus Gethsemani transit ihesus inde suis valedicit

2 et] *inserted at end of* 2. **4** supervenit] V, supervenient. **10** melius est mihi mors quam vita V. **11** est] est ergo V.

•a•

1 Legitur in 2° libro regum iij capitulo quod Joab princeps milicie regis Dauid venit ad abner vt loqueretur ei in dolo quem cum dolose et blande alloqueretur transfixit eum gladio: Joab qui dolose alloquebatur abner significabat iudam qui christum dolose osculatus est et dedit impijs iudeis ad crucifigendum **2** Legitur in j° libro machabeorum capitulo xij quod tryphon venit ad viros de iuda et israel vt eis loqueretur in dolo et eos caperet: Tryphon iste iudam traditorem significat qui dolose ad christum veniens ipsum calumpniose osculans et eum sic impijs iudeis tradidit ad interficiendum **3** Dauid homo pacis mee in quo speraui **4** Salomonis prouerbia xvij Qui vertit linguam incidit in malum **5** JUDAS BETRAYS CHRIST WITH A KISS **6** JOAB BETRAYS ABNER **7** TRYPHON BETRAYS JONATHAN **8** Versus Alloquitur bland[e]: joab hunc perimitque nephande **9** Versus Verba gerens blanda parat arma tryphonque nephanda **10** ysayas iij Ve impio in malum retribucio manuum fiet ei **11** Jeremias [ix] In ore suo pacem cum amico suo loquitur **12** Versus per pacem Criste trahit hijs te proditor iste

4 incidit] incidet V. **8** blande] blanda. **10** manuum] enim; manuum eius V. **11** ix] xi.

s

1 Legitur in gen[e]si xiiij capitulo quod cum Abraham de sede inimicorum rediit [ut] ferret secum magnam praedam quam excussit de inimicis suis tunc melchicedech sacerdos dei summus optulit ei panem & vinum: Melchicedech cristum significat qui panem & vinum id est corporem et sanguinem suum in cena suis discipulis ad edendum et bibendum porrigebat **2** Legitur in exodo xvj capitulo quod dominus praecepit moysi vt diceret populo quod quilibet tolleret de manna celesti quan[t]um sufficeret sibi pro die illa manna autem celeste quod dominus israe-[litic]is dedit significabat panem sanctum scilicet sui sanctissimi corporis quod ipse in cena dedit suis discipulis cum dicebat accipite ex hoc omnes &c **3** Dauid Panem angelorum manducauit homo **4** Prouerbiorum ix Venite comedite panem meum **5** LAST SUPPER **6** MELCHISEDECH OFFERS BREAD & WINE **7** MOSES & THE MANNA **8** Versus sacra notant cristi: quae melchicedech dedit isti **9** Versus Se tenet in manibus se cibat ipse cibus **10** ysaias lv Audite audientes me et comedite bonum **11** Sapientia xvj panem de caelo prestitisti illis **12** Versus Rex sedet in cena turba cunctus duodena

1 genesi] genisi; ut] &. **2** quantum] ?quacum; israeliticis] israellicitis.

V

1 Legitur matthei xxv capitulo quod fatuis virginibus oleum non habentibus cum lampadibus clausa est janua scilicet porta eternae salutis Iste virgines iudeos significant qui etiam retro ceciderunt a domino interrogati super montem oliuarum quem quaeritis id est in disperationem et duriciam cordis ceciderunt et ideo iam sunt in inferno non credentes **2** Legitur in apocalypsis xij capitulo et in ysaya xiiij capitulo quod lucifer cecidit per superbiam de celo cum omnibus suis adherentibus Isti superbi dyaboli iudeos significant qui timuerunt perdere locum et terram eorum et ideo humilem pium ihesum interfecerunt et crucifixerunt et ipsi ceciderunt in foueam quam ipsi fecerant scilicet in infernum viuentes sicut scriptum est in psalmo **3** Trenorum ij En ista est dies quam exspectabamus inuenimus **4** ysaie liij Desiderauimus eum despectum et nouissimum virorum **5** JEWS FALL BACK FROM CHRIST **6** FOOLISH VIRGINS CONDEMNED **7** FALL OF THE ANGELS **8** Versus virginibus fatuis aufertur spes data gnaris **9** Versus Serpens antiquus cecidit de sede repulsus **10** Jeremias xiiij Reportauerunt vasa sua vacua **11** Baruch vj Si ceciderint in terram a semetipsis non resurgunt **12** Versus Sunt sic prostrati Cristum captare parati

11 resurgunt] consurgunt V.

•b•

1 Legitur in iii libro regum xix capitulo quod yesabel regina cum occidisset prophetas domini: tand[e]m helyam prophetam occidere desiderabat: hec impia regina impios iudeos significabat qui verum helyam id est cristum crudeliter et inuidio[se] occidere intendebant quia ipsis eorum malicia[m] praedicando manifestabat **2** Legitur in daniele xiiij° capitulo quod populus babilonicus impius venit ad regem nabugodonisor & dixerunt trade nobis danielem innocentem populus iste iudeos significat qui ad pylatum impetuose ac inportunis vocibus clamabant crucifige crucifige eum et iterum si dimittis hunc non es amicus cesaris: Rex autem iste pylatum significat qui iudeos timens christum innocentem eis tradidit **3** ysayas v Ve qui dicunt malum bonum & bonum malum **4** prouerbia xviij Accipere personam impij in iudicio non est bonum **5** JEWS CONDEMN CHRIST **6** JEZABEL SEEKS ELIAS' LIFE **7** THE KING CONDEMNS DANIEL **8** Versus Femina trux istum: dampnat sic impia cristum **9** Versus Gens haec crudelis: facit in mortem danielis **10** Job xxxvj Causa tua quasi impij iudicata est **11** Amos v Qui conuertitis in absinthium iudicium et iustitiam **12** Versus Est fera plebs ausa dampnare ihesum sine causa

1 tandem] tandam; inuidiose] inuidio; maliciam] malicia. **3** dicunt] dicitis V. **4** in . . . bonum] non est bonum, ut declines a veritate iudicii V.

•c•

1 Legitur in genesi ix capitulo quod noe cum dormisset in tabernaculo suo jacuit in terra nudatus quod cum vidisset filius eius cham derisit eum sed alij filij eius videre noluerunt et eorum oculos obtexerunt: Noe christum significat quem iudei deridentes ipsum coronauerunt et denudauerunt et sic infideles filij ipsum tamquam stultum subsa[n]nauerunt **2** Legitur in iiij° libro regum ij capitulo quod cum helyseus propheta ascendisset in montem bethel occurrerunt ei pueri in clamando et subsannando eum deriserunt et dixerunt ascende calue ascende calue: heliseus significat christum quem sui pueri id est iudei in coronatione & passione deriserunt **3** Dauid Omnes videntes me deriserunt me **4** prouerbiorum xix Parata sunt derisoribus iudicia & mallei percucien[es] **5** CHRIST IS MOCKED **6** NOAH'S NAKEDNESS IS MOCKED **7** CHILDREN MOCK ELISEUS **8** Versus Nuda verenda vidit: patris dum cham male ridet **9** Versus Percutit ira dei: derisores helysei **10** Trenorum iij Factus sum in derisum omni populo meo **11** ysaie primo Blasphemauerunt sanctum ysrael **12** Versus pro nobis criste: probum pateris pie triste

1 subsannauerunt] subsanauerunt. **4** percuciences] percutientes V, percuciencium.

•e•

1 Legitur in genesi xxij capitulo cum Abraham gladium extendisset vt filium immolaret angelus domini ipsum de caelo prohibuit: dicens ne extendas manum tuam super puerum Abraham patrem celestem significat qui filium suum scilicet cristum pro nobis omnibus in cruce immolauit vt per hoc innueret signum amoris paterni **2** Legitur in libro numeri xxi capitulo quod cum dominus vellet populum quem serpentes momorderant de serpentibus liberare: praecepit moysi vt faceret serpentem eneum et eum in ligno suspenderet vt quicumque illum inspiceret: de serpentibus liberaretur serpens suspensus intuitusque a populo cristum in cruce significat quem intu[ere] debet omnis fidel[is] qui a serpente id est dyabolo vult liberari **3** Dauid Foderunt manus meas et pedes meos **4** ysaias liij Oblatus est quia ipse voluit & peccata nostra ipse portauit **5** CRUCIFIXION **6** SACRIFICE OF ISAAC **7** MOSES LIFTS UP THE SERPENT **8** Versus Signantem christum: puerum pater immolat istum **9** Versus Lesi curantur: serpentem dum speculantur **10** Job xl Numquid capies leuiathan hamo **11** Abacuc iij Cornua in manibus eius ibi abscondita est fortitudo eius **12** Versus Eruit a tristi: baratro: nos passio christi

2 intuere] intuitus; fidelis] fideles. **10** An extrahere poteris leviathan hamo V.

•g•

1 Legitur in genesi [xxxvij] capitulo quod cum fratres joseph vellent eum hysmahelitis vendere ipsum tunica sua spoliauerunt & eum in cysternam veterem miserunt joseph iste christum significat qui missus fuit in cysternam hoc est in sepulchrum cum eum amici de cruce posuerunt **2** Legitur in libro jone ij capitulo quod cum ipse jonas ascenderat nauim vt iret tharsis in ciuitatem quamdam facta est tempestas magna in mari & cum misissent sortem inter se qui erant in naui sors cecidit super jonam quem illi apprehendentes miserunt in mare & piscis magnus statim eum deglutiuit in cuius ventre fuit tribus diebus & tribus noctibus jonas cristum significat qui fuit in ventre terrae tribus diebus & tribus noctibus **3** Dauid Excitatus est tanquam dormiens dominus tanquam potens crapulatus a vino **4** Canticorum v Ego dormio et cor meum vigilat **5** ENTOMBMENT **6** JOSEPH PLACED IN THE WELL **7** JONAS IS SWALLOWED **8** Versus Hanc in cysternam: detruditur iste veternam **9** Versus Jonas glutitur: tamen illesus reperitur **10** ysaias xi Et erit sepulchrum eius gloriosum **11** Genesi xlix Requiescens cubabit sicut leo **12** Versus Mirra conditur: et ab hijs cristus sepelitur

1 xxxvij] xxxvj. **11** cubabit sicut] accubuisti ut V.

•d•

1 Legitur in genesi [xxij] capitulo quod cum Abraham et ysaac pergerunt simul abraham portauit gladium et ignem ysaac vero ligna portabat per quam ipse immolari debuit: Iste ysaac qui lignum portauit christum significat qui lignum crucis in quo pro nobis immolari voluit in suo proprio corpore portauit **2** Legitur in iij libro regum xvij capitulo quod helyas clamabat ad mulierem quae ibat ad campum vt ligna colligeret et sibi pulmentum faceret quae respondens ait en duo ligna colligo vt inde mihi faciam et filio meo pulmentum Duo ligna quae haec mulier colligebat ligna crucis significabant quae ligna christus in suo corpore portare colligebat **3** ysaie liij Sicut ouis ad occ[is]ionem ductus est **4** Jheremie xi venite mittamus lignum in panem eius **5** CHRIST CARRIES THE CROSS **6** ABRAHAM & ISAAC **7** WOMAN OF SAREPHTA **8** Versus Ligna ferens criste: te praesignificat puer iste **9** Versus Mistica sunt signa: crucis haec vidue duo ligna **10** Dauid [Venite] propera[t]e currite ad victimam **11** Jheremie xi Ego autem quasi agnus mansuetissimus qui portatur ad victimam **12** Versus Fert crucis hic lignum: christus reputans sibi dignum

1 xxij] xii. **3** occisionem] occionem. **4** venite] *not in* V. **10** Venite] Medice; properate] properare. **11** Ego . . . mansuetissimus] Et ego quasi agnus mansuetus V.

•f•

1 Legitur in genesi ij capitulo cum Adam obdormiuisset dominus costam de latere eius tulit et formauit de ea mulierem: Adam dormiens cristum iam in cruce mortuum significat de cuius latere pro nobis fluxere sacramenta cum miles lancea sua latus cristi aperuit **2** Legitur in exodo xvij capitulo quod cum moyses populum per desertum transduxisset deficiente illis aqua prae aquae penuria moyses cum virga quam in manu tenebat silicem percuciebat et exiuerunt aquae largissimae velud de abisso inulta silex siue lapis christum significat qui nobis aquas salutares scilicet sacramenta de suo latere effudit cum illud lanc[e]a militis in cruce aperiri permisit **3** Dauid Super dolorem uulnerum meorum addiderunt **4** Sacharias xiij Qui[d] sunt plage iste in medio manuum tuarum **5** CHRIST IS OPENED **6** EVE IS DRAWN FROM ADAM **7** MOSES STRIKES THE ROCK **8** Versus Femina prima viri: de costa cepit oriri **9** Versus Est sacramentum: cristi dans petra fluent[u]m **10** Trenorum primo O vos omnes qui transitis per viam attendite & videte **11** Amos viij In die illa occidet sol & radios suos abscondet **12** Versus De cristo munda: cum sanguine profluit vnda

2 lancea] lancia. **4** Quid] Quae V, Quit. **9** fluentum] fluentem. **11** Et erit in die illa, dicit Dominus deus; occidet sol in meridie, et tenebrescere faciam terram in die luminis V.

•h•

1 Legitur in i° libro regum xvij capitulo quod dauid cum goliam gigantem deiecisset in suo proprio gladio ipsum interfecit et caput eius amputauit sic christus quando a mortuis resurrexit hominem de inferno liberauit & a dyabolica potestate exemit & ipsum dyabolum in sua potencia debilitauit **2** Legitur in libro iudicum xiiij capitulo de Sampsone quod cum leo in eum [ir]ruisset ipse leonem apprehendit et interfecit Sampson cristum significat qui leonem id est dyabolum occidit quando de eius potestate hominem liberauit **3** Dauid Contriuit portas ereas & [vectes] ferreos confregit **4** Osee xiij O mors ero mors tua morsus tuus ero inferne **5** CHRIST OPENS LIMBO **6** DAVID KILLS GOLIATH **7** SAMSON KILLS THE LION **8** Versus Signans te criste; golyam conterit iste **9** Versus Vt vis sampsonis: destruxit ora leonis **10** Zacharias [ix] Tu in sanguine testamenti tui emisisti vinctos **11** Genesi xlix Ad praedam fili mi ascendisti **12** Versus Fit cristi morte barathri destruccio porte

2 irruiset] reruisset. **3** vectes] V., victos. **10** ix] ij.

·i·

1 Legitur in libro iudicum xvj capitulo de Sampsone quod ipse media nocte surrexit portasque civitatis ereas ambas sua fortitudine deiecit & extra civitatem secum detulit Sampson cristum significat qui media nocte de sepulchro surgens portas sepulchri deiecit et liber atque poten[s] inde exiuit 2 Legitur in libro Jone prophetae ij capitulo quod cum ipse Jonas fuisset in ventre ceti tribus diebus & tribus noctibus postea piscis eum expuit super terram aridam Jonas qui post tres dies de pisce exiuit significat cristum qui post tres dies de sepulchro exiuit uel resurrexit 3 Dauid Excitatus est tanquam domus dormiens dominus 4 Genesis xlix Catulus leonis iuda filius meus 5 RESURRECTION 6 SAMSON REMOVES THE GATES OF GAZA 7 JONAS IS RELEASED 8 Versus Obsessus torbis: sampson valuas tulit vrbis 9 Versus De tumulo christe: surgens te denotat iste 10 Osee vi In die tertia suscitabit nos sciemus et sequemur eum 11 Sophonias iij In die resurrectionis meae congregabo gentes 12 Versus Quem saxum texit: ingens tumulum ihesus exit

1 potens] potenti. 3 domus] *not in* V; filius meus] ad praedam fili me V. 10 sciemus . . . eum] Et vivemus in conspectus eius. Sciemus, sequemurque ut cognoscamus Dominum V. 11 congregabo] in futurum; Quia judicium meum ut congregem V. 12 ingens] iñgens *preceded by* ? *uncut:*.

·k·

1 Legitur in genesi xxxvij capitulo quod ruben venit et quaesiuit fratrem suum Joseph in cysterna quam cum inuenisset turbatus erat nimis ad fratres suos ait puer non comparet & ego quo ibo ruben iste mariam magdalenam significat qui cum dolore & deuocione christum quaesiuit in sepulchro cum autem responsum ab angelo recepisset quod a mortuis resurrexisset ipsa postmodum eum videre meruit 2 Legitur in libro salomonis canticorum iij capitulo de ipsa sponsa quae quaerendo suum dilectum · ait quaesiui quem diligit anima mea & non inueni illum haec sponsa figuram gerit mari[e] magdalene quae suum dilectum quaesiuit in tumulo & postea in orto inuenit 3 ysaias lv Querite dominum dum inueniri potest inuocate eum dum prope est 4 Dauid Letetur cor quaerentium dominum 5 THREE WOMEN AT THE TOMB 6 RUBEN AT THE WELL 7 THE BRIDE SEEKING HER HUSBAND Quesiui illum et non inuei · canticorum iij 8 Versus Ruben sublatum: puerum timet esse necatum 9 Versus Hec pia vota gerit dum sponsum sedula quaerit 10 michaeas vltimo Ego autem aspiciam ad dominum et expectabo eum 11 Genesi xlix Salutare tuum expectabo domine 12 Versus Quod viuas criste: certum docet angelus iste

2 marie] mariam. 10 Ego autem ad Dominum aspiciam; exspectabo Deum V.

·l·

1 Legitur in daniele xiiij° capitulo quod cum daniel propheta missus fuisset in lacum leonum vt leones eum occiderent mane facto rex venit ad lacum leonum et ad danielem vt videret si adhuc viueret qui cum videret eum viuere gauisus est valde : Rex enim iste mariam magdalenam significat quando maria venit ad monumentum postea dominum suum vidit & quia a mortuis resurrexit gauisa est valde 2 Legitur in cantico canticorum iij° capitulo quod sponsa cum suum dilectum invenisset dixit inueni quem diligit anima mea & iterum tenebo eum & non dimittam eum sponsa haec mariam magdalenam significat quae suum sponsum id est cristum videns ipsum tenere voluit qui sibi taliter respondit noli me tangere nondum enim ascendi ad patrem meum 3 Dauid Non derelinques quaerentes te domine 4 i° regum ij Exultauit cor meum in domino 5 CHRIST IS FOUND BY MARY MAGDALENE 6 DANIEL IS FOUND AMONG THE LIONS 7 THE BETROTHED FINDS THE BELOVED Tenui eum nec dimittam canticorum iij 8 Versus Rex iocundatur hunc vt viuum speculatur 9 Versus Sponso quaesito fruitur iam sponsa cupit[o] 10 Ysaias [lxi] Gaudens gaudebo in domino et exulta in deo 11 Osee ii Adducam eam in solitudinem et ibi loquar ad cor eius 12 Versus Te monstrans piam: solaris criste mariam

3 derelinques] derelinquisti V. 9 cupito] cupita. 10 lxi] lx; et . . . deo] Et exsultabit anima mea in Deo meo V. 11 Adducam] Et ducam V; ibi] *not in* V.

·m·

1 Legitur in genesi [xlv] capitulo quod Joseph vidisset fratres suos terrore concussos & multitudinem timentes ignorantesque quod Joseph esset · dixit eis ego sum frater vestri Joseph nolite timere & sic consolatus est eos: Joseph christum significat qui post resurrexionem suam discipulis simul existentibus apparuit et eos alloquendo consolatus est dicens nolite timere ego sum 2 Legitur in ewangelio luce xv capitulo quod filius cuiusdam div[i]tis ad patrem suum dixit vt sibi partem haereditatis sue daret & cum sibi tradidisset abijt in regionem longiquam & totam substantiam male cons[u]mpsit quo facto ad patrem suum redijt et eum benigne recepit & consolabatur Iste enim pius pater significat illum patrem celestem qui ad suos discipulos veniens eos de sua morte consolatus est & suam resurrexionem manifestauit 3 Dauid Adimplebis me leticia cum vultu tuo 4 Sapientiae primo Et apparuit hijs qui fidem habuere in illum 5 CHRIST APPEARS TO HIS DISCIPLES 6 JOSEPH IDENTIFIES HIMSELF TO HIS BROTHERS 7 PRODIGAL SON 8 Versus Quos vexit pridem blanditur fratribus idem 9 Versus Flens amplexatur: natum pater ac recreatur 10 Ysaias [li] Attendite ad petram vnde exc[isi] estis 11 Ezechiel xxxiiij Ecce ego ipse requiram oues meas et visitabo eas 12 Versus Hijs ihesus apparet: surgentis gloria claret

1 xlv] lxv. 2 divitis] d'rt'; sibi partem] *preceded by otiose stroke*; consumpsit] conscimpsit. 4 apparuit] apparet V; hijs] eis V; habuere] habent V. 10 li] l; excisi] V, excussi.

·n·

1 Legitur in libro iudicum vi° capitulo quod angelus domini venit ad gedeonem dicens ad eum dominus tecum virorum fortissime quia tu ipse populum liberabis & sic factum est: Gedeon enim thomam significat ad quem venit angelus magni consilij scilicet christus et eum confortans in fide: dixit mitte manum tuam in latus meum & cognosce loca clauorum & noli esse incredulus sed fidelis 2 Legitur in gen[e]si xxxij capitulo quod cum angelus domini venisset ad Jacob ipse angelum apprehendens cum eo luctabatur nec eum dimisit nisi eum benedixisset Jacob iste thomam apostolam designat qui angelum id est cristum tangens benedictionem hoc est certificacionem de cristi resurrectione meruit obtinere 3 ysaye lvij [Vias eius vidi] et dimisi eum & reduxi eum 4 Jheremias xxxi Conuerte me & reuertar quia tu dominus deus meus 5 DOUBTING THOMAS 6 GIDEON & THE ANGEL 7 JACOB WRESTLES WITH THE ANGEL 8 Versus Angelus hortatur nequid gedeon vereatur 9 Versus I[srael] est dictus luctans iacob benedictus 10 Dauid letifica domine animam serui tui 11 Zophonias iij Attamen timebis me suscipies disciplinam 12 Versus Te pateris criste · palpari [cedat] vt iste

3 Vias . . . vidi] V, Videns vide eum; et . . . eum[2] et sanavi eum; et reduxi eum V. 2 genesi] genisi. 4 reuertar] convertar V. 9 Israel] Ihrl'. 10 Domine . . . laetifica animam servitui V. 12 cedat] se dat.

·o·

1 Legitur in gen[e]si v capitulo quod enoch deo placuit et translatus est in paradysum enoch enim qui cristo placuit cristum significat qui summo patri placuit ideo in paradysum celestem id est in celum ascendere meruit eum enim in die ascencionis super omnes choros angelorum exaltauit 2 Legitur in iiij libro regum ij capitulo quod cum helyas propheta in curru igneo tolleretur in celum helyseus clamabat dicens pater mi pater mi currus israel et auriga eius helyas christum significabat quem videntes apostoli quos helyseus significabat in celum ascendentem admirati sunt cum christus eis dixit ascendo ad pat[rem] meum 3 Dauid Ascendit deus in iubilatione & dominus in voce [tu]be 4 ysaye lxiij Quis est iste qui venit de edom tinctis vestibus &c 5 ASCENSION 6 HENOCH ASCENDS 7 ELISEUS RECEIVES ELIAS' MANTLE 8 Versus Enoch translatus celestibus est sociatus 9 Versus Celitus effectus helia per aera vectus 10 Deuteronomium [xxxii] Sicut aquila prouocans pullos suos ad volandum 11 Michaeas ij Ascendit iter pandens ante eos 12 Versus Sanctus sanctorum cristus petit astra polorum

1 genesi] genisi. 2 patrem] pateram. 3 iubilatione] iubilo V; tube] V, turbe. 10 xxxii] xxx; pullos . . . volandum] ad volandum pullos suos V. 11 Ascendit . . . pandens] Ascendit enim pandens iter V.

·p·

1 Legitur in exodo [xxxv] capitulo quod dominus dixit ad moysen ascende ad me in montem et dabo tibi duas tabulas testimonij sicut enim moysi lex fuit data & in tabulis lapideis inscripta sic in die pente[ch]ostes fuit lex noua in cordibus fidelium inscripta quando ignis super credentes in vnum congregatos apparuit **2** Legitur in iiij° libro regum xviij° capitulo quod helyas propheta cum imposuisset holocaustum scilicet bouem vnum super lignum et circumstante populo inuocauit dominum et ignis veniens de celo consumpsit omnia & sic credidit populus in domino: Iste ignis celitus significat istum ignem diuinum qui in die pentechostes venit super discipulos et purgauit eos et omnia vicia peccatorum consumpsit **3** Dauid Emitte spiritum tuum et creabuntur **4** Sapientia i Spiritus domini repleuit orbem terrarum &c **5** PENTECOST **6** MOSES RECEIVES THE LAW **7** ELIAS' SACRIFICE IS ACCEPTED **8** Versus Est lex diuina: moysi data v[e]rtice syna **9** Versus Celica flamma venit et plebis pectora lenit **10** Ezechiel xxxvj Spiritum meum ponam in medio vestri **11** Johel ij Super seruos meos [et] ancillas meas effundam **12** Versus Pectora verorum replet almum pneuma virorum

1 xxxiv] xxxij; pentechostes] pentecohostes. **8** vertice] virtice. **11** et] V, *omitted*; meas] in diebus illis V.

·q·

1 Legitur in iiij° libro regum ij capitulo quod cum bersabee mater salomonis fuisset ingressa ad eum in palacium suum ipse rex salomon iussit poni matri sue thronum iuxta thronum suum bersabee virginem gloriosam significat cuius thronus positus est iuxta thronum veri salomonis scilicet ihesu cristi **2** Legitur in libro hester ij° capitulo quod cum regina hester venisset ad regem assuerum in suum pallacium ipse rex assuerus honorando: eam iuxta se posuit hester regina virginem mariam significat quam assuerus id est christus in die assumptionis sue in gloria celesti iuxta se collocauit **3** Dauid Vultum tuum deprecabuntur omnes diuites plebis **4** Canticorum vltimo Que est ista quae assendit per desertum **5** CORONATION OF THE VIRGIN **6** SOLOMON ENTHRONES BETHSABEE **7** ASSUERUS GRANTS ESTHER'S PETITION **8** Versus Ingressam matrem: salomon sibi collacat istam **9** Versus Hester vt ingreditur: et assuerum veneratur **10** ysaias xxxv Gloria libani data est ei decor carmeli et saron **11** Sapientia iiij O quam pulchra est casta generatio cum c[l]aritate **12** Versus Assumendo piam: veneraris christe mariam

4 per desertum] de deserto V. **11** claritate] V, caritate.

·r·

1 Legitur in iij° libro regum iiij° capitulo quod venerunt due mulieres meretrices coram salomonee & contendebant de filijs suis coram iudice de filio oppresso & viuo qui cum non posset aliter iudicare dixit afferte mihi gladium & diuidite infantem viuum et translata sunt viscera mulieris infantis viui et dixit date ei infantem viuum et cessauit iudicare Per salomonem sapientissimum christus intelligitur qui iudicabat iustos & iniustos secundum verum iudicium **2** Legitur in ij° libro regum i° capitulo quod rex dauid post mortem saul mansit in sizilech & veniens vnus a terr[a] amalachitarum iactabat se quod interfecisset cristum domini scilicet saul regem et data est super eo sentencia mortis a dauid quia os eius locutum fuisset aduersus eum & dixit ad armigerum suum irrue in eum & interfice eum Dauid christum significat qui vt amalachitam dauid iudicatur[us] est omnes gentes in equitate vnicuique remunerabit iuxta delicta sua **3** Ecclesiastes iiij Iustum et impium iudicabit dominus **4** i regum ij Dominus iudicabit fines terre **5** LAST JUDGEMENT **6** JUDGEMENT OF SOLOMON **7** DAVID CONDEMNS THE AMALACITE **8** Versus Dicat nunc iuste dandus matri puer iste. **9** Versus Ob domini cristum: sic dauid iudicat istum **10** ysayae ij Iudicabit gentes & arguet populos multos **11** Ezechiel vij Iudicabit te iuxta vias tuas **12** Versus Iudico dampnandos reprobos simulatque nephandos

2 terra] terram; iudicaturus] iudicaturrus. **3** dominus] Deus V. **11** Iudicabit] Indicabo V.

·s·

1 Legitur in libro deuteronomij xi capitulo quod dathan et abiron habitantes in medio israel propter quod mandatum dei non seruauerant absorti sunt a terra cum domibus et tabernaculis suis Per dathan & abiron significantur peccatores non curantes de lege catholica nec decalogi et ingurgitantur in infernum qui est locus peccatorum plenus dolo et igne qui deuorabit eos atque cum dyabolo punientur **2** Legitur in genesi xix capitulo quod propter peccata sodomorum et gomorreorum immisit ignem deus de celo super civitates has atque subuerse sunt ambe Per sodomam et gomorram intelliguntur peccatores terre viuentes secundum desideria corporum eorum excecancia oculos eorum et cum mane exortum fuerit tunc apparebunt omnes peccatores terre atque ad infernum destinabuntur viui et dampnabuntur **3** Sapientia xviij Simili pena seruus cum domino punietur **4** Dauid Fex eius non est exinanita bibent omnes peccatores terre **5** THE DAMNED ENTER HELL **6** DATHAN & ABIRON ARE ENGULFED **7** SODOM & GOMORRHA BURN **8** Versus Hi terre dantur: quia christo non famulantur **9** Versus Ob crimen vite: truduntur sic sodomite **10** Iheremie xxv Perdam ex eis vocem gaudij eorum **11** Job xvj Saturati sunt penis meis **12** Versus Sic affliguntur penis qui praua seqvuntur

2 deus] ?dominus. **3** Simili] Simili autem V; punietur] afflictus est V. **10** Perdam] que V. **11** Saturati] Saciati V.

·t·

1 Legitur in libro Job primo capitulo quod filij sui habebant conuiuia per domos suas unusquisque in domo sua & mittentes pro sororibus suis vt secum comederent et biberent Filij Job sunt sancti qui cotidiana faciunt conuiuia mittentes pro saluandis vt veniant ad gaudium eternum et eternaliter deo fruantur amen **2** Legitur in genesi [xxviij] capitulo quod cum Jacob vidisset occasum solis invenit lapidem quod subposuit capiti suo in sompnis vidit scalam erectam a terra usque in celum & angelos descendentes et dominum innixum scale dicentem sibi: terram in qua dormis tibi dabo & semini tuo in seculum pro iacob subaudi animam fidelem quae cum obdormierit in lapide id est christo obtinebit terram lacte & melle manantem id est regnum celorum **3** Dauid Gaudete Justi in domino & gloriamini omnes recti corde **4** Thobias [xi] Et flere ceperunt pre gaudio **5** CHRIST GATHERS BLESSED SOULS **6** JOB'S FAMILY FEASTS **7** JACOB'S LADDER **8** Versus Job nati gaudent quia sic feliciter audent **9** Versus Angelus est visus Jacob in hoc valde gauisus **10** In libro Iosue i Omnem locum quem calcauerit vestigium tu[u]m **11** Isaiae ultimo letamini cum Iherusalem & exultate in ea omnes qui diligitis eam **12** Versus O pater in celis: me tecum pascere velis

2 xxviij] xxvij. **4** xi] ij; Et . . . gaudio] et coeperunt ambo flere prae gaudio V. **10** tuum] vestri V, tuam.

·v·

1 Legitur in cantico canticorum iiij° capitulo quod sponsus alloquitur sponsam sibi eam sumendo dicit tota pulchra es amica mea et macula non est in te: veni amica mea veni coronaberis Sponsus verus iste est christus qui assumendo eam sponsa[m] quia est anima sine macula omnis peccati et introducit eam in requiem eternam & coronat eam cum corona immortalitatis **2** Legitur in apocalypsis xxi capitulo quod angelus dei apprehendit Ihoannem ewangelistam cum esset in spiritu & volens sibi ostendere archana dei dixit ad eum veni ostendam tibi sponsam uxorem agni angelus loquitur ad omnes in generali vt veniant ad auscultandum in spiritu agnum innocentem christum animam innocentem coronantem **3** Dauid Tanquam sponsus dominus procedens de thalamo suo **4** Ysaye [lxi] Tanquam sponsus decorauit me corona **5** CHRIST GIVES THE CROWN OF ETERNAL LIFE **6** THE GROOM CROWNS THE BRIDE **7** THE ANGEL & ST JOHN **8** Versus Laus animae vere: sponsum bene senti habere **9** Versus Sponsus amat sponsam christus nimis et speciosam **10** E[z]eciel xxiiij Corona tua circumligata sit tibi et calciamenta in pedibus **11** Ozee ij Sponsabo te m[ihi] in sempiternum &c **12** Versus Tunc gaudent animae sibi quando bonum datur omne

1 sponsam] sponsa. **3** dominus] *not in* V. **4** lxi] vj; Tanquam sponsus . . . me] Quasi sponsum decoratum V. **10** Ezeciel] Egeciel; calciamenta in pedibus] calceamenta tua erunt in pedibus tuis V. **11** mihi] m. **12** quando] ?.

BIBLIOGRAPHY

Primary Sources

Baltimore, Walters Art Gallery, MS 182.
Brussels, Bibliothèque Royale Albert Ier, MS II 7619.
— MS IV 194.
— MSS 9018–19, 9020–23.
Ghent, Universiteitsbibliotheek, MS 632.
The Hague, Koninklijke Bibliothek, MS 78 D 39.
— MS 133 E 22.
The Hague, Rijksmuseum Meermanno-Westreenianum, MS 10
    F 3.
Krakow, Muzeum Narodowe, MS 3091.
Liége, Bibliothèque de l'Université, Wittert MS 34.
— Wittert MS 13.
London, British Library, Add. MS 10043.
— Add. MS 15410.
— Add. MS 16951.
— Add. MS 18162.
— Add. MS 29887.
— Add. MS 38122.
— Add. MS 38724.
— Add. MS 39657.
— MS Egerton 1149.
— MS Harley 2966.
— MS King's 5.
— MS Sloane 2571.
— MS Sloane 2692.
— MS Sloane 2726.
— MS Stowe 18.
Munich, Bayerische Statsbibliothek, MS germ. 1102.
Nuremberg, Stadtbibliothek, MS Solger 8°.
Oxford, Blackfriars, MS 1.
Oxford, Bodleian Library, MS Aubrey 31.
— Bodleian Library, MS Aubrey 31.
— MS Auct. D. inf. 2.13.
— MS Buchanan e.11.
— MS Buchanan f.1.
— MS Buchanan f.3.
— MS Canon. Liturg. 17.
— MS Canon. Liturg. 92.
— MS Canon. Liturg. 118.
— MS Douce 30.
— MS Douce 93.
— MS Douce 248.
— MS Douce 374.
— MS Douce 381.
— MS Douce d. 19.
— MS Douce f. 4.
— MS E. D. Clarke 30.
— MS Laud Misc. 7.
— MS Liturg. 98.
— MS Liturg. 400.
— MS Rawl. liturg. g. 6.
St Gallen, Stiftsbibliothek, MS 605.
Windsor, Eton College, MS 177.
Vienna, Österreichische Nationalbibliothek, MS 1856.
— MS 2771–2772.

Secondary Sources

Schiller is cited in the English translation for Vols. I and II, and in the German for Vols. III and IV.

Ameisenowa, Zofja. 'The Tree of Life in Jewish Iconography'. *JWCI*, 2 (1938–39), 326–45.

Andrew, Malcolm R. 'Jonah and Christ in *Patience*'. *MP*, 70 (1972–73), 230–33.

— and Ronald Waldron. *The Poems of the Pearl Manuscript*. London: Edward Arnold, 1978.

Apocalypsis Sancti Johannis [Schreiber Edition III]. Netherlands, fifteenth century. British Library, C.9.d.1.

Arnold, Hugh. *Stained Glass of the Middle Ages in England and France; Painted by Lawrence B. Saint, Described by Hugh Arnold*. 3rd ed. London: Black, 1939.

Auerbach, Erich. 'Figurative Texts Illustrating Certain Passages of Dante's *Commedia*'. *MLN*, 21 (1949), 474–89.

— *Typologische Motive in der mittelalterlichen Literatur*. Schriften und Vorträge des Petrarca-Instituts Köln, 2. Krefeld: Scherpe, 1953.

— 'Figura'. Trans. Ralph Manheim. In *Scenes from the Drama of European Literature*. New York: Meridian, 1959.

Avalle, d'Arco Silvio, ed. *Sponsus dramma delle vergini prudenti e delle vergini stolte*. Milan and Naples: Ricciardi, 1965.

Bagrow, Leo. *History of Cartography*. Rev. R. A. Skelton. London: Watts, 1964.

Baldass, Ludwig. *Jan Van Eyck*. London: Phaidon, 1952.

Banning, Knud. 'Man skriver i Skåne . . . om *Biblia Pauperum*, vers i skånske kallsmalerier'. *Ico Iconographiske Post*, 1 (1979), 3–11.

— 'Biblia Pauperum and the Wall Paintings in the Church of Bellinge. The Book and the Church Wall'. In *Medieval Iconography and Narrative: a Symposium*. Ed. Flemming G. Andersen, Esther Nyholm et al. Odense: Odense Univ. Press, 1980, pp. 124–56.

Barr, James. *Old and New in Interpretation: A Study of Two Testaments*. London: SCM Press, 1966.

Batiffol, Pierre. *Histoire du Bréviaire Romain*. Paris, 1895.

— *The History of the Roman Breviary*. Trans. Atwell M. Y. Bayley. London, 1898.

Baudot, Jules. Trans. [A Priest of the Diocese of Westminster]. *The Roman Breviary: Its Sources and History*. London: Catholic Truth Society, 1909.

— Trans. [The Benedictines of Stanbrook]. *The Breviary: Its History and Contents*. Catholic Library of Religious Knowledge, 4. London: Sands, 1929.

Beadle, Richard. *The York Plays*. London: Edward Arnold, 1982.

Beaulieu, Michèle, and Jeanne Baylé. *Le Costume en Bourgogne de Philippe le Hardi à Charles le Téméraire*. Paris: Presses Universitaires de France, 1956.

Beeke, Anthon. *Alphabet*. Hilversum: de Jong, 1970.

Bégule, Lucien. *L'Église Saint-Maurice, ancienne cathédrale de Vienne en Dauphiné: Son architecture, sa décoration*. Paris: Laurens, 1914.

Behrends, Rainer, with Konrad Kratzsche and Heinz Mettke, comm. Biblia Pauperum Apocalypsis: *The Weimar MS. Fol. max. 4*. Trans. George Baurley and Leonard A. Jones. New York: Hacker Art Books, 1978.

Beissel, Stephan. 'Eine Missale aus Hildesheim und die Anfänge der Armenbibel'. *Zeitschrift für christliche Kunst*, 15, No. 10 (1902), 265–74, 308–18.

Berjeau, Jean Philibert, ed. Biblia Pauperum *Reproduced in Facsimile from One of the Copies in the British Museum: With an Historical and Bibliographical Introduction*. London, 1859.

— *Canticum Canticorum, Reproduced in Facsimile from the Scriverius Copy in the British Museum*. London, 1860. See also *Cantica*.

Berve, Maurus. *Die Armenbibel: Herkunft Gestalt Typologie: Dargestellt anhand von Miniaturen ans der Handschrift Cpg 148 der Universitätsbibliothek Heidelberg*. Beuron: Beuroner Kunstverlag, 1969.

Bible moralisée. See Laborde.

Biblia Patristica: Index des citations et allusions bibliques dans la littérature patristique. Vol. I: *Des Origines à Clément d'Alexandrie et Tertullien*. Paris: Centre National de la Recherche Scientifique, 1975.

Biblia Sacra iuxta Vulgatam Clementinam . . . 4th ed. Matriti: Biblioteca de Autores Cristianos, 1965.

Bing, Gertrud. 'The Apocalypse Block-books and their Manuscript Models'. *JWCI*, 5 (1942), 143–58.

Blair, Claude. *European Armour circa 1066 to circa 1700*. London: Batsford, 1958.

Bliss, Douglas, P. *A History of Wood-Engraving*. London: Dent, 1928.

Bloch, P. 'Typologie'. In Engelbert Kirschbaum, et al. *Lexicon der christlichen Ikonographie*. Vol. IV. Rome: Herder, 1968–74, pp. 395–403.

Block, Katherine S., ed. *The Ludus Coventriae or the Plaie Called Corpus Christi Cotton MS. Vespasian D. viii*. EETS ES, 120. London: Oxford Univ. Press, 1922.

Blum, Pamela Z. 'The Middle English Romance "Iacob and Ioseph" and the Joseph Cycle of the Salisbury Chapter House'. *Gesta*, 8 (1969), 18–34.

Blum, Shirley N. *Early Netherlandish Triptychs: A Study in Patronage*. Berkeley: Univ. of California Press, 1969.

Bodenstedt, Sr Mary Immaculate. *The Vita Christi of Ludolphus the Carthusian*. Washington, D.C.: n. p., 1944.

Boeckler, Albert. *Die Regensburg Prüfeninger Buchmalerei des XII. und XIII. Jahrhunderts*. Munich: A. Reusch, 1924.

Bonaventura, St. *Speculum Beate Marie Virginis*. Augsberg: Anthonium Sorg, 1476.

Bonnell, John K. 'The Serpent with a Human Head in Art and in Mystery Play'. *American Journal of Archaeology*, 21 (1917), 255–91.

Borenius, Tancred. 'The Cycle of Images in the Palaces and Castles of Henry III'. *JWCI*, 6 (1943), 40–50.

Bourke, Patricia. 'The Stained Glass Windows of the Church of St. Neot, Cornwall'. *Devon and Cornwall Notes and Queries*, 33, No. 3 (1974), 65–68.

Bouvet, Frances, ed. *Le Cantique des Cantiques Canticum Canticorum Historia seu Providentia Beatae Mariae Virginis ex Cantico Canticorum*. Les Chefs d'oeuvre de la xylographie. Paris: Les Editions de minuit, 1961.

Bowers, Robert H. *The Legend of Jonah*. The Hague: Nijhoff, 1971.

Branner, Robert. *Manuscript Painting in Paris During the Reign of Saint Louis: A Study of Styles*. Berkeley: Univ. of California Press, 1977.

Breitenbach, Edgar. Speculum Humanae Salvationis: *Eine typengeschichtliche Untersuchung*. Strasbourg: Heitz, 1930.

Breviarum Romanum ex Decreto Sacrosancti Concilii Tridentini Restitutum, S. Pii V. Pontificus Maximi Jussu Editum Clementis VIII. et Urbani VIII. Auctoritate Recognitum cum Officiis Sanctorum Novissime per Summos Pontifices usque ad Hanc Diem Concessis. Mechlinia, 1876.

Breviarium Sacri Ordinis Praedicatorum. Paris, 1743.

Brieger, Peter H., introd. *The Trinity Apocalypse*. 2 vols. London: Eugrammia Press in collaboration with Trinity College, Cambridge, 1967.

Briquet, Charles M. *Les Filigranes. Dictionnaire historique des marques du papier dès leur apparition vers 1282 jusqu'en 1600*. 2nd ed. 4 vols. Leipzig: Hiersemann, 1923.

Brix, Otto. *Über die mittelenglische Übersetzung des* Speculum Humanae Salvationis. Palaestra: Untersuchungen und Texte aus der deutschen und englischen Philologie, 7. Berlin: Mayer and Müller, 1900.

Brooks, Neil C. *The Sepulchre of Christ in Art and Liturgy with Special Reference to the Liturgical Drama*. Univ. of Illinois Studies in Language and Literature, 7, No. 2. Urbana: Univ. of Illinois Press, 1921.

— 'An Ingolstadt Corpus Christi Procession and the *Biblia Pauperum*'. *JEGP*, 35 (1936), 1–16.

Bühler, Curt Ferdinand. *The Fifteenth-Century Book: The Scribes, the Printers, the Decorators*. Philadelphia: Univ. of Pennsylvania Press, 1960.

Buikstra-de Boer, Marianne, and Gary Schwartz, eds. and trans. *All the Paintings of the Rijksmuseum in Amsterdam: A Completely Illustrated Catalogue* . . . Amsterdam: Rijksmuseum, 1976.

Burney, Charles Fox, ed. *The Book of Judges*. London: Rivingtons, 1918.

Buschhausen, Helmut. 'The Klosterneuburg Altar of Nicholas of Verdun: Art, Theology and Politics'. *JWCI*, 37 (1974), 1–32.

Byvanck, Alexander W. *Les Principaux manuscrits à peintures de la Bibliothèque Royale des Pays-bas et du Musée Meermanno-Westreenianum à la Haye*. Paris: Société française de reproductions de manuscrits à peintures, 1924.

— *La Miniature dans les pays-bas septentrionaux*. Paris: Les Éditions d'art et d'histoire, 1937.

— *De middeleeuwsche boekillustratie in de noordelijke Nederlanden*. Maerlantbibliotheek, 10. Antwerp: de Sikkel, 1943.

— and Godefridus J. Hoogewerff. *Noord-Nederlandiche miniaturen in handschriften der 14e, 15e en 16e eeuwen*. 3 vols. 'S-Gravenhage: Nijhoff, 1923–25.

Cabrol, Fernand, and Henri Leclerq, comp. *Dictionnaire d'archéologie chrétienne et de liturgie*. 15 vols. Paris: Librairie Letouzey et Ané, 1903–53.

Calkins, Robert, G. 'Parallels Between Incunabula and Manuscripts from the Circle of the Master of Catherine of Cleves'. *Oud Holland*, 92, No. 3 (1978), 137–60.

Cames, Gérard. *Allégories et symboles dans l'Hortus Deliciarum*. Leyden: Brill, 1971.

Camesina, Albert von, ed., and Gustav Heider, comm. Biblia Pauperum: *Die Darstellungen der* Biblia Pauperum *in einer Handschrift des XIV. Jahrhunderts, aufbewahrt im Stift St. Florian im Erzherzogthume Österreich ob der Enns*. Vienna, 1863.

Cantica Canticorum. Netherlands, c. 1465. British Library, IB.46.

Cantica Canticorum. Pref. Otto Clemen. Zwickauer Facsimile-drucke, 4. Zwickau: n.p., 1910.

Cantica Canticorum: Societatis in Honorem Marées Pictoris Conditae Opus Tricesimum Quartum. Editio Archetypum Anni circiter Millesimi Quadringentesimi Sexagesimi Quinti Imitans. Marées Geselleschaft, 14. Berlin: Ganymede, 1922.

Cappelli, Adriano. *Lexicon Abbreviaturarum: Dizionario di abbreviature latine ed italiane*. 6th ed. Milan: Ulrico Hoepli, 1973. See Pelzer for suppl.

Catholic Encyclopedia. See Herbermann.

Caviness, Madeline. *The Early Stained Glass of Canterbury Cathedral, circa 1175–1220*. Princeton, N.J.: Princeton Univ. Press, 1977.

Cecchelli, Carlo. *La Cattedra di Massimiano ed altri avorii romano-orientali*. Vol. I. Rome: La Libreria dello stato, 1936.

Châtelet, Albert. *Heures de Turin quarante-cinq feuillets à peintures provenant des très belles heures de Jean de France, duc de Berry*. Turin: Bottega d'Erasmo, 1967.

Clausen, Jacob. 'Bibeln i Bellinge. Et eksempel på Biblia Pauperum anvendelse i dansk kalkmalerier'. *Ico Iconographisk Post*, i (1974), 3–11.

Colquhoun, Katherine H. 'A Critical Edition of the Middle English *Speculum Humanae Salvationis*'. Diss. London 1964.

Connick, Charles J. *Adventures in Light and Colour; an Introduction to the Stained Glass Craft*. London: Harrap, 1937.

Conway, William Martin. *The Woodcutters of the Netherlands in the Fifteenth Century*. Cambridge, 1884.

Copinger, Walter A. *Supplement to Hain's Repertorium Bibliographicum or, Collections Towards a New Edition of that Work, in two parts*. 3 vols. London, 1895–1902.

Cornell, Henrik. *The Iconography of the Nativity of Christ*.

Uppsala Universitets Årsskrift, 1 No. 3. Uppsala: Lunde-quistska Bokhandeln, 1924.

— *Biblia Pauperum*. Stockholm: Thule-Tryck, 1925.

Corpus Scriptorum Ecclesiasticorum Latinorum. 85 vols. Vienna: Öesterreichische Akademie der Wissenschaften, 1866–1974.

Cox, Lady Trenchard [Mary D. A.]. 'The Twelfth-Century Design Sources of the Worcester Cathedral Misericords'. *Archaeologia*, 97 (1959), 165–78.

Curtius, Ernst R. *European Literature and the Latin Middle Ages*. Trans. Willard R. Trask. London: Routledge and Kegan Paul, 1953.

Daniélou, Jean. *Sacramentum Futuri : études sur les origines de la typologie biblique*. Études de théologie historique. Paris: Beauchesne, 1950.

— 'La Typologie biblique traditionnelle dans la liturgie du Moyen-Age'. *Settimane di studio del Centro Italiano di Studi sull'Alto Medioevo*, 10 (1963), 141–61.

— *Primitive Christian Symbols*. Trans. Donald Attwater. London: Burns and Oates, 1964.

Darsy, Felix. *Les Portes de Sainte Sabine dans l'archéologie et l'iconographie générale du monument*. Rome: Vatican City, 1957.

Davies, Martin. *Early Netherlandish School*. National Gallery Catalogues. 3rd ed. rev. London: National Gallery, 1968.

Davies, Reginald T., ed. *Medieval English Lyrics: A Critical Anthology*. London: Faber and Faber, 1963.

Deissmann, Gustav A. *Forschungen und Funde im Serai, mit einem Verzeichnis der nichtislamischen Handschriften im Topkapu Serai zu Istanbul*. Berlin and Leipzig: de Gruyter, 1933.

— and Hans Wegener. *Die Armenbibel des Serai, Rotulus Seragliensis Nr. 52*. Berlin and Leipzig: de Gruyter, 1934.

Delaissé, Léon M. J. 'Le Livre d'Heures de Marie Van Vronensteyn, chef d'oeuvre inconnu d'un atelier d'Utrecht, achevé en 1460'. *Scriptorium*, 3 (1949), 230–45, pls 21–32.

— *La Miniature flamande à l'époque de Philippe le Bon*. Milan: Electra Editrice, 1956.

— *Miniatures médiévales de la Librairie de Bourgogne au cabinet des manuscrits de la Bibliothèque Royale de Belgique*. Brussels: Editions de la Connaissance, 1959.

— *A Century of Dutch Manuscript Illumination*. Berkeley and Los Angeles: Univ. of California Press, 1968.

Delisle, Léopold V., introd. *Chantilly le cabinet des livres imprimés antérieurs au milieu du xvie siècle*. Paris: Plon-Nourrit, 1905.

— and Paul Meyer. *L'Apocalypse en français au XIIIe siècle*. Société des ancien textes français. Paris: Firmin-Didot, 1901.

Destombes, Marcel. *Mappaemundi*. Vol. I of *Monumenta Cartographica Vetustioris Aevi A.D. 1200–1500*. Amsterdam: N. Israel, 1964.

Didron, Adolphe N. *Christian Iconography, or the History of Art in the Middle Ages*. Trans. Ellen J. Millington. 2 vols. London: H. G. Bohn, 1851, 1907.

Dionysius de Leuwis. *D. Dionysii Carthusiani, in Quatuor Euangelistas Enarrationes . . .* Vol. I of [Works]. Ed. D. Loer. Cologne, 1532.

Dodgson, Campbell, introd. *Grotesque Alphabet 1464 Reproduced in Facsimile from the Original Woodcuts in the British Museum*. London, 1899.

— *Catalogue of Early German and Flemish Woodcuts Preserved in the Department of Prints and Drawings in the British Museum*. 2 vols. London: British Museum, 1903, 1911.

— 'Two Woodcut Alphabets of the Fifteenth Century'. *Burlington Magazine*, 17 (1910), 362–65.

— *The Weigel-Felix* Biblia Pauperum : *A Monograph*. London: Chiswick Press, 1906.

The Douce Apocalypse. Introd. Averil G. Hassall and William O. Hassall. Faber Library of Illuminated Manuscripts. London: Faber and Faber, 1961.

Drake, Maurice. *The Costessey Collection of Stained Glass Formerly in the Possession of William Jerningham 8th Baron Stafford of Costessey in the County of Norfolk*. Exeter: Pollard, 1920.

Du Cange, Charles du Fresne. *Glossarium ad Scriptores Mediae et Infimae Latinitatis*. 3 vols. Paris, 1678.

Duff, Edward G., and Henry Thomas, comp. *Fifteenth Century English Books: A Bibliography of Books and Documents Printed in England and of Books for the English Market Printed Abroad*. London: Oxford Univ. Press, 1917.

Durrieu, Paul. *Heures de Turin quarante-cinq feuillets à peintures provenant des très belles heures de Jean de France, duc de Berry*. Paris: n. p., 1902.

— *La Miniature flamande au temps de la cour de Bourgogne (1415–1530)*. Paris: Libraire Nationale d'art et d'histoire, 1921.

Edmund of Abingdon. *Edmund of Abingdon: 'Speculum Religiosorum' and 'Speculum Ecclesiae'*. Ed. Helen P. Forshaw. Auctores Britannici Medii Aevi, 3. London: Oxford Univ. Press for the British Academy, 1973.

Ehwald, Rudolf, introd. *Die Biblia Pauperum: Deutsche Ausgabe von 1471*. Facs. Weimar: n. p., 1906.

Einsle, Anton, ed., and Joseph Schönbrunner, introd. Biblia Pauperum : *Facsimile Reproduktion getreu nach dem in der Erzherzoglich Albrecht'schen Kunst-Sammlung 'Albertina' befindlichen Exemplar*. Vienna, 1890.

Eisler, Colin T., introd. *Flemish and Dutch Drawings*. Drawings of the Masters. London: Weidenfeld and Nicolson, 1964.

Encyclopedia of World Art. 15 vols. New York: McGraw-Hill, 1959–67.

Engelhardt, Hans. *Der theologische Gehalt der* Biblia Pauperum. Studien der deutschen Kunstgeschichte, 243. Strasbourg: Heitz, 1927.

England, George A., and Alfred W. Pollard, eds. *The Towneley Plays*. EETS ES, 71. 1879; rpt. London: Oxford Univ. Press, 1966.

L'Éurope gothique, xiie xive siècles. Musée du Louvre Pavillon de Flore. Douzième exposition du Conseil de l'Europe, 1968. Paris: Ministère d'état, affaires culturelles, 1968.

Evans, Joan. *Art in Mediaeval France 987–1498: A Study in Patronage*. London: Oxford Univ. Press, 1948.

— *Dress in Mediaeval France*. Oxford: Clarendon, 1952.

Falke, Otto von, and Heinrich Frauberger, introd. *Deutsche Schmelzarbeiten des Mittelalters und andere Kunstwerke der kunst-historischen Ausstellung zu Düsseldorf 1902*. Frankfurt on Main: J. Baer, 1904.

Field, Richard S., comp. *Fifteenth Century Woodcuts and Metal-cuts from the National Gallery of Art Washington, D.C.*

Washington D.C.: National Gallery of Art [1965?].

Les Figures du vieil testament & du nouuel. Paris: Verard, 1504.

Fisher, John H., gen. ed. *The Medieval Literature of Western Europe: A Review of Research, Mainly 1930–1960.* London: London Univ. Press, 1966.

Formby, Henry. *The Book of the Holy Rosary. A Popular Doctrinal Exposition of its Fifteen Mysteries, Mainly Conceived in Select Extracts from the Fathers and Doctors of the Church with an Explanation of Their Corresponding Types in the Old Testament.* London, 1872.

Forstner, Karl, ed. *Die Salzburger Armenbibel: Codex a IX 12 aus der Erzabtei St. Peter zu Salzburg.* 2 vols. Munich: Pustet, 1969.

Franciscus de Retza. *De Generatione Christi siue Defensorium Inuiolate Castitatis Beatae Virginis Maria.* Germany, 1470.

— *Defensorium Inviolatae Virginitatis Mariae aus der Druckerei der Hurus in Saragossa in Faksimile-Reproduktion.* Introd. W. L. Schreiber. Weimar: Gesellschaft der Bibliophilen, 1910.

Frankl, Paul. *The Gothic: Literary Sources and Interpretation Through Eight Centuries.* Princeton, N. J.: Princeton Univ. Press, 1960.

Friedländer, Max J. *Early Netherlandish Painting.* Trans. of *Die altniederländische Malerei.* 14 vols. 1924–37; rpt. Leyden: Sijthoff, 1969.

— *From Van Eyck to Breugel.* Trans. M. Kay. London: Phaidon, 1965.

Friedman, Lionel J. *Text and Iconography for Joinville's* Credo. The Medieval Academy of America, 68. Cambridge, Mass.: Medieval Academy of America, 1958.

Friend, Albert M., gen. ed. *Studies in Manuscript Illumination.* 7 vols. Princeton, N. J.: Princeton Univ. Press, 1947–77.

Fučič, Branko. 'Biblia Pauperum i Istarske freske'. *Zbornik za umetnostno zgodovino,* 13 (1977), 143–51, pls XLVII–LX.

Gabelentz, Hans von der. *Die* Biblia Pauperum *und* Apokalypse *der grossherzöglichen Bibliothek zu Weimar.* Strasbourg: Heitz, 1912.

Galbraith, K. J. 'The Iconography of the Biblical Scenes at Malmesbury Abbey'. *Journal of the British Archaeological Association,* 28 (1965), 39–56, pls XVII–XXIV.

Gaskell, Philip. *A New Introduction to Bibliography.* Oxford: Clarendon, 1972.

Gerstenberg, Kurt G. *Hans Multscher.* Leipzig: Insel-Verlag, 1928.

Gesamtkalog der Wiegendrucke, herausgegeben von der Kommission für den Gesamtkatalog der Wiegendrucke. 7 vols. Leipzig: Hiersemann, 1925–38.

Gheyn, Joseph van den, ed. *Le Psautier de Peterborough.* Le Musée des enluminures. Haarlem: Kleinmann, n. d.

Gibson, Walter S. *Iconography and Iconology in Western Art from Early Christian Times to the End of the Eighteenth Century: A Selected Bibliography.* [Cleveland]: John G. White Department of Folklore, Orientalia and Chess, Cleveland Public Library, 1975.

Gilby, Thomas, gen. ed. *St. Thomas Aquinas:* Summa Theologicae. 2nd ed. Vol. I–. New York and London: Eyre and Spottiswode, 1964–.

Glorieux, Palémon. *Pour revaloriser Migne.* Mélanges de science religieuse, 9 suppl. Lille: Facultés Catholiques, 1952.

Göbel, Heinrich. 'Die gestickten Wandteppiche des Klosters Wienhausen'. *Cicerone,* 20 (1928), 9.

Goff, Frederick R. *Incunabula in American Libraries: A Third Census of Fifteenth-Century Books Recorded in North American Collections.* 1964; rpt. Millwood, N.Y.: Kraus, 1973.

Goldkühle, Fritz. *Mittelalterliche Wandmalerei in St. Maria Lyskirchen: Ein Beitrag zur Monumentalkunst des Mittelalters in Köln.* Bonner Beiträge zur Kunstwissenschaft, 3. Düsseldorf: Schwann, 1954.

Gougaud, L. 'Muta Praedicatio'. *Revue Benedictine,* 42 (1930), 168–71.

Gough, Michael R. E. *The Origins of Christian Art.* London: Thames and Hudson, 1973.

Graesse, Johann G. Th. *Trésor de livres rares et précieux, ou nouveau dictionnaire bibliographique, contenant plus de cent mille articles de livres rares . . .* 7 vols. Dresden, [1869].

Grodecki, Louis. *The Stained Glass of French Churches.* Trans. Rosemary Edmunds and A. D. B. Sylvester. London: Drummond, 1948.

— 'Les Vitraux allégorique de Saint-Denis'. *L'Art de France,* I (1961), 19–46.

Grotesque Alphabet. See Dodgson.

Guglielmi, Carla F. *Roma: Basilica di S. Sabina.* Fasc. 4 of *Dal Paleocristiano al Romanico.* Vol. I of *Tesori d'arte cristiana.* Bologna: Officine grafiche poligrafici Il Resto del Carlino, 1966.

Guillaume de Deguileville. *Le Pèlerinage de vie humaine.* Ed. Jakob J. Stürzinger. London: Nichols, for the Roxburghe Club, 1893. See also Henry.

Gumbert, Johan P. *Die Utrechter Karthäuser und ihre Bücher im frühen fünfzehnten Jahrhundert.* Leyden: Brill, 1974.

Gurewich, Vladimir. 'Observations on the Iconography of the Wound in Christ's Side, with Special Reference to Its Position'. *JWCI,* 20 (1957), 358–62.

Haastrup, Ulla. 'The Wall Paintings in the Parish Church of Bellinge (dated 1496) Explained by Parallels in Contemporary European Literature'. In *Medieval Iconography and Narrative: A Symposium.* Ed. Flemming G. Andersen, Esther Nyholm et al. Odense: Odense Univ. Press, 1980, pp. 135–66.

Haebler, Conrad. *The Study of Incunabula.* Trans. Lucy E. Osborne. 1933; rpt. New York: Kraus, 1967.

Hain, Ludwig. *Repertorium Bibliographicum in Quo Libri Omnes ab Arte Typographica Inventa Usque ad Annum MD.* Paris, 1826. See Copinger, and Reichling for suppl.

Hassall, Averil G., and William O. Hassall, introd. *The Douce Apocalypse.* Faber Library of Illuminated Manuscripts. London: Faber and Faber, 1961.

Hassall, William O., introd. Bible moralisée *M.S. Bodley 270b.* Oxford: Oxford Micropublications, 1978.

Haussherr, Reiner. 'Sensus Litteralis und Sensus Spiritualis in der *Bible moralisée*'. *Frühmittelalterliche Studien,* 6 (1972), 356–80.

— ed. *Bible moralisée: Faksimileausgabe im Originalformat des Codex Vindobonensis 2554 der Österreichischen Nationalbibliothek.* 2 vols. Reihe Codices Selecti, 40, 40*. Graz: Akademische

Druck- und Verlagsanstalt, 1973.

Hedgeland, J. P. *A Description Accompanied by Sixteen Coloured Plates, of the Splendid Decorations Recently Made to The Church of St. Neot, in Cornwall . . .* London: privately printed, 1830.

Heimann, Adelheid. 'L'Iconographie de la Trinité. I. Une Forme byzantine et son développement en occident'. *L'Art chrétien*, 1 (October 1934), 37–58.

— 'L'Iconographie de la Trinité. II. Les Trois Personnes divines sous une même forme humaine'. *L'Art chrétien*, 1 (November 1934), 19–30.

— 'The Capital Frieze and Pilasters of the Portail royal, Chartres'. *JWCI*, 31 (1968), 73–102, Pls 33–42.

— Rev. of Biblia Pauperum: *Facsimile Edition of the Forty-leaf Blockbook in the Library of the Esztergom Cathedral.* Ed. Erzébet Soltész. Trans. Lili Halápy. Rev. Elizabeth West. *Burlington Magazine*, 3 (1969), 94.

Heinecken, Karl-Heinrich von. 'Kurze Abhandlung von der Erfindung Figuren in Holz zu schneiden und von den ersten in Holz geschnittenen und gedruckten Büchern'. In *Nachrichten von Künstlern und Kunstsachen*. Leipzig: n. p., 1768–1769, pp. 85–240.

Heitz, Paul, introd., and Wilhelm Schreiber, comm. Biblia Pauperum: *Nach dem einzigen Exemplare in 50 Darstellungen . . .* Strasbourg: Heitz, 1903.

Hennecke, Edgar. *New Testament Apocrypha*. Trans. Ernest Best et al. Ed. R. McL. Wilson. 2 vols. London: Lutterworth Press, 1963, 1965.

Henry, Avril. '*Biblia Pauperum*: The Forty-page Blockbook Schreiber Editions I and VIII Reconsidered'. *Oud Holland*, 95, No. 3 (1981).

— ' "Eliseus Raises the Sunamite" in Context: Observations on Some Late Medieval Stained Glass Panels Now in Exeter Cathedral Lady Chapel. Part I'. *Friends of Exeter Cathedral Fifty-Third Annual Report* (1983), 10–17.

— 'The Living Likeness: the Forty-Page Blockbook *Biblia Pauperum* and the Imitation of Images in Utrecht and other Manuscripts'. *Journal of the British Archaeological Association*, 136 (1983), 124–36, pls. XVII–XLVIII. [Cited as Henry (1983ii)]

— '*Biblia Pauperum*: the Forty-Page Blockbook and The Hague, Rijksmuseum Meermanno-Westreenianum, MS. 10.A.15'. *Scriptorium*, 38, No. 1 (1984), 31–41.

— ' "Eliseus Raises the Sunamite" in Context: Observations on Some Late Medieval Stained Glass Panels Now in Exeter Cathedral Lady Chapel. Part II'. *Friends of Exeter Cathedral Fifty-Fourth Annual Report* (1984), 12–18.

— ed. *The Pilgrimage of the Lyfe of the Manhode: A Critical Edition of the Middle English Prose Translation of Guillaume de Deguileville's Pèlerinage de la vie humaine.* Vol. I (Text, Variants and Introduction). EETS OS, 288. Oxford: Oxford Univ. Press, 1985.

— 'The Woodcuts of *Der Spiegel menschlicher Behältnis* in the Editions Printed by Drach and Richel'. *Oud Holland*, 99, No. 1 (1985), 1–15.

— Rev. of *A Medieval Mirror*, Speculum Humanae Salvationis, *1324–1500*, by Adrian Wilson and Joyce Lancaster Wilson. *The Library*, 6th Ser, 8 (1986), 169–71.

— ed. *The Mirour of Mans Saluacioune, a Middle English Translation of* Speculum Humanae Salvationis: *A Critical Edition of the Fifteenth-Century Manuscript Illustrated from* Der Spiegel der menschen Behältnis *Speyer:Drach, c. 1475.* London: Scolar, 1986, Philadelphia: Univ. of Pennsylvania Press, 1987.

— ed. *The Pilgrimage of the Lyfe of the Manhode: A Critical Edition of the Middle English Prose Translation of Guillaume de Deguileville's Pèlerinage de la vie humaine.* Vol. II (Explanatory Notes, Glossary, Bibliography). EETS OS, 292. Oxford: Oxford Univ. Press, 1988 forthcoming.

Herbermann, Charles G., et al. *The Catholic Encyclopedia: An International Work of Reference on the Constitution, Doctrine, Discipline and History of the Catholic Church.* 17 vols. New York: Encyclopedia Press, 1907–14.

Herrade de Landsberg. *Hortus Deliciarum.* Ed. A. Straub and G. Keller. Strasbourg: Schlesier and Schweikhardt, 1901.

Hind, Arthur M. *An Introduction to a History of Woodcut with A Detailed Survey of Work Done in the Fifteenth Century.* 2 vols. 1935; rpt. London and New York: Dover, 1963.

Hindman, Sandra. 'Fifteenth-Century Dutch Bible Illustration and the Historia Scholastica'. *JWCI*, 37 (1974), 131–44.

— *Text and Image in Fifteenth-Century Dutch Bible Illustration.* Corpus Sacrae Scripturae Medii Aevi, Series Miscellanea, 1. Leyden: Brill, 1977.

— and James D. Farquhar. *Pen to Press: Illustrated Manuscripts and Printed Books in the First Century of Printing.* Baltimore: Johns Hopkins Univ. Press, 1977.

Hirsch, Rudolf. *Printing, Selling and Reading 1450–1550.* Weisbaden: Harrassowitz, 1967.

Hochegger, Rudolf. *Über die Entstehung und Bedeutung der Blockbücher.* Beiheft zum Zentralblatt für Bibliothekswesen, 5. Leipzig, 1891.

Hodnett, Edward. *English Woodcuts 1480–1535.* Oxford: Oxford Univ. Press, 1973.

Hoefer, Hartmut. *Typologie im Mittelalter. Zur Übertragbarkeit typologischer Interpretation auf weltliche Dichtung.* Göppingen: Kümmerle, 1971.

Hoffman, Edith. 'Az Esztergomi *Biblia Pauperum*'. *Magyar Müveszet*, 6 (1930), 248–52.

Holt, Elizabeth G., ed. *The Middle Ages and the Renaissance.* Vol. I of *A Documentary History of Art.* New York: Anchor-Doubleday, 1957.

The Holy Bible Douay Version: Translated from the Latin Vulgate (Douay, A.D. 1609: Rheims, A.D. 1582). London: Catholic Truth Society, 1956.

Hoogewerff, Godefridus J. *De Noerd-Nederlandsche schilderkunst.* 5 vols. 'S-Gravenhage: Nijhoff, 1936–47.

Houvet, Étienne, and Yves Delaporte. *Les Vitraux de la cathédrale de Chartres.* 4 vols. Chartres: Houvet, 1926.

Hughes, Robert. *Heaven and Hell in Western Art.* London: Weidenfeld and Nicolson, 1968.

Huizinga, Johan. *The Waning of the Middle Ages: A Study of the Forms of Life, Thought and Art in France and the Netherlands in the XIVth and XVth Centuries.* Trans. F. Hopman. London: Edward Arnold, 1924.

Hulme, Frederick Edward. *The History, Principles and Practice of Symbolism in Western Art.* Rev. ed. Poole: Blandford, 1976.

Hulme, William Henry. *The Middle-English Harrowing of Hell and Gospel of Nicodemus*. EETS ES, 100. London: Oxford Univ. Press, 1907.

Humbert, André. *La Sculpture sous les ducs de Bourgogne (1361–1483)*. Paris: Laurens, 1913.

Les Incunables de la collection Edmond de Rothschild la gravure en relief sur bois et sur métal. Paris: Musée du Louvre, 1974.

Jacobus de Voragine. *The Golden Legend or Lives of the Saints as Englished by William Caxton*. Trans. William Caxton. Ed. F. Ellis. The Temple Classics. 7 vols. London, 1900; rpt. New York: AMS Press, 1973.

James, Montague Rhodes. 'On Fine Art as Applied to the Illustration of the Bible in the Ninth and Five Following Centuries, Exemplified Chiefly by Cambridge MSS.' (including Appendix 'Verses from the Cloister Window of St Albans Abbey'.) *Proc.CAS*, 7 (1888–1891), 31–69.

— 'On the Paintings Formerly in the Choir at Peterborough'. *Proc.CAS*, 9 (1897), 178–94.

— 'On Two Series of Paintings Formerly at Worcester Priory'. *Proc.CAS*, 10 NS. IV (1898–1903), 99–115.

— *The Verses Formerly Inscribed on Twelve Windows in the Choir of Canterbury Cathedral*. Cambridge Antiquarian Society 8° series, No. 38 (1901), 1–42.

— 'The Tapestries at Aix-en-Provence and at La Chaise Dieux'. *Proc.CAS*, 11 (1903–6), 506–14.

— and J. Berenson. *Speculum Humanae Salvationis Being a Reproduction of an Italian Manuscript of the Fourteenth Century*. Oxford: Oxford Univ. Press, 1926.

— *The Apocalypse in Art*. The Schweich Lectures, 1927. London: Oxford Univ. Press, 1931.

— 'Pictor in Carmine'. *Archaeologia*, 94 (1951), 141–66.

— *The Apocryphal New Testament: Being the Apocryphal Gospels, Acts, Epistles, and Apocalypses with Other Narratives and Fragments Newly Translated . . . 1924; corr. rpt. Oxford: Clarendon, 1966.

Jameson, Anna B. *History of Our Lord as Exemplified in Works of Art*. 2 vols. London, 1864.

Jarosławliecka-Gąsiorowska, Marja. *Les Principaux Manuscrits à peintures du Musée des princes Czartoryski, à Cracovie*. Bulletin de la Société française de reproductions de manuscrits à peintures. 18e année. Paris: n. p., 1935.

Jones, Alexander, gen. ed. *The Jerusalem Bible*. London: Darton, Longman and Todd, 1966.

Jubinal, Achille. 'Tapisseries de la Chaise-Dieu'. In his *Les Anciennes Tapisseries historiées, ou collection des monumens les plus remarquables, de ce genre, qui nous soient restés du moyen-âge, partir du xie siècle au xvie inclusivement*. 2 vols. Paris, 1838.

Jungmann, Joseph A. *[Missarum Solemnia]: The Mass of the Roman Rite: Its Origins and Development*. Trans. Francis A. Brunner. Rev. Charles K. Riepe. London: Burns and Oates, 1959.

Kalcken, Gustaaf van. *Peintures ecclésiastiques du moyen-âge, Église St.-Pancrace à Enkhuysen*. Haarlem: Tjeenk Willink, 1919.

Katzenellenbogen, Adolf. *The Sculptural Programs of Chartres Cathedral: Christ, Mary, Ecclesia*. Baltimore: Johns Hopkins Univ. Press, 1959.

Keenan, Hugh T. 'A Check-List on Typology and English Medieval Literature through 1972'. *SLI*, 8 (1975), 159–66.

Kendon, Frank. *Mural Paintings in English Churches during the Middle Ages: An Introductory Essay on the Folk Influence in Religious Art*. London: Bodley Head, 1923.

Kirschbaum, Engelbert, et al. *Lexikon der christlichen Ikonographie*. 7 vols. Rome: Herder, 1968–74.

Kitzinger, Ernst. *Early Medieval Art in the British Museum*. 2nd ed. 1955; rpt. London: British Museum, 1963.

Kloss, Ernst, introd. Speculum Humanae Salvationis, *ein niederländisches Blockbuch*. Munich: Piper, 1925.

Knowles, David. *The Evolution of Medieval Thought*. London: Longmans, 1962.

Knox, Ronald. *The Holy Bible A Translation from the Latin Vulgate in the Light of the Hebrew and Greek Originals . . . 1955; rpt. London: Burns and Oates, 1961.

Koch, Robert A. 'The Sculptures of the Church of Saint-Maurice at Vienne, the *Biblia Pauperum* and the *Speculum Humanae Salvationis*', *Art Bulletin*, 32 (1950), 151–55.

— 'Elijah the Prophet, Founder of the Carmelite Order'. *Speculum*, 34 (1959), 547–60.

— 'New Criteria for Dating the Netherlandish *Biblia Pauperum* Blockbook'. In *Studies in Medieval and Renaissance Painting in Honor of Millard Meiss*. New York: New York Univ. Press, 1977, pp. 253–89.

Koechlin, Raymond. *Les Ivoires gothiques français*. 2 vols. Paris: Picard, 1924.

Kollwitz, Johannes. *Die Lipsanothek von Brescia*. 2 vols. Berlin: de Gruyter, 1933.

Kolve, Verdel A. *The Play Called Corpus Christi*. London: Edward Arnold, 1966.

Konrad, Martin. 'Das Weltgerichtsbild im Stadthause zu Diest'. *Wallraf-Richartz Jahrbuch*, 3–4 (1926–27), 141–51.

Kratzsch, Konrad, Rainer Behrends and Heinz Metz, contributors. Biblia Pauperum Apocalypsis: *Die Weimarer Handschrift*. Leipzig: Insel-Verlag, 1977.

Krautheimer, Richard. *Ghiberti's Bronze Doors*. Princeton, N. J.: Princeton Univ. Press, 1971.

Kristeller, Paul O. introd. Biblia Pauperum. *Unikum der Heidelberger Universitätsbibliothek in 34 Lichtdrucktafeln und 4 Tafeln in Farbenlichtdruck*. Berlin: Cassirer, 1906.

— *Latin Manuscript Books before 1600: A List of the Printed Catalogues and Unpublished Inventories of Extant Collections*. Rev. ed. 1960; rpt. New York: Fordham Univ. Press, 1965.

Kuhn, Charles L. 'Herman Scheerre and English Illumination of the Early Fifteenth Century'. *Art Bulletin*, 22 (1940), 138–56.

Künstle, Karl. *Ikonographie der christlichen Kunst*. 2 vols. Freiburg: Herder, 1926, 1928.

Kurzwelly, Johannes. *Fragment aus der ältesten deutschen Armenbibel-Handschrift*. Suppl. to *Zeitschrift für Bildende Kunst*. Leipzig: E. A. Seeman, 1908.

Laborde, Alexandre de, ed. La Bible moralisée *illustrée conservée à Oxford, Paris et Londres: reproduction intégrale du manuscrit du xiiie siècle . . . 5 vols. Paris: Société française de reproductions de manuscrits à peintures, 1911–27.

Ladurie, Emmanuel Le Roy. *Montaillou: Cathars and Catholics in* a French Village, 1294–1324. Trans. B. Bray. London: Scolar, 1977.

Laib, Freidrich, and Franz J. Schwarz, introd. Biblia Pauperum nach dem Original in der Lyceumsbibliothek zu Constanz. Zurich, 1867.

Lampe, Geoffrey W. H., and K. J. Woollcombe. Essays on Typology. Studies in Biblical Theology. London: SCM Press, 1957.

Lane, Barbara G. Letter [on Hugo van der Goes's Berlin Nativity and the Biblia Pauperum]. Art Bulletin, 58 (1976), 641.

Lapide, Cornelii a. [Steen, Cornelius]. Commentarii in Scripturam Sacram. 1st coll. ed. Venice, 1740; 10 vols. Leyden, 1875.

Latham, Ronald E., comp. Revised Medieval Latin Word-List, Compiled from British and Irish Sources. London: Oxford Univ. Press, 1965.

Leach, Edmund R. TLS, 18 March 1977, pp. 311–12.

Leclercq, Jean. The Love of Learning and the Desire for God: A Study of Monastic Culture. Trans. Catharine Misrahi. 2nd edn. 1974; London: Society for Promoting Christian Knowledge, 1978.

Lehmann, Walter. Die Parabel von den klugen und törichten Jungfrauen. Eine ikonographische Studie mit einem Anhang über die Darstellungen der anderen Parabeln Christi. Diss. Berlin 1913. Berlin: Ebering, 1916.

Lejeune, Jean, and Jacques Steinnon. Art Mosan aux XIe et XIIe siècles. Brussels: L'Arcade, 1961.

Loo, Georges H. de. Heures de Milan troisième partie des Très-belles heures de Notre-Dame enluminées par les peintures de Jean de France, duc de Berry . . . Brussels: G. Van Oest, 1911.

Loriquet, Charles. Les Tapisseries de Notre-Dame de Reims. Description précédée de l'histoire de la tapisserie dans cette ville d'après les documents inédits. Rheims, 1876.

Lumiansky, Robert M., and David Mills, eds. The Chester Mystery Cycle. Vol. I. EETS SS, 3. London: Oxford Univ. Press, 1974.

Lundberg, Per. La Typologie baptismale dans l'ancienne église. Acta Seminarii Neotestamentici Upsaliensis, 10. Leipzig, Lorentz and Uppsala: A.-B. Lundequistka Bokhandeln, 1942.

Luttor, Franz J. Biblia Pauperum. Studie zur Herstellung eines inneren Systems. Mit dem Texte der in der Wiener k.k. Hofbibliothek aufbewahrten Handschrift. Veszprem and Vienna: Buchhandlung der Reichspost, 1912.

Lutz, Jules, and Paul Perdrizet. Speculum Humanae Salvationis texte critique traduction inédite de Jean Mielot (1448): Les sources et l'influence iconographique principalement sur l'art alsacien du XIVe siècle . . . 2 vols. Mulhouse: Meininger, 1907, 1909.

Maas, Paul. Textual Criticism. Trans. Barbara Flower. Oxford: Clarendon, 1958.

Mâle, Émile. The Gothic Image: Religious Art in France of the Thirteenth Century. Trans. from 3rd French ed. Dora Nussey. 1913; rpt. London: Collins, 1961.

— L'Art religieux de la fin du moyen âge en France: étude sur l'iconographie du moyen âge et ses sources d'inspiration. 3rd ed. Paris: Librairie Armand Colin, 1925.

— L'Art religieux du xiiie siècle en France: étude sur l'iconographie du moyen âge et sur ses sources d'inspiration. 6th ed. Paris: Librairie Armand Colin, 1925.

— L'Art religieux du xiie siècle en France: étude sur les origines de l'iconographie du moyen âge. 3rd ed. Paris: Librairie Armand Colin, 1928.

Marks, Richard. 'The Stained Glass of the Collegiate Church of the Holy Trinity, Tattershall (Lincs.)'. Diss. London 1975.

— 'The Glazing of the Collegiate Church of the Holy Trinity, Tattershall (Lincs.): A Study of Late Fifteenth-century Glass-Painting Workshops'. Archaeologia, 106 (1979), 133–56.

Marle, Raimond Van. Iconographie de l'art profane au moyen âge et à la décoration des demeures. 2 vols. The Hague: Nijhoff, 1931.

Marrow, James H. 'Dutch Manuscript Illumination before the Master of Catherine of Cleves'. Nederlandsch kunsthistorische jaarboek, 19 (1968), 51–113.

Martin, Henry. La Miniature française du xiiie au xve siècle. Paris: G. Van Ouest, 1923.

Martin, John R. The Illustration of the Heavenly Ladder of John Climacus. Studies in Manuscript Illumination, 5. Ed. A. M. Friend. Princeton, N. J.: Princeton Univ. Press, 1954.

Maurer, Friedrich, introd. Die religiösen Dichtungen des 11. und 12. Jahrhunderts. Vol. 1. Tübingen: Niemeyer, 1964.

Meditations on the Life of Christ. An Illustrated Manuscript of the Fourteenth Century, Paris Bibliothèque nationale, MS. Ital. 115. Trans. Isa Ragusa. Ed. Isa Ragusa and Rosalie Green. Princeton, N.J.: Princeton Univ. Press, 1961.

Meer, Frederick van der. Apocalypse Visions from the Book of Revelation in Western Art. London: Thames and Hudson, 1978.

Mellinkoff, Ruth. The Horned Moses in Medieval Art and Thought. California Studies in the History of Art, 14. Berkeley: Univ. of California Press, 1970.

Metz, Peter. The Golden Gospels of Echternach. Trans. Ilse Schrier and Peter Gorge. London: Thames and Hudson, 1957.

Meyers, Walter E. 'Typology and the Audience of the English Cycle Plays'. SLI, 8 (1975), 145–58.

Meyvaert, Paul. 'Bede and the Church Paintings at Wearmouth-Jarrow'. Anglo-Saxon England, 8 (1979), 63–77.

Miélot, Jean. Miracles de Nostre Dame Collected by Jean Miélot Secretary to Philip the Good, Duke of Burgundy, Reproduced in Facsimile from Douce Manuscript 374 in the Bodleian Library . . . Introd. George F. Warner. London: Nichols, for the Roxburghe Club, 1885.

— Les Miracles de Nostre Dame compilés par Jehan Miélot secrétaire de Philippe le Bon, Duc de Bourgogne. Comm. A. de Laborde. Paris: Société française de reproduction de manuscrits à peintures, 1929.

Migne, Jacques Paul, ed. Patrologiae Cursus Completus . . . Series Latina. 221 vols. Paris, 1844–64.

— Patrologiae Cursus Completus . . . Series Graeca. 162 vols. Paris, 1857–1912.

Milchsack, Gustav, ed. The Heidelberger Passionspiel. Tübingen, 1880.

Miner, Earl, ed. Literary Uses of Typology from the Late Middle Ages to the Present. Princeton, N. J.: Princeton Univ. Press, 1977.

Minorita, Alexander. *Expositio in Apocalypsim*. Ed. A. Wachtel. Monumenta Germaniae Historica. Quellen zur Geistesgeschichte des Mittelalters, 1. Weimar: H. Böhlaus Nachfolger, 1955.

The Miroure of Mans Saluacionne: A Fifteenth-century Translation into English of the Speculum Humanae Salvationis *and Now for the First Time Printed from a Manuscript in the Possession of Alfred Henry Huth*. London: Roxburghe Club, 1888.

Molsdorf, Wilhelm. *Christliche Symbolik der mittelalterlichen Kunst*. 2nd ed. 1926; rpt. Graz: Akademische Druck- und Verlagsanstalt, 1968.

Mongan, Elizabeth, and Edwin Wolf. *The First Printers and Their Books*. Philadelphia: Free Library of Philadelphia, 1940.

Musper, Heinrich Th. 'Die Urausgabe der niederländischen *Biblia Pauperum*'. *Die graphischen Künste*, NF 2 (1937), 81–84.

— ed. *Die Urausgaben der holländischen* Apokalypse *und* Biblia Pauperum. Munich: Prestel, 1961.

— 'Xylographic Books'. In *The Book through Five Thousand Years*. Ed. Hendrik D. L. Vervliet. London and New York: Phaidon, 1972, pp. 341–47.

Neumüller, Willibrord, comm. Speculum Humanae Salvationis: *Vollständige Faksimileausgabe des Codex Cremifanensis 243 des Benediktinerstifts Kremsmünster*. Facs. and comm. 2 vols. Graz: Akademische Druck- u. Verlagsanstalt, 1972.

New Catholic Encyclopedia. 15 vols. New York: McGraw-Hill, 1967.

Niermeyer, Jan F., completed by C. Van de Kieft. *Mediae Latinitatis Lexicon Minus: A Medieval Latin-French/English Dictionary*. Leyden: Brill, 1976.

Norris, Herbert. *Seculae to Bosworth 1066–1485*. Vol. II of *Costume and Fashion*. London: Dent, 1927.

Orchard, John B., et al., eds. *A Catholic Commentary on Holy Scripture*. London: Thomas Nelson, 1953.

Owst, Gerald R. *Literature and Pulpit in Medieval England. A Neglected Chapter in the History of English Letters and of the English People*. 2nd ed. Oxford: Blackwell, 1961.

The Oxford Dictionary of the Christian Church. Ed. Frank L. Cross and Elizabeth A. Livingstone. 2nd ed. London: Oxford Univ. Press, 1974.

Pächt, Otto, and Jonathan J. G. Alexander. *Illustrated Manuscripts in the Bodleian Library Oxford*. 3 vols. Oxford: Clarendon, 1966–73.

— and Ulrike Jenni. *Holländische Schule*. Vol. III of *Die illuminierten Handschriften und Inkunabeln der Österreichischen Nationalbibliothek*. Vienna: Österreichische Akademie der Wissenschaften, 1975.

— and Dagmar Thoss. *Französische Schule I, II*. Vols. I and II of *Die illuminierten Handschriften und Inkunabeln der Österreichischen Nationalbibliothek*. Vienna: Österreichische Akademie der Wissenschaften, 1974, 1977.

Panofsky, Erwin, ed. and trans. *Abbot Suger on the Abbey Church of St.-Denis and Its Art Treasures*. Princeton, N.J.: Princeton Univ. Press, 1946.

— *Early Netherlandish Painting: Its Origins and Character*. Charles Eliot Norton Lectures, 1947–48. 2 vols. Cambridge, Mass.: Harvard Univ. Press, 1953.

Parker, Elizabeth. 'A Twelfth-Century Cycle of New Testament Drawings from Bury St. Edmunds Abbey'. *SIAP*, 31 (1969), 263–302.

Parkes, Malcolm. 'The Literacy of the Laity'. In *The Medieval World*. Vol. I of *Literature and Western Civilisation*. Ed. David Daiches and Anthony Thorlby. London: Aldus, 1973, pp. 555–77.

Parshall, Peter W. Letter [on Hugo van der Goes's Berlin *Nativity* and the *Biblia Pauperum*]. *Art Bulletin*, 58 (1976), 639–41.

Partridge, Astley C. *English Biblical Translation*. London: André Deutsch, 1973.

Pelzer, Auguste. *Abréviations Latines médiévales: Supplément au Dizionario di abbreviature latine ed italiane de Adriano Cappelli*. Louvain: Publications Universitaires, 1964.

Perdrizet, Paul. *Étude sur le* Speculum Humanae Salvationis. Paris: Champion, 1908.

Petrus de Riga. *Aurora Petri Rigae Biblia Versificata*. Ed. Paul E. Beichner. 2 vols. Medieval Studies, No. 19. Notre Dame, Ind.: Univ. of Notre Dame Press, 1965.

Pfaff, Richard W. *New Liturgical Feasts in Later Medieval England*. Oxford: Clarendon, 1970.

Pfeiffenberger, Selma. 'Notes on the Iconology of Donatello's *Judgement of Pilate* at San Lorenzo'. *RQ*, 20 (1967), 437–54.

Pickering, Frederick P. *Literature and Art of the Middle Ages*. Trans. and rev. London: Macmillan, 1970.

Pilinski, Adam. Bible des Pauvres, *reproduite en fac-similé; sur l'exemplaire de la Bibliothèque Nationale*. Paris, 1883.

Planchenault, René. *L'Apocalypse d'Angers*. Paris: Caises nationale des monuments historiques et des sites, 1966.

Pollard, Arthur W. 'The Transference of Woodcuts in the XV and XVI Centuries'. *Bibliographica*, 2 (1896).

— comp. *British Museum Catalogue of Books Printed in the XVth Century Now in the British Museum*. Vols I and IX. London: British Museum, 1908 and 1962.

Porter, Arthur Kingsley. *Romanesque Sculpture of the Pilgrimage Roads*. 10 vols. Boston: Marshall Jones, 1923.

Post, Regnerus R. *The Modern Devotion. Confrontation with Reformation and Humanism*. Studies in Medieval and Reformation Thought, 3. Leiden: Brill, 1968.

Prideaux, Edith K., and George R. H. Shafto. *The Bosses and Corbels of Exeter Cathedral an Illustrated Study in Decorative and Symbolic Design*. London: Chatto and Windus, 1910.

Proctor, Robert G. C. *An Index to the Early Printed Books in the British Museum: From the Invention of Printing in the Year MD. with Notes of Those in the Bodleian Library*. 2 parts. London: Kegan Paul, Trench, Trübner, 1898–1938 (Pt. 2, section 2, 3, Quaritch). Suppl. 1888–1902; London: Chiswick Press, 1900–03.

Le Psautier de Saint Louis: Manuscrit latin 10525 der Bibliothèque Nationale, Paris. Comm. Marcel Thomas. Codices Selecti Volumen, 37. Graz: Akademische Druck- u. Verlagsanstalt, 1972.

Purvis, John S. 'The Use of Continental Woodcuts and Prints by the "Ripon School" of Woodcarvers in the Early Sixteenth Century'. *Archaeologia*, 85 (1935), 107–28.

Puyvelde, Leo van. *The Flemish Primitives*. Trans. Doris I. Wilton. London: Collins, 1948.

Rackham, Bernard. *The Ancient Glass of Canterbury Cathedral.* London: Lund Humphries for the Friends of Canterbury Cathedral, 1949.

Réau, Louis. *La Bourgogne: La Peinture et les tapisseries.* Paris: G. van Oest, 1929.

— *Iconographie de l'art chrétien.* 6 vols. Paris: Presses Universitaires de France, 1955-59.

Reichling, Dietrich, ed. *Appendices ad Hainii Copingeri Repertorium Bibliographicum. Additiones et Emendationes.* 7 pts. Monachii, n. p., 1905-1914.

Renders, Émile. *Jean van Eyck et le Polyptyque: deux problèmes résolus.* Brussels: Librairie Générale, 1950.

Ricci, Corrado. *Ravenna.* Bergamo: Instituto Italiano d'arti grafiche, 1913.

Rickert, Margaret. 'The Illuminated Manuscripts of Meester Dirc van Delf's Tafel van den Kersten Ghelove'. *JWAG*, 12 (1949), 79-108.

Röhrig, Floridus. *Der Verduner Altar.* Vienna: Herold, 1955.

— 'Rota in Medio Rotae. Ein typologischer Zyklus aus Österreich'. *Jahrbuch des Stiftes Klosterneuburg*, NF 5. Klosterneuburg: Klosterneuburger Buch- und Kunstverlag, 1965.

Ross, Woodburn O., ed. *Middle English Sermons Edited from British Museum MS. Royal 18 B. xxiii.* EETS, OS. 209 (1960).

Rothe, Edith. *Mediaeval Book Illumination in Europe.* London: Thames and Hudson, 1966.

Rushforth, Gordon M. 'Seven Sacraments Compositions in English Medieval Art'. *The Antiquaries Journal*, 9 (1929), 83-100.

— *Medieval Christian Imagery as Illustrated by the Painted Windows of Great Malvern Priory Church Worcestershire Together with a Description of All the Ancient Glass in the Church.* Oxford: Clarendon, 1936.

Sandler, Lucy F. 'Peterborough Abbey and the Peterborough Psalter in Brussels'. *Journal of the British Archaeological Association*, 3rd ser., 33 (1970), 36-49.

— *The Peterborough Psalter in Brussels and Other Fenland Manuscripts.* London: Harvey Miller, 1974.

Sartor, Marguerite. *Les Tapisseries, toiles peintes et broderies de Reims.* Rheims: Michaud, 1912.

Saxtorph, Neils M. *Jeg ser pa kalkmalerier: alt hvad der findes i danskskirker.* Copenhagen: Politiken, 1979.

Scheler, August. *Trouvères belges (nouvelle série) Chansons d'amour, jeux-partis, pastourelles, satires, dits et fabliaux, par Gonthier de Soignies, . . . Raoul de Houdenc etc.* Louvain, 1879.

Scheller, Robert W. *A Survey of Medieval Model Books.* Introd. trans. D. A. S. Reid. Haarlem: Bohn, 1963.

Schiller, Gertrud. *Ikonographie der christlichen Kunst.* 4 vols. Gütersloh: Gütersloher Verlagshaus Gerd Mohn, 1966-76.

— *Iconography of Christian Art.* Vols. I and II trans. from 2nd ed. London: Lund Humphries, 1971.

Schlosser, Julius von. *Schriftquellen zur Geschichte der karolingischen Kunst.* Vienna, 1892.

— *Quellenbuch zur Kunstgeschichte des abendländischen Mittelalters.* Vienna, 1896; rpt. Hildesheim: George Olms, 1976, pp. 317-22.

— *Materialien zur Quellenkunde der Kunstgeschichte.* Vol. I: *Mittelalter.* Sitzungsberichte der kaiserlichen Akademie der Wissenschaften in Wien, 3. Vienna: Alfred Hölder, 1914.

Schmidt, Gerhard. *Die Armenbibeln des XIV. Jahrhunderts.* Veröffentlichungen des Institutes für österreichische Geschichtsforschung, 19. Graz and Cologne: Herman Böhlaus, 1959.

Schmidt, Ph. *Die Illustration der Lutherbibel 1522-1700.* Basel: Friedrich Reinhardt, 1962.

Schmitt, Otto. *Gotische Skulpturen des Freiburger Münsters.* 2 vols. Frankfurt-on-Main: Anstalt, 1926.

— et al., eds. *Reallexikon zur deutschen Kunstgeschichte.* Vols. I and VI. Stuttgart: Metzler, 1933-57.

Schrade, Hubert. *Ikonographie der christlichen Kunst, die Sinngehalte und Gestaltungsformen.* Berlin: Gruyter, 1932.

Schramm, Albrecht. *Der Bilderschmuck der Frühdrucke.* 3 vols. Leipzig: Deutsches Museum für Buch und Schrift, 1922-20 [sic].

Schreiber, Wilhelm L. *Manuel de l'amateur de la gravure sur bois et sur métal au XVᵉ siècle.* 8 vols. Hiersemann, 2nd ed. 1926-30; rpt. Stuttgart and Nedeln: Kraus Reprint, 1969.

Schretlen, Martinus J. A. *Dutch and Flemish Woodcuts of the Fifteenth Century.* London, 1925; rpt. New York: Hacker Art Books, 1969.

Semff, Michael. 'Die Holzreliefs der Türen des Gurker Westportals'. *Österreichische Zeitschrift fur Kunst und Denkmalpflege*, 33 (1979), 1-16.

Seyffert, Oskar. *A Dictionary of Classical Antiquities Mythology-Religion-Literature-Art.* 1891; rev. and ed. Henry Nettleship and J. E. Sandys. London: Allen and Unwin, 1957.

Shorr, Dorothy C. 'The Iconographic Development of the Presentation in the Temple'. *Art Bulletin*, 28 (1946), 17-32.

Silber, Evelyn. 'The Early Iconography of the *Speculum Humanae Salvationis*: the Italian Connection in the Fourteenth Century.' Diss. Cambridge 1982.

— Rev. of *A Medieval Mirror, Speculum Humanae Salvationis, 1324-1500*, by Adrian Wilson and Joyce Lancaster Wilson. *Burlington Magazine* (August, 1986), 609.

Smalley, Beryl. *The Study of the Bible in the Middle Ages.* 2nd ed. Oxford: Oxford Univ. Press, 1952.

Smeyers, Maurits. *La Miniature.* Typologie des sources du moyen âge occidental, Fasc. 8. Turnhout: Brehpols, 1974.

— 'De Invloed der blokboekeditie van de *Biblia Pauperum* op het getijdenboek van Maria van Vronensteyn'. *De Gulden Passer*, 53 (1975), 307-25.

Smith, John C. D. *A Guide to Church Woodcarvings Misericords and Benchends.* London: David and Charles, 1974.

Soltész, Erzébet. Biblia Pauperum: *Facsimile Edition of the Forty-leaf Blockbook in the Library of the Esztergom Cathedral.* Trans. Lili Halápy. Rev. Elizabeth West. Budapest: Corvina, 1967.

Sotheby Parke Bernet. *Catalogue of Valuable Printed Books of the 15th and 16th Century Including a Block-book: The Property of the Carl and Lily Pfortzheimer Foundation, Inc. . . . 12 June 1978.* London: Sotheby Parke Bernet, 1978.

Sotheby, Samuel Leigh. *Principia Typographica: The Blockbooks Issued in Holland, Flanders, and Germany during the Fifteenth Century.* 3 vols. London, 1858.

Speculum Humanae Salvationis. See James and Berenson; Lutz and Perdrizet; Neumüller; Henry.

Stange, Alfred. *Deutsche gotische Malerei 1300–1430.* Königstein im Taunus: Langewiesche, 1964.

Stegmüller, Friedrich. *Repertorium Biblicum Medii Aevi.* 7 vols. Matriti: Instituto Francisco Suárel, 1950–61.

Steinmann, Ernst. 'Die Tituli und die kirchliche Wandmalerei im Abendlande vom v. bis zum xi. Jahrhundert'. Leipzig, 1892.

Stern, Henri. 'Quelques problèmes d'iconographie paléochrétienne et juive'. *Cahiers Archéologiques*, 12 (1962), 99–113.

— 'Les mosaïques de l'église de Sainte-Constance à Rome'. *Dumbarton Oaks Papers*, 12 (1958), 157–218.

Stevenson, Allan H. 'Beta-radiography and Paper Research'. VII International Congress of Paper Historians, Communications. Oxford: TS, 1967.

— 'The Quincentennial of Netherlandish Blockbooks'. *BMQ*, 31 (1966–67), 83–87.

Strand, Kenneth A., ed. *Essays on the Northern Renaissance.* Ann Arbor: Ann Arbor, 1968.

Strohem, Paul. 'The Malmesbury Medallions and Twelfth-Century Typology'. *Mediaeval Studies*, 33 (1971), 180–87.

Stucky, Monique. *Les Tapisseries de l'apocalypse d'Angers.* Lausanne: Payot, 1973.

Thomas Aquinas. *The 'Summa Theologica' of St. Thomas Aquinas Literally Translated by the Fathers of the English Dominican Province.* 2nd ed. 22 vols. London: Burns, Oates and Washbourne, 1921–32.

Thomas Cantimpratensis. *Der bien boeck.* Swolle: Peter Van Os, 1488.

Thomas, Lucien-Paul. *Le 'Sponsus' (Mystère des vierges sages et des vierges folles) suivi des trois poèmes limousins et farcis du même manuscrit.* Paris: Presses Universitaires de France, 1951.

Thomas, Michael. 'Zur kulturgeschichtlichen Einordnung der *Armenbibel* mit *Speculum Humanae Salvationis*'. *Archiv für Kulturgeschichte*, 52 (1970), 192–225.

Thomson, Samuel H. *Latin Bookhands of the Later Middle Ages 1100–1500.* London: Cambridge Univ. Press, 1969.

Thurston, Ada, and Curt F. Bühler, comp. *Checklist of Fifteenth Century Printing in the Pierpont Morgan Library.* New York: The Pierpont Morgan Library, 1939.

Tietze, Hans. 'Die Handschriften der Concordantia Caritatis des Abtes Ulrich von Lilienfeld'. *Jahrbuch der k.k. Zentralkommission für Erforschung und Erhaltung der Kunst- und historischen Denkmale*, NF 3 ii (1905), 29–63.

Timmers, J. J. M. *Symboliek en iconographie der christelijke kunst.* Roermonde-Maaseik: Romen & Zonen-Uitgevers, 1947.

Tischendorf, Constantinus de. *Evangelia Apocrypha Adhibitis Plurimus Codicibus Graecis et Latinis Maximam Partem Nunc Primum Consultis atque Ineditorum Copia Insignibus.* Lipsia, 1876.

Toesca, Pietro. *San Vitale of Ravenna: the Mosaics.* London: Collins, 1954.

Toulmin Smith, Lucy, ed. *York Plays The Plays Performed by the Crafts or Mysteries of York on the Day of Corpus Christi in the 14th, 15th and 16th Centuries Now First Printed from the Unique Manuscript in the Library of Lord Ashburnham.* Oxford, 1885; rpt. New York: Russell and Russell, 1963.

The Town of Stamford. Royal Commission on Historical Monuments England: An Inventory of Historical Monuments. London: HMSO, 1977.

Trenkler, Ernst. *Das Schwartze Gebetbuch: Handschrift 1856 der Österreichischen Nationalbibliothek.* Kunstdenkmäler, 5. Vienna: Deuticke, 1948.

The Trinity College Apocalypse. See Brieger.

Tristram, Ernest W. *English Medieval Wall Painting. The Twelfth Century.* London: Oxford Univ. Press for the Pilgrim Trust, 1944.

Tuve, Rosemond. *Allegorical Imagery: Some Mediaeval Books and Their Posterity.* Princeton, N. J.: Princeton Univ. Press, 1966.

Twining, Edward F. *A History of the Crown Jewels of Europe.* London: Batsford, 1960.

Ulbert-Schede, Ute. 'Das Andachtsbild des kreuztragenden Christus in der deutschen Kunst von den Anfängen bis zum Beginn des 16. Jahrhunderts: Eine ikonographische Untersuchung'. Diss. Munich 1966.

Underwood, Paul A. 'Second Preliminary Report on the Restoration of the Frescoes in the Kariye Camii at Istanbul by the Byzantine Institute'. *Dumbarton Oaks Papers*, 11 (1957), 174–220.

— *The Kahriye Djami.* 4 vols. London: Routledge and Kegan Paul, 1967–75.

Unterkircher, Franz, and Gerhard Schmidt, comm. *Österreichische Nationalbibliothek in Wien. Illuminierte Handschriften in Faksimile. Die Wiener* Biblia Pauperum: *Codex Vindobonensis 1198.* 3 vols. Graz, Vienna, Cologne: Styria, 1962.

Vacant, Jean M., and E. Mangenot, et al. *Dictionnaire de théologie catholique contenant l'exposé des doctrines de la théologie catholique leurs preuves et leur histoire.* 15 vols and indices. Paris: Letouzy & Ané, 1899–1950.

Vaughan, Richard. *Philip the Bold: The Formation of the Burgundian State.* London: Longmans, 1962.

— *Philip the Good: The Apogee of Burgundy.* London: Longmans, 1970.

— *Charles the Bold: The Last Valois Duke of Burgundy.* London: Longmans, 1973.

— *Valois Burgundy.* London: Allen Lane, 1975.

Vavassore, Giovanni A., comp. *Opera noua contemplatiua p. ogni fidel christiano laquale tratta de le figure del testamento vecchio . . .* Venice, [1510?].

Vermeeren, Petrus J. H. 'Het Passyonael van den Heyligen in het Brits Museum te Londen (MS Add. 18162)'. *Het Boek*, 33 (1959), 193–210.

Vetus Latina. Ed. Bonifatius Fischer. Vols. I (2nd ed.). Freiburg: Herder, 1963 and II, 1951.

Viller, Marcel, gen. ed. *Dictionnaire de spiritualité, ascétique et mystique, doctrines et histoire.* Paris: Beauchesne, 1932–.

Villette, Jean. *La Résurrection du Christ dans l'art chrétien du iie au viie siècle.* Paris: Laurens, 1957.

Villon, François. *Oeuvres.* Ed. Auguste Longnon. 4th ed. Les Classiques français du moyen âge. Paris: Champion, 1961.

Vincent of Beauvais. *Speculi Maioris Vincenti Bvrgvndi Praecvlis Belvacensis, Ordinis Praedicatorum . . .* Vol. I. Venice, 1591.

Vloberg, Maurice. *L'Eucharistie dans l'art.* 2 vols. Paris: Artaud, 1946.

Vulgate Bible. See *Biblia Sacra.*

Wald, Ernest T. de. 'Observations on Duccio's *Maesta*'. In *Late Classical and Mediaeval Studies in Honor of Albert Mathias Friend Jr.* Ed. Kurt Weitzmann. Princeton, N. J.: Princeton Univ. Press, 1955, pp. 362–86.

Walther, Johann L. *Lexicon Diplomaticvm, Abbreviationes Syllabarum et Vocvm in Diplomatibvs Codicibvs Seculo VIII. ad XVI. vsque Occvrrentes Exponens . . .* Göttingen, 1747.

Watson, Arthur. *The Early Iconography of the Tree of Jesse.* London: Oxford Univ. Press, 1934.

— 'Mary in the Burning Bush'. *JWCI,* 2 (1938–39), 69–70.

Wayment, Hilary. *The Windows of King's College Chapel, Cambridge.* Corpus Vitrearum Medii Ævi, Great Britain, Suppl. No. 1. London: Oxford Univ. Press for the British Academy, 1972.

Weckwerth, Alfred. 'Die Zweckbestimmung der *Armenbibel* und die Bedeutung ihres Namens'. *Zeitschrift für Kirchengeschichte,* 68 (1957), 225–58.

Weis-Liebersdorf, Johan E. *Das Kirchenjahr in 156 gotischen Federzeichnungen. Ulrich von Lilienfeld und die eichstätter Evangelienpostille: Studien zur Geschichte der* Armenbibel *und ihrer Fortbildungen.* Studien zur deutschen Kunstgeschichte, 160. Strasbourg: Heitz, 1913.

Weitzmann, Kurt. 'Observations on the Cotton Genesis Fragments'. In *Late Classical and Mediaeval Studies in Honor of Albert Mathias Friend Jr.* Ed. Kurt Weitzmann. Princeton, N. J.: Princeton Univ. Press, 1955, pp. 112–31.

Werner, Wilfried, ed. *Das Blockbuch von den Zehn Geboten 1455/58.* Dietikon: Urs Graf, 1981.

Wessel, Klaus. *Der Sieg über den Tod. Die Passion Christi in der frühchristlichen Kunst des Abendlandes.* Berlin: Evangelische Verlagsanstalt, 1956.

Whittredge, Ruth, ed. '*La Nativité et Le Geu des trois roys:* Two Plays from Manuscript 1131 of the Bibliothèque Sainte Geneviève, Paris'. Diss. Bryn Mawr 1944.

Wilk, Barbara. 'Die Darstellung der Kreuztragung Christi und verwandter Szenen bis um 1300'. Diss. Tübingen 1969.

Willshire, William H. *A Descriptive Catalogue of Early Prints in the British Museum.* Vol. I: *German and Flemish Schools.* London, 1879.

Wilson, Adrian, and Joyce Lancaster Wilson. *A Medieval Mirror,* Speculum Humanae Salvationis, *1324–1500.* Berkeley: California Univ. Press, 1985. See Henry, and Silber, for reviews.

Winkler, Friedrich. *Die flämische Buchmalerei des XV. und XVI Jahrhunderts.* Leipzig: Von Seeman, 1925.

— 'Ein Kölnisches Gebetbuch aus der Mitte des 15. Jahrhunderts'. *Wallraf-Richartz-Jahrbuch,* NF 1 (1930), 110–13.

Woolf, Rosemary. 'The Effects of Typology on the English Mediaeval Plays of Abraham and Isaac'. *Speculum,* 32 (1957), 805–25.

— *The English Mystery Plays.* London: Routledge and Kegan Paul, 1972.

Wormald, Francis. *English Drawings of the Tenth and Eleventh Centuries.* London: Faber and Faber, 1952.

Zehnder, Frank, and Alistair Smith, et al. *Late Gothic Art from Cologne [Catalogue of] a Loan Exhibition 5th April to 1st June 1977.* London: National Gallery, 1977.

Zestermann, August C. A. *Die Unabhängigkeit der deutschen xylographischen* Biblia Pauperum *von der lateinischen xylographischen* Biblia Pauperum. Leipzig, 1866.

APPENDICES

A. Extant Impressions of Schreiber Edition I

I have not been able to compare any copies directly with each other. Such a process would reveal more evidence than is apparent on microfilm.

Dresden   Sächsische Landesbibliothek

Sig. **a** is rubbed; **g, h, ·q·, ·m·** are slightly cropped; **·i·** bears scribbles; **·v·** is missing (a leaf from S.X has been substituted). In the facsimile these pages are replaced with pages from the Chantilly copy. There is some overwriting, particularly on **·c·, ·d·, ·e·, ·g·1, 2, ·h·1**; the footprint in **·o·5** should be empty; the disciple on Mary's right in **·p·5** should not appear moustached.

Zurich   Zentralbibliothek

Complete, but more frequently and severely cropped than the Dresden copy (e.g., **ṗ, r, s, t, ·a·, ·b·, ·c·, ·g·, ·h·, ·o·, ·p·, ·t·**).

Chantilly   Musée Condé

Complete, bound, in good condition except for overwriting in **p, q, s, ·i·, ·o·, ·v·**; smudging on **r, ·a·, ·l·** (which is bound in upside down); variable in density and colour of ink: **c** and **d** are very dark; **·t·** is very faint.

London   British Museum Print Room

Mounted on cards. Wants **b** and **c**, and is considerably mutilated. The impression is a late one.

New York   Pierpont Morgan Library

Wants **·v·**. Some colouring washed off, blurring outlines. Some overdrawing. Untypical in showing text darker than pictures. Copious annotation on the blank pages and occasionally on the printed ones (e.g., **i, k, ·d·, ·g·, ·h·, ·i·, ·k·, ·r·**). Probably the copy noted by Schreiber, *Manuel*, IV, 4, as sold to Quaritch in 1906 (Soltész, p. XXVI, n. 88).

St Gallen   Stiftsbibliothek

Rubricated, some annotation (e.g., **s**).

The following were not considered for the facsimile, being coloured or fragmentary.

Alnwick   Formerly the property of His Grace the Duke of Northumberland; sold 27 Nov. 1986 (Sotheby's lot. 148) to Antiquariat Heribert Tenschert, Rottalmünster.

Bound, uncropped. Wants **·m·, ·s·, ·t·**; **a** and **v** severely damaged. The impression is a late one.

Brussels   Bibliothèque Royale Albert Ier

Coloured.

Esztergom	Esztergom Cathedral Library
	Coloured.
Paris	Louvre, Rothschild Collection
	Coloured.
Vienna	Österreichische Nationalbibliothek
	Very clear, uncropped, in better condition than the Dresden and even the Chantilly copy, but unfortunately wants all twenty leaves of the first alphabet, and ·a·, ·o·, ·p·, ·q·, ·r·, ·s·, ·t·, ·v·, This remarkable fragment came to my notice too late to be considered for the facsimile, but in any case it lacks all but one of the leaves which, faulty in the Dresden copy, were substituted from the Chantilly.

Small fragments of S.I are in:

The Hague	Museum Meermanno-Westreenianum
	Sigs **g** and **h** only.
London	British Library
	Sigs ·s·, ·t·, ·v·, are used to make up the S.VI coloured edition whose classmark is IB.43.

According to Stevenson *BMQ* (1967), p. 84, there may be another copy in Leningrad: exhaustive enquiry has failed to trace it.

Only the first four quite uncoloured copies listed, and the Vienna fragment, have been examined to establish the order in which they were made. (The complete task forms part of my study of the paper of all extant copies of all editions of the forty-page *Biblia Pauperum*, in progress.) The five so considered are referred to as D, Z, C, L, V in the following summary of evidence.

L is much later than D, Z, C, V.
Splits absent in D, Z, C, V occur in **d, e, f, g,** ·**k**· (a rare vertical split), ·**q**·. Portions of the ink-bearing line present in D are missing in **r6,** ·**b·6,** ·**o·7**.

C is later than D.
Details whole in D but broken in C are: **b** column 4 and border, ·**o**· base of column 3; ·**o**· column 4 is more broken than in D.

Z is later than D.
The following details, whole in D, are broken: **e** column 4, **n** top-right border, **o** bottom border and top of left border, ·**r**· left border and **7**; ·**o**· column 4 is more broken than in D.

The Z/C relationship is doubtful. It seems most likely that C is later than Z since **b** column 4 and right border, whole in Z, are broken in C, and **h8** in C shows worse splits than in Z. On the other hand, it is hard to explain why in some respects Z seems later than C: whole in C but broken in Z are ·**o**· column 4, ·**r**· left border.

The D/V relationship is also doubtful, and comparing microfilms of such early impressions, which show very few breakages, is perilous: the left-hand block border in ·**l**· seems more broken in D than in V, but on the other hand, the same border in ·**h**· is more broken in V than in D.

It ought to be mentioned that the St Gallen copy, excluded by its rubrication from consideration for the facsimile, is nevertheless an early impression, preceding Z (column 1 in ·**k**·, normal in St Gallen, is displaced in Z), though it is later than D (·**o**· column 4, whole in D, is broken).

The conflicting evidence just cited (which does nothing to cast doubt on D's being the earliest extant uncoloured copy both in good condition and almost complete) highlights the weakness of this whole argument from the part to the whole. Even when more evidence from provenance, watermarks, and colouring becomes available, it will be difficult to prove that some copies were not at an early stage made up from other impressions of S.I. The above evidence is therefore no more than a guide.

B. The Prophets' Hats

With surprisingly few exceptions, the prophets (the 'authors' of Prophecies **3**, **4**, **10**, **11** on each page of the *Biblia Pauperum*) wear their own identifying hats, as if the designer wished each prophet to be recognisable. In this way, perhaps, the frequency of the Psalms' testimony might be obvious in the frequency with which the picture of David appears; on the other hand, the variety of testimonies given might be apparent in the large number of prophets appearing only once. Certainly the overall consistency in allocation of hats is evidence of the designer's attention to detail—so much so that one wonders if the few inconsistencies point to corruption in transmission rather than to carelessness in design. This (and one other factor, as we shall see) may suggest that we do not have the first edition of this blockbook ever printed.

For simplicity I have named each style of hat after the signature at which it first appears: for example, the tall crown-encircled hat with nodding brims worn by David as Psalmist is called **a4** because it first appears there. It appears in front or side view thirty-four times in the 'prophet' position, at **c3**, **d3**, **e4**, **g3**, **h3**, **i4**, **k3**, **l4**, **m4T** (the subject of transposition. as explained below), **n4**, **n11**, **o3**, **p4**, **q4**, **r3**, **s3**, **·a·3**, **·c·3**, **·d·10**, **·e·3**, **·f·3**, **·g·3**, **·h·3**, **·i·3**, **·k·4**, **·l·3**, **·m·3**, **·n·10**, **·o·3**, **·p·3**, **·q·3**, **·s·4**, **·t·3**, **·v·3**. This consistency is maintained even in four of the main scenes in which David appears: **e7**, **h6**, **o6**, **·h·6**. On only four occasions does it break, and three of those are with good reason: at **n6** he is bareheaded in penance; at **n6** (top), **·h·6**, and **·r·7** he is simply crowned, appearing as king; only at **c6** is he shown enthroned and hatted, where his hat does not show the correct nodding brim. This aberration is interesting: Friedländer (IV. 99) observes that a puzzling painting by the Master of the Legend of St Barbara, which he illustrates on his pl. 63, was compared with the scene in the *Biblia Pauperum* to identify the subject as David receiving Abner. David wears the same hat in both pictures. The designs are not very similar, but perhaps a common source lies behind the painting (dated post-1470) and the blockbook.

In the list of David's appearances in the prophet position, above, **m4** was followed by **T**. This indicates that it is one of five most interesting occasions on which the hats show clearly that figures next to each other or their Prophecies (**3**, **4** or **10**, **11**) have been transposed. I have numbered these appearances as they occur in the blockbook, following them by **T** to indicate that they have been transposed: thus, as his scroll and name show, David at **m4T** should be at **m3**. As Conway (p. 6) observed: 'it is not likely that this would have happened in the original edition of the book, but a mistake of the kind might very easily creep into a copy'. Possibly this transposition is due to the block-cutter's working from a print for the transposed figures: if this is the case, it is evidence that the text and illustrations were cut at different times (perhaps by different people, as the often poor quality of the lettering would suggest in any case).

Transposition occurs also at **a10**, **11** (Jeremias and Ezechiel),

f3, 4 (Nahum and Osee), **l10, 11** (Job and the author of 1 Kings), **m10, 11** (Habacuc and Malachias). The evidence for these transpositions is as follows. Ezechiel wears **a11T** at **i10, n3, ·m·11, ·p·10, ·r·11, ·v·10**. That Jeremias is himself, in spite of his being labelled 'Ezechiel', is clear from the fact that he is hatless at **a10T, e10, g10, v10, ·a·11, ·d·4, ·d·11, ·n·4, ·s·10**. Perhaps this bareheaded mode is a sign of his penitential tone: compare King David's bareheadedness in penance, already mentioned.

The designer may sometimes be distinguishing between different works by a supposed author, by giving him differing hats. As author of Lamentations, for example, Jeremias wears **v3** at **·c·10** and **·f·10**. Only once is his hat inconsistent: at **g11** he wears **k10**, worn only once elsewhere—by the author of 2 Kings.

Transposition of Nahum and Osee is proved not by the identity of Nahum (who appears nowhere else in the book) but by that of Osee, who wears **f4T** at **g11, h4, h10, p3, ·h·4, ·i·10, ·l·11, ·v·11**. Evidence of the transposition of Job and the author of 1 Kings is clearer. Job wears **k11** at **l10T, ·b·10, ·e·10** (confusingly, at **·s·11** he wears **o10**, an oddly unpredictable hat first worn, also incorrectly, by Zacharias, and then at **q3** by the author of Genesis, who usually wears **·g·11**, as at **·h·11, ·i·4, ·k·11**). However, the author of 1 Kings wears **l11T** at **·l·4** and **·r·4**.

Evidence for the transposition of Habacuc and Malachias is that the former wears **b10** at **m10T** and **·e·11**, and that the latter wears **d4** at **m11T**. Finally, evidence for the first transposition mentioned, that of David and Isaias at **m3, 4**, is the most abundant. David's consistently hatted appearances (thirty-four as prophet and four in scenes) have already been listed, and Isaias wears **b4** at **c4, c10, e3, i3, k4, m3T, s10, v4, ·a·10, ·b·3, ·c·11, ·d·3, ·e·4, ·g·10, ·k·3, ·l·10, ·m·10, ·n·3, ·o·4, ·q·10, ·r·10, ·t·11, ·v·**. This remarkable consistency is broken only once: at **a3**, where he unaccountably wears the hat worn at **c11** by the author of Numbers ('Balaam'); this hat is also worn at **·q·4** by the author of the Song of Songs, who at **o4** and **·g·4** wears one of a quite different style.

Two other prophets are hatted consistently. Micheas wears **b11** at **t3, ·k·10, ·o·11**; Amos wears **p10** at **·b·11** and **·f·11**. A number appear only once, so their normality cannot be assessed: Nahum at **f3T** has already been mentioned as a transposition; Daniel is at **b3**, Aggeus at **r10**, Jonas at **t10**, Joel at **·p·11**, the author of Ecclesiastes at **·r·3** (perhaps a version of **v11**, worn by Baruch, but it seems more extreme), Josue at **·t·10**. At **l3** Moses appears horned and hatless, as he does in the scenes at **f6, n7, ·f·7, ·p·6**, though he is hatted at **b6** (in spite of Soltész's identification there is no evidence that Moses is shown in **b7**) and at **i6**. (One would think him horned only after the giving of the law, at which he became 'radiant' or 'horned' [see p. 118] in Exodus xxxi, were it not for his being horned at **·f·7**, which is from Exodus xvii.)

The remaining prophets show occasional inconsistencies, but on the whole are steadily identifiable. Zacharias wears **d10** at **f10, h11, i11, n10, o11, p11, r11, ·f·4, ·h·10**, but at **o10**, in spite of his normal appearance opposite at **o11**, he unaccountably wears the 'unpredictable' hat already mentioned. Sophonias is inconsistent once, wearing at **·n·11** not **d11**, worn also at **f11** and **·i·11**, but an otherwise unique hat. Baruch's personal hat cannot be identified since he appears only twice, wearing a different hat each time (**t4** and **v11**, but the two styles are similar).

Solomon is a special case, analogous to Jeremias in his wearing of different hats to suggest different *personae*. If we follow the medieval tradition by which he is the author of the Song of Songs, Proverbs, and Wisdom, we find him wearing three kinds of hat

—but not simply a special hat for each book. As the author of the Song he wears **o4** at **·g·4** (a hat slightly deeper than Osee's), but he wears a different hat at **·q·4**. As the author of Proverbs he wears **g4** at **q10, s4, ·b·4, ·c·4**; as the author of Wisdom he wears this same **g4** at **s11, ·m·4, ·p·4, ·q·11**. On three occasions he is simply crowned: for Proverbs at **r4** and **·a·4**; for Wisdom at **·s·3** (Tobias wears this crown too on his appearance at **·t·4**, perhaps because in some manuscripts of the Bible his book follows the Wisdom section; he is hatless at **t11**, like the author of Deuteronomy at **·o·10**).

In at least one case a hat may tell us something about a crux. At the Prophecy attributed to Osee in **h4**, which is not to be found in his book or indeed in the Bible, the prophet concerned is wearing Osee's hat. This suggests that the identification 'Osee' is not simply the result of textual corruption: the designer thought the Prophecy was Osee's.

There is probably much more to be made of these hats. Biblical scholars may be able to justify the anomalies in terms of medieval understanding of the relation among the books or authors of the Bible. Iconographers may find that these 'personal' hats had or formed precedents. It might even be possible for a fashion historian to account for the allocation of styles to persons. There is enough evidence of the designer's deliberation in hatting his prophets to make the search worthwhile, and there are enough questions raised by his deliberation to justify this account of his practice, and the departures from it.